Riddles of Existence

A Guided Tour of Metaphysics
New Edition

The questions of metaphysics are among the deepest and most puzzling. What is time? Am I free in my actions? What makes me the same person I was as a child? Why is there something rather than nothing?

Riddles of Existence makes metaphysics genuinely accessible, even fun. Its lively, informal style brings the riddles to life and shows how stimulating they can be to think about. No philosophical background is required to enjoy this book. It is ideal for beginning students. Anyone wanting to think about life's most profound questions will find *Riddles of Existence* provocative and entertaining.

Earl Conee is Professor of Philosophy at the University of Rochester, New York.

Theodore Sider is Frederick J. Whiton Professor of Philosophy at Cornell University, New York.

Riddles of Existence

A Guided Tour of Metaphysics

New Edition

Earl Conee and Theodore Sider

CLARENDON PRESS · OXFORD

OXFORD
UNIVERSITY PRESS

Great Clarendon Street, Oxford, OX2 6DP,
United Kingdom

Oxford University Press is a department of the University of Oxford.
It furthers the University's objective of excellence in research, scholarship,
and education by publishing worldwide. Oxford is a registered trade mark of
Oxford University Press in the UK and in certain other countries

Published in the United States of America by Oxford University Press
198 Madison Avenue, New York, NY 10016, United States of America

British Library Cataloguing in Publication Data
Data available

Library of Congress Control Number: 2014937007

ISBN 978-0-19-872404-9

Printed in Great Britain by
Clays Ltd, St Ives plc

CONTENTS

LIST OF FIGURES

PREFACE TO THE
NEW EDITION (2014)

There is more to metaphysics than was taken up in the first edition. In the past century, many philosophers have thought hard about what (if anything) ethical evaluations are really about, and in the past few decades, many philosophers have been thinking hard about what (if anything) metaphysical research accomplishes. This second edition includes two new chapters, 'The Metaphysics of Ethics' (Conee) and 'Metametaphysics' (Sider), which give friendly critical attention to leading answers to these exciting questions.

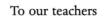
To our teachers

Introduction

You have a choice before you. Will you continue reading this book? Take your time, make up your mind . . . OK, time's up. What is your decision?

If you have reached this sentence, your decision must have been *yes*. Now, think back to your decision. Was it a *free* decision? *Could* you have put the book down? Or did you *have* to keep reading?

Of course you could have put the book down; of course your decision was free. We human beings have free will.

Not so fast. We human beings are made of matter, tiny particles studied by the sciences. And the sciences, especially physics, discover laws of nature that specify where these particles must move. Given the forces that were acting on the particles, your body *had* to move the way it did, and so you had to continue to read. How then was your decision free?

This is the problem of free will. It is a tough problem. We all believe that we have free will, and yet scientific laws govern the matter making up our bodies, determining what we will do next. So do we have free will? Chapter 6 discusses this problem in depth, and suggests a certain answer. But it is not so important to us that you agree with our answer. What we really hope is that you come to appreciate the importance of such problems and develop reasoned opinions of your own.

Grappling with the problem of free will, as with most other metaphysical issues, requires no specialized knowledge. The conflict between free will and science lies in what we already know. What philosophy teaches us is how to reflect on what we already know in a particularly careful and thoughtful way. It is truly astonishing what problems emerge from this kind of reflection!

The problem of free will is just one example of a metaphysical problem. Broadly and vaguely speaking, metaphysics addresses fundamental questions about the nature of reality. What are the basic ingredients of reality? What is their ultimate nature? Could reality have been different? And where do human beings fit into reality? Indeed, why does reality contain anything at all?

Philosophers at colleges and universities teach and write about metaphysics. They pursue deep questions about life, meaning, and the world. Bookstores also have large sections called Metaphysics or Metaphysical Studies, containing books on deep questions about life, meaning, and the world. But these books are rarely written by academic philosophers. Why is that?

The main reason is that what most philosophers write is too technical and specialized. That's a shame. Philosophy is exciting and important, and understandable by anyone. There may also be another reason. Academic philosophers try to be as rational as they can in their writings. They criticize one another's ideas ruthlessly in pursuit of the truth. This makes for controversies rather than soothing certainties, which some people don't like. But that's also a shame. The controversies are fun and enlightening. Philosophy is an intellectual quest, governed by rigorous standards designed to help us figure out what is really true.

Who's it For?

This book is for anyone interested in finding out about metaphysics. We don't take for granted any background in philosophy. The book is understandable without supplemental readings or instruction by a teacher.

As a textbook, it is flexible. The chapters are short and can be used independently of one another. The most accessible chapters come first; beyond that, the ordering has no great significance. In an introductory philosophy course, a section about metaphysics might use two or three chapters. A metaphysics course might use any or all of the chapters.

Who's it By?

It's by a couple of professors of philosophy. We each wrote six chapters. Though we collaborated on them all, we did not try to make the book read as if it were the work of one author. We hope that stylistic differences make for a pleasant and stimulating variation in tone.

What's it About?

The first ten chapters take up major topics in metaphysics; the last two chapters discuss the nature of metaphysics. The chapters deal selectively with their issues. The goal is to take a serious look at these topics, without exhausting them—or the reader! A brief list of suggested further readings appears at the end of each chapter.

Chapter 1, Personal Identity (Sider)

Think back ten or twenty years into your past. You now have little in common with that earlier you. You look different. You think differently. And the matter now making you up is almost completely different. So why is that person *you*? What makes persons stay the same over time, despite such drastic changes?

Chapter 2, Fatalism (Conee)

Fatalism claims that everything is fated to be exactly as it is. Why believe that? Over the centuries, there have been intriguing arguments proposed in favor of it. We investigate how well these arguments work.

Chapter 3, Time (Sider)

Time can seem like the most mundane thing in the world, until you really start to think about it. Does time flow? If so, what could that mean? How fast does it flow, and can one travel back in time, against the current?

Chapter 4, God (Conee)

Does God exist? Yes, some say; and they claim to prove it. We examine some proposed proofs.

Chapter 5, Why Not Nothing? (Conee)

Why is there anything at all rather than nothing? Can we even understand this question? If so, what sort of answer might it have?

Chapter 6, Free Will and Determinism (Sider)

We all believe that we are free to act as we choose. But the business of science is to discover the underlying causes of things. Given science's excellent track record, it's a reasonable guess that it will one day discover the causes of human actions. But if our actions are caused by things that science can predict and control, how can we have free will?

Chapter 7, Constitution (Sider)

'If you hold a clay statue in your hand, you are actually holding two physical objects, a statue and a piece of clay. For if you squash the statue, the statue is destroyed but the piece of clay keeps on existing.' This argument seems to establish a very strange conclusion: two different objects can share exactly the same location. Can that be correct? If not, where did the argument go wrong?

Chapter 8, Universals (Conee)

Any two red apples have many things in common: most obviously, each is red and each is an apple. Some philosophers say that what the apples share are universals, such as *redness* and *applehood*. Universals are very strange entities. For instance, redness seems to be in thousands of places at once: wherever any red object is located, redness itself is there. Do these universals really exist?

Chapter 9, Possibility and Necessity (Sider)

Not all truths are created equal. It is true that Michael Jordan is a great basketball player, and it is true that all bachelors are unmarried. Although each of these is a truth, there is a big difference between them. The first truth might have been false: Jordan might have decided never to play basketball. But the second truth could not have been false: bachelors are necessarily unmarried. What makes these truths so different?

Chapter 10, *The Metaphysics of Ethics (Conee)*

Moral judgments can matter a lot to us. But when we say things like 'she is a good person' or 'that act is wrong', are we talking about any ways that people or acts really are? If so, what in the world are those ways? If not, what are we doing?

Chapter 11, *What is Metaphysics? (Conee)*

After reading ten chapters about ten different metaphysical issues, you might expect to have a clear idea of what metaphysics is. But it is remarkably difficult to identify a unifying feature common to every metaphysical topic. We examine some ideas about the nature of metaphysics itself.

Chapter 12, *Metametaphysics (Sider)*

Sometimes it's good to take a deep breath, step back, and think about what you're doing. In the case of metaphysics this leads to questions like these: Why care about metaphysics? Can we know the truth about metaphysics? And is metaphysics really about reality, as it purports to be, or is it only an elaborate game with words?

CHAPTER I

Personal Identity

Theodore Sider

The Concept of Personal Identity

On trial for murder, you decide to represent yourself. You are not the murderer, you say; the murderer was a *different person* from you. The judge asks for your evidence. Do you have photographs of a mustachioed intruder? Don't your fingerprints match those on the murder weapon? Can you show that the murderer is left-handed? No, you say. Your defense is very different. Here are your closing arguments:

I concede that the murderer is a righty, like me, has the same fingerprints as I do, is clean-shaven like me. He even looks exactly like me in the surveillance camera photographs introduced by the defense. No, I have no twin. In fact, I admit that I remember committing the murder! But the murderer is not the same person as me, for I have changed. That person's favorite rock band was Led Zeppelin; I now prefer Todd Rundgren. That person had an appendix, but I do not; mine was removed last week. That person was 25 years old; I am 30. I am not the same person as that murderer of five years ago. Therefore you cannot punish me, for no one is guilty of a crime committed by *someone else*.

Obviously, no court of law would buy this argument. And yet, what is wrong with it? When someone changes, whether physically or psychologically, isn't it true that he's 'not the same person'?

Yes, but the phrase 'the same person' is ambiguous. There are two ways we can talk about one person's being the same as another. When a person has a religious conversion or shaves his head, he is *dissimilar* to how he was before. He does not remain **qualitatively** the same person, let us say. So in one sense he is not 'the same person'. But in another sense he *is* the same person: no other person has taken his place. This second kind of sameness is called **numerical** sameness, since it is the sort of sameness expressed by the equals sign in mathematical statements like '2+2=4': the expressions '2+2' and '4' stand for one and the same number. You are numerically the same person you were when you were a baby, although you are qualitatively very different. The closing arguments in the trial confuse the two kinds of sameness. You have indeed changed since the commission of the crime: you are qualitatively not the same. But you are numerically the same person as the murderer; no *other* person murdered the victim. It is true that 'no one can be punished for crimes committed by someone else'. But 'someone else' here means someone numerically distinct from you.

The concept of numerical sameness is important in human affairs. It affects whom we can punish, for it is unjust to punish anyone numerically distinct from the wrongdoer. It also plays a crucial role in emotions such as anticipation, regret, and remorse. You can't feel the same sort of regret or remorse for the mistakes of others that you can feel for your own mistakes. You can't anticipate the pleasures to be experienced by someone else, no matter how qualitatively similar to you that other person may be. The question of what makes persons numerically the same over time is known to philosophers as the question of **personal identity**.

The question of personal identity may be dramatized by an example. Imagine that you are very curious about what the future will be like. One day you catch God in a particularly good mood; she promises to bring you back to life five hundred years after your death, so that you can experience the future. At first you are understandably excited, but then you begin to wonder. How will God insure that it is *you* in the future? Five hundred years from now you will have died and your body will have rotted away. The matter now making you up will, by then, be scattered across the surface of the earth. God could easily create a new person out of new matter who resembles you, but that's no comfort. You want *yourself* to exist in the future; someone merely like you just won't cut it.

This example makes the problem of personal identity particularly vivid, but notice that the same issues are raised by ordinary change over time. Looking back at baby pictures, you say 'that was me'. But why? What makes that baby the same person as you, despite all the changes you have undergone in the intervening years?

(Philosophers also reflect on the identity over time of objects other than persons; they reflect on what makes an electron, tree, bicycle, or nation the same at one time as another. These objects raise many of the same questions that persons do, and some new ones as well. But persons are particularly fascinating. For one thing, only personal identity connects with emotions such as regret and anticipation. For another, *we* are persons. It is only natural that we take particular interest in ourselves.)

So how could God make it be you in the future? As noted, it is not enough to reconstitute, out of new matter, a person physically similar to you. That would be mere qualitative similarity. Would it help to use the same matter? God could gather all the protons, neutrons, and electrons that now constitute your body but will then be spread over the earth's surface, and form them into a person. For good measure, she could even make this new person look like you. But it wouldn't *be* you. It would be a new person made out of your old matter. If you don't agree, then consider this. Never mind the future; for all you know, the matter that now makes up your body once made up the body of another person thousands of years ago. It is incredibly unlikely, but nevertheless possible, that all the matter from some ancient Greek statesman has recycled through the biosphere and found its way into you. Clearly, that would not make you numerically identical to that statesman. You should not be punished for his crimes; you could not regret his misdeeds. Sameness of matter is not sufficient for personal identity.

Nor is it necessary. At least, *exact* sameness of matter isn't necessary for personal identity. People survive gradual changes in their matter all the time. They ingest and excrete, cut their hair and shed bits of skin, and sometimes have new skin or other matter grafted or implanted onto their bodies. In fact, normal processes of ingestion and excretion recycle nearly all of your matter every few years. Yet you're still you. Personal identity isn't especially tied to sameness of matter. So what is it tied to?

The Soul

Some philosophers and religious thinkers answer: the **soul**. A person's soul is her psychological essence, a non-physical entity in which thoughts and feelings take place. The soul continues unscathed through all manner of physical change to the body, and can even survive the body's total destruction. Your soul is what makes you *you*. The baby in the pictures is you because the very same soul that now inhabits your body then inhabited that baby's body. So God can bring you back to life in the future by making a new body and inserting your soul into it.

Souls might seem to provide quick answers to many philosophical perplexities about identity over time, but there is no good reason to believe that they exist. Philosophers used to argue that souls must be posited in order to explain the existence of thoughts and feelings, since thoughts and feelings don't seem to be part of the physical body. But this argument is undermined by contemporary science. Human beings have long known that one part of the body—the brain—is especially connected to mentality. Even before contemporary neuroscience, head injuries were known to cause psychological damage. We now know how particular bits of the brain are connected with particular psychological effects. Although we are far from being able to completely correlate psychological states with brain states, we have made sufficient progress that the existence of such a correlation is a reasonable hypothesis. It is sensible to conclude that mentality itself resides in the brain, and that the soul does not exist. It's not that brain science *disproves* the soul; souls *could* exist even though brains and psychological states are perfectly correlated. But if the physical brain explains mentality on its own, there is no need to postulate souls in addition.

Also, soul theorists have a hard time explaining how souls manage to think. *Brain* theorists have the beginnings of an explanation: the brain contains billions of neurons, whose incredibly complex interactions produce thought. No one knows exactly how this works, but neuroscientists have at least made a good start. The soul theorist has nothing comparable to say, for most soul theorists think that the soul has no smaller parts. Souls are not made up of billions of little bitty soul-particles. (If they were, they would no longer provide quick answers to philosophical perplexities about identity over time. Soul theorists would face the same difficult philosophical questions the rest of us face. For instance: what makes a soul the same over time, despite changes to its soul-particles?) But if souls have no little bitty soul-particles, they have nothing like neurons to help them do their stuff. How, then, do they do it?

Spatiotemporal Continuity and the Case of the Prince and the Cobbler

Setting aside souls, let's turn to scientific theories, which base personal identity on natural phenomena. One such theory uses the concept of **spatiotemporal continuity**. Consider the identity over time of an inanimate object such as a baseball. A pitcher holds a baseball and starts his windup; moments later, a baseball is in the catcher's mitt. Are the baseballs the same? How will we decide? It is easiest if we have kept our eyes on the ball. A **continuous series**—a series of locations in space and time containing a baseball, the first in the pitcher's hand, later locations in the intervening places and times, and the final one in the catcher's mitt—convinces us that the catcher's baseball is the same as the pitcher's. If we observe no such continuous series, we may suspect that the baseballs are different. Now, we don't usually need this method to identify a person over time, since most people look very different from one another, but it could come in handy when dealing with identical twins. Want to know whether it is Billy Bob or Bobby Bill in the jail cell? First compile information from surveillance tape or informants. Then, using this information, trace a continuous series from the person in the jail backward in time, and see which twin it leads to.

Everyone agrees that spatiotemporal continuity is a good practical guide to personal identity. But as philosophers we want more. We want to discover the *essence* of personal identity; we want to know *what it is* to have personal identity, not merely how to tell when personal identity is present. If you want to know whether a man is a bachelor, checking to see whether his apartment is messy is a decent practical guide; if you want to tell whether a metal is gold, visual inspection and weighing on a scale will yield the right answer nine times out of ten. But having a messy apartment is not the *essence* of being a bachelor, for *some* bachelors are neat. Weighing a certain amount and appearing a certain way are not the essence of being gold, for it is possible for a metal to appear to be gold (in all superficial respects) but nevertheless not really *be* gold. (Think of fool's gold.) The true essence of being a bachelor is being an unmarried male; the true essence of being gold is having atomic number 79. For in no possible circumstance whatsoever is something a bachelor without being an unmarried man, and in no possible circumstance is something gold without having atomic number 79. All we require of practical guides for detecting bachelors or gold is that they work most of the time, but philosophical accounts of essence must work in all possible circumstances. The **spatiotemporal continuity theory** says that spatiotemporal continuity is indeed the essence of personal identity, not just that it is a good practical guide. Personal identity just *is* spatiotemporal continuity.

The theory must be refined a bit if it is really to work in every possible circumstance. Suppose you are captured, put into a pot, and melted into soup. Although we can trace a continuous series from you to the soup, the soup is not you. After being melted, you no longer exist; the matter that once composed you now composes something else. So we had better refine the spatio-temporal continuity theory to read as follows: persons are numerically identical if and only if they are spatiotemporally continuous via a series of *persons*. You are connected to the soup by a continuous series all right, but the later members of the series are portions of soup, not people.

Further refinements are possible (including saying that any change of matter in a continuous series must occur gradually, or saying that earlier members of such a series *cause* later members). But let's instead press on to a very interesting example introduced by the seventeenth-century British philosopher John Locke. In Locke's example, a certain prince wonders what it would be like to live as a lowly cobbler. A cobbler reciprocally dreams of life as a prince. One day, they get their chance: *the entire psychologies of the prince and the cobbler are swapped.* The body of the cobbler comes to have all the memories, knowledge, and character traits of the prince, whose psychology has in turn departed for the cobbler's body. Locke himself spoke of souls: the souls of the prince and the cobbler are swapped. But let's change his story: suppose the swap occurs because the brains of the prince and the cobbler are altered, without any transfer of soul or matter, by an evil scientist. Although this is far-fetched, it is far from inconceivable. Science tells us that mental states depend on the arrangement of the brain's neurons. That arrangement could in principle be altered to become exactly like the arrangement of another brain.

After the swap, the person in the cobbler's body will remember having been a prince, and will remember the desire to try out life as a cobbler. He will say to himself: 'Finally, I have my chance!' He regards himself as being the prince, not the cobbler. And the person in the prince's body regards himself as being the cobbler, not the prince. Are they right?

The spatiotemporal continuity theory says that they are not right. Spatiotemporally continuous paths stick with *bodies*; they lead from the original prince to the person in the prince's body, and from the original cobbler to the person in the cobbler's body. So if the spatiotemporal continuity theory is correct, then the person in the cobbler's body is really the cobbler, not the prince, and the person in the prince's body is really the prince, not the cobbler.

Locke takes a different view; he agrees with the prince and the cobbler. If he is right, then his thought experiment refutes the spatiotemporal continuity theory. Here is a powerful argument on Locke's side. Suppose the prince had previously committed a horrible crime, knew that the mind-swap would occur, and hoped to use it to escape prosecution. After the swap, the crime is discovered, and the guards come to take the guilty one away. They know nothing of the swap, and so they haul off to jail the person in the prince's body, ignoring his protestations of innocence. The person in the cobbler's body (who considers himself the prince) remembers committing the crime and gloats over his narrow escape. This is a miscarriage of justice! The gloating person in the cobbler's body ought to be punished. If so, then the person in the cobbler's body is the prince, not the cobbler, for a person ought to be punished only for what he himself did.

Psychological Continuity and the Problem of Duplication

Locke took the example of the prince and the cobbler to show that personal identity follows a different kind of continuity, **psychological continuity**. According to the new theory that Locke proposed, the **psychological continuity theory**, a past person is numerically identical to the future person, if any, who has that past person's memories, character traits, and so on— whether or not the future and past persons are spatiotemporally continuous with each other. Locke's theory says that the gloating person in the cobbler's body is indeed the prince and is therefore guilty of the prince's crimes, since he is psychologically continuous with the prince. As we saw, this seems to be the correct verdict. But Locke faces the following fascinating challenge, presented by the twentieth-century British philosopher Bernard Williams.

Our evil scientist is at it again, and causes Charles, a person today, to have the psychology of Guy Fawkes, a man hanged in 1606 for trying to blow up the English Parliament. Of course, it might be difficult to tell whether Charles is faking, but if he really does have Fawkes's psychology, then, Locke says, Charles *is* Guy Fawkes. So far, so good.

But now our scientist perversely causes this transformation *also* to happen to another person, Robert. Coming to have Fawkes's psychology is just an alteration to the brain; if it can happen to Charles, then it can happen to Robert as well. Locke's theory is now in trouble. Both Charles and Robert are psychologically continuous with Fawkes. If personal identity is psychological continuity, then both Charles and Robert would be identical to Fawkes. But that makes no sense, since it would imply that Charles and Robert are identical to each other! For if we know that

$$x = 4 \text{ and } y = 4$$

then we can conclude that

$$x = y.$$

In just the same way, if we know that

$$\text{Charles} = \text{Fawkes and Robert} = \text{Fawkes}$$

then we can conclude that

$$\text{Charles} = \text{Robert.}$$

But it is absurd to claim that Charles = Robert. Though they are now psychologically similar (each has Fawkes's memories and character traits), they are numerically two different people. This is the **duplication problem** for Locke's theory: what happens when psychological continuity is duplicated? (Or triplicated, or quadruplicated . . .)

Williams chose spatiotemporal over psychological continuity because of the duplication problem. Before we follow him, let's think a little harder about spatiotemporal continuity. Just as a tree can survive the loss of a branch, a person can survive the loss of certain parts, even very large parts. You are still the same person if your legs or arms are amputated. Yet losing a part causes a certain amount of spatiotemporal discontinuity, since the region of space occupied by the person abruptly changes shape. Thus, 'spatiotemporal continuity' should be understood as meaning *sufficient* spatiotemporal continuity, in order to allow for change in parts while remaining the same thing or person.

How much continuity is 'sufficient' spatiotemporal continuity? Imagine that you have incurable cancer in the right half of your body but are healthy in the left. This cancer extends to your brain: the right hemisphere is cancerous while the left hemisphere is healthy. Fortunately, futuristic scientists can separate your body in two. They can even divide the brain's hemispheres and discard the cancerous half. You are given a prosthetic right arm and right leg, an artificial right half of your heart, and so on. You need no prosthetic right brain hemisphere, though, because the remaining healthy left hemisphere eventually functions exactly as your whole brain used to function. (Though fictional, this is not wholly far-fetched: the hemispheres of the human brain really can function independently when disconnected, and duplicate some—though not all—functions of each other.) Surely the person after the operation is the same as the person before: this operation is a way to save someone's life! But the operation results in a fairly severe spatiotemporal discontinuity, since the continuity between the person before and the person after is only the size of half the body. Moral: even the continuity of only half the body had better count as sufficient for personal identity.

But now the spatiotemporal continuity theory faces its own duplication problem. Let us alter the story of the previous paragraph so that the cancer is only in your brain, but is present in both hemispheres. Radiation treatment is the only cure, but it has a mere 10 percent chance of success. These odds are not good. Fortunately, they can be improved. Before the radiation treatment, the doctors divide your body—including the hemispheres—in two. Each half-body gets artificially completed as before; then the radiation treatment of the cancerous brain-halves begins. This gives you two 10 percent chances of success rather than one. But now comes the twist in the story: suppose the unlikely outcome is that *each* hemisphere gets cured by the treatment. So the operation results in two persons, each with one of your original hemispheres. Note that each is 'sufficiently' spatiotemporally continuous with you, since we agreed that a half-person's worth of continuity counts as sufficient. The spatiotemporal continuity theory then implies that you are identical to each of these two new persons, and we again have the absurd consequence that these two new persons are identical to each other.

Each of our theories, Locke's psychological continuity theory and the spatiotemporal continuity theory, faces the duplication problem. A single *original person* can be *continuous*, whether psychologically or spatiotemporally, with two *successor persons*. Each theory says that personal identity is continuity of some kind. So the original person is identical to each successor person, which then implies the absurdity that the successor persons are identical to each other. How should we solve this problem?

Some will be tempted to give up on scientific theories and instead appeal to souls. Continuity, whether psychological or spatiotemporal, does not determine what happens to a soul. When a body is duplicated, the soul in the original body might be inherited by one of the successor bodies, or by the other, or perhaps by neither, but not by both. While this is a tidy solution, it is unsupported by the evidence: there still is no reason to believe that souls exist. It would be better to somehow revise the scientific theories to take the duplication problem into account. (If we succeed, we will still need to decide between psychological and spatiotemporal continuity, or some combination of the two. But set this aside for the remainder of the chapter.)

As we originally stated the scientific theories, they said that personal identity is continuity. We could restate them to say instead that personal identity is **non-branching** continuity. Continuity does not *normally* branch: usually only one person at a time is continuous with a given earlier person. In such cases there is personal identity. But the duplication examples involve branching, that is, two persons at a time who are both continuous with a single earlier person. So according to the restated theory, there is no personal identity in such cases. Neither Charles nor Robert is identical to Guy Fawkes. You do not survive the double-transplant operation.

Unlike the claim that the successor persons are identical to each other, this is not absurd. But it is pretty hard to accept. Imagine that, before the operation, you receive some good news: the left-hemisphere person will survive the division operation. Excellent. But now, if the modified spatiotemporal continuity theory is correct, then if the right-hemisphere person survives in addition, you will not survive. So it is *worse* for you if the right-hemisphere person survives. You must hope and pray that the right-hemisphere person will die. How strange! The news that the left-hemisphere person would survive was good; news that the right-hemisphere person would also survive just seems like more good news. How could an additional piece of good news make things much, much *worse*?

Radical Solutions to the Problem of Duplication

Duplication is a really knotty problem! Perhaps it is time to investigate some radical solutions. Here are two.

Derek Parfit, the contemporary British philosopher, challenges a fundamental assumption about personal identity that we have been making, the assumption that personal identity is *important*. Earlier in this chapter we assumed that personal identity connects with anticipation, regret, and punishment. This is part of the importance of personal identity. The last paragraph of the previous section assumed another part: that it is very bad for you if no one in the future is identical to you. That is, it is very bad to stop existing. Parfit challenges this assumption that identity is important. What is really important, Parfit says, is psychological continuity. In most ordinary cases, psychological continuity and personal identity go hand in hand. That is because, according to Parfit, personal identity is non-branching continuity, and continuity rarely branches. But in the duplication case it does branch. In that case, then, you cease to exist. But *in the duplication case*, Parfit says, ceasing to exist is not bad. For even though you yourself will not continue to exist, you will still have all that matters: you will have psychological continuity (a double helping, in fact!).

Parfit's views are interesting and challenging. But can we really believe that utterly ceasing to exist is sometimes insignificant? That would require a radical revision of our ordinary beliefs. Are there other options?

We could instead reconsider one of our other assumptions about personal identity. The duplication argument assumes that if personal identity holds between the original person and each successor person, we get the absurd result that the successor persons are the same person as each other. But this absurd result follows only if personal identity is numerical identity, the same notion that the equals sign ($=$) expresses in mathematics. We made this assumption at the outset, but perhaps it is a mistake. Perhaps 'personal identity' is *never* really numerical identity. Perhaps all change *really does* result in a numerically distinct person. If so, then we would not need to say that branching destroys personal identity. For we could go back to saying that personal 'identity' is continuity (whether psychological or spatiotemporal—that remains to be decided). In branching cases, a single person can stand in the relationship of 'personal identity' to two distinct persons; that is not absurd if personal identity is not numerical identity. We would still need to distinguish mere qualitative similarity ('he's not the same person he was before going to college') from a stricter notion of personal 'identity' that connects with punishment, anticipation, and regret. But even this stricter notion would be looser than numerical identity.

Can we really believe that our baby pictures are of people numerically distinct from us? That too would require radical belief revision. But sometimes, philosophy calls for just that.

FURTHER READING

John Perry's anthology *Personal Identity* (University of California Press, 1975) is an excellent source for more readings on personal identity. It contains a selection from John Locke defending the psychological continuity view, a paper by Derek Parfit arguing that personal identity is not as significant as we normally take it to be, a paper by Thomas Nagel on brain bisection, and many other interesting papers. Perry's introduction to the anthology is also excellent.

Another good book, also called *Personal Identity*, is co-authored by Sydney Shoemaker and Richard Swinburne (Blackwell, 1984). The first half, written by Swinburne, defends the soul theory of personal identity, and is especially accessible. The second half, written by Shoemaker, defends the psychological continuity view.

Bernard Williams introduces the problem of duplication in 'Personal Identity and Individuation', in his book *Problems of the Self* (Cambridge University Press, 1973).

CHAPTER 2

Fatalism

Earl Conee

Introduction

Open possibilities are open to choice or chance. This status matters to us. We are hopeful about the positive possibilities. We worry about the threatening ones. We take an open possibility to be unsettled, up-in-the-air.

In contrast, fated things are out of anyone's control, bound to be. This status matters differently to us. If something fated looks bad, we try to resign ourselves to it. If something fated looks good, we are glad about it. We take anything fated to be a given.

Some philosophers have tried to prove that all of reality—everything that ever happens, every entity that ever exists, and every condition that things are ever in—all was forever fated to be as it is. This is the doctrine of **metaphysical fatalism**.

There are several things to set aside right away, because metaphysical fatalism does not say or imply that they are true. First, metaphysical fatalism is not about being fated by the Fates. The Fates are three ancient Greek mythical goddesses who were believed to decide human destiny. No philosopher thinks that those goddesses exist and determine our lives. Philosophers agree that nothing is fated by the Fates.

Metaphysical fatalism says that there is a kind of necessity to every actual thing. This does not imply that 'everything happens for a reason'. Metaphysical fatalism is about an impersonal necessity, not a reason or purpose. Also, metaphysical fatalism does not imply that we have a destiny where certain things would have to happen to us, no matter what. Rather, it implies that we must be exactly as we are, in exactly the situations that we are actually in. Furthermore, this fatalism does *not* imply that effort is futile. It allows that some efforts cause improvements— although it does imply that both the efforts and the resulting improvements were fated. Fatalists acknowledge that we do not always *know* what is going to happen. They say that everything in the past, present, and future must be as it is, regardless of what anyone knows about what will be.

Moreover, metaphysical fatalism does not tell us to be 'fatalistic', that is, to regard the future with resignation or submission to fate. No particular attitude is automatically justified. Fatalism even allows a cheerful optimism to be justified—maybe things are fated to go well and attitudes of resignation and submission do no good.

Finally, the necessity that metaphysical fatalists attribute to everything is not the necessity of causes to produce their effects. Clearly, many things are determined in advance by physical laws and prior conditions. If everything that ever happens is determined in this way, then what philosophers call **determinism** is true.[1] The melting of some ice that is heated above water's freezing point is inevitable. This seems enough to say that the heating makes the melting 'fated' to occur. But the truth of determinism would not be even partial support for metaphysical fatalism. Fatalism is not about being physically or causally determined. It is about something more abstract, something that does not depend on how things go in nature. Determinists hold that

[1] For more about determinism, see 'Free Will and Determinism', Chapter 6.

the present and future are causally determined by the past and the physical laws, but there could have been a different past or different laws. The metaphysical fatalists' view is that, even if determinism is not true, there are no open possibilities at any point in history. Their claim is that each thing in the past, present, and future has always been fixed and settled. It all must be exactly as it is, whether or not it was causally determined. Metaphysical fatalists think that the sheer presence of anything in the world gives the thing a necessity. Why? Fatalists present **arguments**—lines of reasoning—to try to prove their thesis. Let's look at some main fatalist arguments and see how well they work.

The Sea Battle

The ancient Greek philosopher Aristotle gives us our first argument. Here is a short story about some predictions.

> A sea battle may well take place tomorrow. Today, someone predicts that it will happen tomorrow and someone else predicts that it won't. Neither of the predictors knows what is going to happen. They are both just guessing.

That is the whole story. It is not a work of art. But our Aristotelian fatalist uses it to argue for something profound.

The Sea Battle argument begins as follows.

> *First Assumption*: Either the prediction that the battle will happen is true, or the prediction that it won't happen is true.

This First Assumption seems sensible, although it will not go unchallenged. Let's continue with the reasoning.

> *Second Assumption*: If a statement is true, then it has to be true.

This too initially seems right, though again we'll think more about it. From these two assumptions the fatalist derives the following.

> *Initial Conclusion*: Whichever prediction about the battle is true, it has to be true.

If a prediction has to be true, then it describes a necessary fact. So now the fatalist derives this.

> *Second Conclusion*: Whether or not a battle will take place at sea tomorrow, whichever will happen is something that has to be—it is necessary.

This conclusion is fatalistic. And there is more to come. So far, the Sea Battle argument is just about one predicted event. Metaphysical fatalism is about everything. A conclusion about everything can be reached by generalizing from the reasoning about the sea battle. Nothing in the story makes its battle especially prone to having the status of being settled in advance. So, to the extent that the argument about the battle succeeds, an unrestricted conclusion about everything else seems to be equally well supported.

One less-than-universal aspect of the story is that predictions have been made. That is not crucial, though. The argument does not use the predicting as a basis for implying the necessity of what is predicted. If the argument succeeds, then it would be *the reality of the situation* that makes the predicted fact necessary, not the predicting of it. Thus, the whole truth about the future would be necessary, whether predicted or not. So it looks as though, if the fatalist succeeds in proving the Second Conclusion, then there is no real further obstacle to proving the following.

> *General Fatalistic Conclusion*: Whatever will be, has to be.

Before evaluating the Sea Battle argument, we should note two further things about it. First, battling involves choice. Frequently, fatalism is regarded as being about our having freedom of choice. Choice is an important focus for fatalistic arguments, because choices are some of our favorite examples of open possibilities. We think that there are free choices that really could have gone either way.[2] But the fatalists' conclusion is not limited to excluding freedom of choice. The General Fatalistic Conclusion asserts that the whole future is necessary. If this conclusion is right, then it applies as well to the things that are supposed to be matters of chance according to science. For instance, according to contemporary physics, the time of the radioactive decay of a uranium atom is not physically determined. Two uranium atoms can be in exactly the same physical condition until one decays and the other does not. Yet the Sea Battle sort of argument applies here just as well. Consider two predictive statements made before noon, one saying that some particular uranium atom will decay at noon and the other denying that the atom will decay at noon. The rest of the Sea Battle argument transfers over to the example. We get the fatalistic conclusion that the state of the atom at noon, whether decayed or not, has to be.

The General Fatalistic Conclusion is only about the future. Full-blown metaphysical fatalism is about everything, past, present, and future. This is not an obstacle to fatalism, though. The Sea Battle argument reaching the General Fatalistic Conclusion about the future does all of the hard work. The past and present are easy for the fatalist to deal with. It is quite plausible that the past is just as the fatalist says it is—the whole past is fixed and settled. The same goes for the present. If anything is in some condition at present, then the thing's current condition is fixed and settled. The present is too late to do anything about the present!

Thus, past and present look ripe for fatalism. If the Sea Battle argument shows that the future is fixed and settled too, then the

---

[2] 'Free Will and Determinism', Chapter 6, is about this.

way seems clear for a final comprehensive fatalist conclusion: there are no open possibilities at all at any time.

Objections

Arguments rely on their assumptions. If an argument has a premise that is obviously untrue, then the argument is definitely a failure. Arguments that are taken seriously in metaphysics are seldom that bad. If one strikes us that way, we should strongly suspect that we have not understood it. Arguments can fail less conclusively, though. Another thing that keeps an argument from proving its conclusion is the existence of an unresolved doubt about a premise. Raising doubts about premises is how the Sea Battle argument is most often faulted. Let's see how well the premises stand scrutiny.

Some philosophers have objected to the Sea Battle argument's First Assumption, the premise saying that one of the two predictions about the battle is true in advance. This assumption is one version of a principle known as the **Law of the Excluded Middle** (**LEM**). Our version excludes any middle ground between the truth of a statement and the truth of its denial.

> LEM. Concerning any statement, either it is true or its denial is true.

At least at first, LEM appears irresistible. How could a statement be untrue while the statement denying that it was true—its denial—was untrue too? That would seem to require an unfathomable 'reality gap'—an intermediate condition between being and not being. And this could not be like a ghostly haze, since even being a ghostly haze is a way of being! Yet some philosophers have opposed the Sea Battle argument by arguing against LEM. They have contended that LEM applies only to statements that assert settled facts, such as statements about what has already happened. The critics say that other statements, like ones about a potential sea battle that may or may not take place, have no truth yet. The prediction that the battle will occur is not now true, and neither is its denial, because nothing that exists right now makes either one true. Both predictions are presently indeterminate rather than true. The critics conclude that LEM is false.

This criticism has a serious drawback. Suppose that Alice predicted yesterday, 'There will be a thunderstorm in Cleveland tomorrow', and in fact there is a thunderstorm in Cleveland today. It is only natural to think that Alice *got it right yesterday.* This means that what Alice said was already true when she said it. Maybe at the time no one *knew* whether or not it was true. Maybe at the time its truth was *unsettled.* Still, when we do find out about the storm today, we say that her prediction was correct. If so, then the prediction was not indeterminate yesterday after all. This seems to apply to predictive statements quite generally. If the future bears them out, then we regard what they say of the future as having been true when they were still predictions. The objection to the LEM denies that they were true in advance. So the objection is in trouble.

An opponent of LEM might be unimpressed. An opponent might first repeat the point that when a predicted event is not now a settled fact, there is nothing around now to *make* the prediction true. The opponent could then add that any statement is true only if something makes it true. Conceding that people *regard* these predictions as having been true when made, the opponent might insist that this need for a truth-maker shows that the predictions couldn't have *been* true in advance. This restores the conclusion that LEM is wrong about them.

Though this criticism is reasonable, there is a good reply. The reply is that, because predictions are *about* the future, what makes them true or untrue is *in* the future, not in the present. There does not have to be anything around *now* to make them true. In fact, now is too early. So long as things turn out in the future as predicted, then the predictions are made true now by those later developments. The truth-makers for accurate predictions are in the future, right where they belong.

LEM is looking difficult to refute. Other critics of the Sea Battle argument focus on its Second Assumption: if any statement is true, then it has to be true. The classic objection to this assumption begins by observing that the assumption has more than one meaning. The critics say that on the interpretation of its meaning where the assumption is correct, it does not help the argument. On the interpretation where it helps, it is not correct. Specifically, the assumption is correct if it means this.

> SA1: It has to be that if a statement is true, then the statement is true.

SA1 is impeccable. What it says must be the case is only that if a statement is true, then it is true. That is truly trivial. SA1 does not tell us that any statement *has to be* true if it's true. Compare: If a wall is red, then it's red. That is a necessary fact. It applies to all walls, including a formerly brown wall that was just painted red. Yet it surely does not tell us that the wall *has to be* red. Of course the wall doesn't have to be red—it was recently brown!

Likewise, the conditional claim—a statement is true if it's true—asserts a necessary fact. But it does not tell us that being *true* is all it takes for a statement to *have to be* true. Yet that is precisely what the Sea Battle needs to derive its conclusion—it needs true statements thereby *having to be* true. Looking back at the reasoning, we see that the argument uses the Second Assumption to draw the initial conclusion that there are predictions that *have to be* true. If any assumption brings into the argument this necessity for predictions, it is the Second Assumption, the one that we are now interpreting as SA1. Since SA1 does not bring in any such necessity, the argument's initial conclusion just does not follow logically if the argument uses SA1.

The Sea Battle argument does get what it needs for its initial conclusion to follow logically if the following interpretation of the Second Assumption is part of the argument.

SA2: If a statement is true, then that statement has to be true.

SA2 does say that being true is enough for a statement to be necessary. So SA2 asserts the necessity of true predictions that the Sea Battle argument needs. But why believe SA2? To all appearances, some truths are **contingent**, that is, they are actually true but they need not have been true. We think that any lucky guess about something in the future that is not now settled is actually true, but not necessary. The truth of the guess derives from the occurrence later of what was guessed to happen. Yet SA2 says that even those lucky guesses about the apparently unsettled future would state necessary facts. SA2 says that just being true is enough to make any truth have to be true.

For us to find SA2 credible, we would have to find something about just being true that brings with it necessary truth. Nothing comes to mind. Being true by itself seems to allow that some things just happen to be true. Something that is true by a fluke is true, it just isn't true by any necessity. The only temptation to think otherwise is a deception. We can be deceived by confusing SA2 with SA1. When we keep our minds clear of that confusion, though, SA2 is not reasonable to believe. Thus, either way we interpret the Second Assumption in the Sea Battle argument, the argument looks flawed at that point.

Past Predictions

The Sea Battle argument tries to use present truth to secure future necessity. We have seen that present truths may instead be secured by how the future happens to turn out. But what if something in the past guaranteed a specific future? After all, we are confident that once things are in the past, they are unalterable. So if the past secures the future, then the future is now necessitated.

Metaphysical fatalism has been defended on the basis of the claim that the truth about everything, including the future, already *existed* in the past. By virtue of existing in the past, this comprehensive truth is a fixed fact. This status of being settled in virtue of being past is sometimes called **accidental necessity**. The word 'accidental' here signifies that the fixity of the past is not absolutely necessary. There might have been a wholly different past instead. But once things are in the actual past, they do seem fixed and settled. So this is an 'accidental' sort of necessity. We think that the future is not likewise settled, at least not all of it. Choices and chance developments seem open, with some potential to turn out in different ways. The Past Predictions argument seeks to show that the accidental necessity of the past carries over to the whole future.

A bit of philosophical terminology will be useful. The substance of a statement is what philosophers call a **proposition**. A proposition is what is said in a statement; it is the thought behind the words. Translations of the statement into another language aim to capture the same proposition in other words. Propositions are what we believe and otherwise think about when truth is at stake. If I predict that many good deeds will be done tomorrow, then the prediction is the proposition that many good deeds will be done tomorrow. If you hope that many good deeds will be done tomorrow, then this hope of yours has as its content the same proposition as my prediction.

These are propositions, *if* there really are any such entities. The existence of propositions is controversial among philosophers (as is the existence of everything else!). In any case, with the term 'proposition' understood in this way, we are ready for the Past Predictions argument.

First Assumption: For any way that things will be in the future, there existed in the past a true proposition to the effect that things would be that way.

The first assumption is about propositions that are contents of available predictions. It is not limited to the predictions that anyone has actually made. It says that the contents of all available true predictions existed in the past, whether or not anyone ever stated the predictions by asserting the propositions. The assumption says that an accurate prediction was always there to be made.

The First Assumption will be critically discussed soon.

Second Assumption: Every aspect of the past is accidentally necessary.

This Second Assumption needs investigating. Clearly, everything we ordinarily regard as being in the past is fixed and settled—the unchangeable status that we are calling accidentally necessary. The Second Assumption goes beyond that, though, to claim that every last detail of the past of any sort is accidentally necessary. We'll look into that.

Preliminary Fatalistic Conclusion: The truth in the past of each true predictive proposition is accidentally necessary.

If the truth of predictive propositions about everything in the future is accidentally necessary, then that locks in the whole future. So we have arrived at this.

General Fatalistic Conclusion: The future in every detail is accidentally necessary.

Both assumptions of the Past Predictions argument are questionable. It is easy to have doubts about the existence of the countless unstated propositions that are required by the First Assumption. Does everything about the future correspond to some predictive proposition that existed in the past? Certainly, almost none of those predictions is ever actually made by anyone. Why think that the unstated predictive propositions exist?

An adequate investigation of the existence of propositions would take an extensive metaphysical inquiry. Though it would be terrifically interesting, it would be a very long digression here. Fortunately, we need not investigate this in order to appreciate the core of the Past Predictions reasoning. The argument would reach an impressive fatalistic conclusion even if it were scaled back to actual predictions so as to avoid this issue. People have actually predicted the sorts of things that we think remain open to future resolution. Some predictions have been made about apparently open choices. People have managed to predict—if only by luck—what someone later chose with all apparent freedom. Some accurate predictions have been made about other apparently open possibilities, such as the radioactive decay of a particle. The rest of the Past Predictions argument tells us that at least the actually predicted future outcomes have the accidental necessity of the corresponding true predictions. That is a fatalistic enough result to be remarkable. Predicted outcomes of these kinds seem to remain open just as much as ones that aren't predicted by anyone. This scaled-back version of the argument skips the whole question of the existence of unstated truths. So let's restrict our thinking to actual predictions and proceed.

The Second Assumption of the Past Predictions argument is that every aspect of the past is accidentally necessary. True? When we consider the past, we tend to think of things that are *wholly in the past*: major historical events, our own previous adventures, and other things that are clearly purely in the past. Those are settled aspects of the past. Thinking of them makes the Second Assumption seem right. But what is crucial for the argument is whether certain *other* aspects of the past are in the same boat—the past truth of each true predictive statement.   .

The predictions have been made. So the past *existence* of the predictions is settled. A prediction's *truth*, though, is not something that is entirely accounted for by the past. A prediction is about the future. Because of this, if the prediction is true, then *future circumstances* are what make it true. This is just another way to say that things in the future settle the truth of the prediction. So, as long as some future things are currently unsettled, the truth of their past prediction is unsettled as well. It is reasonable for us to believe that some of the future remains open. We have just seen that, if this is so, then the truth of predictions about those aspects of the future remains unsettled too. Thus, it now looks as though the Past Predictions argument runs into trouble that is fundamentally the same as the problem for the Sea Battle argument. The problem arises here as the dubious assumption that *every* aspect of the past, even the truth of a prediction about the future, is accidentally necessary merely because it is in the past.

Necessary Conditions

I cannot finish off a mile-long run right now. Why? Because I need to have run almost a mile just before now, so that I can now complete the running of a mile. Yet I have not been running. So I cannot finish a mile run at this point.

This explanation seems to say that there is a certain necessary condition for my finishing a mile run—my having run almost a mile—and the absence of this condition renders me unable to complete a mile run. The first assumption of our next fatalistic argument says that, quite generally, the absence of a necessary condition for an alternative always closes off the possibility of that alternative.

> *First Assumption*: Something is fixed and unalterable if any necessary condition for not having the thing is absent.

(Restated in more positive terms: If something has an open alternative, then all that is needed for the alternative to exist is present.)

This First Assumption merits careful consideration. We'll investigate it after seeing the rest of the reasoning. The other assumption in the Necessary Conditions argument is rationally irresistible. It just says that any condition is needed in order to have that very condition.

> *Second Assumption*: Any condition is a necessary condition for itself.

To appreciate how these two assumptions work together to rule out any open alternatives, let's think about an example. Suppose that Cathy is about to make a choice between accepting a job offer and not accepting it. Suppose that Cathy will choose to accept the offer. Could her not choosing to accept be an open alternative at this point, before she chooses? Well, what conditions would have to hold, in order for Cathy not to choose to accept? For Cathy to avoid the choice to accept, at a minimum she would have not to choose to accept. In other words, a necessary condition for Cathy not choosing to accept is that very condition itself: that Cathy will not choose to accept the offer. As the Second Assumption says, that condition is a nonnegotiable necessary condition for itself. Again, it is part of our example that Cathy will choose to accept. So a necessary condition of this not happening is absent, now and forever. The First Assumption of the argument says that when any necessary condition for something not happening is absent, the thing is fixed and unalterable. So it follows from the two assumptions that Cathy's actual choice is already fixed and unalterable before she makes it.

The same reasoning applies equally well to any apparently open possibility, whether or not choice is involved. Concerning any actual thing at any time, some necessary condition for not having that thing is absent—if nothing else, the missing necessary condition is the very condition of not having the thing at the time. So the argument arrives at the following conclusion.

> *Fully Fatalistic Conclusion*: All actual entities, events, and circumstances, past, present, and future, are fixed and unalterable down to the last detail.

To begin a critical examination of the Necessary Conditions argument, let's rethink the explanation presented earlier of why we regard past facts as fixed and unalterable. We observed that my finishing a mile run is not an open possibility at times like now when I haven't been running. We also observed that my having run almost a mile is a necessary condition for my finishing a mile, and that condition is absent. But is the absence of a necessary condition really the explanation of why I cannot now finish a mile run? Here is a rival explanation. To finish a mile run now, I'd have to cause different things to have happened prior to now. I'd have somehow to cause it to be the case that I have been running. But as a matter of fact, I cannot do anything now that would cause me to have been running, nor can anything else now cause me to have been running.[3] This incapacity to supply the needed condition is why I can't finish a mile run now.

Once this account is offered, it seems a better explanation. Generally, we regard the events of the past as not subject to any current causal influence. Our confidence in the fixity of the past derives from that.

Even if this is a better account of why we think that past facts are unalterable, so far this is no objection to the core of the Necessary Conditions argument. It is no reason to deny the

---

[3] Our chapter about time defends the *possibility* of backward causation. The topic there is whether there *could have been* a reality where causes run backward in time. Even if such an alternative reality is possible, this does not tell us that any such causes are *actually available*.

claim of the First Assumption that something is unalterable when a necessary condition of an alteration is absent. But once we don't need *that* claim to understand the fixity of the past, we can see that the claim is doubtful on its own. Let's revisit Cathy's choice. We must concede that, whichever choice Cathy makes, some necessary condition of the alternative is *absent*. Does that absence, all by itself, make her stuck with her actual choice? It seems not. She need not be stuck with it, if the missing condition is *available* to her. If she is *able* to supply all missing necessary conditions, then no necessary condition stands in her way.

We have no reason to doubt that Cathy is able to supply the needed conditions. The necessary condition discussed, that of her not choosing to accept the offer, *seems* available as she considers the choice. Maybe there is some hidden reason why it is not really available. But the reason is *not* just that her non-acceptance is a necessary condition, and it is absent. Analogously, the mere absence of, say, a person, doesn't imply that the person is *unavailable*. The person may be ready and waiting to be present. Likewise, we have no good reason to think that the mere absence of a necessary condition for something locks in its unavailability. This undercuts the reasonableness of the First Assumption of the Necessary Conditions argument.

So the argument is in trouble. The mere absence of a necessary condition does not seem to *guarantee* its unavailability. The First Assumption might be defended on another basis. It could be contended that absent necessary conditions never *actually are available*. This would be enough. We would be just as stuck with the actual situation if the necessary conditions for something else were never in fact available. Are they ever available?

Consider this challenge: If there are available alternatives that make for open possibilities, then how come no allegedly open possibility has ever been *realized*? Never once has something true at a time turned into something that was untrue at that very time. No truth was ever actually avoided. So why think that the makings for such a thing are actually *available*?

In confronting these questions, we should think carefully about what we are denying if we deny that all is fixed and settled. If we say that an actual future truth is not fixed and settled, then we are *not* saying or implying that something true at a time can be made untrue *too*. We are saying, concerning something true in the future, that it has some potential to be untrue *instead*. We are thinking that some truths have an *unrealized potential* to be *just* untrue, *never* true. To defend this thought, we need not directly answer the questions just raised. We need not look for something that has the status of being true at a time and show how it could become *also* untrue or it could *change into* being untrue at the time. Yet the challenge posed by the questions asks us for an example of something true at a time that *realizes* the potential to be untrue at the time. So we need not meet this challenge.

How might we defend our belief in the existence of the potential, if not with the sort of examples that the challenge asks for? We could start by arguing that some future events— maybe choices, maybe physically undetermined events—are not necessitated in any known way. This would include arguing that the fatalists' efforts to prove otherwise fail. Also, we might find evidence that certain pairs of scenarios are duplicates of one another in every way that seems relevant. Yet in one member of the pair, one of our candidates for being an open possibility occurs; in the other member of the pair, the other alternative occurs. If we find such pairs, then in each case the paired duplicate argues that nothing made the one possibility occur rather than the other—it just chanced to happen that way. For instance, two flips of a coin, controlled in every known way to be exact duplicate flips in exact duplicate conditions, might be found to result in the coin landing on different sides. Wouldn't it be most reasonable to say that each flip had a chance to end up the other way? Finally, we might have a well-confirmed scientific theory that implies that some outcomes remain undetermined until they occur. These are reasons that we can have to think that there are open possibilities.

God Knows

Maybe an all-knowing God exists.[4] If so, does that make fatalism true too? Metaphysical fatalism might seem to follow readily from the existence of God, using the following argument.

> *First Assumption*: If God knows everything, then God knows in advance all truths about the whole future.

That seems safe, though we shall see that some have objected to it.

> *Second Assumption*: If God knows any given truth about the future, then any potential for that truth to be untrue would be a potential for God to be mistaken about it.

To see what the Second Assumption says, suppose that God knows that a particular flipped coin will land heads up. According to the Second Assumption, any potential for the coin not to land heads up would be a potential for God to have the mistaken belief that it will land heads up. The heads-up outcome is what God thinks and knows in advance. So if the future turned out the other way, the Second Assumption implies that God would still have this same belief and it would be untrue. We'll soon think more about that assumption.

> *Final Assumption*: It is impossible for God to be mistaken about anything.

---

[4] We investigate this in our 'God' chapter.

We can take it for granted that the Final Assumption is correct. We can assume that this is the sort of God we are considering—a God who is never mistaken under any possible conditions.

> *Conditionally Fatalistic Conclusion*: If God knows everything, then the whole future is fixed and unalterable.

This conclusion does not assert any fatalism. Deriving fatalism about the future would require the added assumption that an all-knowing God does exist. Still, it is interesting to consider whether or not the existence of an all-knowing God implies that the whole future is fixed. We are now investigating that.

One line of opposition to the God Knows argument holds that, contrary to the First Assumption, God knows everything without knowing anything in advance. The opponent claims that God is outside of the time in which we exist—that is, the sequential time of before and after, the time of past, present, and future. God exists 'in eternity'. Eternity is not in sequential time. Eternity is not before, during, or after anything. So God does not know anything 'in advance', since this requires existing in time before something happens and knowing that it will happen. God exists in eternity instead. The objection concludes that this allows God to know everything without having any advance knowledge.

Existence outside of past, present, and future is difficult to understand. Whatever such existence amounts to, though, it does not seem to ruin the core of the God Knows argument. The argument essentially relies on God having *exhaustive* knowledge, not *advance* knowledge. To see this, we can replace 'in advance' in the argument with 'in eternity'. To the extent that we can understand the resulting reasoning, it seems to have the same merits as the original. Suppose that God knows in eternity what is in our future—the future relative to us now. If so, then any potential for our future to be otherwise is a potential for something God knows to be untrue. The God Knows argument tries to persuade us that potential of that sort implies an impossible mistake by God. If the argument succeeds, then we could not avoid the conclusion by locating God in eternity. So this is not a promising source of doubt about the reasoning.

What about the Second Assumption of the God Knows argument? It says that if there is some potential for a true predictive statement not to be true, even though God knows it to be true (in advance or in eternity), then that is a potential for God to make a mistake. This claim is doubtful. Why would God be stuck believing something, whether or not it was true? God's knowledge could be more flexible.

For instance, maybe God knows all by 'seeing' all. Thus, God knows how things will be in our future by perfectly perceiving how things are at later times. Perception of a fact always derives from that fact. So God's perceptual knowledge of future facts derives from the facts perceived. If God knows by perception how our future will be, then God *derives from our future* the complete information that God has about it.

If this is how God's knowledge of our future works, then a potential for things to *be* otherwise in our future would be accompanied by a potential for God to have *perceived* otherwise. The future facts would have been different and God would have perceived them to be facts. Had things been otherwise, God would have derived different future information (in advance or in eternity). God would have known the alternative truths instead of having any mistaken beliefs.

This casts doubt on the Second Assumption of the God Knows argument. It shows us that one sort of knowledge by God of the future, combined with the existence of some potential for an alternative future truth, does *not* imply the possibility of God making a mistake. The combination only implies a potential for something that is actually known by God to have been untrue— and perhaps known by God to have been untrue. It does not imply a potential for anything untrue to have been mistakenly believed by God.

A Final Note

None of the arguments for metaphysical fatalism has turned out to seem successful. Nonetheless, a popular fatalistic saying remains appealing: 'What will be, will be.' There is no denying that this states a fact. Did we overlook the wisdom of this saying in our search for support for fatalism?

Actually, there is no metaphysical fatalism in the saying. It does not say that anything *has to be*. People do sometimes use these words to express an attitude of resignation toward whatever the future holds. But any good basis for that attitude is something beyond the sheer content of the saying. The fact that it states does not warrant any attitude, fatalistic resignation or otherwise. It claims nothing one way or the other about whether we control the future or whether the future is already settled. It simply says: however things will be, that is how they will be— however they get to be that way. This is not fatalism.

People sometimes take the saying to assert that whatever is *destined* to be, will be. That is not what it literally says, since it does not mention destiny. But people do take it that way. It sounds more fatalistic on this interpretation. It really isn't, though. It does not say how much of the future is destined, *if any*. Everyone, including those who deny all destiny, can agree that 'whatever' is destined, will be. Those who deny all destiny can consistently add that this is an empty truth, because nothing is destined.

'What will be, will be' is a good thing to say, for all that. It often comforts people. It just doesn't give us any reason to accept metaphysical fatalism.

This chapter opposes arguments for metaphysical fatalism. The following are a couple of works by defenders of fatalistic arguments. They include arguments that we have discussed. Several editions of a book by Richard Taylor are listed, because his defense of fatalism changes notably in succeeding editions of his book.

Steven M. Cahn, *Fate, Logic and Time* (Ridgeview, 1967).

Richard Taylor, 'Fate', in *Metaphysics* (Prentice-Hall, 1963, 1974, 1983, 1992).

An issue with close connections to fatalism is the compatibility of God's knowledge of our future with our having freedom. Here is a collection of essays about that.

John Martin Fisher (ed.), *God, Foreknowledge, and Freedom* (Stanford, 1989).

CHAPTER 3

Time

Theodore Sider

The Flow of Time

It is strange to question the nature of time, given how fundamental time is to our experience. As a child I wondered whether
fish are conscious of water or whether they experience it uncon-
sciously, as we experience the air we breathe. Time is even more
ubiquitous than water or air: every thought and experience takes
place in time. Questioning the nature of time can be dizzying.

Yet it is worth questioning. The ordinary conception of time,
once you start to think about it, seems to make no sense! For we
ordinarily conceive of time as being something that *moves*. 'Time
flows like a river.' 'Time marches on.' 'Time flies.' 'As time goes
by.' 'The past is gone.' 'Time waits for no one.' 'Time stood still.'
These clichés capture how we tend to think about time. Time
moves, and we are caught up in its inexorable flow. The problem
with this way of thinking is that time is the standard by which
motion is defined; how then could time itself move? This is
metaphysics at its best. Look at the world hard enough, and
even the most mundane things are revealed as mysterious and
wonderful.

Let's examine this idea of time's motion, or flow, more carefully, by comparing it to the motion of ordinary objects. What does it mean to say that a *train* moves? Simply that the train is located at one place at one moment in time and at other places at later moments in time (see Figure 1). At time t_1, the train is in Boston. At later times t_2, t_3, and t_4, the train is located at places further south: New York, Philadelphia, and finally, Washington. The motion of the train is defined by reference to time: the train moves by being located at different places at different times. If at every moment the train stayed in the same place—Boston, say— then we would say that the train did not move.

Ordinary objects move with respect to time. So if time itself moves, it must move with respect to some other sort of time. But what would that other time be?

The way in which time seems to move is by the *present moment's* moving. Initially the present moment is noon. Later the present is 3.00 p.m. Still later it is 6.00 p.m., and then 9.00 p.m., and so on. Since motion is defined by reference to time, the

| t_1 | Boston | New York | Philadelphia | Washington |

| t_2 | Boston | New York | Philadelphia | Washington |

| t_3 | Boston | New York | Philadelphia | Washington |

| t_4 | Boston | New York | Philadelphia | Washington |

Fig. 1. **The movement of a train defined by reference to time**

present moment, if it is moving, must have these four different locations at four different times, t_1, t_2, t_3, and t_4 (Figure 2), just as the moving train had four different locations at four different times. But the diagram is confusing. It mentions the times noon, 3.00, 6.00, and 9.00, but it also mentions four other times, t_1, t_2, t_3, and t_4. These are the times with respect to which the present moment is moving. What are these other times? In what sort of time does time itself move?

One possibility is that t_1, t_2, t_3, and t_4 are part of a *different* sort of time, call it **hypertime**. Just as trains move with respect to something else (time), time itself moves with respect to something else (hypertime). Most motion takes place with respect to the familiar timeline, but time itself moves with respect to another timeline, hypertime.

Hypertime is a bad idea. You can't simply stop there; you need more, and More, and MORE. Hypertime is supposed to be a sort of time. So if ordinary time moves, surely hypertime moves as well. So hypertime must move with respect to yet another sort of time, hyper-hyper time. That time must also move, which

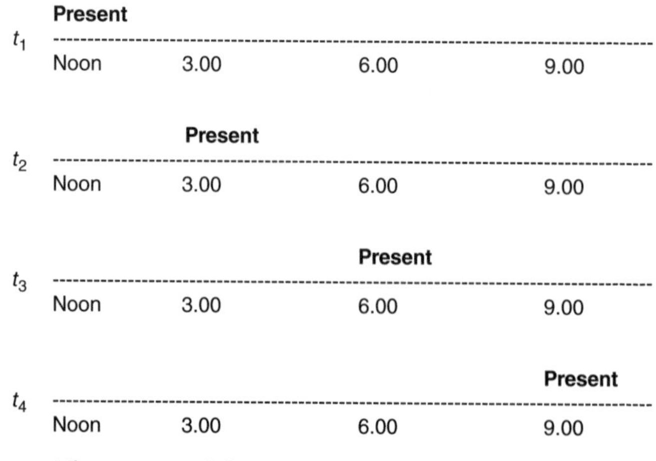

Fig. 2. The moving of the present moment

introduces hyper-hyper-hyper time. And so on. We are stuck with believing in an infinite series of different kinds of time. That's a little much. I can't *prove* that this infinite series does not exist, but surely there are better options. Let's see if we took a wrong turn somewhere.

Instead of being part of hypertime, perhaps t_1, t_2, t_3, and t_4 are just part of ordinary time. In particular, t_1, t_2, t_3, and t_4 could just be the times noon, 3.00, 6.00, and 9.00. According to this view, time moves with respect to itself. Is that plausible?

Although it's nice to be rid of hypertime, there is something strange about this picture. It's not that it isn't *true*. Noon is indeed present at noon, 3.00 is present at 3.00, and so on. But these facts seem *trivial*, and therefore insufficient to capture a genuine flow of time. This can be brought out by comparing time to space, and comparing *present* to *here*. Consider the spatial locations on the train track connecting Boston to Washington. Anyone in Boston can truthfully say 'Boston is *here*'. Likewise, anyone in New York can say 'New York is here'. The same goes for Philadelphia and Washington. So Boston is 'here in Boston', New York is 'here in New York', and so on, just as noon is present at noon, 3.00 is present at 3.00, and so on. But space doesn't move. The line in space connecting Boston with Washington is static. The mere fact that members of a series are located at themselves does not make that series move, whether that series consists of points of time or locations in space.

The Space-Time Theory

Time's motion has us all tangled up in knots. Maybe the problem is with that idea itself. According to some philosophers and scientists, our ordinary conception of time as a flowing river is hopelessly confused, and must be replaced with the **space-time theory**, according to which *time is like space*.

Graphs of motion from high-school physics represent time as just another dimension alongside the spatial dimensions. The graph pictured here (Figure 3) represents a particle that moves through time in one spatial dimension. This particle begins at place 2 in space at the initial time 1, then moves toward place 3, slows down and stops at time 2, and finally moves back to place 2 at time 3. Each point in this two-dimensional graph represents a time t (the horizontal coordinate of the point) and a location in space p (the vertical coordinate). The curve drawn represents the particle's motion. When the curve passes through a point (t, p), that means that the particle is located at place p at time t.

A more complicated graph (Figure 4) represents time alongside two spatial dimensions. (It would be nice to represent all three spatial dimensions, but that would require a four-dimensional graph and so a much more expensive book.) These more complicated graphs are called **space-time diagrams**. (Even the high-school physics graph is a simpler kind of diagram of space-time.) Space-time diagrams can be used to represent all of history; everything that has ever happened or ever will happen can fit into a space-time diagram. This particular diagram represents a dinosaur in the distant past and a person who is born in AD 2000. These objects stretch out horizontally in the graph

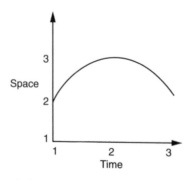

Fig. 3. High-school physics graph of a particle moving through time

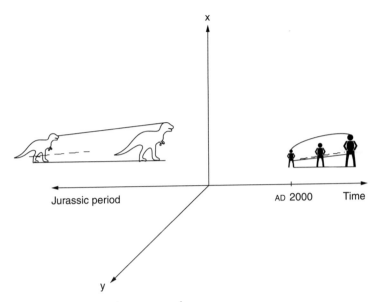

Fig. 4. Space-time diagram

because they last over time in reality, and time is the horizontal axis on the graph: the objects exist at different points along the horizontal time axis. They stretch out in the other two dimensions on the graph because dinosaurs and people take up space in reality: the objects exist at different points along the vertical, spatial, axes.

In addition to the dinosaur and the person themselves, some of their **temporal parts** are also represented in the diagram. A temporal part of an object at a time is a temporal cross-section of that object; it is that-object-at-that-time. Consider the temporal part of the person in 2000: 🕴. This object is exactly the same *spatial size* as the person in 2000. But the temporal part is not the same *temporal size* as the person; the temporal part exists only in 2000 whereas the person exists at later times as well. The person herself is the sum total of all her temporal parts:

. Notice how the person is tapered: the earlier temporal parts (those on the left of the diagram) are smaller than the later ones. This represents the person's growth over time.[1]

In contrast to the ordinary conception of moving or flowing time, then, the space-time theory says that reality consists of a single unified space-time, which contains all of the past, present, and future. Time is just one of the dimensions of space-time, alongside the three spatial dimensions, just as it appears to be in the space-time diagrams. Time does not flow; time is like space.

Well, time isn't *completely* like space. For one thing, there are three spatial dimensions but only one temporal dimension. And time has a special *direction*: past to future. Space has no such direction. We do have words for certain spatial directions: up, down, north, south, east, west, left, right. But these are not directions built into space itself. Rather, these words pick out different directions depending on who says them. 'Up' means away from the earth's center on a line that passes through the speaker; 'North' means toward the Arctic pole from the speaker; 'Left' picks out different directions depending on which way the speaker is facing. In contrast, the past to future direction is the same for everyone, regardless of his or her location or orientation; it seems to be an intrinsic feature of time itself.[2]

Still, according to the space-time theory, time and space are analogous in many ways. Here are three.

First, in terms of *reality*. Objects far away in space (other planets, stars, and so on) are obviously just as real as things here on Earth. We may not *know* as much about the far-away objects as we know about the things around here, but that doesn't make the far-away objects any less real. Likewise, objects

[1] Temporal parts are discussed further at the end of Chapter 7.
[2] Actually, as we'll see in Chapter 12, not everyone agrees with this.

far away in time are just as real as objects that exist now. Both past objects (such as dinosaurs) and future objects (human outposts on Mars, perhaps) exist, in addition to objects in the present. Distant objects, whether temporally or spatially distant, all exist somewhere in space-time.

Second, in terms of *parts*. Material objects take up space by having different parts. My body occupies a certain region of space. Part of this region is occupied by my head, another by my torso; other parts of the region are occupied by my arms and legs. These parts may be called my spatial parts, since they are spatially smaller than I am. The corresponding fact about time is that an object lasts over a stretch of time by having different parts located at the different times within that stretch. These parts are the temporal parts mentioned above. These temporal parts are just as real objects as my spatial parts: my head, arms, and legs.

Third, in terms of *here* and *now*. If I say on the phone 'here it is raining' to a friend in California, and she replies 'here it is sunny' (Figure 5), which one of us is right? Where is the *real here*, California or New Jersey? The question is obviously misguided. There is no 'real here'. The word 'here' just refers to whatever place the person saying it happens to be. When *I* say 'here', it means New Jersey; when my friend says 'here', it means California.

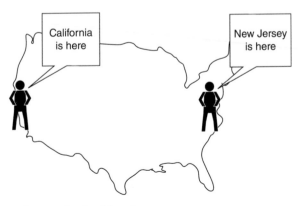

Fig. 5. Where is the 'real here'?

Neither place is *here* in any objective sense. California is here for my friend, New Jersey is here for me. The space-time theory says an analogous thing about time: just as there is no objective here, so there is no objective *now*. If I say 'It is now 2005', and in 1606 Guy Fawkes said 'It is now 1606', each statement is correct (Figure 6). There is no single, real, objective 'now'. The word 'now' just refers to the time at which the speaker happens to be located.

Arguments Against the Space-Time Theory: Change, Motion, Causes

We have met two theories of time. Which is true? Does time flow? Or is time like space?

The space-time theory avoids the paradoxes of time's flow; that counts in its favor. But the believer in time's flow will retort

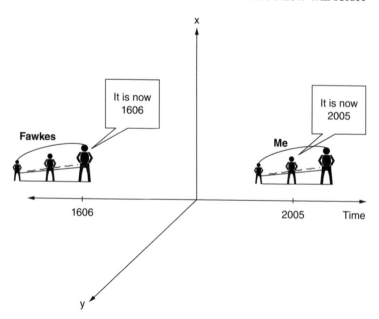

Fig. 6. 'Now' for me and for Guy Fawkes

that the space-time theory throws the baby out with the bath-water: it makes time *too much* like space. For starters, she may say that the alleged analogies between space and time suggested in the last section don't really hold:

> Past and future objects do *not* exist: the past is gone, and the future is yet to be. Things do *not* have temporal parts: at any time, the *whole* object is present, not just a temporal part of it; there are no past or future bits left out. And 'now' is *not* like 'here': the present moment is special, unlike the bit of space around here.

Each of these claims could take up a whole chapter of its own. But time is short, so let's consider three other ways the defender of time's flow might argue that time is not like space. First, regarding *change*:

> Compare change with what we might call 'spatial hetero-geneity'. Change is having different properties at different times. A person who changes height starts out short and then becomes taller. Spatial heterogeneity, in contrast, is having different properties at different *places*. A highway is bumpy at some places, smooth at others; narrow at some places, wide at others. Now, if time is just like space, then having different properties at different times (change) is no different from having different properties at different places (spatial heterogeneity). Look back at the space-time dia-gram. Change is variation from left to right on the diagram, along the temporal axis. Spatial heterogeneity is variation along either of the two spatial dimensions. The two are analogous, according to the space-time theory. But that's not right! Spatial heterogeneity is wholly different from change. The spatially heterogeneous highway doesn't *change*. It just sits there.

Second, regarding *motion*:

Things can move any which way in space; there's no particular direction in which they are constrained to travel. But the same is not true for time. Moving back and forth in time makes no sense. Things can only travel forward in time.

Third, regarding *causes*:

Events at any place can cause events at any other place; we can affect what goes on in any region of space. But events can't cause events at just any other time: later events never cause earlier events. Although we can affect the future, we cannot affect the past. The past is fixed.

The first objection is right that the space-time theory makes change somewhat similar to spatial heterogeneity. But so what? They're not *exactly* the same: one is variation over time, the other is variation over space. And the claim that change and spatial heterogeneity are *somewhat* similar is perfectly reasonable. So the first objection may be flatly rejected.

The second objection is more complicated. 'Things move back and forth in space, but not back and forth in time'—is this really a disanalogy between time and space? Suppose we want to know, for a certain true statement about space, whether the analogous statement is true of time. The twentieth-century American philosopher Richard Taylor argued that we must be careful to construct a statement about time that really is analogous to the statement about space. In particular, we must *uniformly reverse ALL references to time and space* to get the analogous statement. And when we do, Taylor argued, we will see that time and space are more analogous than they initially seemed.

To illustrate. Our true statement about space is this:

Some object moves back and forth in space.

Before we can reverse the references to time and space in this statement, we need to locate all those references, including any that are not completely explicit. For instance, the word 'moves' conceals a reference to time. When these references are made explicit, our statement becomes:

> *Moving back and forth in space*: Some object is at spatial point p_1 at time t_1, point p_2 at time t_2, and point p_1 at time t_3.

(See Figure 7.) Now we're in a position to construct the analogous statement about time—to reverse *all* references to time and space. To do so, we simply change each reference to a time into a reference to a point in space, and each reference to a point in space into a reference to a time. This is what we get:

> *Moving back and forth in time*: Some object is at time t_1 at spatial point p_1, time t_2 at point p_2, and at time t_1 at point p_3.

And we get the graph for this new statement (Figure 8) by swapping the 'Time' and 'Space' labels on Figure 7.

Our question now is: is this second statement correct? Can an object 'move back and forth in time' in this sense? The answer is in fact *yes*, for a fairly humdrum reason. To make this easy to see, let's make the 'moving back and forth in time' graph look like our earlier diagrams by flipping it so that its temporal axis is horizontal (see Figure 9). It should be clear that the diagram represents an object that is first, at t_1, located at *two* places, p_1 and

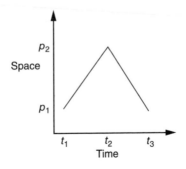

Fig. 7. Moving back and forth in space

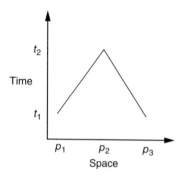

Fig. 8. Moving back and forth in time, temporal axis vertical

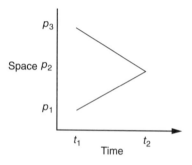

Fig. 9. Moving back and forth in time, temporal axis horizontal

p_3, and then, at t_2, is located at just one place, p_2. This sounds stranger than it really is. Think of a clapping pair of hands. At first the two hands are separated—one is located at place p_1, the other at p_3. Then the hands move toward each other and make contact. The pair of hands is now located at place p_2. Finally, suppose the pair of hands disappears at time t_2. This kind of scenario is what the diagram is representing. So things *can* 'move back and forth in time', if that statement is understood as being truly analogous to 'moving back and forth in space'. We were deceived into thinking otherwise by neglecting to reverse *all* references to time and space. The statement 'things move back and forth in space' contains an implicit *reference dimension*, namely time, for it is with respect to time that things move in space. When we construct the statement 'things move back and forth in time', we must change the reference dimension from time to space. When we do, the resulting statement is something that can indeed be true.

The third objection is the most challenging and interesting. It is true that we do not actually observe 'backward causation', that is, the causation of earlier events by later events. This represents a *de facto* asymmetry between space and time—an asymmetry in the world as it actually is. But a deeper question is whether this asymmetry is built into the nature of time itself, or whether it is just a function of the way the world happens to be. The question is: *could* there be backward causation? *Could* our actions now causally affect the past?

If time is truly like space, then the answer must be *yes*. Just as events can cause events anywhere else in space, so too events can in principle cause other events anywhere in time, even at earlier times. But this has a very striking consequence. If backward causation is possible, then *time travel*, as depicted in books and movies, ought to be possible as well, for it ought to be possible to cause ourselves to be present in the past.

Time travel may never *in fact* occur. Perhaps time travel will never be technologically feasible, or perhaps the laws of physics prevent time travel. Philosophy cannot settle questions about physics or technology; for speculation on such matters, a better guide is your friendly neighborhood physicist or engineer. But if time is like space, there should be no prohibition *coming from the concept of time itself*: time travel should at least be conceptually possible. But is it?

A familiar kind of time travel story begins as follows: 'In 1985, Marty McFly enters a time machine, sets the controls for 1955, pushes the button, waits, and then arrives in 1955 ...' Any time travel story must contain this much: the use of some sort of time travel device and subsequent arrival in the past. But even this much seems to conceal a contradiction. The troublesome bit is the end: 'and *then* arrives in 1955'. The suggestion is that McFly *first* pushes the button, and *second* arrives in 1955. But he pushes the button in 1985, which is *after* 1955.

This is an example of a so-called paradox of time travel. One attempts to tell a coherent story involving time travel, but ends up contradicting oneself. Saying that McFly arrives in 1955 both after and before he pushes the button is contradicting oneself. And if there is no way to tell a time travel story without self-contradiction, then time travel is conceptually impossible.

This first paradox can be avoided. Is the arrival after or before the pushing of the button? *Before*—1955 is before 1985. What about 'and *then*'? Well, all that means is that McFly *experiences* the arrival as being after the button-pressing. Normal people (i.e. non-time travelers) experience events as occurring in the order in which they truly occur, whereas time travelers experience things out of order. In the sequence of McFly's experiences, 1985 comes before 1955. That's a very strange thing, to be sure, but it does not seem conceptually incoherent. (What determines the order of McFly's experiences? Later members of the sequence of his experiences contain memories of, and are caused by, earlier members of the sequence. When McFly experiences 1955, he has memories of 1985, and his 1985 experiences directly causally affect his 1955 experiences.)

Yet a more potent paradox lurks. Let's continue the story from *Back to the Future*: 'Back in 1955, the dashing McFly inadvertently attracts his mother, overshadowing his nerdy father. As the union of his parents becomes less and less likely, McFly begins to fade away into nothingness.' The problem is that a time traveler could undermine his own existence. He could cause his parents never to meet; he could even kill them before he is ever born. But then where did he come from? Back to paradox!

That McFly begins to fade away into nothingness shows that the writers of *Back to the Future* were aware of the problem. But the fade-out solves nothing. Suppose McFly fades out completely after preventing his parents from meeting. He still existed before fading out (it was he, after all, who prevented his parents from meeting). Where then did he come from in the first place? Whatever its literary merits, as a work of philosophy *Back to the Future* fails miserably.

Let's not be too hard on careless screen-writers and authors. (We can't all be philosophers.) Though it's not easy, paradox-free time travel stories can be told. The movie *Terminator* is an excellent example:[3]

> In the future, machines take over the world and nearly destroy the human race. But the machines are eventually thwarted by the human leader John Connor. On the verge of defeat, the machines fight back by sending a machine, a 'Terminator', back to the past to kill John Connor's mother, Sarah Connor, before John is born. John Connor counters by sending one of his men, Kyle Reese, back to the past to protect Sarah Connor. The Terminator nearly succeeds, but in the end Reese stops him. (Reese dies, but not before conceiving a child with Connor's mother, Sarah Connor. The baby, we later learn, grows up to be John Connor himself!)

This story never contradicts itself. It would if the Terminator killed Sarah Connor, since we are told in the beginning of the story that Sarah Connor lived and had a son, John Connor, whose future exploits are the cause of the presence of the Terminator in the past. But since Sarah Connor survives, the story remains consistent.

---

[3] *Terminator 1*, that is. *Terminator 2* appears to be incoherent. It says in the beginning that Cyberdyne systems learned the technology behind Skynet by studying the hand of the corpse of a T-800 Terminator from the future. Then at the end, after the T-800 is melted (Schwarzenegger's thumbs-up to Furlong), the movie suggests that Skynet is never created and Judgment Day is avoided. Where then did the time-traveling Terminators come from? *Terminator 3* does better: it never suggests that Judgment Day is avoided. Yet there are remaining questions, for instance about the true date of Judgment Day. *Terminator 1* is by far the best of the three, from a philosophical (as well as cinematic) point of view.

The failure of *some* time travel stories (such as *Back to the Future*) to remain consistent shows nothing, since other consistent stories can be told. The similarity of time and space has survived: there is no conceptual impossibility with backward causation and time travel.

There are numerous close calls in *Terminator*. Again and again, Sarah Connor narrowly escapes death. It would appear that on any of these occasions, she could easily have died. Yet we know that she must survive, because her son is John Connor. So it seems that she is not really in danger; she cannot die. But there is the Terminator in front of her. The danger seems very real. Back into paradox?

Not at all. What is strange about a time travel story is that we are told the end of the story first. We, the audience, learn early on that John Connor exists in the future. Later we find his mother endangered before he is ever born. We, the audience, know she will survive (if we trust the screen-writers to be consistent!), but that does not mean that *in the story* her danger is unreal.

A very peculiar thing arises when the time traveler himself knows how the story will end. Think of Reese. He knows that the Terminator will fail, since he knows that John Connor exists: it was Connor that sent him back to the past. Yet he fears for Sarah Connor's life, works hard to protect her, and in the end gives his life to save her. Why doesn't he just walk away and save himself? He *knows* that Sarah Connor is going to survive.

Or does he? He *thinks* he remembers serving a man called John Connor. He thinks he remembers Connor defeating the machines. He *thinks* Connor's mother was named Sarah. He *thinks* this woman he's defending is the same Sarah Connor. He *thinks* this woman has not yet had children. So he's got lots of evidence that this woman he's defending will survive. But then he sees the Terminator advance. He sees it effortlessly killing everyone in its path, searching for someone named Sarah Connor. Now it advances on the woman he's defending. It raises its gun. Reese's confidence that this woman will survive now wavers. Perhaps she is not John Connor's mother after all. Or, if he's sure she is, perhaps she's already had a child. Or, if he's quite sure she hasn't, perhaps he's made some other mistake. Perhaps all of his apparent memories from the future are delusions! Such self-doubt is ordinarily far-fetched, but it becomes increasingly reasonable with each step of the Terminator. As certain as he once was that Sarah Connor will survive, he has become equally certain about the danger presented by the Terminator: 'It can't be bargained with! It can't be reasoned with! It doesn't feel pity, or remorse, or fear. And it absolutely will not stop, ever, until you are dead!' He thinks 'I'd better be sure.' He raises his gun.

FURTHER READING

Peter van Inwagen and Dean Zimmerman (eds.), *Metaphysics: The Big Questions* (Blackwell, 1998): this anthology contains a number of readings on time (as well as readings on many other metaphysical topics). Some highlights: 'Time', by J. M. E. McTaggart, makes the shocking claim that time is unreal! Two articles by A. N. Prior argue against the space-time theory. 'The Space-Time World', by J. J. C. Smart, defends the space-time theory. 'The Paradoxes of Time Travel', by David Lewis, argues that time travel is possible.

This article by Richard Taylor lays out a fascinating series of analogies between space and time: 'Spatial and Temporal Analogies and the Concept of Identity', *Journal of Philosophy*, 52 (1955), 599–612.

In addition to the conceptual issues about time travel discussed in this chapter, there are many interesting scientific issues as well. The following article is available online: Frank Arntzenius and Tim Maudlin, 'Time Travel and Modern Physics', <http://plato.stanford.edu/entries/time-travel-phys/>.

CHAPTER 4

God

Earl Conee

'Religion is entirely a matter of opinion, of course, and you are as entitled to your religious opinions as I am to mine.' We've all heard that. We may have said it ourselves. It seems to be a safe and sensible judgment, until we stop trying to be so agreeable and take it seriously. Then it starts to look like a premature judgment, maybe even a dogmatic one.

When a disputed topic is entirely a matter of opinion, there is no better reason to take one side than another. So if religion is entirely a matter of opinion, then either the reasons for and against any religious view balance out evenly, or there are no reasons at all. But that's not credible. Religious thinkers and their opponents have offered lots of reasons and we have no good basis just to assume that they always balance out.

Religion and metaphysics overlap on the question of God's existence. It is a metaphysical matter because part of metaphysics, **ontology**, concerns the most basic kinds of beings. God is basic. For one thing, God is the creator of the universe, if God exists. It would be of tremendous metaphysical interest to learn that at least all of physical reality depends for its existence on the creative choice of one being.

Several lines of reasoning are aimed at establishing that God exists. We'll investigate three sorts of arguments where many of the surrounding issues are metaphysical.

Getting It All Started

Effects

Our first version of an argument for God's existence relies on one fact about the world. The fact is that some things are caused to happen. Many things that are taking place now are clearly effects of various causes. This includes things that are happening to you right now. You see these words as an effect of light that is beamed to your eyes and you understand these words as an effect of your learning English and applying your knowledge of it.

Okay, so there are effects. What is the connection to God's existence?

We next observe that the causes of effects are themselves caused. Those causes in turn have their causes, and so on.

The reasoning from this point that gets us to God's existence is not supposed to rely on anything that we find out by observing the world around us. We are supposed to see its force by thinking about the relation of cause and effect. First we note that a sequence of cause and effect might go back indefinitely. But could it go back forever? The argument asserts that each causal sequence must have gotten started. There must have been a first cause that was not caused, to get each sequence into existence. Thomas Aquinas was the major medieval proponent of this sort of argument. Aquinas observed that, if you take away the cause, then you take away the effects. We see effects. He inferred that there must be some first cause of the existing effects. The argument concludes that the first cause of all is the creator of the universe, God.

The argument proceeds in two phases. The **premises** of the argument are the assumptions that it relies on. The **conclusion** of each phase is the claim that is supposed to be proven by that phase.

First Cause Argument

Phase 1

> *Premise 1*: There are effects.
> *Premise 2*: Any effect derives eventually from a first cause.
> *Conclusion 1*: There is a first cause.

The second phase builds on the first. It starts with the conclusion that Phase 1 is supposed to prove. It adds another assumption and draws the First Cause argument's final conclusion.

Phase 2

> *Conclusion 1*: There is a first cause.
> *Premise 3*: If there is a first cause, then it is God.
> *Conclusion 2*: God exists.

We have to select ways to understand 'God' and 'exists'. People mean various things by 'God'. Sometimes someone's 'God' is whoever the person idolizes. It might be the person's favorite musician. This meaning is no good for present purposes. It is not a major metaphysical matter whether or not any given musician exists (however major a musical matter it is). In contrast, it is metaphysically huge to find out about the existence of a being like this: a creator of the universe who is all-knowing, all-powerful, and morally perfect. We'll understand 'God' so that **God** is a being who is all-knowing, all-powerful, morally perfect, and the creator, if 'God' applies at all. By using the word only for a being with these extreme attributes, we make the issue of God's existence a topic of metaphysical significance and we use a meaning that is recognizable to those in Western religious traditions.

We'll understand '**exists**' in a broad way. 'Exists' applies to anything that is in reality at all, whether past, present, or future, whether in space or not. What 'exists' does not apply to are merely apparent realities, the merely mythical, the illusory, the fictional.

An argument relies on its premises. They must be entirely reasonable to believe if the argument is to establish its conclusion. If there is some serious unresolved doubt about a premise, then the argument does not prove its conclusion.

Let's consider Premise 2 ('P2' for short). The claim made by P2—that any sequence of cause and effect must have gotten started—holds a powerful grip on many people. It can seem just obvious that a series of things must have a first one. This grip loosens, though, when we try to spell out anything that would justify this claim. Exactly why can't each cause in a series have its own cause, with no beginning?

'No beginning' must be rightly understood. It just means that nothing is first in the series. There are familiar precedents for this. The series of numbers known as the integers has no first one. The integers include -1, which is preceded by -2, which is preceded by -3, and so on. The integers go back infinitely.

This infinity is not mind-boggling. We don't have to think of all of the integers separately. We understand the **infinity** adequately if we get the idea that each integer has a new integer as its predecessor. This arrangement is an understandable way for a sequence to exist while having 'no beginning'.

We see how the negative integers are arranged. Why couldn't causes and effects be arranged that way too? Why couldn't there be causes preceding effects backward in time infinitely into the past with no beginning? We cannot *picture* a whole infinite series like that. But we cannot do this picturing just because we have no way to picture the series' 'far end', since it has none. We still do understand the structure of the series, without a picture. So again, what reason do we have to deny the possibility of an infinite series of causes and effects that is structured in the same way? Nothing comes to mind.

This possibility undercuts the credibility of P2. P2 is supposed to be worth assuming because we are supposed to see the need for a first cause in order to have a causal sequence at all. P2 is doubtful if we don't see the need. And now we don't.

Trouble for the First Cause argument does not stop there. Phase 2 has a weakness as well, namely, P3. Suppose that a causal series has some first cause. P3 asserts that the first cause is God in particular. Why so?

Here is an answer: only almighty God is great enough for self-creation. So God can exist without having something else as a cause. Anything other than God has to have help in order to exist.

This answer assumes that each thing has to have a cause. It assumes that either the cause is something other than the effect, or the cause and the effect are one and the same. The answer claims that only God is fit to be a self-cause.

Why must each thing have any cause at all, though? It seems possible that something just happens without being caused at all. This possibility does not imply that anything is so powerful, or otherwise magnificent, that it causes itself. For all we can tell by thinking about causes and effects, it is possible that something just does happen in nature, without a cause, and it starts a causal series. Whether or not this ever actually happens, we don't seem to have any way to exclude it as impossible. So thinking about causes and effects does not give us any good basis to accept the claim made by P3 that any first cause is God.

There is a different defense of the claim that God is a special sort of cause. The new idea is that God is so great that God does not need to get caused into existence. In contrast, all lesser beings require help in order to exist.

But what does greatness have to do with getting caused? Why couldn't some tiny insignificant particle just pop into existence without anything making it exist, and then cause other things? An uncaused first cause of that metaphysically minor sort appears to be possible. This appearance casts doubt on P3.

Maybe there is a need for God as the first cause that stems from a need for *explanations*. We could not correctly *explain why* a first cause just pops up, because there would be no explanation. Is that an objection to the possibility? Yes, *if* we have some assurance that everything has some correct explanation. The claim that there is an explanation for everything is known as the **Principle of Sufficient Reason**.

The Principle of Sufficient Reason requires an explanation for the existence of any first cause. The principle also raises questions about infinite causal series that do not have a first cause. Maybe each item *in* an infinite series is explained as an effect of prior causes. But according to the Principle of Sufficient Reason, that is not all that needs explaining. The *whole series* is something too. The principle requires an answer to the question of what explains why the whole series exists. Thus, first causes and infinite series of causes both require explanation, according to the principle.

A first response to the question that the principle raises about infinite causal series is that the whole series may have a derivative explanation. Perhaps when each event in the series has been explained, the combination of all of those explanations explains the whole thing.

That first response may seem fishy. Maybe each element in the series *causes* the next one. But do those causal facts entirely *explain* why that particular contingent series exists at all?

Suppose not. The Principle of Sufficient Reason requires that there be some explanation. But what assures us that this principle is true? When we think about how things might possibly have gone, it seems possible that some things just do exist with no explanation. Why not? The situation would be intellectually disappointing. But what guarantee do we have that intellectual satisfaction is always available? The Principle of Sufficient Reason declares that explanations always exist. Again, why believe it? The lofty title, 'Principle of Sufficient Reason', doesn't make the principle true. And loftily labeled principles are plentiful. The **Principle of Insufficient Reason** says that some things have no explanation. The two principles conflict. Thinking about possibilities seems to tell us that each of the principles might have been true. Thinking about how things might be gives us no reason to believe that the Principle of Sufficient Reason in particular is the one that is actually true.

If nothing assures us that the Principle of Sufficient Reason is true, then the principle does not help the argument. It does not justify our denying apparent possibilities that go against P3. For instance, it seems possible that everything started with the Big Bang, rather than God, and the Big Bang has no explanation. Until we have a sound basis for denying that any such possibility obtains, P3 is in doubt.

Dependents

Here is an interestingly different version of the argument. The new version is about a non-causal sort of dependence. **Ontological dependence** consists in one thing needing another simultaneously, in order to support its existence. The idea eludes precise definition, but it has one clear sort of illustration. Consider a tuna salad sandwich. At any given time, the sandwich derives its existence from the existence of the bread, the tuna salad, and any other ingredients that compose it. Without them, it would be nothing. The sandwich's ingredients do not cause it to exist. Rather, they give it existence directly. The sandwich 'ontologically depends' on its ingredients. Anything that does *not* depend in this way on any other entity is **ontologically independent**.

Using this idea of ontological dependence, the new version of the argument otherwise goes just like the previous one.

Ontological Dependence Argument

Phase 1

> *Premise 1*: There are ontologically dependent things.
>
> *Premise 2*: Anything ontologically dependent derives its existence eventually from something ontologically independent.
>
> *Conclusion 1*: Something ontologically independent exists.

Phase 2

> *Conclusion 1*: Something ontologically independent exists.
>
> *Premise 3*: If something ontologically independent exists, then God exists.
>
> *Conclusion 2*: God exists.

The claim made by P1 about the existence of ontological dependence is fully credible. Many things, such as a tuna sandwich, illustrate its truth. P2 is supposed to be true because an endless sequence of ontological dependence is supposed to be blatantly impossible. P3 is supposed to be true because only God is powerful and knowledgeable enough to be able to exist independently of all other entities.

We can be efficient here. The doubts about the Ontological Dependence argument parallel the doubts about the First Cause argument.

First, concerning P2, exactly why couldn't there be an endless sequence of ontological dependents? For instance, why not an endless sequence of bigger parts depending for their existence on ever-smaller parts? The sheer infinity of the sequence does not make it inconceivable. We saw that we can conceive of a beginningless series by considering the negative integers. If it is otherwise impossible, why is that? Until we see a good reason, P2 stands in doubt.

And why does only God qualify as ontologically independent? Suppose that there are point-sized physical particles that have no parts. Why think that they would have to depend on anything just to exist?

Until we have a good answer to this question, we have grounds to doubt that God is uniquely qualified for ontologically independence, as P3 claims.

Designing the World

When we stand back from the previous arguments and consider what they try to do, they seem amazingly ambitious. The only facts about the world around us that the arguments use are the facts that there are effects and that there are ontologically dependent things. Simple, abstract, neutral facts like those seem far removed from the existence of an all-knowing, all-powerful, morally perfect creator. It is no wonder that arguments on that meager basis turn out to fall short of proving God's existence.

The actual facts of the world are much more wonderful than just any old effects and dependencies that might have existed. Maybe some awe-inspiring facts about how things actually are can serve to establish God's existence.

Suppose that the whole universe was unplanned and purely accidental. What would it be like? We can apply to this question what we've observed about accidents. Accidents make messes. Car crashes, bridge collapses, and accidents generally, result in disarray. Yes, once in a while there is a fortunate accident where some structure happens to develop. Some inadvertently spilled paint occasionally forms some neat shape. But that is highly exceptional. And if the accidents keep coming, any structure in the situation eventually dissolves. Further accidental paint spills obliterate a pretty pattern. So, if the universe was entirely accidental, then our observations lead us to expect that it would display disorderly disarray, with the occasional pattern emerging briefly.

That is not what we find. Instead, we find an abundance of examples of organized structures resembling complex machines. The most impressive machine-like structures that we know of involve life. The examples range from the intricate interrelationships of components within single cells to the tremendous complexities of whole organisms and eco-systems. The composing material at sub-cellular levels is also highly organized, from the structures of molecules to the structures of atoms and subatomic particles. On larger scales we find planetary systems, galaxies, and groups of galaxies.

We have observed how order gets introduced. What we observe is that machine-like order is imposed by minds. We see such order arise by design in everything from simple tools to amazingly intricate systems like computers and ocean liners. We do observe mindless robotic devices at work on assembly lines, arranging materials into planes, trains, and automobiles. But it always turns out that minds designed the system.

What does this comparison tell us about the origin of the universe? Proponents of a design argument for God's existence contend that it makes a strong case for a divine mind behind the whole thing. They contend that the universe has machine-like structure throughout. They add that the only mind up to the task of planning all this is the mind of the divine creator, God.

First Version

Here is our first version of this reasoning, in two phases.

Demonstration by Design

Phase 1

> *Premise 1*: The universe exhibits intricate machine-like structure on every scale of space and time.

Premise 2: The only possible way for the universe to exhibit such structure is for it to have been intelligently designed.

Conclusion 1: The universe was intelligently designed.

Phase 2

Conclusion 1: The universe was intelligently designed.

Premise 3: If the universe was intelligently designed, then it was designed by God.

Conclusion 2: God exists.

P2 links the claim made by P1 about order in the universe to the conclusion of Phase 1 so that the conclusion follows inescapably. By doing this, though, P2 runs afoul of the possibility of the improbable. Consider the most orderly arrangement imaginable of the largest universe imaginable. Call it a MOHU, for 'Maximally Orderly Huge Universe'. If we somehow knew that we were in a MOHU, it would be ridiculous to assume that our MOHU happened to exist for no reason. That is so unlikely as to be virtually impossible. The problem for Phase 1 is that the accidental existence of a MOHU is only virtually impossible, not quite just plain impossible. No matter how much structure the MOHU has, its materials might possibly have happened to arrange themselves that way in a fluke random occurrence. If we doubt this, our doubts can be worn away. We must acknowledge that some minimal structure could arise by chance, say, a simple shape arising from random fluctuations. How about just a little more structure? No doubt that is less likely, but still, it is a possibility. How about a little more, and more, and more? We find ourselves acknowledging the possibility of a structure exactly like a Rolls Royce arising at random. And we can't stop there. Only the likelihood decreases; we never reach any impossibility. Finally we have to admit that random typing by monkeys might possibly type out Hamlet. No defensible stopping place exists and we end up acknowledging the possibility of a chance MOHU. P2 denies this possibility, and that is bad for P2

Second Version

There is an alternative version of the reasoning. Some arguments render their conclusions highly reasonable, though they offer something short of proof. If considerations of design could do that for the conclusion that God exists, it would be an important result. We said that a chance MOHU was possible. It would be highly unreasonable, though, on finding ourselves in a MOHU, to think that it was a chance MOHU. We would be seeing maximally orderly arrangements everywhere. They would almost certainly exist for some reason, either in the nature of the MOHU's laws or in the mind of a creator. It would be way more sensible to deny that our MOHU existed by a fluke of chance. If we could be shown that affirming God's existence is as reasonable as denying that a MOHU happened by chance, then the claim that God exists would be very strongly supported. Even somewhat weaker support would be plenty interesting.

Let's return to what our observations show us about the origin of organized structure. Our observations make it grossly implausible that much machine-like order arose by accident. The claim that this order exists by chance seems a very poor *explanation* of it. In contrast, the claim that the order implements a planned design renders its existence understandable to us. Proponents of a design argument can offer God's design as the best explanation of the structure that we find in the universe. To capture this idea, we can replace P2 of the Demonstration by Design with a claim about explanation.

Best Explanation by Design

Phase 1

> *Premise 1*: The universe exhibits machine-like structure on every scale of space and time.

> *Premise 2e*: The best explanation of the universe exhibiting such structure is that the universe was intelligently designed.

So probably:

> *Conclusion 1*: The universe was intelligently designed.

Phase 1 assumes that the best explanation of something is probably true. Phase 1 offers no *proof* that its conclusion C1 is true. But if it succeeds, then it gives very good reason to believe C1.

Phase 2

> *Conclusion 1*: The universe was intelligently designed.
> *Premise 3*: If the universe was intelligently designed, then it was designed by God.
> *Conclusion 2*: God exists.

Not questioning P1 for now, how credible is P2e? Initially, it seems quite plausible. What could explain the high level of order that we observe as well as the explanation claiming that the order resulted from an intelligent plan?

Here is a rival hypothesis: unplanned physical laws exist—laws of physics, chemistry, biology, and the other sciences—and these laws, operating on the physical materials in the universe, produce the high level of order. This natural sort of explanation does work. It gives an explanation of the machine-like organization that we observe in things like molecules, marsupials, and marshes. We can understand how some laws, operating on some materials that were in a position to develop into orderly arrangements by conforming to the laws, would yield the highly orderly systems that we find in the universe. It is a long story that science has yet to complete in detail. The point is that we see that this is one way to explain the development of the order.

An explanation saying that the order implements a creator's plan also works. We understand that machine-like order could have come about by implementing an intelligent design. P2e says that the latter explanation is best. But so far, the two explanations seem equally capable of explaining the phenomenon in question. So why think that the design explanation is better?

It is sometimes complained that the purely physical explanation just takes for granted that the physical laws and materials that exist produce the observed order. 'Yes,' it is conceded, 'we can understand the presence of order, given the presence of physical laws and materials that just happen to go together to produce it. But this only pushes back the phenomenon requiring explanation: why is there this remarkable combination of physical materials and laws that mesh together so as to produce the observed high level of organization?'

Notice what this reply concedes. It acknowledges that the physical account explains the existence of the order. The complaint is that the physical account relies on something else, the combination of laws and the arrangement of materials, and they call for explanation.

This reliance does not show that the physical explanation is worse than the explanation by design. The designing creator explanation relies on things too. It relies on the existence of an intelligent designer, the designer's plan for the universe to be as it is, and the designer's capacity to implement that plan in the universe. The existence of these things could use explaining too. It would be arbitrary simply to rest content with no explanation of them.

It is far from clear which explanation is in better shape here. A powerful intelligent being who planned and created the whole universe would be the most amazing thing in the world. Such a being can seem much *more* remarkable than the existence of natural laws and materials that happen to work together to generate the observed order. After all, we acknowledged some possibility of natural things just happening to produce a high degree of order, however unlikely it was. Is a designing creator even *that* likely? If the existence of the right physical ingredients calls for explanation, then the existence of a designing creator cries out for explanation.

Some have claimed that God's existence is self-explanatory; others have denied that it requires explanation. These claims are seriously obscure and doubtful. The first one seems to say that God exists because God exists. That's just bewildering. It never explains anything just to repeat what needs explaining. An all-powerful God would have what it takes to sustain a *continued* existence, if God exists. But God's existence in the first place is what we are concerned about now. Similarly, it is baffling to be told that God's existence requires no explanation. Why not? If there is some good reason to take for granted God's existence, why doesn't that reason also apply to the laws and materials of the physical account? Why do they still need explaining?

If there is anything finally better about the design explanation, it remains to be seen. Until it is definitely seen, P2e stands in doubt.

What about P1? Is the universe really so well organized all over the place? That is doubtful. On the largest spatial scale that we currently observe, the galaxies are not randomly distributed. They tend to cluster. But that's it. They are not arrayed in some pinwheel pattern or any other fancy structure. Being somewhat clumped together is not an impressive type of organization. Similarly, on the smallest spatial scale that we currently have information about, the scale of particles composed of quarks, we have trios of quarks bound closely together and jiggling about. That is not much like a complicated machine. When we look far back and far forward in time, the leading current cosmological views find considerably less intricate organization than is present today. Going far back toward the Big Bang, the theories say that things become ever less machine-like in structure. Going far forward toward the Big Chill, the theories say the same thing. So P1 is open to serious doubt.

We could replace P1 with a premise about the more localized order that is more clearly present in the world. But the smaller the portion of reality that displays machine-like order, the more probable it is that the order is accidental. Recall that our observations of accidents allow occasional patterns to be purely accidental effects of natural laws in operation. Does the extent of machine-like order in the whole world, throughout all of space and time, rise above that level? This is a question of detailed fact with no obvious answer.

There are other kinds of order that are sometimes cited in design arguments. One kind is the order that consists in the unbroken regularity of the operation of *natural laws*. This order is present throughout the known universe, including regions where machine-like structure is absent. If we replace P1 with a claim about the existence of this lawful order, does that make a better case for a designing creator?

The second premise will have to be adjusted too. It will have to claim that intelligent design best explains this lawful order. This new premise is open to doubt. When it comes to machine-like order, we are familiar with how minds introduce it. We have observed minds producing machines. But when it comes to something as perfectly uniform as the operation of a natural law, we have not observed minds implementing any such thing. Natural laws are like rules. Minds do invent rules. But intelligent minds in our experience do not enforce the same rules with no variation, ever, no matter what. Attributing such order to an intelligent design does not enable us to understand why the order exists, at least until we see a good enough reason for the absolute constancy.

This is an initial ground for doubt. Some views about God offer candidate reasons for God to institute unvarying laws. Also, according to some religious views natural laws are not perfectly constant, since they have been miraculously violated. These views in turn are disputed.

Another sort of order that some people point to as evidence of design is a kind of fine-tuning among physical magnitudes.

According to current theories, if certain basic physical magnitudes had not been almost exactly the quantities that they are, they would have disallowed the development of complex atoms, much less human life. Does this argue that the universe was designed for us to exist in it?

Again, there is some ground for doubt. Suppose that human life depends on some exactly appropriate basic magnitudes in nature. Still, human life occupies an extremely small fraction of the known universe and it is extremely recent by cosmological standards. If the universe was designed for us by a mind intelligent and powerful enough to adjust physical magnitudes so that we would eventually get here, why didn't the mind produce us more efficiently?

Again, the initial doubt may be answerable. Perhaps the huge lifeless portion of space and time serves other intelligent purposes. Such purposes have been proposed, and disputed.

This issue will not be resolved here. There is no brief way to decide the merits of replacing our first premise with one about these other sorts of order. However the best version of the first premise finally works out, Phase 2 of the Design arguments has a problem that deserves our attention.

The doubts that were just raised about explanations by design are similar in spirit to some of David Hume's ideas in his wonderful work, *Dialogues Concerning Natural Religion*. P3 in Phase 2 is subject to some of Hume's other powerful points. For one thing, Hume suggests that we make use of *more specific details* in our observations of the origins of order. For instance, any large building project in our experience has multiple designers who have limited knowledge and ability. The universe was the largest building project of them all, if it was created by design. So our experience would lead us to expect a huge team of limited designers for such a project, rather than one all-knowing all-powerful God. Do we know anything else that overrides this lesson of experience? If not, then P3 is highly questionable.

Conceptually Guaranteeing God

A **concept** is a way of classifying something in our thinking. All of us have approximately a zillion concepts. We have the concept of a mammal, the concept of molasses, the concept of a toy, the concept of friendship, the concept of gravity, the concept of eyesight, the concept of danger, the concept of a boringly long list, and so on. A **singular concept** is a classification that brings to mind a single thing, if the concept applies at all. Singular concepts are familiar. Examples from ordinary life abound. When Donna's dachshund Dobson is in Donna's house alone, he is fond of luxuriating on the sofa, occupying his chosen pillow in regal comfort. While Dobson is doing this, we can bring him to mind in many ways—for example, by conceiving of him as the pooch on the couch, as the dachshund on the pillow, and as the dog in the house. These are singular concepts that apply to Dobson.

One important line of thinking has it that God is the greatest being that anyone could bring to mind. If so, then one singular concept of God is the concept of the greatest conceivable being. We'll need the phrase 'greatest conceivable being' a lot. Let's abbreviate it with its initials: **GCB**.

Almost a thousand years ago the medieval philosopher Anselm argued that the GCB concept has to apply to an existing entity who is God, because of facts that we can discover by appreciating the nature of the concept itself. The reasoning is called 'Anselm's ontological argument'.[1] In one version or another, ontological arguments are particularly appealing to many philosophers. This appeal has something to do with the remarkable fact that we are supposed to be able to find out, just by

---

[1] The aim of this chapter in considering Anselm's argument is to think about whether it shows that God *actually* exists. In the chapter 'Why Not Nothing?' two other ontological arguments are discussed. The aim there is to determine whether they can show that a *necessary* being exists, whether or not the being qualifies as God.

thinking correctly, all that we need to know to see them prove their point. They are pure philosophy with a powerful payoff—*if* they work. The ontological argument that we'll consider is a reconstruction of Anselm's highly influential reasoning.

It'll be helpful to have a label for what a singular concept singles out. In other words, we want a term for the entity that meets the specifications of the concept, if anything does. The concept of Donna's dog, for instance, calls for a dog that is the one owned by Donna. The concept applies to such a dog, or it does not apply. Let's label the entity that is singled out by a singular concept the **target** of the concept.

Typical singular concepts need not have a target. Consider the concept of the spoon on the moon. If a single spoon happens to be on the moon—maybe an astronaut left one there—then this concept has that spoon as its target. Otherwise the concept of the spoon on the moon has no target. Either way, the concept of the spoon on the moon is one of our concepts. The same goes for the singular concept of the pooch on the couch, the singular concept of the farthest star from the Earth, and so forth.

Key question: Could our GCB concept lack a target?

No, according to Anselm. He asks us to suppose that the GCB concept has no target. In other words, suppose that the GCB does not exist. Anselm argues that if this were so, then we could form another concept that would be a concept of something greater than the GCB. Starting with our GCB concept, we can add the idea of existing. This gives us the concept of the existing GCB (the **EGCB** for short). Anselm holds that under circumstances where no GCB existed, our EGCB concept would be the concept of something greater than the GCB. The reason is that existing is a better status than not existing and we would be explicitly requiring existence in our EGCB concept.

But wait! Anselm points out that there is no possible way for us to form a concept of any being that is greater than the greatest conceivable one. The GCB is the greatest being that we can conceive of—it says so right in the concept itself. Therefore we *cannot* conceive of a greater being. Yet in the situation just described, we are supposed to *be* conceiving of a greater being. Since this is impossible, as we just saw, we must have assumed something untrue in setting up the situation. Anselm holds that the only questionable assumption in the setup is the initial one, the assumption that the GCB concept does not have a target. If that assumption is the mistake, then the GCB concept *does* apply to something. So the target of the GCB concept, the GCB, exists. The GCB is God. So God exists. This reasoning can be summarized as follows.

Anselm's Ontological Argument

Phase 1

> *Temporary Assumption (TA)*: The GCB concept has no target.

Now add this premise:

> *Premise 1*: If the GCB concept has no target, then the EGCB concept is a concept of something greater than the GCB concept.

From TA and P1, infer:

> *Temporary Conclusion (TC)*: The EGCB concept is a concept of something greater than the GCB concept.

Add another premise:

> *Premise 2*: No concept is a concept of something greater than the GCB concept.

Premise 2 says that TC is untrue, so the temporary assumption TA that got us TC must be false. In other words, infer:

> *Conclusion 1*: The GCB concept does have a target.

Phase 2

> *Conclusion 1*: The GCB concept does have a target.
> *Premise 3*: If the GCB concept does have a target, then the GCB exists.
> *Conclusion 2*: The GCB exists.

Phase 3

> *Conclusion 2*: The GCB exists.
> *Premise 4*: The GCB is God.
> *Conclusion 3*: God exists.

Let's start our critical consideration of this argument on a positive note by contemplating P3. It is entirely okay. If a singular concept has a target, then the concept does apply to some existing thing. For example, since the singular concept of Donna's dog has the real dog Dobson as a target, Donna's dog exists.

Now let's consider the final assumption, P4. It seems pretty credible at first that God is the GCB. But maybe we can conceive of something greater than God. Such as? Well, consider someone with limited abilities who overcomes adversity and acts heroically. In a way, such a person seems to be better than any being of unlimited power and knowledge who is morally flawless. That sort of being is too knowledgeable and powerful to be heroic. Maybe heroism is one feature of a conceivable being who would be overall greater than a being who has the power and knowledge of the traditional God.

This is debatable. God could still turn out to be the greatest. For instance, the greatness of God might consist in God's having all of the important positive properties, like knowledge, ability, and moral goodness, to a *maximum* extent. That sounds like an unbeatable combination.

This idea that God has the maximum degree of greatness is a risky one, though. The important positive properties may not all have a *possible* maximum. For example, part of being morally good is doing good. Yet no matter how much good someone does, it seems *possible* to have done more good. So moral goodness may not have a maximum. If not, then we don't get the GCB by conceiving of a being who is *maximally* morally good, because we get an impossible being. Any being that does exist and is good surely outdoes the greatness of any impossible being. Thus, the maximum idea of God is a problematic way to try to establish God as the GCB.

Much more thinking is needed to draw a justified conclusion about the truth of P4. But regardless of how well Phase 3 with P4 works out, successful reasoning through Phase 2 would be nothing to sneeze at. A proof of Phase 2's conclusion, C2, would be mighty metaphysically interesting. Establishing the actual existence of the greatest conceivable being would show us something wonderful about reality.

P1 and P2 are taken for granted in Phase 1. If either one of them is untrue, then C1 is not proven in Phase 1. Without success in Phase 1, the whole argument collapses. Let's think more about P1.

P1 says that if the GCB concept has no target, then the EGCB concept is 'of' something greater. The interpretation of the small word 'of' turns out to be crucial to assessing the argument. Two interpretations should be distinguished. First, for a concept to be 'of' a greater being, on one interpretation, is for a greater being to be the concept's target. This interpretation gives us:

> *P1.1*: If the GCB concept has no target, then the target of the EGCB concept is a greater thing than the target of the GCB concept.

If the GCB concept has no target, then it is easy for some other concept to have a greater target. The other concept would just have to apply to something that is greater than nothing. Again, anything good is greater than nothing. So a concept of a good thing that exists would qualify as having a greater target than the GCB concept. But would the EGCB concept in particular have a greater target, as P1.1 says?

Suppose that the GCB concept has no target. Recall that this means that the GCB concept does not apply to anything. If nothing is the greatest conceivable being, then nothing is the *existing* greatest conceivable being either. Thus, if the one concept applies to nothing, then so does the other. Since they both lack targets, the greatness of their targets is the greatness of nothing—worthless! Therefore, if the GCB concept has no target, then the GCB concept and the EGCB concept would be *tied at zero* for the greatness of their targets. This denies the P1.1 claim that the EGCB concept would have a *greater* target. So if we have interpreted P1 correctly as P1.1, then it is untrue.

There is another interpretation of P1. The new idea is that if the GCB concept has no target, then the EGCB concept demands more greatness than does the GCB concept. In other words, if no GCB exists, then in the competition for being our way of conceiving of the greatest being that we can possibly conceive of, the EGCB concept would beat out the GCB concept. Both concepts clearly require extreme greatness to apply. But according to P1 as we are now interpreting it, in the absence of a real GCB, the EGCB concept would require the greater greatness. This gives us:

> P1.2: If the GCB concept has no target, then the greatness needed for the EGCB concept to apply is more than the greatness needed for the GCB concept to apply.

P1.2 does not stand scrutiny. The GCB concept goes all out in its demand for greatness—it demands 'the greatest'. It demands maximal greatness, whether or not its demand is met. For example, existing appears to be part of what it takes to be the greatest thing that we can conceive of. Any 'things' that could have existed, but don't exist, at most could have been great. 'They' aren't great. 'They' aren't anything, much less anything great. If this appearance that existence is needed for greatness is correct, then the GCB concept demands existence just as much as the EGCB concept. If this appearance is incorrect, then the

EGCB concept does not demand more greatness by explicitly demanding existence.

There is just no way for the GCB concept to be beaten in this competition. The GCB concept requires 'the greatest', and that's that! Yet P1.2 alleges that under one particular condition—the non-existence of the GCB—the EGCB concept demands more greatness. That must be a mistake. The existence or non-existence of a GCB does not alter what any concept demands for its application. A concept's demands for its application are what make it the concept that it is. For example, the concept of chocolate is the concept of chocolate, rather than the concept of vanilla, or the concept of strawberry ice cream, or any other concept, because the concept of chocolate is the one that demands for its application precisely chocolate, nothing more or less. A concept's demands are just built into it. The non-existence of the GCB doesn't affect what the EGCB concept demands, including whether the EGCB concept demands something greater than the GCB concept demands. And we've just seen that the EGCB concept does *not* demand anything greater. So on this other interpretation P1 is also untrue and does not help Anselm's ontological argument. Phase 1 of the argument relies on the truth of some interpretation of P1. Since the argument needs Phase 1 to work in order to get anywhere, the argument goes nowhere if our criticism is correct.

Putting it All Together

We have found problems in each of the arguments for God's existence that we have considered. Let's not leap to any conclusions. Even if we had found problems in all arguments that are ever made for God's existence, it would not follow that God does not exist. Entities whose existence cannot be proven by us might exist. They might exist without being in any revealing sort of relation to us. God could be like that. Or God could be revealed by an argument that we have not considered.

Let's not leap away from any conclusions either, though. The arguments that we have seen for God's existence do not work.

Sometimes each clue to a crime on its own does not mean much, while together they argue powerfully for a certain culprit. Likewise, the thoughts from several arguments might work better in combination. The most reasonable belief that we can have about something is one based on *all* relevant available evidence. So before we draw any conclusive conclusions about God's existence, we would do best to look at the combined strength of our arguments.

There are initial indications of an improved case. For instance, it seems to become more reasonable to think that the universe had God as first cause when we add in the observations from our discussion of the design argument that support the idea that the universe displays various sorts of order. On the other hand, the doubts raised about whether the universe really is organized as though by an intelligent designer carry over as doubts that God was its first cause.

Assessing the strength of a combined case for God's existence would require assessing together everything in the First Cause and Design arguments, and the Ontological argument as well. Having done this, we would still not be in a position to draw the most rational conclusion. More evidence exists. There are other arguments for God's existence. There are arguments against God's existence too. The most prominent one—the **Problem of Evil**—contends that an all-powerful, all-knowing, morally perfect being would never allow all of the bad things that exist in this world, and so no such being exists. Several versions of this argument have been developed. They have in turn received intense critical scrutiny. All of that is more of the evidence available on the topic of God's existence. And then there's the challenge of assembling and weighing the totality of the evidence . . . We never said that metaphysics was quick and easy!

There's no need to get discouraged, either. We have looked into the merits of the major metaphysical arguments for God's existence. So we have a serious investigation well under way.

FURTHER READING

Philosophy on the topic of God's existence comprises a huge literature. Here are two significant recent books. The first one is favorably disposed toward arguments against the existence of God; the second one is favorably disposed toward arguments for the existence of God.

Jordan Howard Sobel, *Logic and Theism* (Cambridge University Press, 2004).

Richard Swinburne, *The Existence of God*, 2nd edn. (Oxford University Press, 2004).

CHAPTER 5

Why Not Nothing?

Earl Conee

Introduction

Suppose that you find pickles in your potato soup. You ask indignantly, 'Why are there pickles in my potato soup?' You are told that Mort put them in when he prepared your soup. He did so because good old Bob told him, as a prank, that you favor pickles in your potato soup.

You may well remain dissatisfied, but the presence of the pickles has been explained to you. It is not an exhaustive explanation. It takes much for granted. It doesn't explain Bob's desire to play a prank or Mort's capacity to make soup. More fundamentally, it doesn't explain the existence of Mort, Bob, or the pickles. A fuller explanation would explain those things. It too would take a lot for granted, though, probably including some background conditions and general principles of psychology and biology.

The explanatory structure of this example seems to be completely typical. Seemingly, any answer to any question has to take something for granted. Explanations use some things to explain others.

But then there is the following metaphysical question, where taking anything for granted appears to be disallowed. Also, it seems to be as basic as a question can get.

Q: Why is there something, rather than nothing?

Q asks why there is anything at all. Any answer to Q that is based on something seems to be immediately disqualified. Whatever the basis for the answer, Q asks for an explanation of why that basis exists in the first place. Yet how could an answer be any good if it is not based on anything?

What is the Question?

We should be sure that we are focusing on a metaphysical question. We should set aside nearby scientific ones. According to established science, the whole universe emerged from an explosion, the Big Bang. If so, then one question we can ask is this:

QBB: What explains the Big Bang—why did it happen?

There is no established scientific answer to QBB. But it is a scientific issue. An answer might give a typical sort of causal explanation of the Big Bang. Such an explanation would identify one or more events and conditions that made the Big Bang happen in accordance with natural law. Or an answer might use just natural laws. It might be discovered that one or more basic laws of nature entail that the Big Bang was inevitable, or that it was more or less probable.

In any case, with a little further thought we'll see that Q definitely does not ask for an explanation of the Big Bang that cites causes or laws. In fact, the main question that Q seems to be asking looks altogether unanswerable.

To clarify the metaphysical question, let's consider the most minimal alternative reality that we can specify. This is an absolutely empty reality—no material objects, no dimensions of space or time, just nothing. And by 'nothing' here we truly mean: nothing! Our maximally minimal reality does not include any objects or dimensions; it does not include any natural laws or any tendencies. It is empty in every way. Let's call it 'W'.

This W at least appears to have been a possible alternative to the actual situation. One question that Q can ask is the following one:

QM: Why there is anything more to reality than W?

If QM is what Q asks, then scientific replies to the question about the Big Bang—in terms of causes or laws—seem disqualified. Those replies tell us why something happened, namely, the Big Bang, by relying on at least one other thing that explains its occurrence, such as a cause or a law. But QM asks about the existence of those other things too, since W includes none of them. QM asks why anything exists of any sort at all. So it seems that an answer to this question cannot take for granted the existence of any sort of thing, not even a natural law. All answers available from science seem to take for granted at least one such entity without explaining why it exists.

Do We Get the Question?

Do we really understand QM? After all, we have no familiarity with the phenomenon of there being nothing at all. In fact, calling it a 'phenomenon' is an overstatement. Nothingness is the absence of all phenomena, and everything else. The mind boggles.

On second thought, though, the mind doesn't stay boggled. Let's start with the word 'nothing'. A reality in which nothing exists is just a reality in which there isn't anything—no thing of any kind. We get that idea. We cannot *imagine* it. A silent blank void is as close as we can come, and that is not nothing. It is a spatial region with no sound, light, or matter. That is something. But understanding a topic of a question does not require being able to imagine that topic. For instance, we can understand questions that are about amazement. We have a good idea of what amazement is. Yet we have no mental image of amazement. We can imagine, say, Amanda's being amazed. But that is only an image of Amanda making some typical display of amazement. It is not an image of the psychological state of amazement itself. Likewise, we have some understanding of what possibility is. We can picture specific possible things, but not their possibility. Yet we do not have a problem with understanding the topics of amazement and possibility well enough to comprehend questions about those topics. So if there is a problem understanding what QM is asking, it is not that we cannot imagine what it is about.

More positively, here is a reason to think that we do understand the question. We understand each word in QM. The word 'why' comes closest to making trouble. This is not because we draw a blank. It is just that we lack full clarity about it. The 'why' asks for explanation. Explanations differ. The question does not specify what sort of explanation is sought. In any case, we do see that it asks for an explanation. This is enough to make sense of the question. In addition to understanding the words in QM separately, we also see how they relate grammatically. We can put them together and comprehend the whole thing. We can show our understanding by rephrasing QM with four easy words: why is there anything? We do get the question.

To say that we understand a question is not to suggest that the question is easy to investigate, much less to answer. In the case of QM, it is not even easy to say what would qualify as an answer. In fact, answering QM seems hopeless, at least at first. How could there be an explanation that does not rely on anything?

Necessitarianism

Perhaps all explanations do rely on something. According to one important tradition on this topic, though, that fact does not prevent us from solving the problem posed by Q. The tradition says that we can explain why the possible reality that actually exists has something in it, unlike the maximally empty W, by showing that W is not even possible. We can understand why there is something rather than nothing, by seeing that there has to be something. More specifically, we can be shown that one or more particular somethings have to exist. These would be **necessary beings**, that is, beings that exist in any and all possible situations. By seeing why one or more necessary beings exist, we understand why there is actually something. We understand that this turns out to have been inevitable.

Suppose that we can also see that each thing relied on to establish the existence of some necessary being is itself a necessary being. If so, then we do not have to worry about the fact that we are relying on things to explain things. If we really can see that they are all inevitable, then we are left with no reason to wonder why they actually exist.

This necessitarian approach sounds promising in form, but it is dubious in substance. If it is correct, then we were making a mistake in thinking of the totally thing-free W as a possibility. Yet exactly what would be impossible about W? Just that it lacks objects? But how could that be impossible? Temporary emptiness of some spatial region is possible. Once we grant this, there seems to be no upper limit on how much space can be empty and for how long. So why not a whole empty reality? Is W impossible because it lacks all natural laws? But what could be inevitable about laws of nature? Some things could have happened by chance rather than by law. Why couldn't reality have been entirely lawless? And if some possible reality with objects and events in it is lawless, then why would there have to be natural laws if there were no objects? So again, just what is impossible about W?

Godly Necessitarianism

Necessitarians have answers to these questions. There is a major division in necessitarian approaches at this point between theological necessitarians and non-theological ones. According to one main theological view, God is a necessary being. God would exist under any possible circumstances. So there could not have been nothing.

We should note an initial doubt about Godly necessitarianism. It is subject to a problem of vanishing possibilities. We are talking about the traditional God here. God has to be the all-knowing, all-powerful, perfectly loving, and benevolent creator of the universe. Apparent possibilities vanish when we ask what sort of a reality such a being would allow to exist. For instance, it seems clear that there are some evils that God would not allow— perhaps the existence of suffering for no good reason, or the existence of unjustified human degradation. So, if the traditional God is a necessary being, such evil is not possible. The appearance that the evil was even possible would be an illusion. Yet we can spell out in as much detail as we like how things go in a reality that includes such evils but not God. Leaving God out of the situation does not give any appearance of making it an impossibility. So its impossibility is dubious.

And that is not all. Would God allow a reality in which there was no sentient life? Seemingly not. Seemingly, a perfectly loving and benevolent being would want to share existence with sentient creatures, and have those creatures do very well in their lives. An all-powerful being would be able to create thriving sentient beings. So no possible reality would be without them, if God exists necessarily. Thus, many more apparent possibilities would turn out to be merely apparent.

Note that the *existence* of God does not make this trouble. It can be that God actually exists. As long as God is not a necessary being, worthless and repugnant possibilities do not have to be allowed by God in order for them to be possible. It can be that God is not in those alternative realities to prevent such inexcusably miserable things. It is the assumption of a *necessary* God that gives rise to the problem of vanishing possibilities. That is the very assumption of interest to us here, though, since it is the assumption that implies that there could not have been nothing.

The problem gets worse. Apparently, any flaw or defect of any kind would be avoidable, with no net cost, by one who had sufficient knowledge and power. A being with boundless love, power, and benevolence would avoid all defects. So it seems that wherever such a being exists, the world would be entirely lacking in defects. And the same goes for any other imperfection—it would be banished. If this is correct, then only perfection is even possible, if God is necessary. Yet that seems to leave out virtually all of the possibilities! Almost everything that we would otherwise have thought to be possible is less than perfect. All of that would turn out to be impossible. Amazing! Thus, there seems to be a high price in credibility to pay for thinking that God is a necessary being. So why think so?

Ontological Arguments for a Necessary Being

Let's look into a classic sort of argument for a necessary God, an ontological argument.[1] Our initial version of it will have two

[1] The ontological arguments in this chapter aim to prove the necessary existence of a being who is traditionally identified as God. The ontological argument of the 'God' chapter aims to prove the actual existence of God. Both versions to be discussed in this chapter derive primarily from Rene Descartes's

phases. The first assumption of the first phase is the claim that the concept of God is the concept of a being who is maximally perfect. If that is not your concept of God, it does not matter for present purposes. We are looking for a necessary being to answer our present question. If the necessary being happens to fit your concept of God, or otherwise qualify as God, then that is an additionally interesting and important fact. But it is actually incidental to present purposes.[2] We will not even use the term 'God' in our formulation of the argument. The current argument aims to establish the existence of a necessary being by using the concept of the most perfect being. We can scrutinize the merits of this reasoning, whatever the connection turns out to be between the most perfect being and other understandings of God.

Let's begin with a preliminary sketch of the argument. It is about a concept. **Concepts** are our ideas; they are our ways of thinking about things. The first assumption of our first version of the argument asserts the existence of a particular concept. It says that there is a concept of something that is maximally perfect. The other assumption of the first phase of the argument is that it is impossible for anything to be maximally perfect without existing. Relying on these assumptions, the first phase concludes that something that is maximally perfect exists.

The second phase of the argument adds the third and final assumption. This is where necessary existence comes in. The claim of the final assumption is that necessary existence is implied by maximal perfection. Using this assumption together with the conclusion of the first phase, the argument draws the final conclusion: something maximally perfect exists necessarily (!).

Here is the whole thing in a nutshell.

presentations of the argument in his *Meditations* and *Replies to Caterus*, though they are not primarily intended to be historically faithful renditions of his reasoning. The first version owes most to the *Meditations*.

[2] The focus is reversed in the chapter 'God'.

First Ontological Argument

Phase 1

> *Premise 1*: There is a concept of something that is maximally perfect.
>
> *Premise 2*: Anything that is maximally perfect must exist.
>
> *Conclusion 1*: Something that is maximally perfect exists.

Phase 2

> *Conclusion 1*: Something that is maximally perfect exists.
>
> *Premise 3*: Anything that is maximally perfect exists necessarily.
>
> *Conclusion 2*: Something maximally perfect exists necessarily.

If this argument succeeds, then our hypothetical entirely empty alternative reality W turns out to be impossible. A perfect being has to exist, no matter what.

This argument has strengths. Initially, Premise 1 ('P1' for short) looks safe. We do have that *concept* at least, don't we? Well, we'll see . . . Meanwhile, the claim of P2 seems even safer. Doesn't a thing have to exist, in order to be maximally perfect? After all, doesn't a thing have to exist, just in order to be pretty good, or mediocre, or even bad, much less perfect?

Actually, this has been doubted. For instance, isn't it a fact that Santa Claus is a very good fellow, distributing all of those presents every year? Yet Santa does not exist. So existence is not required in order to be good.

On reflection, though, that reasoning looks faulty. It is not really so that Santa is good, period. And this is not because of any scandalous hidden truth establishing that Santa is bad. It is just that no Santa exists to be in any condition at all, good, bad, or otherwise. Rather, the fact in the vicinity is just that, *according to the Santa folklore*, Santa is good. This fact does not imply that Santa is actually good, any more than it implies that Santa exists.

Anyway, P2 is defensible even if some fictional character manages to be good without existing. P2 says that to be *maximally* perfect, a thing must exist. Maybe unreal things like Santa can be good, maybe even perfect in some ways. As long as the uppermost level of perfection is reserved for existing things, that is all the second assumption says. And that is plausible. Unreal things, however glorious in their own way, are rather ethereal and inconsequential in comparison to anything great that actually exists.

P3 is also plausible. It is easy to believe that necessary existence is in some way better than contingent existence. Necessary existence is definitely more impressive. Perhaps this is because necessary existence has a special sort of perfection not shared by contingent existence.

But let's reconsider the initial assumption, P1, which says that there is a concept of something that is maximally perfect. Again, this initially seems beyond doubt. We can just consult our inventory of concepts and, sure enough, we have the concept of something maximally perfect. Doesn't that settle the existence of a concept of something maximally perfect?

Yes and no. The meaning of P1 turns on how we take the ambiguous word 'of' in its wording. Here is an analogous case with the same ambiguity. Suppose I say, 'There is a painting of an animal on my wall.' This sentence is ambiguous—what I say might be true in two drastically different ways. First, it might be that a painting on my wall is 'of' an animal, because it is a portrait of a particular animal, say, a certain moose that the artist saw. Using 'of' in this way, our claim attributes a relationship between two existing things: the canvas on my wall and that moose. The claim says that the one portrays the other in paint.

But equally, it might be that I have a painting 'of' an animal by having on the wall a painting that represents a mythical animal, say, a hippogriff. It is still correctly called a painting 'of' an animal, but now in a new sense. Hippogriffs do not exist. No actual animal was painted. The new meaning is that it would take a certain sort of animal for the painting to portray something real. In effect, the painting specifies how part of the world would have to be for the painting to have been drawn from life. It would take the existence of a hippogriff for the painting to be an accurate depiction of something. When a painting requires an animal in this way—in order to be drawn from life—that is something else that we call a painting 'of' an animal.

The same goes for concepts. You do not have a concept 'of' something as being maximally perfect, understanding 'of' in the first way, unless you are related to some existing thing by conceiving it to be maximally perfect. The two of you have to exist and you have to be conceptually related to it. In contrast, you have a concept 'of' something as maximally perfect, understanding 'of' in the second way, if you have a concept that applies to something only if that something is maximally perfect. The concept specifies a standard. It calls for the utmost perfection. Unless that level of perfection is there, the concept does not apply. But the concept can exist and specify maximal perfection in order to apply, without actually applying. We still say that it is the concept 'of' something maximally perfect. We say this to signify that the concept requires maximal perfection for it to apply, just as something can be a painting 'of' a hippogriff because the painting requires an actual hippogriff to be an accurate depiction.

Equipped with this distinction, we can interpret P1. P1 says that there is a concept 'of' something that is maximally perfect. Is that true? Well, if we take the 'of' in the second way, then there is such a concept. We do have the idea of being maximally perfect. At least, we have this idea abstractly, however unsure we may be about details of what makes for the highest level of perfection. We have the idea of something having whatever it takes to be most perfect. So we must agree that this concept exists. Interpreted in this way, P1 is true.

But now comes trouble for the argument. When we combine this interpretation of P1 with P2, the conclusion of the first phase does not follow. P2 says: anything that *is* maximally perfect must exist. So, in order for P2 to help to imply the first phase conclusion, namely, that a maximally perfect being exists, P2 has to work in combination with a claim to the effect that something *is* maximally perfect. Yet P1 now does not say that anything is maximally perfect. P1 says only that a concept exists that has maximal perfection as a requirement for its application. P1 does not imply that this requirement is met. Thus, when we understand the 'of' in P1 in this way, Phase 1 of the argument goes wrong.

Understanding 'of' in P1 the other way makes one large improvement. The conclusion of the first phase now follows. P1 now says all of this: there is a concept and there is a something, these two are related in such a way that the first is a concept of the second, and the second is maximally perfect. So now P1 implies that something *is* maximally perfect. Thus, since P2 says that whatever is maximally perfect must exist, it follows that something maximally perfect does exist, just as the conclusion says.

Taking P1 in this way, with the 'of' relating a concept to an existing thing, why believe it? Only this much is clear: there is a concept that applies to something that is maximally *perfect, if it applies at all.* When we had P1 saying *only* that much, though, we were back with the other interpretation and its problem. The argument needs P1 to claim something beyond that. It needs P1 to claim that there is something to which the maximal perfection concept *does* apply. So we need a good answer to the question: why believe that it applies? If we already knew that a most perfect thing existed, then we could use that knowledge to justify this claim about the concept applying. But we don't already know that. It is what we're trying to see proven. Without knowing that, we lack justification for believing the claim that the concept applies. So P1 stands in need of justification. An argument with an unjustified assumption does not prove anything.

Thus, either way we read the 'of' in the first assumption, this version of the ontological argument for a necessary being appears to fail in its first step.

In our quest for a necessitarian answer to Q, we seek something that exists necessarily. In the version of the ontological argument that we just considered, the inference to necessary existence occurs in the second phase. We have seen that the reasoning gets into trouble before that. So we didn't even get to anything about necessary existence. We should briefly look at a version that involves necessary existence from the beginning.[3]

The new version begins by assuming that the 'essential nature' of the maximally perfect being includes existing necessarily. Something's **essential nature** is the combination of features that the thing has to have in order to exist and that makes it what it fundamentally is. Therefore, whatever features we discover in a thing's essential nature must characterize it, no matter what its circumstances are—including its actual circumstances. Again, the assumption says that necessary existence is one of the features in the essential nature of the maximally perfect being.

The other assumption in the new version spells out an inescapable connection between a feature being in a thing's essential nature and the thing *having* that feature. The assumption is that if necessary existence is included in something's nature, then the thing exists necessarily. These two premises yield the conclusion that the maximally perfect being exists necessarily.

Second Ontological Argument

Premise 1: The essential nature of the maximally perfect being includes existing necessarily.

---

[3] This second version is suggested by some of what Descartes says in his *Replies to Caterus*.

Premise 2: If necessary existence is included in the essential nature that some being has, then the being exists necessarily.
Conclusion: The maximally perfect being exists necessarily.

One good thing about this version is that the second assumption, P2, is not seriously disputable. If a being has necessary existence in its essential nature, then that being has necessary existence—that's for sure.

Support for the new P1 derives from some thinking about perfection that is familiar to us. The supporting idea is that when we reflect on what goes into the loftiest heights of perfection, one feature that we find included is that of having the most impressive sort of existence, namely, necessary existence. That reflection seems to be the best defense of P1.

Trouble for the Second Ontological Argument is familiar too. The current P1 includes the phrase 'the essential nature *of* the maximally perfect being'. There is that 'of' again. On one reading, this phrase has the premise say, among other things, that the maximally perfect being exists and has a nature. If the first assumption says that, then it ruins the argument. The argument is supposed to prove that a maximally perfect being exists. An argument cannot prove anything that it just assumes to be true by having a premise that asserts it.

On the other hand, P1 may be just claiming something about a requirement for a concept to apply. P1 can be interpreted as saying that there is a concept that applies to a most perfect being, if at all, and in order for it to apply, the being must have an essential nature that includes necessary existence. All of that is plausible. It does not assume that a most perfect being exists. So let's read P2 that way.

Familiar trouble arises. Now the needed logical link to the conclusion has been lost. The second premise, P2, makes a claim about 'the essential nature that some being has'. So in order for P1 to link with the claim made by P2, P1 has to be about a being that *has* some nature. Yet as we now read P1, it does not say that anything has any nature. It just specifies a requirement for a concept to apply. So the two premises do not work together to imply the conclusion.

Thus, either way we read P1, the reasoning fails to prove the existence of a necessary being. Let's try something else.

Ungodly Necessitarianism

A necessitarian answer to the question of why anything exists does not require anything as exalted and wonderful as a maximally perfect thing. Any necessary being of any sort, however otherwise unexciting, would fill the bill. The entirely empty reality W would turn out to be impossible. There are numerous humbler candidates for the status of necessary being.

Let's use the label 'W*' for a definitely *possible* reality that is as empty as it is possible to be. *If* it is possible for there to be nothing at all, then W* is identical to W. But if more is needed for W* to have been a genuine possibility, then W* includes the least more that makes it possible. The following is a new necessitarian reason to think that W* must contain something, and so W is not possible.

How would things be in W*? 'Things' may be the wrong word, because there is as close as possible to nothing in W*. But still, there is a factual situation in W*. It is a fact about W* that it is as empty as can be, for instance. We should rephrase our question. What would be true in W*? Well, for instance, W* would lack all moose, since no moose is a necessary being. It seems to follow that it would be true in W* that there are no moose.

Aren't truths something, though? For instance, it is an actual truth *that there are moose*. In saying this, it seems that we are referring to an entity that is that particular truth. The standard philosopher's term for this sort of thing is **proposition**. If we state that there are moose, a proposition is what we state; if we believe that there are moose, the same proposition is what we believe. Any truth is a proposition. And since the proposition that there are moose is a truth, it exists. In general, in order to be in any condition at all, an entity has to exist. In some other possible realities, in W^* for instance, that proposition is another way. It is false in W, because there are no moose there. Since the proposition is in the condition of being false there, the proposition exists there. Any proposition is either true or false about any possible conditions. So if we take this line about propositions, we can conclude that any proposition is a necessary being.

Thus, the minimal possible reality W^* is *not* the absolutely empty W, because W^* has propositions in it. The general necessitarian answer to the question of why reality is not absolutely empty is that some things have to exist. The present version of necessitarianism says specifically that there have to exist the truths of each possible reality, and the falsehoods too.

Was it really legitimate, though, to infer the existence in W^* of the proposition that there are no moose? There would have been no moose, were W^* to have been the real world. That is actually true, and it is about W^*. So it might follow that this proposition *actually* exists. But why does the proposition that there are no moose, or any other proposition, have to exist *in W^* too*? There would be no moose in W^*, but how exactly does that imply that there would exist in W^* an entity that is the substance of the claim that there are no moose? We said that there is a factual situation in W^*. Maybe that is only loosely accurate. Maybe the strict truth is this. Here in the actual world, where we are reasoning about W^*, there do exist facts that are about how things would be in W^*. But, were W^* to have been the actual world, there would have been no factual situation. There would have been nothing, not even the truth that there was nothing. Why not think that W^* is the absolutely empty W after all?

Minimal Contingency

Whether or not there are any necessary beings, an important version of Q remains to be considered:

QC: Why is there anything that does not have to exist?

Our minimally occupied possible reality, W^*, includes necessary beings if there are any. But W^* includes nothing **contingent**. In other words, W^* includes nothing that exists without having to exist. Yet the actual situation is clearly populated by things that do not have to exist: moose, moons, muons, moors, and more. QC does not ask why all of the particular real things exist. (That is a good question, but a different one.) QC asks why any unnecessary thing exists. QC asks why there is any contingency, anything beyond the absolute minimum.

Anthropic Explanation

An anthropic explanation might seem helpful here. **Anthropic explanations** seek to account for some phenomenon by pointing out how the phenomenon is required in order for us to exist and thus to be in a position to investigate it. In the present instance, the idea would be something like this. Any possible reality must contain a multitude of contingent things, in order for us to exist in that reality and ask QC. At the very least, it must contain us. We are not necessary beings. So it is no wonder that the actual world has contingent things in it and is therefore not the minimally occupied W^*.

It is doubtful that this anthropic account answers QC satisfactorily. The account gives a good answer, but it is an answer to a different question. Suppose that we were asking this:

QWC: Why does the world in which we exist include contingent things?

QWC takes it for granted that we are in the world, and asks why contingent things are present with us. If that is something we wonder about, then it seems to be directly responsive to point out that we are contingent ourselves. That observation seems capable of removing any puzzlement about why a reality with us in it has contingencies.

Unlike QWC, QC does not ask about what accompanies us in the actual world. It is true that, if there were no contingent things, then we would not exist to ask QC. But QC asks about our existence just as much as it asks about the existence of any other contingent thing. When we are asking QC, we are asking why any contingent thing at all actually exists. A reply that just identifies something that is required for us to exist is unresponsive to this question.

Godly Explanation

God might seem helpful in answering QC. If God is a necessary being, then God is in our minimal possible reality, W. We can assume that God has the power to create contingent things. It seems that God's reasons for creating contingent things would explain why they exist too.

But we have also seen that a necessary God gives rise to a problem of vanishing possibilities. Here, the problem plays itself out as a difficulty about what contingencies God could create. First, perhaps under any possible circumstances God would have exactly the same reasons for creating, and God would use those reasons in the very same way to decide what to create. If so, then it seems that God would always create exactly the same reality. We are assuming that God is a necessary being. Given this, just one creation would be the only possible created reality. It would not even be contingent, since it would exist along with God in the one combination of circumstances that was even possible.

This is a problem, because it surely seems that there are many different contingent possibilities. For instance, there are actually various hummingbirds in various places. Had their habitats happened to develop differently, hummingbirds would have been more or less differently distributed. That gives every appearance of being a possibility. There are countless similar ones. It is difficult to believe that the seeming existence of multiple possibilities is entirely misleading.

Let's try something else. Suppose again that there is a necessary God. But now suppose that in different possible realities God has different reasons for creating. If so, then those differences allow for the different contingencies. There would be the different possible created outcomes, none of them necessary.

But then the initial differences in God's reasons would turn out to be the origin of the contingencies. All differences would stem from these variations in God's reasons. Assuming all of this, QC would turn out to be asking: why do any of these variations in God's reasons exist? To answer QC, we would need to explain why God has any particular batch of these reasons. It is quite difficult to think of some way that allows God's reasons for creating to differ at all. God couldn't have overlooked anything, since we are assuming that God is all-knowing. It looks as though God would have to have all reasons. Since any variation in reasons seems impossible, we have no hint of something that could have induced any variation in them.

A third alternative does somewhat better. Perhaps God's reasons for creating leave ties among possible creations. That is, there might be alternative contingent realities that are exactly equally best at fulfilling all of God's purposes. The different possibilities arise from God's ability to choose freely from among these alternatives. In each different alternative reality,

God makes a different free choice about which of these creations to bring about.

The main trouble with this new answer is that it can account for only a narrow range of possibilities. Recall that it is part of this explanation that God is a necessary being. So there is no possible reality without God. The possible creations by God as we are now understanding them drastically restrict the possibilities. In all possible realities God's reasons for creating are fulfilled. Yet many other things appear to have been possible. For example, all of the following seem possible: thoroughly boring mindless realities that would have been of no value by any standard, unfortunate realities where the bad outweighs the good, and fairly nice realities where most lives are worth living while none are terrific. It is not credible that these alternatives would flawlessly fulfill the reasons that a perfect God would have for creating. Thus, the free choices of a necessary God would reject all of these apparent possibilities. Such choices could explain only contingencies that would perfectly fulfill perfect purposes.

Since we apparently see more possibilities than that, we have to keep looking for their explanation. On the other hand, if God is not necessary, then at best God is part of the present problem and not its solution. Wherever God does exist, God is one of the contingencies for which we seek an explanation by asking QC. And wherever God does not exist, God is not there to make any choices that might explain contingent things.

Tendentious Explanation

If God doesn't help us to answer QC then what about goodness? Let's consider the idea that good things that can exist have an innate tendency to exist. The more perfect possible things have a greater tendency to exist than the less perfect. The better things are overall in a possible reality, the stronger is the tendency of that possibility to be actual.[4]

Various things are credibly regarded as good, including benevolent deeds, pleasant experiences, beautiful art, and enriching relationships. When we survey the candidates for goodness, it becomes clear that all reasonable candidates involve the existence of contingent things like people and experiences. In contrast, it is clear that our maximally empty possible reality W^* is thoroughly neutral in value. W^* is too blank to be any good. In the view about goodness that we are considering, then, W^* is just barely possible. It does not have the propensity to exist that better possibilities possess. Thus, the new explanation of why there is something beyond the contents of W^* is that the actual existence of contingent good things manifests the intrinsic tendency of possible good things to exist.

The idea that the good tends to exist is comforting. It has three problematic features, though. The least fundamental problem is that the idea seems unjustifiably optimistic. Why is it *good* things that have this tendency, rather than bad or neutral things? Of course any decent person finds the good more attractive than the other two, and so decent people are drawn to produce and preserve the good. But this cannot explain why there are any contingent things at all. The claim is that there is a tendency to exist that each possible good thing has on its own, without the assistance of appreciative people who already exist. It is the alleged tendency to exist that the good possibilities have on their own that needs some defense.

That problem is not fundamental, because there is an equally satisfactory explanation of contingent things that lacks this bias toward the good. It could be claimed instead that all contingent things, good, bad, or indifferent, have a propensity to exist. This

---

[4] Leibniz, one of the leading philosophers of the seventeenth century, proposed something along these lines.

would provide the core of the same sort of explanation. Again, W* world would be just barely possible. The actual world would display countless manifestations of the tendency toward existence of contingent things.

A second and more basic problem with this idea is the obscurity of the relevant tendency. Our understanding of tendencies seems to require that they be possessed by existing things and explained by existing things. For instance, fragile things have a tendency to break. The breaking does not already exist and may never exist. Some fragile things never break. But all things that *have* this tendency do exist, and the tendency is accounted for by the structure and environment that those things actually have. A possessor of tendencies might be remarkably hollow. Current physics asserts a tendency for particles to form in empty space. But if so, this is a tendency of something actual, space, and it is explained by something actual, physical law. We are totally unfamiliar with a tendency that is had by something merely possible that does not exist.

This obscurity is part of a wider problem. Having a tendency to exist is having a certain feature. Yet the explanation attributes this feature to things that merely *might have existed*. It is difficult to make sense of mere possibilities having any features at all. We can understand how various specifications *would* specify things having certain features *if* those specifications were realized. We have a much harder time with the idea that some alleged entity, although it is no real thing, nonetheless manages to have the feature of tending to exist. *What* has the feature? An unreal thing? Isn't the phrase 'an unreal thing' like the phrase 'a fake duck'? Just as fake ducks are not ducks at all, unreal things are not things at all. There are no such things! And if there are no such things, then there are no such things to have any tendencies.

Even if we could make sense of the idea that some possible contingencies have a tendency to exist, there would remain a different sort of fundamental problem for the view. What reason do we have to think that any such tendency claim is true? Compare this claim that contingencies tend to exist with the opposite claim. It could be claimed that it is *difficult* to get into existence. It could be claimed that all contingent things are prone *not* to exist, while the 'easy emptiness' of W^* had a strong tendency to be realized. This view would conclude that the actual world contains contingencies by a fluke. The existence of contingencies would run contrary to the tendency among possibilities.

This opposite hypothesis seems no less credible than the other one. The problematic fact for any tendency-style explanation is that we have no reason to believe in any such tendency.

Statistical Explanation

Here is a final idea about why there is anything real that does not have to exist. As we have repeatedly noted, it is plausible that diverse contingencies are possible. Some seemingly possible realities contain life and some do not; some are governed by laws of nature and some are not; some contain good things and some do not; some contain only sorts of things that we have thought of and some do not. It is plausible that there are infinitely many of these possibilities.

Our minimal possibility W^* is of course a possibility. There is convincing reason to think that W^* is importantly unique. In the end, it does seem that reality could have lacked all contingent things. Given this, W^* includes only what must be, if there are any such things. Furthermore, what must be does not vary. There is no multiplicity of alternative realities, each of which includes only necessary things, but without containing all necessary things. If a thing is truly necessary, it is included in every last possible reality. Thus, W^* must have in it all necessary beings (if any), and only necessary beings. Also, no change is necessary.

So any necessary beings in W^* do not change. They are just there.

If all of this is correct about W^*, then there must be just one minimal alternative reality. There is no way for two possible realities to contain the unchanging necessary beings, and nothing else. There would be no difference between 'them' at all, and so there would be just one possibility, not two. W^* is the unique minimal possible reality.

Thus, it seems clear that there are infinitely many possible realities with various contingencies, and only one possible reality without any contingencies. Each alternative reality is entirely possible. Each might have been the actual world. But now we are dividing the range of possibilities into those with at least one contingent thing and those with none. This yields infinitely many possibilities on one side and a single possibility on the other. From this perspective we can see that some contingency was *almost* bound to exist. The presence of some contingency was the closest thing to inevitable. If the one alternative reality without any contingency had been the actual world, that happenstance would have been a fluke of the most gigantic proportions.

Recall QM:

QM: Why is there anything more to reality than the empty W?

The current statistical sort of response answers QM as well as it answers QC. If there are no necessary beings, then W^* is the empty W. So then W is the one and only alternative reality with no contingent thing. And again, something contingent was all but inevitable.

The same facts about infinite-versus-one seem to support another illuminating conclusion about answering Q. The statistical facts don't justify our reasoning like this: 'The nothing alternative, W, was just one of infinitely many possibilities, and the rest all have something more than nothing in them. They all were possible. So now I see why there isn't nothing.' The 'see why' part of that reasoning is wrong. We still don't see why the possibility W *didn't* become actual.

Here is a very close analogy. Suppose that I buy a lottery ticket in a big and random lottery, maybe an infinitely large one, and I find out later that my ticket lost. I understand that there were all those other tickets and mine was only one. I understand that it was a random drawing where only one was selected. I see that my odds were small, maybe infinitesimal. Still, I don't see why mine *wasn't* selected. All I see about that is this. My ticket happened to be one of those that didn't happen to turn up. It wasn't bound to lose. It just happened to lose.

In that sort of lottery we can't see why a ticket lost. There couldn't be any explanation like that. All the tickets had a chance. There was nothing special about the one selected and nothing disqualifying about the others. It happened by chance *instead of* there being a reason why it happened.

Maybe the same goes for explaining why W isn't the actual world. One of the possible alternative realities has to be the actual one, because they are all of the possibilities. The way that one of them got to be the actual one wasn't a random drawing— nothing already existed to do any selecting from the possibilities. But just like the tickets in a random drawing, the possibilities all had a chance and there was no reason why the 'winner' was selected. In the same way, the empty possibility W was mega-unlikely and it didn't happen to turn up. Much as we'd like to see why that didn't happen, we can't. That sort of explanation is impossible.

These observations do not quite completely explain why anything contingent exists. W^* remains a possibility. We have not seen a conclusive reason why the minimal possibility was not realized. What we may have seen is why it was *virtually* necessary that something more existed.

Conclusion

We have seen various candidate answers to our two main questions:

> *QM*: Why is there anything more to reality than the empty W?
>
> *QC*: Why is there anything that does not have to exist?

None of the answers is completely satisfactory. The statistical answer does not quite tell us why the maximally minimal possibility W^* did not turn out to be actual. Maybe this is as good an answer as we can get, though. We think that countless alternative realities could have been actualities, one of them being W^*. If so, then there cannot be an airtight reason why any one of them did not turn out to be the actual reality. They all had a chance.

FURTHER READING

Three essays that are worthwhile as further reading are 'On Explaining Existence' by Nicholas Rescher, 'Why is Reality as it is?' by Derek Parfit, and 'Why is there Something rather than Nothing?' by Robert Nozick. (The question addressed in Derek Parfit's paper is the question of why everything is as it is, which is different from our question of why anything exists, although it includes our question.) These essays are conveniently gathered together as the first section, 'Existence', of the following collection.

Steven D. Hales, *Metaphysics: Contemporary Readings* (Wadsworth, 1999).

CHAPTER 6

Free Will and Determinism

Theodore Sider

The Problem

Suppose you are kidnaped and forced to commit a series of terrible murders. The kidnaper makes you shoot a first victim by forcing your finger to squeeze the trigger of a gun, hypnotizes you into poisoning a second, and then throws you from an airplane, causing you to squash a third. Miraculously, you survive the fall from the airplane. You stagger from the scene, relieved that the ordeal is over. But then, to your amazement, you are apprehended by the police, who handcuff you and charge you with murder. The parents of the victims scream obscenities at you as you are led away in disgrace.

Are the police and parents fair to blame you for the killings? Obviously not, for you have an unassailable excuse: you did not act of your own **free will**. You couldn't help what you did; you could not have done otherwise. And only those who act freely are morally responsible.

We all believe that we have free will. How could we not? Renouncing freedom would mean no longer planning for the future, for why make plans if you are not free to change what will happen? It would mean renouncing morality, for only those who act freely deserve blame or punishment. Without freedom, we march along pre-determined paths, unable to control our destinies. Such a life is not worth living.

Yet freedom seems to conflict with a certain apparent fact. Incredibly, this fact is no secret; most people are fully aware of it. We uncritically accept free will only because we fail to put two and two together. The problem of free will is a time bomb hidden within our most deeply held beliefs.

Here is the fact: *every event has a cause*. This fact is known as **determinism**.

We all believe in causes. If scientists discovered debris in the upper stratosphere spelling out 'Ozzy Osbourne!', they would immediately go to work to discover the cause. Was the debris put there by a renegade division of NASA comprised of heavy-metal fans? Was it a science project from a school for adolescent geniuses? If these things were ruled out as causes, the scientists would start to consider stranger hypotheses. Perhaps aliens from another planet are playing a joke on us. Perhaps the debris is left over from a collision between comets, and the resemblance to the name of the heavy-metal singer is purely coincidental. Perhaps different bits of the debris each have different kinds of causes. Any of these hypotheses might be entertained. But the one thing the scientists would *not* contemplate is that there simply is no cause whatsoever. Causes can be hard to discover, or coincidental, or have many different parts, but they are always there.

It's not that uncaused events are utterly inconceivable. We can imagine what it would be like for an uncaused event to occur. For that matter, we can imagine what it would be like for all sorts of strange things to occur: pigs flying, monkeys making 10,000 feet tall statues from jello, and so on. But it is reasonable to believe that no such things *in fact* occur. Likewise, it is reasonable to believe that there are in fact no uncaused events—that is, it is reasonable to believe in determinism.

Our belief in determinism is reasonable because we have all seen science succeed, again and again, in its search for the underlying causes of things. Technological innovations owe their existence to science: skyscrapers, vaccination, rocket ships, the internet. Science seems to explain everything we observe: the changing of the seasons, the movement of the planets, the inner workings of plants and animals. Given this track record, we reasonably expect the march of scientific progress to continue; we expect that science will eventually discover the causes of everything.

The threat to freedom comes when we realize that this march will eventually overtake us. From the scientific point of view, human choices and behavior are just another part of the natural world. Like the seasons, planets, plants, and animals, our actions are studyable, predictable, explainable, controllable. It is hard to say when, if ever, scientists will learn enough about what makes humans tick in order to predict everything we do. But regardless of when the causes of human behavior are *discovered*, determinism assures us that these causes *exist*.

It is hard to accept that one's own choices are subject to causes. Suppose you become sleepy and are tempted to put down this book. The causes are trying to put you to sleep. But you resist them! You are strong and continue reading anyway. Have you thwarted the causes and refuted determinism? Of course not. Continuing to read has its own cause. Perhaps your love of metaphysics overcomes your drowsiness. Perhaps your parents taught you to be disciplined. Or perhaps you are just stubborn. No matter what the reason, there was some cause.

You may reply: 'But I felt no compulsion to read or not to read; I simply decided to do one or the other. I sensed no cause.' It is true that many thoughts, feelings, and decisions do not *feel* caused. But this does not really threaten determinism. Sometimes the causes of our decisions aren't consciously detectable, but those causes still exist. Some causes of behavior are preconscious functions of the brain, as contemporary psychology teaches, or perhaps even subconscious desires, as Freud thought. Other causes of decisions may not even be mental. The brain is an incredibly complicated physical object, and might 'swerve' this way or that as a result of certain motions of its tiniest parts. Such purely physical causes cannot be detected merely by directing one's attention inward, no matter how long and hard and calmly one meditates. We can't expect to be able to detect all the causes of our decisions just by introspection.

So: determinism is true, even for human actions. But now, consider any allegedly free action. To illustrate how much is at stake here, let's consider an action that is horribly morally reprehensible: Hitler's invasion of Poland in 1939. We most certainly blame Hitler for this action. We thus consider him to have acted freely. But determinism seems to imply that Hitler was not free at all.

To see why, we must first investigate the concepts of **cause** and **effect**. A cause is an earlier event that *makes* a later effect happen. Given the laws of nature,[1] once the cause has occurred, the effect *must* occur. Lightning causes thunder: the laws of nature governing electricity and sound guarantee that, when lightning strikes, thunder will follow.

Determinism says that Hitler's invasion of Poland was caused by some earlier event. So far, there is little to threaten Hitler's freedom. The cause of the invasion might be something under Hitler's control, in which case the invasion would also be under his control. For instance, the cause might be a decision that Hitler made just before the invasion. If so, then it seems we can still blame Hitler for ordering the invasion.

---

[1] Chapter 9 discusses laws of nature.

But now consider this decision itself. It is just another event. So determinism implies that it too must have a cause. This new cause might be an even earlier decision Hitler made, or something his advisers told him, or something he ate, or, more likely, a combination of many factors. Whatever it is, call this cause of Hitler's decision to invade Poland 'c'. Notice that c also caused the invasion of Poland. For as we saw above, a cause is an earlier event that makes a later event happen. Once c occurred, Hitler's decision had to occur; and once that decision occurred, the invasion had to occur.

We can repeat this reasoning indefinitely. Determinism implies that c must have an earlier cause c_1, which in turn must have an earlier cause c_2, and so on. The resulting sequence of events stretches back in time:

$$\ldots c_2 \rightarrow c_1 \rightarrow c \rightarrow \text{the decision} \rightarrow \text{the invasion}$$

Each event in the sequence causes the invasion, since each event causes the event that occurs immediately after it, which then causes the next event occurring immediately after that one, and so on. The final few events in this sequence look like ones under Hitler's control. But the earlier ones do not, for as we move back in time, we eventually reach events before Hitler's birth.

This argument can be repeated for any human action, however momentous or trivial. Suppose an old man slips while crossing the street, and I laugh at him instead of helping him up. Using the above chain of reasoning, we can show that my laughter was caused by events before my birth.

Things now look very bad for freedom. Hitler no longer seems to have had a free choice about whether to invade Poland. I seem to have had no choice but to laugh at the old man. For these actions were all caused by things outside our control. But then what was morally wrong about what Hitler or I did? How can we blame Hitler for invading Poland if it was settled before his birth that he would do it? How can we blame me for laughing? How can we blame anyone for anything?

We can restate the challenge to freedom in terms of physics. Any action or decision involves the motion of sub-atomic particles in one's body and brain. These sub-atomic particles move according to the laws of physics. Physics lets us calculate the future positions of particles from information about (i) the previous states of the particles, and (ii) the forces acting on the particles. So, in principle, one could have examined the sub-atomic particles one hundred years before the invasion of Poland, calculated exactly how those particles would be moving one hundred years later, and thereby calculated that Hitler would invade Poland. Such calculations are far too difficult to ever complete in practice, but that doesn't matter. Whether or not anyone could have completed the calculations, *the particles were there*, before Hitler's birth, and the fact that they were there, and arranged in the way that they were, made it *inevitable* that Hitler would invade Poland. Once again, we have found a cause for Hitler's invasion that already existed before Hitler was born. And the existence of such a cause seems to imply that Hitler's invasion of Poland was not a free action.

And yet, it *must* have been free, for how else can we *blame* him for this despicable act? The time bomb has exploded. Two of our most deeply held beliefs, our belief in science and our belief in freedom and morality, seem to contradict each other. We must resolve this conflict.

Hard Determinism

The simplest strategy for resolution is to reject one of the beliefs that produce the conflict. One could reject free will, or one could reject determinism.

The rejection of free will in the face of determinism is called **hard determinism**. Think of the hard determinist as a hard-nosed intellectual who tolerates no softies. Free will conflicts with science, so free will has got to go. Here is a typical hard determinist speech:

> We must get used to the idea that no one is really responsible for anything. Belief in freedom and moral responsibility was a luxury of a pre-scientific age. Now that we have grown up, we must put aside childish ways and face the facts. Science has disproved the existence of freedom and morality.

Can we live with this depressing philosophy? Philosophers must seek the truth, however difficult it may be to accept. Maybe hard determinism is one of those difficult truths. Hard determinists might attempt 'damage control', arguing that life without freedom is not as bad as one might think. Society might still punish criminals, for instance. Hard determinists must deny that criminals *deserve* punishment, since the crimes were not committed freely. But they can say that there is still a use for punishment: punishing criminals keeps them off the streets and discourages future crimes. Still, accepting hard determinism is nearly unthinkable. Nor is it clear that one *could* stop believing in free will, even if one wanted to. If you find someone who claims to believe hard determinism, here's a little experiment to try. Punch him in the face, really hard. Then try to convince him not to blame you. After all, according to him, you had no choice but to punch him! I predict you will find it very difficult to convince him to practice what he preaches.

Hard determinism is a position of last resort. Let's see what the other options look like.

Libertarianism

If the hard determinist is the intellectually hard-nosed devotee of science, the **libertarian**[2] has the opposite mindset. Libertarians

[2] The use of the word 'libertarian' in politics is unrelated.

resolve the conflict between free will and determinism by rejecting determinism. Their guiding thought is that *people are special*. The march of science, subjugating observed phenomena to exceptionless law, is limited to the non-human realm. For libertarians, science is good as far as it goes, but it will never succeed in completely predicting human behavior. Humans, and humans alone, transcend the laws of nature: they are free.

What makes people so special? Some libertarians answer that we have souls, non-physical sources of consciousness, which make choices that are not controlled by laws of nature. Others say that humans are indeed purely physical systems, but that they are not subject to the natural laws that govern other physical systems. Either way, laws of nature do not wholly determine human behavior.

Although libertarians are clear on what freedom *isn't*—namely, determinism—they have a little more trouble telling us what freedom *is*. They do not want to say that freedom is merely uncaused action. Saying *that* would equate freedom with *randomness*, and libertarians don't want to do that. Here's why.

Suppose Mother Teresa discovers a hand-grenade in an orphanage in Calcutta. As you might expect, she picks up the hand-grenade in order to dispose of it safely. But now an utterly uncaused event occurs: to her horror, her hand suddenly pulls out the pin and throws the grenade into the heart of the orphanage. The grenade explodes, resulting in mayhem and destruction. When I say 'uncaused', I really mean that there is *no* cause, none whatsoever. As I am imagining the example, the action of pulling the pin and throwing the grenade was not caused by any decision on Mother Teresa's part; nor did it have an external physical cause. No dormant dark side of Mother Teresa's personality has finally come to light. She has no nervous tic. Her hand simply flew up from absolutely no cause whatsoever. This clearly is *not* a free action. We could not blame Mother Teresa; she is the victim of a cruel accident.

The alarming thing for libertarians is that Mother Teresa seems *unfree* precisely because her action was uncaused. Freedom now appears to *require* causation. This obviously threatens the fundamental libertarian claim that the key to the problem of freedom is indeterminism of human action. Libertarians must somehow distinguish between free undetermined action and randomness.

Some libertarians address this problem by postulating a special kind of causation that only humans wield, called **agent causation**. Ordinary mechanistic causation, the kind studied in physics and the other hard sciences, obeys laws. Mechanistic causes are repeatable and predictable: if you repeat the same cause again and again, the very same effect is guaranteed to occur each time. Agent causation, on the other hand, does not obey laws. There is no saying which way a free human being will exercise her agent causation. The very same person in exactly similar circumstances might agent-cause different things. According to the theory of agent causation, you act freely when (i) your action is not caused in the ordinary, mechanistic way, but (ii) your action *is* caused by you—by agent causation. If you freely decide to eat Wheaties one morning rather than your usual helping of Apple Jacks, it would have been impossible to predict beforehand which cereal you would choose. Nevertheless, your choice was not a random occurrence, for you yourself caused it. You caused it by agent causation.

It is unclear whether agent causation really solves the problem of randomness. Consider what an agent-causation theorist would say about your freely making a difficult decision. There are two important factors in decision-making: what you desire, and what you believe is the best means to achieve that desire. If you are undecided whether to vote Democrat or Republican in a US presidential election, for instance, this is because some of your beliefs and desires favor a Democratic vote, and others favor a Republican vote. Suppose that, in the end, the set favoring a

Democratic vote wins out. A libertarian would say that mechanistic causes that occurred in the past did not determine this outcome. It was you yourself, via agent causation, that selected the Democratic vote. Your selection was subject to no laws; it was unpredictable. This activity of agent causation was not caused by your beliefs and desires. But now—and here is the problem—since the selection was not causally based in your beliefs and desires, it seems entirely *detached* from you. The selection did not emerge from what you know about the candidates and what sort of leader you want for your country. Your vote didn't arise from who you are. It just appeared in the world, as if by magic. Given this, it would be odd to praise or blame you for it. And this suggests that it was unfree.

Whether or not libertarianism relies on agent causation, its most worrisome feature is its clash with science. First, libertarians must reject the possibility of an all-encompassing psychology. Human behavior would be governed by the laws of such a science, and libertarians deny that human behavior is controlled by any laws. But the clash does not end there. Libertarians must also reject the possibility of an all-encompassing *physics*. The realms of psychology and physics cannot be neatly separated, for human bodies are physical objects, made up of subatomic particles. An all-encompassing physics could predict the future motions of *all* particles—even those in human bodies—based on the earlier states of particles. Since libertarians say that human behavior cannot be scientifically predicted, they must deny the possibility of such a physics. According to libertarians, if physicists turned their measuring instruments on the subatomic particles composing a free person, formerly observed patterns would break down.

This attitude toward science seems rash. Here in the twenty-first century, we have the benefit of hindsight on various disagreements between science, on the one hand, and religion and philosophy, on the other. Remember the Catholic Church's decision to censor Copernicus and Galileo for saying that the Earth moves around the Sun. No one wants to repeat that mistake. And remember the dramatic successes of science, both theoretical and technological. Of course, science is not infallible. But a philosopher had better have *very* good reasons to declare that an existing science is just plain wrong, or that a certain kind of scientific progress will never happen. One's philosophy should avoid colliding with or limiting science.

Our choices look grim. On the one hand, there is the dismal philosophy of hard determinism, which robs life of all that is distinctly human and worthwhile. On the other hand, there is the radically anti-scientific philosophy of libertarianism—which, given the problem of randomness, may not even succeed in salvaging free will.

Interlude: Quantum Mechanics

Before moving on, we should investigate a side issue: whether **quantum mechanics** bears on the problem of freedom. Quantum mechanics is a theory about the behavior of tiny particles. This theory was developed in the early part of the twentieth century and continues to be accepted by physicists today. Quantum mechanics (or at least, a certain version of it) is a radically indeterministic theory. It does not predict with certainty what will occur; it only gives *probabilities* of outcomes. No matter how much information you have about a particle, you cannot predict with certainty where it will be later. All you can say is how likely it is that the particle will be found in various locations. And this is not a mere limitation on human knowledge. The particle's future position is simply not determined by the past, regardless of how much we know about it. Only the probabilities are determined.

In the previous sections I was ignoring quantum mechanics. For instance, I assumed that if a cause occurs, its effect *must* occur, even though quantum mechanics says that causes merely make their effects probable. Why did I ignore quantum mechanics? Because randomness is not freedom. Let us try a little thought experiment. First pretend that quantum mechanics is incorrect and physics is truly deterministic. The threat to human freedom that this presents is what we have been talking about so far in this chapter. Next, in each person's brain, add a little lottery, which every so often randomly causes the person to swerve one way rather than another. This is like what quantum mechanics says really happens: there is an element of randomness to what events occur. Does the threat to freedom go away? Clearly not. If the original, wholly determined person had no free will, then the new, randomized person has no free will either; the lottery injects only randomness, not freedom or responsibility. And as we learned from the case of Mother Teresa, randomness does not mean freedom. If anything, randomness undermines freedom.

A libertarian might concede that quantum randomness is not *sufficient* for freedom, but nevertheless claim that quantum randomness *makes room for* freedom, because it makes room for agent causation. Imagine that it is 1939, and Hitler has not yet decided to invade Poland. He is trying to decide what to do among the following three options:

Invade Poland
Invade France
Stop being such an evil guy and become a ballet dancer

Quantum mechanics assigns probabilities to each of these possible decisions; it does not say which one Hitler will choose. Suppose, for the sake of argument, that the probabilities are as follows:

95.0% Invade Poland
4.9% Invade France
0.1% Become a ballet dancer

After assigning these probabilities, the work of quantum mechanics is complete. According to some libertarians, agent causation now steps in. After quantum mechanics sets the probabilities, Hitler himself chooses, by agent causation, which decision he will in fact make. Physics sets probabilities, but *people*, by agent causation, ultimately decide what occurs.

If this picture were correct, then my criticism of libertarianism as being anti-scientific would be rebutted: agent causation could peacefully coexist with quantum mechanics. In fact, though, the coexistence picture makes agent causation a slave to quantum-mechanical probabilities.

Imagine running the following interesting (if wildly unethical) experiment. First produce one million exact clones of Hitler as he was in 1939. Then, in one million separate laboratories, reproduce the exact conditions that Hitler faced before he decided to invade Poland. Put each clone in his own laboratory and deceive him into thinking that it is really 1939 and that he is in charge of Germany. Then sit back and watch. Record how many clones attempt to invade Poland, how many attempt to invade France, and how many attempt to become ballet dancers. The coexistence picture says that you will observe a distribution of behaviors that roughly matches the probabilities listed above, for the coexistence picture says that quantum mechanics correctly gives the probabilities of outcomes. Thus, you will observe around 950,000 clones trying to invade Poland, around 49,000 trying to invade France, and around 1,000 practicing ballet. If you repeat the procedure again and again, you will continue to observe outcomes in approximately the same ratios. (The more times you repeat the experiment, the closer the total ratios will match the probabilities, just as the more times one flips a coin, the closer the ratio of heads to tails approaches one-to-one.) If you change the laboratory conditions faced by the clones, so that quantum mechanics predicts different probabilities, you will observe a new distribution of behaviors that fits the new probabilities. The distribution keeps following what quantum mechanics says.

What good then is agent causation? It seems to mindlessly follow the probabilities, having no effect of its own on the distribution of outcomes. This sort of agent causation is empty; it adds nothing to freedom or responsibility. Agent causation, if it is to be worth anything, must be capable of disrupting the probabilities given by quantum mechanics. There can be no peaceful coexistence: agent causation theorists must clash with science. Quantum mechanics does not help the agent-causation theorist. So I will go back to ignoring quantum mechanics.

We are back to the grim dilemma. Apparently, we must reject science or reject freedom. Yet neither option seems at all appealing.

Compatibilism

Many philosophers believe that there is a way out of this dilemma. Others think that this way out is a big mistake. You must decide for yourself.

The way out is called **compatibilism**. According to compatibilists, our discussion took a wrong turn all the way back when we said that the available options were rejecting freedom or rejecting determinism. Compatibilists say that this overlooks a third option. We can have our cake and eat it too: we can retain *both* freedom and determinism. That way we can preserve both our science and our humanity. The argument in the first section, which concluded that freedom and determinism are opposed to each other, was a mistake. Free will is in fact compatible with determinism. The alleged conflict is an illusion, based on a misunderstanding of the concept of free will. Our actions (or at least their probabilities) are indeed caused by events before our births. But they are often free despite this.

To explain what compatibilists are up to, let's first consider some examples. Imagine a very young boy with a serious misunderstanding of the concept of a *man*. This boy thinks it is part of the definition of the word 'man' that men never cry. As far as he knows, the men in his family never cry, the men on television never cry, and so on. He believes that his father is a man, of course, but one day he sees his father crying. The boy becomes very confused. Two of his beliefs now conflict: his belief that his father is a man and his belief that his father is crying. Which should he give up? Should he decide that his father is not a man after all? Or should he decide that his father was not really crying—that he was only cutting up onions, say? Obviously, he should do neither. Instead, he should clear up his conceptual confusion about the nature of manhood. Then he will see that his beliefs about his father's manhood and about his father's crying are compatible after all.

Here is a second example. How would you define the word 'contact', as in 'Barry Bonds' bat made contact with the baseball'? If you are like most people, your first answer is probably something like this: *things are in 'contact' when there is no empty space between them.* But now remember your high-school science. Baseballs and bats are made up of atoms. These atoms consist of nuclei and surrounding clouds of electrons. When one atom approaches another, the electrons of the atoms repel one another with electromagnetic forces. The closer together the atoms get, the stronger the forces become. Eventually the forces become so strong that they push the atoms away from each other. This occurs when the atoms get very close to each other, but before their clouds of electrons start to overlap. Thus, as Bonds' bat closed in on the baseball, the outermost atoms of the bat began to repel the outermost atoms of the ball, until eventually the ball came to a halt and flew in the opposite direction. At every moment there was some space between the bat and the ball. In fact, there is *never* absolutely zero space between bats and balls, nor between fists and jaws, fingers and computer keyboards, or any other things we consider to be in contact. Yet we all believe that contact regularly occurs. So we have another apparent conflict, this time between our belief in high-school science and our belief that things are regularly in contact. Should we renounce one of these beliefs? Obviously not. We should instead reject the proposed definition of 'contact'. Those who accept that definition are in a sense conceptually confused. For things can be in contact even when there is a small amount of space in between them. (What then is the correct definition of contact? Tough question! What about: *things are in contact when there is no visible space in between?* This is only a start.)

The compatibilist makes a similar claim about free will. Determinism seems to conflict with freedom only because we misunderstand the concept of freedom. If 'free' meant 'uncaused', then the conflict would be real. But that's not what 'free' means. (Remember Mother Teresa.) Once we clear up our conceptual confusion, the conflict will vanish. Then we can believe in *both* free will and determinism. Properly understood, they were never really opposed.

So far so good. But if 'free' doesn't mean 'uncaused', what *does* it mean? The compatibilist wants to say, roughly, that *a free action is one that is caused in the right way.* When you were kidnaped and forced to commit murders, your actions were unfree because they were caused in the *wrong* way. Free actions, such as Hitler's invasion of Poland, my writing of this chapter, and your reading it, also have causes, but they are caused in the *right* way. All actions have causes, but having a cause doesn't settle whether an action is free. Whether it is free is settled by what kind of cause it has. If free actions are those that are caused in the right way, as this definition says, then an action can be *both* free *and* caused.

Thus, given this definition, freedom and determinism do not conflict.

Hard determinists and libertarians may object that all causes should be treated alike. So long as my choice is caused by events before my birth, it is unfree; it does not matter *how* it is caused. But for some purposes, compatibilists can reply, it is clear that causes are not all alike. Causing a running back to fall by tackling him is legal football; causing him to fall by shooting him with a crossbow is not. The rules of football treat some causes differently from others. According to compatibilists, we can think of freedom and morality in an analogous way. Morality, like football, has rules. These rules treat some causes differently from others. If an action is caused in a certain way—the right way—then the rules of morality count that action as free. But if an action is caused in the wrong way, then the rules count that action as unfree.

It is admittedly strange that my actions can be free even though they were caused by events that occurred before I was born. Some philosophers reject compatibilism on this basis. But given the implausibility of hard determinism and libertarianism, compatibilism at least deserves a fair hearing.

Compatibilists must refine their theory, though. When they say that free actions must be caused 'in the right way', what exactly does that mean? Examples were given: Hitler's invasion was caused in the right way; murders coerced by your kidnaper were caused in the wrong way. But examples are not good enough. We need a definition.

Here is a first stab: a *free action is one that is caused by the person's beliefs and desires*. This checks out with some of the examples. When kidnaped, your beliefs and desires did not cause you to shoot the first victim or to fall from the airplane onto the third. You did not want to do these things; your actions were caused by the beliefs and desires of your kidnaper. So the proposed definition correctly counts your behavior in those cases as *not* being free. It also correctly counts Hitler's invasion as being free, since the invasion was caused by Hitler's sinister beliefs and desires. Likewise, since my beliefs and desires caused me to write this chapter, and yours caused you to read it, these actions are also free, according to this definition.

But the definition's success does not last. Recall the second victim, whom you poisoned while you were hypnotized. If your kidnaper hypnotized you into *wanting* to poison the victim, then the poisoning *was* caused by your beliefs and desires. So the definition says that you were free. Yet you obviously were *not* free. So the definition is wrong. The compatibilist needs a better definition.

When you were hypnotized, you acquired beliefs and desires against your will. So maybe we should change the definition to say: *a free action is one that is caused by the person's beliefs and desires, provided that the person has freely chosen those beliefs and desires.* But this definition is **circular**: the word 'free' is used in its own definition. If circular definitions were kosher, we could have used a much simpler one: *a free action is one that is free.* But this is clearly unhelpful. Circular definitions are unacceptable.

(Circularity aside, it's not even clear that the modified definition is correct. I have freely decided to continue to work on this chapter. My decision was caused by my desire to complete this book. Is it *really* true that I have freely chosen this desire? I doubt it. I want to complete the book simply because that's the kind of guy I am. I didn't choose to have this desire; I just find myself having it. But this doesn't seem to undermine the fact that my decision to continue working is free.)

What about this then: *a free action is one that is caused by the person's beliefs and desires, provided that the person was not compelled by another person to have those beliefs and desires?* This new definition raises as many questions as it answers. What does the word 'compelled' mean here? (Philosophers always ask questions like this.) When you think about it, 'compelled' in its ordinary sense means something like: 'caused so as to destroy freedom'. But then it is circular to define 'free' in terms of 'compelled', for 'compelled' is itself defined in terms of 'free'. The circularity is not so blatant as when the word 'free' itself was used in the definition, but it is circularity all the same. So the compatibilist had better not be using 'compelled' in its ordinary sense.

The definition would not be circular if 'compelled' just meant 'caused'. But then the definition wouldn't work. Recall my free decision to continue to work on this chapter. The definition requires that this decision is caused by my beliefs and desires, and it is—by my desire to complete the book. The definition further requires that this desire is not caused by any other person. But one of the causes of this desire *does* involve other people: my parents instilled diligence and a love of learning in me. So if causal involvement by another person renders a desire compelled, then my desire to continue working is compelled. We all believe and desire as we do in part because of our causal interactions with others; no one is an island. So if 'compelled' meant 'caused', the definition would imply that no one ever does anything freely. That's not what the compatibilist intends.

Another problem with the definition is that not all compulsion is by another person. A kleptomaniac compulsively desires to steal, and so steals. But he is not free; he cannot help his compulsive desires. Yet the definition counts him as free. For his stealing is caused by his beliefs and desires, and he is not compelled *by another person* to have those beliefs and desires. We could just delete 'by another person'. The definition would then read: *a free action is one that is caused by the person's beliefs and desires, provided that the person was not compelled to have those beliefs and desires*. But the problem of the meaning of 'compelled' remains. It cannot mean 'caused' (given determinism, all beliefs and desires are caused). It cannot mean 'caused so as to not destroy freedom' (that would be circular).

Let's take one final crack at a definition: *a free action is one that is caused by the person's beliefs and desires, provided that those beliefs and desires flow from 'who the person is'*. The idea of 'who the person is' needs to be explained. As a human being moves toward adulthood, she gradually develops her character, her moral beliefs and habits, her self-conception, and other qualities that give her 'an identity'. It is these qualities, which make her distinctive from a personal and moral point of view, that I am referring to when I speak of who a person is. Who an adult person is is partly a matter of upbringing and circumstance, but also partly a matter of choice. As we mature we shape ourselves; and even after reaching adulthood we continue to reflect on ourselves, and try to change if we aren't living up to our ideals. So when the definition says that the beliefs and desires must flow from who the person is, this means that the beliefs and desires must be 'in character' for that person: they must fit with the character, moral beliefs and habits, and self-conception that the person has shaped for herself over time (and continues to fine-tune). In the example at the beginning of the chapter, after you snap out of your hypnotized state, you will be inclined to protest that poisoning the second victim does not result from 'who you are'. It is out of character for you. Even though you desired to poison him at the time (because of the hypnosis), that desire conflicts with the values by which you have always lived. The case of the kleptomaniac is trickier, but here too we can say that even though her thievery is caused by her beliefs and desires, it may not be free. For suppose that even though she has always found herself desiring to steal, this desire has always been unwelcome to her. She has always tried to resist the desires—sometimes successfully, but unfortunately, sometimes not. Further, suppose that she believes that stealing is morally wrong. Given all these facts about who she is—her moral beliefs, her desire not to desire to steal, and her pattern of resisting her desires to steal—the desire to steal does not flow from 'who she is'. The definition therefore says that her stealing is not free.

This last definition may be on the right track, but there is still work to be done. First, the definition says that your desires under hypnosis do not flow from 'who you are' because they do not match the desires you usually have; they are uncharacteristic. But many perfectly ordinary free actions are caused by uncharacteristic desires. Though I am generally a nice person, a couple of times in my life I have irritably snapped at someone. Despite being uncharacteristic for me, my snapping was obviously a free action. So my desire to snap had better count as flowing from 'who I am'. Somehow, the definition must treat my desire to snap differently from your hypnotized desire to poison—even though each desire is out of character.

Second, compare two ways of *changing* 'who one is'. Way one: someone permanently brainwashes me into becoming a horrible person. The brainwashing is so thorough that for the rest of my life I want nothing more than to harm people. At first, my actions seem out of character. But soon everyone forgets my former good qualities and regards me as a monster. Are my subsequent actions free? The question is hard, but it seems that they are at least partially unfree, since the new, evil 'who I am' results from brainwashing. Way two: I undergo *moral transformation*. After recognizing that my life is going badly and in need of reform, I change 'who I am', perhaps with the help of a spiritual leader, therapist, or other moral guide. (Moral transformation can also go from better to worse: we have all heard stories of promising young people who make the wrong decisions, fall in with the wrong crowd, and become self-destructive and immoral. The members of the 'wrong crowd' serve as negative moral 'guides'.) Unlike brainwashing, moral transformation does not destroy free will. But in each case, one acts in accordance with 'who one is', though that has changed under the influence of other people. Somehow, the definition must treat these cases differently.

Coming up with a good compatibilist definition of freedom is no piece of cake. Then again, who ever said it should be easy? Defining anything interesting is hard. (A few paragraphs ago, we couldn't even define a measly word like 'contact'.) And look at the alternatives to compatibilism: libertarianism ('I know from my armchair that physics is incomplete!') and hard determinism ('I reject everything good about humanity!'). If our first attempts to give a compatibilist definition of freedom don't succeed, we should just keep trying.

FURTHER READING

Gary Watson's anthology *Free Will* (Oxford University Press, 1982) contains a number of interesting papers on free will. See especially the papers by Roderick Chisholm, Peter van Inwagen, A. J. Ayer, and Susan Wolf. Chisholm defends libertarianism, van Inwagen gives a careful argument against compatibilism, Ayer defends a simple form of compatibilism, and Wolf defends a sophisticated form of compatibilism and also discusses compatibilist definitions of freedom like the final one discussed in the chapter.

Timothy O'Connor, *Persons and Causes* (Oxford University Press, 2000) defends libertarianism.

CHAPTER 7

Constitution

Theodore Sider

The Antinomy of Constitution

> It is impossible to hold just one material object—an ice cube, or a soda can, or a clay statue—in one's hand. Wherever there appears to be only a single material object, there are in fact two.

Only a philosopher would dream of arguing for such a thing. As Bertrand Russell once said, 'the point of philosophy is to start with something so simple as not to seem worth stating, and to end with something so paradoxical that no one will believe it'. But mere shock value is not the aim. Philosophers grapple with arguments that have counter-intuitive conclusions because these arguments reveal hidden complexity in the world, even at the mundane level of ice cubes, soda cans, and statues.

Here is the argument for the counter-intuitive claim we began with. Ice cubes, soda cans, and clay statues are made up of matter. An ice cube is made up of water molecules, a soda can of aluminum, a clay statue of clay. So wherever there is a material object, there is also another object: a **quantity (piece) of matter**. Where there is an ice cube, there is also a quantity of water; where there is a soda can, there is a piece of aluminum; where there is a clay statue, there is a piece of clay. The ice cube, soda can, and statue are *made up of*, or **constituted** by, these quantities of matter. But they are not the same objects as the quantities of matter. For consider: the quantity of water making up the ice cube existed long before the ice cube was made. And if the ice cube is allowed to stand at room temperature, it will melt and so be destroyed, but the quantity of water will continue to exist. A sculptor begins with a piece of clay. By shaping it into the right form, she creates a statue, which did not exist beforehand. If she tires of the statue, she can squash it and so destroy it, though squashing it does not destroy the piece of clay. Thus the piece of clay is not the same object as the statue, for it exists before the statue does and continues to exist after the statue is destroyed. Think of it this way. The sculptor began with a piece of clay. That's one object. She then created a new object, the statue. That's a second object. So after she finished sculpting, there existed two objects, the piece of clay and the statue. Thus when I hold a statue in my hand, there are actually two objects there, a statue and a piece of clay. There appears to be only one, but there are really two.

The conclusion of this reasoning is that the statue and piece of clay are two different objects. But this is very hard to accept. Think of how similar to each other these objects are. For one thing, they are located in exactly the same place. Also, they are made up of exactly the same matter, which in turn means that they have exactly the same size, shape, weight, color, and texture. They are even more similar to each other than two duplicate billiard balls fresh from the factory, for such billiard balls are made up of different matter, and have different spatial locations. Given the similarity between the statue and the piece of clay, isn't it absurd to claim that they are two different objects? And yet they are; they must be, because the piece of clay existed before the statue, and could exist after the statue is destroyed.

This is an example of what the twentieth-century American philosopher W. V. O. Quine calls an **antinomy**: apparently sound

Antinomy

Sound reasoning leading to an apparently absurd conclusion. Philosophers prize antinomies, because they are bound to teach us something. Once caught in the antinomy, we cannot rest content with the status quo; something has to give. Either the apparently sound reasoning is not sound after all, or else the apparently absurd conclusion is not as absurd as it seems. Our job is to figure out which.

Assumptions of the Antinomy

To start, we must identify the crucial assumptions in the antinomy of constitution, especially any tacit assumptions we may be making without noticing. The most obvious assumption is:

> **Creation**: The sculptor really does create the statue—that is, the statue did not exist before the sculptor sculpted it.

The argument also makes some less obvious assumptions:

> **Survival**: The sculptor does not destroy the quantity of clay by forming it into a statue.
>
> **Existence**: There really are such objects as statues and pieces of clay.

useful heuristics perhaps

And finally, the conclusion of the argument must really be absurd for the antinomy to bite:

> **Absurdity**: It is impossible for two different objects to share the same matter and spatial location at a single time.

Assuming there are no other assumptions we have missed, we must reject Creation, Survival, Existence, or Absurdity, in order to resolve the antinomy. Investigating these assumptions will shed light more generally on the nature of material objects.

The Just-Matter Theory

Let's begin with Creation, which says that the statue only began to exist when the sculptor shaped the piece of clay into statue form. Someone who wanted to deny this assumption could say instead that the sculptor creates nothing, but simply *changes* the piece of clay. Painting a red barn green creates nothing; it only changes the color of the barn. Likewise, it may be said, the sculptor merely changes the shape of the piece of clay from a rather lumpy shape into a statue shape.

This would avoid the absurd conclusion that two different material objects share the same matter. Just as the previously red barn is the same barn as the subsequently green barn, so the previously lumpy-shaped piece of clay is the same piece of clay as the subsequently statue-shaped piece of clay. When you hold the statue in your hand, you are holding just one thing: a piece of clay with a statue shape.

This response may be based on a general theory of the nature of material objects. Consider the **just-matter** theory, according to which hunks (quantities, pieces) of matter are the *only* objects that exist. A hunk of matter is defined by the matter making it up. The only way to create a hunk of matter is to create some new matter. Merely rearranging pre-existing matter creates no new hunks, it only changes old hunks. That is what happens when the sculptor shapes the piece of clay into statue form. Likewise, the only way to destroy a hunk of matter is to destroy some of its matter. Rearranging or even scattering the matter changes, but does not destroy, the hunk. So squashing the statue destroys nothing. The piece of clay has gone back to having a lumpy shape, but it still exists.

The just-matter theory leads to shocking conclusions—perhaps as shocking as the absurd conclusion of the antinomy that we're trying to avoid. We ordinarily think of sculptors as creating things. Likewise, we ordinarily think that freezing water in a freezer tray or shaping aluminum in a factory *creates* ice cubes and soda cans. The just-matter theory denies this. It says that the ice cube in your drink existed before it was frozen, though it would not then have been called an ice cube; your soda can existed long before it was shaped in the factory, though it would not then have been called a soda can.

A wrecked car is towed to a junkyard, where it is crunched, taken apart, and sold for scrap material. This destroys the car, right? Wrong, according to the just-matter theory! The quantity of matter we formerly called 'the car' has merely been scattered. All that metal (and plastic and rubber) still exists, sold to various people in different locations. Since none of the matter itself has been destroyed, the hunk of matter remains. The object we used to call 'the car' still exists, though we can no longer call it a car since it no longer has a car shape.

Strikes me as correct

An even more extreme example: when Socrates died over two thousand years ago, his body was buried and then slowly rotted. By now, the matter that once composed him has been dispersed over the Earth's surface; some of it has even escaped the planet altogether. Still, none of that matter itself has perished. So according to the just-matter theory, Socrates still exists. Or, more accurately, the object we formerly called 'Socrates' still exists. We can no longer call it 'Socrates' or a 'person', since it no longer has a human form; it is now a scattered object, like a deck of cards strewn across a table. But it still exists. For similar reasons, the just-matter theory implies that you yourself existed thousands of years ago, for the piece of matter that is now you existed then. It was not then a person, since it was scattered across the Earth, but it existed nevertheless.

Maybe in the end we should accept these strange claims that the just-matter theory makes. But let's first look at some other options.

better to speak of 'Socrates' as a unique set, and when the set is scattered, it no longer exists

The Takeover Theory

We might instead reject Survival. In order to derive the absurd conclusion that the sculptor's work results in two different objects, we needed to assume that she created the statue (Creation), but we also needed to assume that she did not destroy the original piece of clay (Survival). For if creating the statue destroys the piece of clay, then at each point in the process there is only a single object, and we avoid the antinomy's conclusion.

Can a piece of clay *really* be destroyed simply by reshaping it? Though that's hard to believe, it shouldn't be dismissed out of hand. As we'll see, *every* response to the antinomy requires saying something a little strange. (That's what makes the antinomy of constitution such a good one.) We should instead ask for more information: *how* does reshaping the piece of clay destroy it? What general theory of objects justifies this claim?

The best answer is the **takeover theory**. An object, such as a piece of clay or a statue, is made up of certain particles of matter. Depending on how a group of particles are arranged, they will constitute an object of a certain **sort**, for instance, the sort *piece of clay* or the sort *statue*. When the clay particles in our antinomy were arranged in a lumpy way, they constituted a piece of clay. Later, after being moved around by the sculptor, they were arranged so as to constitute an object of a different sort, a statue. But according to the takeover theorist, particles can only constitute one object at a time. So as soon as the particles are arranged in statue form, the sort *statue* **takes over** from the sort *piece of clay*: the piece of clay stops existing, and in its place a new object, a statue, starts to exist. The particles no longer constitute the original piece of clay; that piece of clay no longer exists. The particles now constitute a different object, a statue.

An object's sort determines what kinds of changes the object can, and cannot, survive. Objects of the sort *statue* must retain a statue shape. So if the statue is squashed, and ceases to be statue-

The members of the set & their relations, spatio temporal, matter in the *Constitution* ~ 141 constitution shaped, that statue stops existing; the sort *statue* hands control of the particles back to the sort *piece of clay*, and an object distinct from the statue comes into existence. At any one time, only one sort has control of the particles; at any one time, those particles make up just one object.

The takeover theory agrees with the just-matter theory that only one object can be constituted by a group of particles at a time. But the just-matter theory says that the sort of the constituted object, no matter how the particles are arranged, is always the sort *quantity of matter*, whereas the takeover theory says that the sort differs depending on how the particles are arranged. Appropriately arranged particles can constitute statues, ice cubes, or soda cans. This is certainly an advantage for the takeover theory: it means that not all objects are defined by their matter. Whether objects of sorts like *statue* and *person* persist through various changes does not depend merely on whether their matter continues to exist; how the matter is arranged is significant. Statues, for instance, go out of existence when they are squashed, even if their matter continues to exist. Neither are persons defined by their matter. Thus Socrates no longer exists according to the takeover theory: when his body rotted, the sort *corpse* took over from the sort *person*, and the person that formerly existed—Socrates—ceased to be.

Still, on balance, the takeover theory seems worse than the just-matter theory. It says that the piece of clay is destroyed when the sort *statue* takes over from the sort *piece of clay*. One can destroy a piece of clay just by kneading it into a statue shape. Try convincing someone of *that* at your local bar! (Many would admit that a piece of clay can be 'transformed' into a statue, but the takeover theory denies a 'transformation', which is a way of continuing to exist, and insists on a replacement.) So *each* theory says something unintuitive about the changes objects can and cannot survive: the just-matter theory says that persons can exist after rotting and disintegration; the takeover theory says that pieces of clay *cannot* exist after acquiring more artistic shapes. So far the score is even, one strike against each theory. But now compare the theories in a more abstract way: which has a more intuitively satisfying *rule* for what objects exist? The just-matter theory has a clear rule: all objects are hunks of matter. The takeover theory provides no such clear rule. It does tell us what objects exist in some cases. It tells us, for example, that the sort *statue* takes over when the piece of clay is sculpted, and that the sort *person* relinquishes its hold when a person disintegrates. But what *general* rule tells us in *all* cases when one sort takes over from another?

Imagine a takeover theorist from Mars. Instead of sorts like *statue* and *piece of clay,* beloved of Earthly takeover theorists, Martian takeover theorists speak of sorts like:

> *outpiece*: piece of clay located outdoors, no matter how shaped,
> *inpiece*: piece of clay located indoors, no matter how shaped.

Earthly takeover theorists say that when a piece of clay is made into a statue, it stops existing and a statue takes its place. Of course, whether the clay is indoors or outdoors is irrelevant to what objects exist. Martian takeover theorists see things very differently. They view the world in terms of inpieces and outpieces, not statues and pieces of clay. When an outpiece is brought indoors, they say, the sort *inpiece* takes over, the outpiece goes out of existence, and a new inpiece comes into existence. This inpiece exists so long as the clay is indoors. Whether it is shaped into statue form is irrelevant to what object exists. But if it is taken outdoors, it stops existing and is replaced by an outpiece.

Earthly and Martian takeover theorists agree that the conclusion of the antinomy is absurd; they agree that there are never two distinct material objects made of the same parts. So each must think that the other is mistaken about what the correct sorts are, and about what objects exist. For consider the sculptor, inside her house, about to begin sculpting. The Earthling and the Martian agree that she holds a single object in her hand, but they disagree over what its sort is. The Earthling thinks that the object is a piece of clay, which will be destroyed when sculpted into a statue. The Martian thinks that it is an inpiece, which will survive being sculpted but will be destroyed when taken outdoors. They cannot both be right, since the same object cannot both continue and cease to exist. Thus our own Earthly takeover theorist must say that the Martian is mistaken: inpieces and outpieces simply do not exist.

But how can this claim be justified? The Earthly takeover theorist's choice of sorts suspiciously mirrors the words we humans here on Earth happen to have coined. We could have invented different words; we could have gone the way of the Martians and introduced words for inpieces and outpieces rather than statues and pieces of clay. If we had, the Earthly takeover theorist must say, then we would have been mistaken in nearly all our judgments about when objects come into and go out of existence, for the true objects are pieces of clay and statues, not inpieces and outpieces. It is nothing short of a miraculous coincidence that reality just happens to contain objects matching *our* current words rather than those of the Martians. Believing in pieces of clay and statues to the exclusion of inpieces and outpieces would be anthropocentric.

Nihilism

Takeover and just-matter theorists agree that in any given case there is a single sort of object present. The former's choice of *which* sort of object exists is suspiciously anthropocentric. The latter's choice is more objective, but has counter-intuitive consequences.

Since it is so hard to choose what sort of object exists in a given case, perhaps we should say that *no* sort of object exists. This is what the **nihilist** says. Thus, the nihilist challenges the assumption of Existence, according to which statues and pieces of clay are existing entities. If there simply are no such things as statues or pieces of clay (or inpieces or outpieces), then our antinomy does not get off the ground.

Is it wholly absurd to deny the existence of pieces of clay and statues? After all, we can just see pieces of clay and statues, can't we? Philosophers seek the *truth*; they are not merely trying to provoke, or annoy, or say whatever they can get away with. They often make surprising or unfamiliar claims, but these claims must always be reasonable; they should not directly contradict the evidence of our senses. Otherwise, even if we don't know exactly how to refute the philosopher, we may justifiably write him off as playing an idle game.

In fact, denying the existence of statues and pieces of clay isn't wholly absurd, and doesn't contradict the evidence of our senses. Consider the immense number of sub-atomic particles that make up what we call the statue. The nihilist agrees that these particles exist; she doesn't reject the existence of *everything*. Now, most of us think that, in addition to these septillion or so particles arranged in statue form, there also exists a septillion-and-first entity, namely the statue itself, which is composed of the septillion particles. But according to the nihilist, there is no statue. There are only the septillion particles, arranged in statue form; there is no septillion-and-first entity. In fact, according to the nihilist, the *only* things that exist are **particles**, that is, things with absolutely no smaller parts. Even protons and neutrons do not exist, for those things contain quarks as parts. Only the ultimate particles of physics (for instance, quarks and electrons) exist. The nihilist avoids the conclusion that the statue and the piece of clay are two things made up of the same matter by saying that neither the statue nor the piece of clay exists at all. Indeed, no objects larger than a particle exist—not even you yourself! There is no you; there are only particles arranged in person form.

Nihilism is not wholly absurd because everyday sensory experiences do not tell us whether there exist only particles, or whether there exist in addition objects composed of those particles. I (or rather, a number of particles arranged 'me form') look in front of me and have a certain sensation, apparently of a computer screen. But that same sensation could be produced by mere particles arranged 'computerscreenwise'. How could I tell whether, in addition to the particles, there is also the computer screen? Even those of us who believe in computer screens agree that they look, feel, and smell as they do because of the arrangement of their septillion or so microscopic bits. So we must admit that the bits would look, feel, and smell the same regardless of whether they compose a septillion-and-first thing.

But even if nihilism isn't wholly absurd, and can't be disproven by simple observation, it is still pretty absurd. After all, following Rene Descartes, the seventeenth-century French philosopher, I can't disprove by simple observation that I'm not on Mars dreaming an extremely vivid dream. (Descartes himself thought that he could prove the existence of a benevolent God who would protect him from being so drastically mistaken, but his arguments are unconvincing.) I might pinch myself to see whether I am dreaming, but I could just be dreaming the pinch! Yet, philosopher though I am, I don't doubt for a moment that I'm currently located on the planet Earth. It seems reasonable to simply ignore the outlandish possibility that I'm dreaming on Mars. Now, it's hard to say exactly when it is reasonable to ignore such possibilities. But perhaps nihilism is outlandish enough to be in the same category as the dream scenario: difficult to refute but safe to ignore.

Anyway, nihilism may not even work on its own terms. It assumes that the world is ultimately made up of particles—that is, things with no smaller parts. But perhaps there are no such things as particles. Have you ever (late at night, perhaps in an altered state) entertained the hypothesis that our entire universe is just a tiny speck in a giant other universe? And that within each atom of our universe, there exists a whole other tiny universe? And that in each of the 'atoms' of this tiny universe there is contained yet another universe? If this sequence continued forever there would be no particles, since each object would contain smaller parts. I suppose these thoughts are as idle as Descartes's dream hypothesis, but a less psychedelic version is more worrisome: perhaps each particle contains smaller parts, if not an entire universe. When chemistry first discovered the atom, no one knew that atoms had smaller parts. Then protons, neutrons, and electrons were discovered. Still later, scientists learned that even protons and neutrons have smaller parts: quarks. As scientists develop more and more powerful tools, electron microscopes and whatnot, they keep telling us of smaller and smaller objects. Perhaps this process will continue without end; perhaps every object, no matter how small, has still smaller parts. In each of these scenarios, no particles exist, since every object has smaller parts. Now, *absolute nihilism*, which says that no objects at all exist, not even particles, is too silly to take seriously, for it cannot explain the evidence of our senses that objects at least appear to exist. So in either scenario, there must exist *some* objects; and given how the scenarios were described, these objects must have smaller parts. Nihilism would therefore be false in either scenario. Moreover, if some objects with smaller parts do exist, then there is no reason to deny that statues and pieces of clay are among these objects. And if so, we still face the antinomy of constitution. Nihilism does not help in the imagined scenarios, the second of which, at any rate, may for all we know be correct.

Cohabitation

Like the assumptions of Creation and Survival, the Existence assumption is hard to question. Since these are the only assumptions made by the argument, we are slowly being backed into a corner. The only remaining possibility is to question our assumption that the conclusion of the argument is absurd: in other words, to reject Absurdity. Perhaps two material objects can, after all, share the same matter and spatial location at the same time. We can call this the hypothesis of **Cohabitation**, for it says that the same region of space can be inhabited by more than one object.

Our problem has been to choose what sort of object sits in the sculptor's hand. The just-matter theorist says: *a piece of matter*. The takeover theorist says: a *statue*. The nihilist refuses to choose, and says: *neither*. The defender of Cohabitation also refuses to choose, and says: *both*.

Cohabitation seems strange, but are there any *reasons* against it? Yes; here are two. First, just before the sculptor squashes the statue-shaped clay, she allegedly holds in her hand two objects: a statue and a piece of clay. Then she presses her hands together, squashing the clay. According to the defender of Cohabitation, this destroys only one of the objects: the statue is destroyed while the piece of clay carries on. But the sculptor squashed the piece of clay just as hard as she squashed the statue; she exerted the same pressure with her hands on each object. So, we must conclude, the statue is far more vulnerable to squashing than the lump; it is much more delicate. But how can that be? The statue is *exactly like* the piece of clay in all of its physical characteristics. It is made up of exactly the same matter as the piece of clay, arranged in exactly the same configuration.

Second, the very idea that the same parts could make up *two* things clashes with the concept of a part. Here's an absurd story: 'A woman once decided her house needed a change, so she painted every part of it bright orange. But even though all its parts changed color, the house itself did not change color at all; it stayed exactly the same.' The story is absurd because it supposes that the house is something over and above its parts. Like any whole object, a house is in some sense nothing more than its parts taken together. But if this is right, then we must reject Cohabitation. If a whole is nothing more than its parts, then the same parts cannot form *two* wholes; otherwise one (or both) of the wholes would have to be different from its parts.

Four-Dimensionalism

We are running out of options! The argument for the antinomy made only three assumptions: Creation, Survival, and Existence, none of which is easy to deny. Defenders of the just-matter theory reject Creation, but are committed to the counter-intuitive claim that Socrates still exists. Takeover theorists reject Survival, but face the charge of anthropocentrism. Nihilists reject Existence, but are left with a theory too radical to believe. So the conclusion of the argument—that statues and pieces of clay are distinct objects made up of the same matter—follows. But accepting the conclusion, and therefore Cohabitation, itself faces two powerful arguments. What to do?

A remaining theory of material objects allows us to accept Cohabitation and to rebut the two arguments. That theory is **four-dimensionalism**.

Begin with the theory that 'time is like space', as discussed in Chapter 3. Think of time as a fourth dimension, alongside the three spatial dimensions. This is clearest in pictures. Consider the space-time diagram, Figure 4, that we saw in Chapter 3. The relevant feature of the diagram is that it depicts objects as having **temporal parts** as well as spatial parts, which is the core claim of four-dimensionalism. We tend to think only of spatial parts: a person's hands and feet, a car's doors and steering wheel. A person's spatial parts are spatially smaller than that person: they occupy smaller spatial regions than the entire person. But the four-dimensional perspective reveals temporal parts as well. A person's temporal parts are temporally smaller than the person: they exist in a smaller temporal interval than the entire person. The diagram pictures a dinosaur, a person, and their temporal parts. Let's focus on the person:

and her temporal parts:

👤, 👤, and 👤.

Can more poetic

Each of these temporal parts exists at only one time, just as each of a person's smallest spatial parts exists at only one place. The person as a whole consists of all her parts put together, both temporal and spatial.

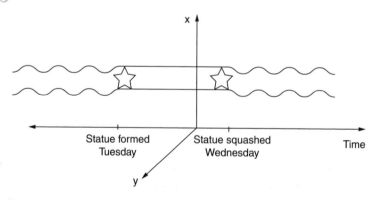

Fig. 10. Four-dimensional perspective on the clay statue

Consider the statue and piece of clay from the four-dimensional perspective (Figure 10). The diagram depicts a piece of clay which first has a lumpy shape, then is formed into a statue of a star, then is squashed back into a lumpy shape. The diagram depicts Cohabitation, since it depicts the statue as being a different object from the piece of clay. The piece of clay is the entire object, which begins long before being shaped into statue form and lasts long after being squashed:

The statue, on the other hand, is an object that exists only when the piece of clay is star-shaped:

As Figure 10 shows, the statue is part of the piece of clay. So the statue and the piece of clay are two different objects, just as you are a different object from your hand. Thus, four-dimensionalism embraces the conclusion of the antinomy, namely that the statue and piece of clay are two different objects.

We saw that Cohabitation faces two objections. Given the four-dimensional picture, the objections melt away. Let's take them in reverse.

The second objection was that Cohabitation violates the principle that a single set of parts cannot compose two different wholes. In fact, from the four-dimensional perspective, the principle is not violated at all. The space-time diagram clearly shows that the statue and the piece of clay do *not* have exactly the same parts. The piece of clay has more parts than the statue, since it has temporal parts located to the future of the statue:

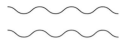

as well as to the past of the statue:

The statue and piece of clay only *appeared* to have the same parts because we were neglecting the fourth dimension of time.

The first objection asked how the statue can be so fragile when it is made of the same material as the sturdy piece of clay. To answer this objection, let us continue to press analogies between space and time. One useful spatial analog of the statue and the piece of clay is a long road and one of its smaller parts. US Route 1 runs up the east coast of the United States all the way from Florida to Maine; a short section in Philadelphia is called the Roosevelt Boulevard. The Roosevelt Boulevard is *part* of Route 1. They are of course two different roads, since Route 1 extends much longer (in space). But no one wonders why the Roosevelt Boulevard is so fragile as to stop existing at the city limits of Philadelphia, despite the fact that it is made of exactly the same asphalt within the city limits as is Route 1. Its termination at the city limits is merely the result of a decision by the good people of Philadelphia to use the words 'The Roosevelt Boulevard' for a mere part of Route 1. This analogy shows why the first argument against Cohabitation is misguided, given the four-dimensional picture. Why does only the statue go out of existence upon squashing? Answer: this is merely the result of our choice to use the word 'statue' only for the statue-shaped temporal parts of a piece of clay.

If you are still inclined to worry that the first objection threatens four-dimensionalism, this may be because of a mistaken picture of the two objects in the sculptor's hand, namely, a picture of two objects 'directly' present. If I touch your nose, I am in a sense touching two things, you and your nose. But your nose is the only thing I touch directly. I touch *you* indirectly, *by* touching your nose, which is part of you. The correct picture of the two objects in the sculptor's hand is analogous. There is just one object directly in the sculptor's hand, namely the current temporal part common to both the statue and the piece of clay. The statue and the piece of clay themselves are in the sculptor's hand only indirectly, by containing a temporal part that is directly in the sculptor's hand.

If both the statue and the piece of clay were directly present in the sculptor's hand, then perhaps the survival or destruction of these entities would depend on their current physical characteristics, in which case we would indeed face the question of how the statue could be so fragile when the piece of clay is so robust. But since the only thing directly in the sculptor's hand is the current temporal part of both the statue and the piece of clay, what happens afterwards is just a function of the physical characteristics of the temporal part and what she does to it. If she squashes it, then there will be further temporal parts with lumpy shapes; if she leaves it alone, then those temporal parts will continue to be statue-shaped. There remains the question of what we will *call* various aggregates of temporal parts, depending on what those further temporal parts are like. We only call statue-shaped aggregates 'statues'. So if the sculptor squashes the statue and the further temporal parts have lumpy shapes, only the aggregate terminating at the squashing counts as a 'statue'.

Note that four-dimensionalism avoids the charge of anthropocentrism that the takeover theory faces. The English language contains a word ('statue') for collections of statue-shaped temporal parts of clay. It contains no words for collections of *indoor* or *outdoor* temporal parts of clay. Nevertheless, such collections exist. These objects are what the Martians would call 'inpieces' and 'outpieces'. Four-dimensionalism says that these strange collections are just as real as our familiar statues and pieces of clay. Compare the collection of segments of US Route 1 that are located within cities whose names begin with the letter 'A'. We have no word for this 'Route A', but it exists; it is just as real an object as Route 1. Thus, four-dimensionalists must admit the existence of inpieces and outpieces, *in addition* to statues and pieces of clay.

Some philosophers think inpieces and outpieces are strange entities, and dislike four-dimensionalism accordingly. Others dislike four-dimensionalism because they doubt that time is like space. Still others are suspicious of temporal parts: instantaneous objects popping into and out of existence at every moment. I myself have no problem with these things. Accepting inpieces and outpieces on an equal footing with statues and pieces of clay is an excellent way to avoid the charge of anthropocentrism leveled against the takeover theorist. Treating time like space has been fruitful in contemporary physics. As we have seen in this chapter, it is fruitful in metaphysics as well. Instantaneous objects popping into and out of existence? Perhaps that is a bit of a surprise. But any solution to the antinomy of constitution is bound to have some surprising feature. Otherwise the antinomy would not have vexed metaphysicians for so long.

FURTHER READING

The following article concerns antinomies and their importance in philosophy: W. V. O. Quine, 'The Ways of Paradox', in his book *The Ways of Paradox and Other Essays* (Random House, 1966).

Chapter 3 of Roderick Chisholm's book, *Person and Object* (Open Court, 1976) defends the just-matter theory (which is often called 'mereological essentialism').

Michael Burke defends the takeover theory (though he does not give the theory that name) in this fairly technical article: 'Preserving the Principle of One Object to a Place: A Novel Account of the Relations Among Objects, Sorts, Sortals, and Persistence Conditions', in Michael Rea (ed.), *Material Constitution* (Rowman & Littlefield, 1997).

Inpieces and outpieces are based on Eli Hirsch's 'incars' and 'out-cars', introduced on p. 32 of his book *The Concept of Identity* (Oxford University Press, 1982). The primary question of Hirsch's book is: how do material objects continue to exist over time?

For further reading on nihilism, a good source is Trenton Merricks's book *Objects and Persons* (Oxford University Press, 2001), especially chapters 1 and 2. Merricks is not a true nihilist, since he believes in persons as well as particles. Close enough—he does not believe in statues or pieces of clay.

Chapter 1 of my book *Four-Dimensionalism* (Oxford University Press, 2001) is an accessible presentation of four-dimensionalism. Chapter 5 is a more technical discussion of the problem of constitution.

Judith Jarvis Thomson's paper 'Parthood and Identity Across Time' criticizes four-dimensionalism and defends cohabitation, and is also an excellent general introduction to the antinomy of constitution. It can be found in the *Material Constitution* anthology mentioned above.

CHAPTER 8

Universals

Earl Conee

Introduction

Much of metaphysics is mind-expanding, especially **ontology**—
the part of metaphysics that is about the most basic kinds of
things. Philosophers engaged in ontology often argue that we
can find remarkable entities hidden in plain view. The entities are
supposed to be embedded in some familiar facts. They are
supposed to become apparent to us, once we think in the right
way. According to opponents of the entities, their apparent
existence is an illusion. Whoever is right, we gain a better
understanding of the world by appreciating this sort of dispute.

Think of three typical Red Delicious apples. It is a mundane
fact about them that they have several things in common. For
instance, they are red, they have grown on a tree, they are
composed of organic molecules, and they taste bad (that last
one is the sorry truth about Red Delicious apples, in spite of their
self-congratulatory name).

In line with some standard philosophical terminology, let's use
the term **property** for any feature of anything or anyone. Properties include color, shape, composition, location, temperature,
age, distance from the Washington Monument, ownership,

mood, perceptual condition, educational status, marital status, and so on. A property is any way at all that something could be. We are assigning the term 'property' to those things, *if* they exist. So we are not sneaking in a controversial assumption here. Maybe there really are no such things as properties.

A bit more standard terminology: a property that can be a feature of more than one thing is called a **universal**. In other words, a universal is a way that numerous things could be—*if* universals exist.

We noted the mundane fact that three Red Delicious apples have things in common. This seems to be a fact that we can equally well state by saying that there are properties that the apples share. Properties that are shared are features of more than one thing, so they qualify as universals. Apples can't go around sharing universals that don't exist. These simple points seem to establish that universals exist.

The dispute over the existence of universals is one of the most durable debates in metaphysics. Can it really be that a few simple observations show conclusively that universals exist?

No. The question of whether or not universals really exist turns out to be highly challenging. Once we start thinking about them, universals are difficult to deny. The simple reasoning that we have just seen argues in favor of their existence, and there are other good reasons to accept them as well. If universals exist, then every object in the world has some. They are all over the place. Once they are pointed out, it can seem that no reasonable person could deny their existence. Yet the existence of universals turns out to be troubling and doubtful on several grounds. It can seem that universals would make problems and solve none. There are philosophical alternatives to accepting the existence of universals, but we shall see that the alternatives have troubles of their own.

Positive Reasons

Why not conclude that the existence of universals is proven by plain facts like the facts about shared features of apples that we have just considered? Would that be 'too easy'? What's wrong with easy? If the reasoning fails, exactly where does it go wrong?

We might try denying that the three apples have any properties in common. After all, strictly speaking, the apples do not have precisely the same color, and they differ in details of their chemical composition. Encouraged by these points, we might try to go all the way with this line and maintain that the apples have nothing truly in common.

This line is tough to defend. For one thing, it is difficult to get around the fact that one respect in which the apples are exactly alike is that they are apples. This seems to tell us that they have in common the property *being an apple*.

There is also serious science to contend with. Physics tells us that all electrons have exactly the same charge. So according to physics the electrons have this property in common. Charge is a property of electrons that plays a basic role in extremely well confirmed physical explanations of much of what happens in the world. It seems that we would have to argue against a basic claim of established science to deny that charge is a universal.

For another thing, suppose that we could finally defend the conclusion that no two things are exactly alike in any way. Still, the differences between the properties of things would appear accidental. For instance, even if the charges of all electrons turn out to differ minutely, that seems to be just a way that things happen to be. No matter what charge any particular electron has, couldn't another electron at least happen to have exactly the same charge? Why not? What could absolutely guarantee that all charges are of different magnitudes? Nothing comes to mind. So the charge of any electron is a universal, since it is a sharable property, even if it is not actually shared. Although many things that are very similar in some way turn out to differ subtly, there are some ways that many things at least could have been. These are universals.

Here is another route to the existence of universals. Clearly, we see objects. But we also see the colors of some objects. Likewise, we see and feel the shapes and textures of some objects. The colors, shapes, and textures of objects are ways that those objects are, properties of the objects. Each of these properties is a way that other things are, or could have been. Since we see and feel the properties, they exist. They are sharable properties, and so they are universals.

Can this reasoning be reasonably resisted? We might try being skeptical about perception. Sometimes we make perceptual errors. We see something as having a feature that it does not have. Some philosophical skeptics about perception use such acknowledged facts of our perceptual fallibility to raise doubts that we ever *know* what perceptible features objects have.

The merits of such skepticism constitute a large issue in the area of philosophy that primarily deals with knowledge, **epistemology**. For present purposes, though, a defender of universals does not even have to dispute the skepticism. A strong perceptual argument remains for the existence of universals. Suppose that you see an apple as red. It can be granted that you do not thereby know that the apple is red, or even know that the apple exists. Nonetheless, it can be contended that the color red must be something. It is the color that you see the apple as having. So there must be such a color, even if this apple does not have it, and even if nothing has it. The mere fact that red is a way that you see an apple as being seems to imply that there exists such a way for things to be. Since multiple things at least could have been this color, it is a universal.

A further argument for universals deserves our attention, an argument about meaning. The argument focuses on what we are doing when we use language to formulate our thoughts.

Consider simple sentences of the subject-predicate form, 'X is F', where 'X' stands for the subject (what the sentence is about) and 'F' stands for the predicate (what the sentence says about the subject). This is the structure of countless sentences, such as 'Alice is amused', 'Bob is baffled', and 'Carol is considerate'. When we use this sort of sentence to state something that we think, it is clear that the 'X' part, the subject, singles out our topic. What does the predicate 'F' contribute to saying what we mean? The natural answer is that we intend the 'F' part to say *how we take the subject to be*. In other words, we intend the predicate 'F' to express a property that we think X has, namely, the property *being F*. This intention is not often actively on our minds. But if we reflect, this intention is our best idea about what we are using the predicate for. When we think that Bob is baffled, *being baffled* is a way that we are thinking Bob is. So, there must be such a thing as this property. In these subject-predicate sentences, what we mean by the predicate is a property that many things can have. Therefore, what we mean by such a predicate is a universal.

Here is one last fast argument for universals. Red and blue are two different colors. So there exist two colors (at least). Any color is a sharable property. So universals exist.

We have seen reasons to think that an abundance of universals exist—colors and other perceived qualities, scientific magnitudes, and the meanings of unlimited numbers of predicates. Let's call a defender of the existence of all these universals a **universalist**. Why not agree with the universalists?

Doubts

We began with the fact that apples have things in common. But maybe this casually worded statement is misunderstood and inflated by the universalist. It sounds fishy to argue that apples or electrons have 'things' in common, and therefore these 'things', universals, exist. Just calling an apple 'an apple' does not seem like talking about two things: the apple and something else. Yet that is what the universalist argument implies we are doing. We are supposed to be saying something about both the apple and *being an apple*. That doesn't ring any bells. All we seem to be doing is classifying an apple as an apple.

The case for universals may not be in trouble here, though. Maybe we are talking about universals without realizing it. First, we should not confuse the claim that universals are **things** with the claim that universals are material objects. The universalist's claim is not that universals are entities of the very same type as protons, people, and pulsars—individual objects. Universalists just claim that universals are real, they are actual, and they are not merely apparent or illusory. They may exist and yet be different in nature from individual objects.

Also, in arguing that some true assertions about apples imply that universals exist, a universalist is not making a claim about what we actively think when we talk about apples. Perhaps we have a universal in mind only tacitly, as was suggested in the argument from meaning. The claim is that a universal has to exist for some of our factual assertions about apples to be true. This is supposed to follow because of what we actually assert, whatever we actively think that we are doing. When we classify apples as apples, for instance, universalists say that something could qualify to be classified as an apple only by exemplifying *being an apple*.

In any event, this point about seeming misinterpretation does not argue *against* universals. At most, it casts doubt on some lines of argument for universals.

The existence of universals does pose problems, however. Let's investigate the hypothesis that *being red* is a universal that is shared by the three Red Delicious apples. How does the universal relate to the apples? For one thing, where is it? There seem to be only two live possibilities for its location, and neither of them is attractive.

The first possibility is that universals do not exist in space. They exist, but nowhere. Things like apples that have universals are in space, but not the universals themselves.

This non-spatial alternative creates mysteries. How do we see the color of an apple, if the color is not there where the apple is? In fact, isn't it as obvious that we see the color located there, on the surface of the apple, as that we see the apple? More generally, if a universal is nowhere, then how does it get connected to some particular spatial objects and not others, in order to be had by some and not had by the others?

These may not be unanswerable questions. But the non-spatial possibility does not seem promising.

The other live possibility is that a universal is present wherever an instance of it exists. So *being red* is present where each of our three Red Delicious apples is, and where each other red thing is too. At least this puts the universal in the right place to be seen by looking at red things.

The whole universal *being red* cannot be just where one apple is, because other things are instances of the same universals. Is the universal scattered about in space, with part of it at the location of each red thing?

A scattered existence of parts would undercut the universalist theory. Universalists say that each of our three Red Delicious apples is red because they have one and the same thing in common, the universal *being red*. If each apple has at its location just its own part of the universal, then it seems to follow that what any one apple has is different from what any other one has. It seems to follow that they do not share the universal after all.

Suppose we try instead the idea that *being red* is located *in its entirety* where each red thing is. In this view, the apples definitely have something in common, the whole universal. The view seems to say something impossible, though. If the whole of the universal is where one apple is, how could that same universal be somewhere else too?

This turns out *not* to be blatantly impossible. We should distinguish 'wholly' from 'solely.' The claim we are now considering about the location of a universal is not the claim that the universal is *solely* in the spatial region occupied by that apple, and also elsewhere. That's blatantly impossible! The claim is rather that the whole thing is in a spatial region occupied by an apple, and the same whole thing is also simultaneously elsewhere. If it's wholly one place, then *all* of it is there. But this does not come right out and say that it is *only* there. So we do not contradict ourselves by adding that it is elsewhere too.

Multiple location is troubling, though. Universalists propose that the same whole thing—a universal—can be in more than one place at the same time. Well, if it can happen to universals, then why can't it happen to concrete things like *car parts* too? Imagine that some car is parked parallel to the curb with its right tires touching the curb. So, part of the car is definitely well within a foot of the curb. But maybe that part is multiply located. Maybe, say, the 13 inch wide portion of the car that is closest to the curb is somewhere else too. Maybe that whole portion is also on the other side of the car, doing double duty as both the left and the right 13 inch wide outer portion of the car. (The idea is that the same 13 inch wide car part is on both sides of the car, but the part has a different configuration on each side to give the car its actual shape.) The rest of the car— the middle between the 13 inch wide outer portion—is definitely more than a foot away from the curb. So the *whole* car—all of its parts—is more than a foot away from the curb (although part of the car is *also* located within one foot of the curb). Now suppose that the law reads, 'It is prohibited for any whole parked car to be more than a foot from a curb.' With multiple whole location of car parts, you could earn a parking ticket no matter how carefully you parked! If the law said instead, 'Part of the car must be within a foot of the curb', then that law would *not* be broken in our example. But it's more metaphysically informative to think about the case where the law happens to read the other way.

The multiple location of car parts seems silly. In the case of material things, we are strongly inclined to think that the spatial basis that we use to distinguish parts *has to work*. Suppose it does. We have no idea why it would work in some cases but not others. So maybe it has to work *across the board*. If that is true, then the universalist is mistaken in thinking that universals can be wholly located in many places at once. But then the universalist is in real trouble. The trouble is that, apart from multiple whole location, there seems to be nothing acceptable to say about the location of universals.

Another problem arises when we consider further the alleged role of universals in perception. Sometimes we see the color of a ripe Red Delicious apple. Suppose that this is seeing the universal *being red*. Does the universal itself have a color? There appears to be trouble for universals, no matter how this question is answered.

Suppose that the universal is colored red. Then it seems unproblematic that we see red when we see that universal. We see the color of the apple, and now we are saying that this color, the universal *being red*, is colored red.

On this alternative, though, there seem to be too many red things. There is a red apple and a red universal. We are supposed to be seeing the color of the apple. But now another red thing seems to get in the way, the color of the red universal. If that is what we see when we look at the apple, then it seems that we are not really seeing the apple's color after all, but rather we are seeing its color's color. And does *that* color have a color, or is it colorless? We are off on a wild goose chase. Something has gone wrong.

Suppose instead that *being red* is not itself colored red. We'd better assume that it is not green or yellow either, since any other color would equally get in the way of seeing the apple's color, and it would present us with the wrong color to boot. So we'd better assume that *being red* is colorless. On this alternative, when we see the color of the apple, we are seeing a colorless universal.

In familiar examples of seeing a colorless thing, such as seeing clean water, we don't see a color. So how come when what we are seeing is the colorless color of an apple, we see red? Again, something has gone wrong. Now we have trouble for both of the two possible alternatives concerning the color of universals.

Another doubt about universals arises in connection with relations. So far we have discussed only universal features, that is, ways that one thing can be on its own, such as *being happy* and *being an apple*. Universalists hold that there are also ways that things can relate to each other. They call ways of relating **relations**. Many relations seem to have multiple examples, just like features of single things. For instance, suppose that each of us has a brother. Yours is Bob and mine is Paul. Then it seems that there is a relation that you bear to Bob—the *brotherhood* relation—and I bear that same relation to Paul. If you and I are each carrying something, then we both bear the *carrying* relation to something; if we are each the same age as some movie star or other, then we both bear the *same-age-as* relation to someone, and so forth. These are examples where one relation seems to hold in many cases. According to universalists, these relations too are universals.

The new problem for universals concerns instantiation. To *instantiate* a property is simply to have that property. For example, when you are happy, universalists claim that you are instantiating the universal property, happiness. This claim seems to imply that there is a *relation* between you and happiness, namely, instantiation. Suppose that we apply the universal theory to instantiation, just as it is supposed to apply to other ways that things are related. Then your being happy includes you, happiness, and a third thing, instantiation, that relates you to happiness. This same relation of instantiation would likewise relate any other universal property to the things that have the property. So the universalist view implies that instantiation is a universal, a universal that is a relation. This seems to be what the theory has to say, and by itself, it does not seem bad.

But this is only the beginning. The theory now finds three things in the fact that you are happy: you, happiness, and instantiation. Yet if there are these three things in that fact, then they are related in a certain way. You are related to instantiation and happiness by bearing the instantiation relation to happiness. Concerning this claim, though, if it states a fact, then another application of the universalist view seems to imply that there is a fourth thing involved. The theory seems to imply that there is a 'bearing-to' relation that holds among the three things: you, happiness, and instantiation.

If there is any such fourth thing, then it does not stop there. Those four are also related, and so the theory says that there are five, and they are related, and so on without end.

We have witnessed an explosion of relations that do nothing but make connections between a thing and a property that it has. This seems way too complicated. When you are happy, your happiness is a condition that you are in; it is how you are. The connection seems immediate. Yet now we have a universalist theory telling us that there are endlessly many relations intervening between you and your happiness. It is difficult to believe in all of those relations, even for someone who considers universals sympathetically.

The extra relations are implied by the same explanatory principle that universalists use to infer the existence of ordinary relations. Universalists hold that related things are always related by some entity that is a relation. If that sort of principle has limits, what are they?

A universalist might say that instantiation is special. It is the maximally intimate relation that connects a thing to the thing's own properties. In this special case, the relation relates things directly without itself bearing any relation to the things that it relates. But however intimate a relation it is, how does it manage to relate those things without being related to them? And if instantiation can do that somehow, then why cannot things generally just be related, without any relation universals at all?

A Final Ground for Doubt

We are about to see that some other reasons for thinking that there are universals also seem to go overboard. For example, in the argument from meaning, a claim is made about a role that we intend for the predicates of subject-predicative sentences. The claim is that we think of a universal (at least tacitly) and we intend the predicate of a sentence to ascribe that universal to the sentence's subject. When we think that Alice is amused, we think of amusement in connection with Alice. For a wide variety of cases like this thought about Alice, the claim about attributing a universal when we apply a predicate seems harmless and maybe even correct. But there is a very powerful argument that requires us to deny that this is what we are always doing when we predicate. If the reasoning succeeds, it is a big problem for universalists. We'll see that it makes trouble for the main arguments for universals.

To appreciate this threatening line of reasoning, we can begin by noting the interesting fact that some properties seem to be instances of themselves. For example, all properties are, if nothing else, properties. If we apply a universalist view here, we infer that all properties share the universal, *being a property*. If absolutely *all* properties have this property, then so does that very property, *being a property*. It too exemplifies the universal, *being a property*. In other words, it is an instance of itself—a phenomenon that we can call **self-instantiating**.

Okay, that's interesting, at least a little. But it seems to be an isolated oddity. Most universals do not appear to be instances of themselves. To take a pretty much random example, we have no good reason to think that *being happy* is itself happy. In fact, that is out of the question. A universal is supposed to be a mere way of things. It does not have a mind capable of happiness. For another example, *being an apple* is no apple. When we count apples, we surely do not leave any apples out of our count by not including *being an apple* in the total!

It is easy to convince ourselves that universals are mostly like *being happy* and *being an apple* in that they are *not* self-instantiating. So we can formulate something that we believe as follows:

Being happy is not self-instantiating.

Now trouble arises. One assumption in the meaning argument for universals definitely goes wrong here. The meaning argument assumes that, in a sentence like this one about *being happy*, we use the predicate to attribute a universal to the subject. But in the case of predicating the denial of self-instantiation, it turns out that we *cannot* have in mind a universal that we intend the predicate to stand for. It would be the universal of *non-self-instantiation*. We cannot have in mind a universal of *non-self-instantiation*, because no such universal can exist.

To see why, suppose that a universal of *non-self-instantiation* did exist. Call this hypothetical universal 'UN'. If UN exists, then either UN does instantiate itself, or it does not. We will try each of these alternatives. It will turn out that both alternatives are impossible. That result reflects very badly on the existence of UN. Because UN implies the impossible, UN is itself impossible. UN cannot exist.

First, suppose that UN instantiates itself. Recall that UN is the universal that things have in virtue of which they do not instantiate themselves, if UN exists. So anything that instantiates UN, which we are now supposing includes UN, does *not* instantiate itself. This directly contradicts our current supposition that UN *does* instantiate itself. So our supposition must be mistaken. Since the supposition that UN *does* instantiate itself is a mistake, it clearly follows that UN does *not* instantiate itself.

So maybe that's the way it is. UN does not instantiate itself. What is the problem with that? Let's assume that UN does not instantiate itself and see what follows. We should again focus on what UN is supposed to be. UN is the universal that things have in virtue of which they do not instantiate themselves, if UN exists. Now we are assuming that UN exists *and does not instantiate itself.* So UN would be an *instance* of the universal that makes for things not instantiating themselves. Which universal is that? Well, if it exists, it is UN. So we have derived that UN *does* instantiate itself from the assumption that it does not. Since our current supposition that UN does not instantiate itself thus implies its own contradiction, this supposition too turns out to imply the impossible. So the supposition must not be true. In other words, it is not so that UN does not instantiate itself. Putting this more positively, we have derived that UN *does* instantiate itself.

We have just established that if UN exists, then it instantiates itself. Before that, we established that if UN exists, then it does not instantiate itself. Thus, if UN exists, an impossible contradictory situation is implied. No truth implies an impossibility. So we must conclude that UN does not exist. This might seem to be nothing more than a special problem for the peculiar candidate universal, UN. There's no such universal—but so what? Why is it worth the trouble of going through this fairly complicated reasoning?

The answer is that the reasoning undercuts the arguments for universals. We can argue for the existence of UN in the very same ways that universalists argue for the existence of any universal. These ways cannot succeed in establishing the existence of UN, since we've just seen that UN does not exist. So there must be something wrong with the arguments for universals. That is a big deal.

For instance, the reasoning about meaning begins with an apparent psychological fact about something that we intend each predicate to do for us. We are supposed to intend the predicate to stand for a universal. The argument infers that the intended universals exist. Now we see that in at least one case the intention cannot get us a universal. Since UN does not exist, there is no such thing for us to mean by the predicate 'does not instantiate itself'. If the reasoning about meaning definitely does not prove the existence of a universal in this case, why think that it *ever* works?

Our first argument for universals, the argument about apples having things in common, becomes similarly suspect. The something-in-common reasoning can be applied to properties as well as to apples. The properties of *being happy* and *being an apple* seem to have much in common. They are both properties, both are instantiated by many things, and so on. Crucially, each does not instantiate itself. From this, by the standard universalist inference, we would have it that *non-self-instantiation*, UN, is something that those properties share. Yet we have seen that UN does not exist. Since this sort of reasoning does not *always* work, why think that it *ever* does?

The argument from the apparent use of certain universals in science is not as conspicuously subject to the same problem. But in the end, the problem is there. Science does not appeal to UN to explain physical phenomena. But the argument from science infers, for instance, that charge is a universal. It gets this consequence from the fact that there are scientific explanations that assert the presence of the same charge in many things. Maybe the truth of such claims does not really require the existence of a universal. Maybe they manage to be true in whatever way the following claim succeeds in being true:

> One way in which *being an apple* is the same as *being happy* is that each does not instantiate itself.

This statement is unlikely to turn up in a normal conversation. But it is true. It is true somehow, without any help from UN. So maybe the scientific claim that electrons have the same charge likewise manages to be true without any help from a universal.

Thus, the argument for the conclusion that UN does not exist turns out to be unnerving to a universalist. It makes all of the inferences to existence of universals look dubious. On further investigation, these doubts about the existence of universals may not hold up. The problems do make many philosophers doubtful of the universalist view.

Alternatives

What are the philosophical alternatives to accepting the existence of the abundance of universals accepted by the universalist?

Sparse Universals

The nearest alternative view is that there are universals, but not nearly as many as the universalist accepts. There is not a different universal every time there is some apparent difference in the ways of things. Rather, universals are comparatively sparse. In particular, there are no negative universals, like *not being an apple* and *non-self-instantiation*. Perhaps there are also no universals that serve as meanings of ordinary predicates like 'happy' and 'red'. David Armstrong, a leading contemporary proponent of the sparse universals idea, holds that only properties used in scientific explanations are genuine universals.

This new approach has drawbacks. It might seem to have the advantage of avoiding the problem of UN in a principled way, by denying reality to all 'negative' universals. The notion of negativity is nebulous, though. For instance, the predicate 'unoccupied space' sounds very negative. But what about 'empty space'? That seems to mean the same thing, without being at all clearly negative. And what about 'pure space'? That seems to mean the same thing again, while sounding positively positive. Even *non-self-instantiation* itself might be characterized as the property of being 'only externally instantiated', which is not clearly negative. So if the view is described in part as a denial that 'negative' universals exist, then this part of the view is gravely obscure.

Another problem for a sparse approach to universals is that of finding a defensible principle to identify the genuine universals. Do the predicates of all self-proclaimed 'sciences' symbolize genuine universals? Including political science? Creation science? If not, what are the restrictions? Also, there is fully legitimate science that turns out to be mistaken. Do predicates in a mistaken scientific theory identify genuine universals? If so, then why is a mistaken theory a better guide to reality than a complete fiction? If not, then maybe no current scientific predicate identifies a universal, because we may not yet have any scientific theory that is entirely correct. Maybe no one will pursue science long enough and well enough to find the whole truth. If so, then there will never be an entirely true and complete science to rely on in order to specify the real universals. But then which are the sparse universals that actually exist, if not those used by the true and complete science?

The sparse approach does not solve the problem about the location of universals. No matter how few universals are instantiated, they pose the problematic alternatives of multiple location and lack of location. So that difficulty remains.

A final problem is that the sparser are the universals that a philosophical view invokes, the more difficult it is for the view to explain the things for which universals seem suited. For one example of principled austerity about universals, there is the elegant worldview that defers entirely to basic physics. It holds that all that is real is the minimum that is needed to explain the most basic physical states and changes in things. Concerning universals, the view is that only the basic predicates of the ultimate and true physics symbolize universals. This elegant sparse universal theory seems not to provide for some facts about genuine possibilities. For instance, it seems to be a fact that some other properties could have been the fundamental physical properties of things. For instance, physicists draw inferences about how the universe would have developed differently if various alternative properties had been the basic magnitudes. Suppose it is a fact that there are certain alternative properties that could have been physically fundamental. If so, then the sparse universalism that admits the existence of only the properties of the actual ultimate physics is incomplete. The properties that might have been fundamental are left out.

Tropes

One step farther away from the abundance of universals accepted by the universalist is the theory of 'tropes'. A trope is a property. It is a way that some one thing is. But a trope is a particular thing, not a universal. Each trope can be instantiated by only one entity. The red color of a particular fire hydrant is one trope; the color of any other hydrant is another trope, even if the hydrants are the very same shade of red. (In fact, strictly speaking, each red part of a hydrant has its own trope of redness.)

'Tropical theory', as we can call it, seems to avoid the location difficulty for universals. Since a trope has one instance, each trope can be wholly located in the one place where its instance is. Tropical theory is well equipped to agree with the argument that concluded that a universal of *non-self-instantiation* does not exist. Suppose that you are happy. Then one trope is your happiness—it is yours alone. Your happiness trope does have *a* property of *non-self-instantiation*. That property is a trope. Does this particular *non-self-instantiation* trope that is had by your happiness also have itself? No. Precisely because it is a trope, it has only one instance. And again, that instance is your happiness. So it definitely does not have any other instance, including itself.

(Since that trope of *non-self-instantiation* does not instantiate itself, it might have its own *different* trope of *non-self-instantiation*. So there may be an infinite sequence here, but at least there is no contradiction. That is an improvement.)

Tropical theories have troubles of their own, though. For instance, suppose that it is a fact that two fire hydrants just happen to be *identical* in shape. Why is that a fact, in spite of the non-identity of their shape tropes? Typically, a tropical theorist will say that the shape tropes of the two hydrants are correctly said to be 'identical' when those shape tropes *maximally resemble* one another. What we casually call 'identity' of shape is really just a maximal likeness of shapes.

The shapes we count as identical need not be maximally alike, however. Suppose that the two hydrants are exactly alike in shape, but they differ in size. The shape trope of the larger hydrant is spread out over a larger area than is the shape trope of the smaller hydrant. Suppose that a third hydrant matches the first one in both shape and size. If so, then the shape tropes of the first two hydrants are not *maximally* alike. They are not as much alike as are the shape tropes of the first and the third hydrants, which are alike in both shape and size. Yet this does not interfere at all with the fact that first two hydrants are identical in shape. Tropical theorists need another explanation of this sort of identity.

Sets

Theorists who take the next step away from abundant universals agree about the existence of lots of universals. They seek to identify universals with certain things that are familiar from other inquiries. The classic version of this view holds that each universal is identical to a set of things. The universal being red, for instance, is the set of things that are red.

Sets are familiar mathematical objects, useful for various theoretical purposes. A key fact about sets is that they are identical exactly when they have the same members. The membership of a set is the whole story about which set it is. Because of this, sets are often described by simply itemizing their members within curly brackets, for example, {Art, Bill} is the set whose members are Art and Bill, while {1, 2, 3, ...} is the set of the positive integers. Sets are very well understood in some ways. It would be intellectually comforting if universals turned out to be sets.

The view that a universal is a set of instances diverges from abundant universalism in some cases. The abundant theory allows there to be different universals wherever there is any apparent difference in how things are. For example, 'phlogisticated air' was supposed to be air that is infused with the substance phlogiston, and this was supposed to help to explain combustion. It turns out that there is no such substance. So nothing really has the property *being phlogiston*. Salem, Massachusetts was supposed to have had resident witches who were dealing with the Devil. But it did not. Nothing really had the property *being a Devil-dealing Salem witch*. The properties, *being phlogiston* and *being a Devil-dealing Salem witch*, seem quite different from one another. The former would be exemplified by air and it would help to explain fire; the latter would be exemplified by people and it would imply engaging in supernatural transactions. The set view, though, does not allow for different universals here. A basic fact about sets is that there are two sets only when their memberships differ. The membership of the set of things that are phlogiston is exactly the same as the membership of the set of things that are Devil-dealing Salem witches. In each case, there are none. So in each case the set of instances is the set with no members, the null set. Yet in light of the apparent differences, how could there be just one universal here?

Another drawback of the set view concerns the composition of facts. Simple facts seem to be composed of the things that make them true. For instance, the fact that you are happy (assuming that it is a fact) definitely involves you. So it seems fine to include you in the constitution of that fact. The fact also involves happiness, if there is such a universal. So that universal seems to belong in the constitution of the fact, too. But the fact that you are happy seems not to involve Oprah Winfrey at all (unless you are Oprah Winfrey, in which case, congratulations!—and please consider instead the example of the fact that Ellen Degeneres is happy. We can suppose too that your happiness does not derive from Oprah (or Ellen) in any way, just to keep her out of it altogether). Yet Oprah is a happy person. So she is a member of the set of happy individuals. A set is somehow made up of its members. Thus, if happiness is identical to the set of happy individuals, then Oprah is in some way involved in the make up of happiness. She would be thereby involved in the fact that you are happy. That seems wrong.

Nominalism

The most drastic departure from abundant universalism goes all the way away. Classic nominalism holds that there are no properties at all, no universals of any sort, whether sets or not, and no tropes. There are only particular objects. We apply a word like 'red' to many things, but not because those things share a universal. Since nominalism dispenses with universals, it seems to have none of the troubles that we have been considering.

Nominalists have to be careful in order to succeed in doing without universals while appealing to words. The word 'red', for example, seems to have many instances, both written and spoken. Each word thus appears to have the generality that is characteristic of universals. To cope with this, many nominalists restrict their theories to using only particular written marks and sounds instead of words. When I pronounce 'red' and you pronounce 'red', we say 'the same word' with these two sounds. Nominalists try to account for this sort of 'same-word' fact while denying that any universal is shared by the two sounds.

The main difficulty for nominalism is to explain the phenomena that give rise to arguments for the existence of universals. For instance, there is the basis for our last fast initial argument for universals. It relies on the nearly indisputable fact that blue is a color. This seems to be a fact about the property *being blue*. How can it be a fact, if there is no such thing as that property?

Nominalists have proposed paraphrases. They have claimed that sentences stating facts that appear to require the existence of properties really state no such facts. They have used other sentences to try to show this. These other sentences are supposed to say the same as the originals, while not even appearing to require universals.

In particular, 'Blue is a color' seems to be about the universal *being blue*. Its subject term, 'Blue', seems to refer to that property. A nominalist can claim that the same fact is also stated in this way: 'Each blue thing is a colored thing.' In this sentence, the word 'blue' does not appear to refer to an object, because it is not a noun. The word here is just an adjective.

Nominalists who say this have to be able to explain how these adjectives work while using nothing but particular objects. That is not easy. Why does the word 'blue' apply to the things that it does, and not apply to other things? A nominalist can say, 'The word "blue" applies as it does because English speakers chose "blue" as a term for blue things and consequently it applies to things that are indeed blue.'

This nominalist claim relies on our prior understanding of the word 'blue'. That is not cheating, though. We are not asking how to interpret the word. We are just asking why the word applies as it does, given how we understand it.

The answer seems to leave something out, however. It does not tell us what makes it true that those things are blue. This is not a *causal* question. Nominalists can offer common sense and science about what causes some things to become blue and what causes some things to stay blue. But as for explaining what a thing's being blue consists in, nominalists must say, 'The things that are blue just are blue, and that is the end of the story.'

Explanations all end somewhere, but it is difficult to be satisfied with this stopping place.

Nominalists can observe that we do not add an awful lot of explanatory oomph just by saying, 'What makes it true that an object is blue is that there is an entity, the universal *being blue*, and the object instantiates that entity.' For full understanding, we need to know more about the alleged universal and more about instantiation. And we have seen trouble in attempts to explain these things. Yet in spite of the troubles, invoking a universal does seem to be the start of an explanation of what something's being blue consists in. The nominalist refuses all further explanation here.

Whether or not the nominalist position about this is acceptable, the nominalist paraphrasing tactic to avoid commitment to the existence of universals while explaining the truth of sentences seemingly about universals sometimes fails. Other sentences seemingly about universals cannot be paraphrased in the same way as 'Blue is a color'.

Consider the sentence 'Sloth is a vice.' That is true. But it does not say the same thing as the paraphrase, 'Every slothful thing is a vicious thing.' The latter sentence is *not* true. Someone who has the relatively minor vice of sloth may be otherwise so virtuous that he or she is in no sense vicious.

A replacement for this paraphrase is available: 'Every slothful thing has at least one vice.' That matches the original sentence in that it is true too. Trouble for a nominalist arises from the noun 'vice' at the end. It appears that 'vice' refers to something that the sentence says is had by any slothful thing. Seemingly, this would be the property *being a vice*. Nominalists deny that any property exists. So they need a different paraphrase, or a different account of the truth of the sentence.

Nominalists also need some explanation of plausible claims that seem to be explicitly about properties. We illustrated a problem for sparse universalists with the claim: 'some other properties could have been the fundamental physical properties of things'. This claim appears to be a truth about properties. Nominalists must deny that. They may say that it is true, but not really about properties, or they may say that it is not really true at all. To defend either claim, they have explanatory work to do.

Conceptualism

The word 'apple' applies to many things—the apples. Why? Universalists say that the word applies to things that share the universal that we associate with 'apple', namely, being an apple. As we saw, universalism has trouble, including problems of location and instantiation. Nominalists agree that the word 'apple' applies to the apples, but they deny that anything common to the apples makes the word apply to them. As we saw, nominalism has trouble, including the difficulty in accounting for the application of an adjective without relying on an entity that gives the word its application. Maybe we can split the difference between the two approaches and come out all right.

Conceptualism is the view that the things that confer generality on our words are certain things in our minds, namely, concepts. A **concept** is a means by which we can think of things. We have the concept of a boat. Our concept of a boat applies to boats, and not anything else. The concept is general in that way. By adopting the word 'boat' to stand for this concept, we give the word the general application to boats that the concept has built into it. That is the account of conceptualism. The account gives conceptualists something with the desired generality—the concept—while allowing them to deny that any one entity is shared by all of the boats.

(An aside about philosophy and practical life: conceptualism can be thought of as a friendly compromise. Neither universalism nor nominalism is entirely vindicated, while each is borne out to some extent. That seems nice. But the compromising character of conceptualism is a neutral fact about it, not a strength. We don't need to make peace and move on. The metaphysical problem of universals is neither a war nor a game. The problem is a purely intellectual challenge. If conceptualism retains what is correct in universalism and in nominalism and conceptualism offers an adequate explanation of the phenomena under consideration, then it solves the problem. Some who accept other views might still reject it because it leaves out features of the other views that they cherish. Their rejection would not affect the merits of the solution. The philosophical aim is to know the truth of the matter, not to achieve reconciliation among disputants. On the other hand, if conceptualism does not solve the intellectual problem, then we can decline to accept it without being in any trouble. We can decline to accept all of the alternatives. We don't need a solution to this problem in order to go on with our lives. It is not a practical difficulty that must be solved in order to live well. We can keep thinking about it at our leisure.)

Back to the issue. Conceptualism confronts criticism. The simple argument for universals that got us started uses some mundane facts, such as the fact that three Red Delicious apples are alike in having grown on a tree. This seems to be a fact constituted entirely outside of our minds. It is constituted partly by the apples. Perhaps the rest of the constitution of the fact is a universal that the apples share, or perhaps it is a resemblance among some tropes that each apple instantiates, or perhaps it is something else. In any case, it seems that the rest of the fact is something that pertains to the apples and not to us. Conceptualists locate the apples out there, but not the rest of the fact. A mental thing, the concept of having grown on a tree, is supposed to be the rest of what explains the fact that the apples have in common having grown on a tree. Yet the mind seems to be the wrong place to locate any part of that fact.

Explaining how a concept gets its particular application is also problematic. We are familiar with one initially promising way to give some things a kind of multiple application, but it turns out not to help. We can give multiple application to a word by a procedure of pointing and stipulating. The procedure does not rely on any common element in the things to which it applies. For instance, we can start with a meaningless term, say, 'blurg'. We can stipulate that the things to which 'blurg' applies are those that we point at, and then point at this thing, that thing, and the other thing. Thereafter, the term 'blurg' applies to this, that, and the other, whether or not they have anything in common.

This procedure does not develop a *concept* of a blurg though. The term 'blurg' does not get associated with any *way of thinking* of the three things. We have simply labeled those things as 'blurg' without attaching any general meaning to the label. Also, even if some procedure like this could assign some concept an application, the concept thereby applies only to the things that we have singled out. Yet generally our concepts are not restricted in that way. For instance, there are constantly new and previously unknown things to which our concept of blue applies—they are new blue things. Clearly we did not single them out in setting up our concept of blue. So a 'blurg'-like specification of a concept's application would not explain why the concept of blue applies to the new things.

A conceptualist can say that we do not have to *do* anything to assign things to concepts. When we acquire concepts, they are already equipped with applications. Concepts have their applications intrinsically. They just do apply to certain things—that is their nature.

An account of concept application that stops there is problematic. It compares unfavorably to the nominalist explanation of why general words apply as they do, and we were none too happy about that one. The nominalist says that the word that we intend for blue things, 'blue', applies to those things because they are blue and that's that. However incomplete this account may be, it must be at least part of the truth that 'blue' applies to things because they are blue. In contrast, the conceptualism that we are now considering holds that the concept of blue applies where it does *because it just does*. This is not in virtue of anything we do to relate the concept to blue things and it is not in virtue of anything about the blue things themselves. End of story. That answer indicates no basis in the blue things for the application of the concept. Yet something about blue things surely seems to be part of why they are truly called 'blue'.

These are not conclusive objections to conceptualism. They do make for troubling explanatory challenges to the view.

Conclusion

We have seen problems for many approaches to the question of whether universals exist. There is more philosophy about this, but it doesn't get any easier. The problem of universals is a tough one. A consolation is that it is intellectually enriching to appreciate the strengths and weaknesses of the alternative approaches.

FURTHER READING

D. H. Mellor and Alex Oliver (eds.), *Properties* (Oxford University Press, 1997) is a collection of recent essays about universals by defenders of several approaches. The introductory chapter very helpfully describes the included essays.

Alex Oliver, 'The Metaphysics of Universals', *Mind*, 105 (1996), 1–80, is a critical survey of recent philosophical work on universals. It includes an extensive bibliography.

CHAPTER 9

Possibility and Necessity

Theodore Sider

The Problem of Possibility and Necessity

Given a team of scientists, unlimited time and resources, and enough patience, you could observe a lot about the world. You could observe the behavior of electrons, protons, atoms, molecules, organisms, societies, planets, stars, and galaxies. But there are some facts about the world that you could not observe, no matter how big your research budget was. You could only see how the world *is*, not how it *could have been* or *had to be*. That is, you could not observe *possibilities* and *necessities*.

Possibilities are things that could have happened, even if they didn't actually happen. Suppose you and your scientists come across a gambler throwing dice. Suppose the gambler throws double sixes. The dice *could have* come up double ones instead. (Or a one and a two, or any other combination.) *In actuality*, double ones did not occur, but they could have. There are many alternatives to actuality, big and small. In actuality, Germany lost the Second World War, but things might have turned out otherwise. In an alternative possible history, Germany wins. In actuality, there are no unicorns, or 10-feet-tall humans, but there could have been, had history unfolded differently.

Not everything is possible. Unlike unicorns and 10-feet-tall humans, round squares and married bachelors are impossible. In no alternative history are there round squares or married bachelors. Squares *must* be non-round; bachelors *must* be unmarried. Things that must occur are called **necessities**. If you drop a stone, it necessarily falls. If a number is even, it necessarily is divisible by two.

Since you and your scientists only observe what actually happens, you will never observe what might have occurred. In a sense you *will* observe necessities, since things that must happen *do* happen. But you won't observe *that they are necessary*, only that they are actual. David Hume, the Scottish philosopher, pointed this out in the eighteenth century. Let go of a stone and you will see it fall, but you won't see the *necessity* of its falling; you won't see that it *must* fall. Drop stones again and again, and you will see them fall each time, but you will never observe anything more than a regularity—a repeating pattern.

Possibility and necessity are related. To say that something is possible is to say that its failure to happen is not necessary. Unicorns are possible because it is not necessary that they fail to exist. To say that something is necessary is to say that its failure to happen is not possible. It is necessary that all bachelors are unmarried because married bachelors are not possible. Musts and mights are really two sides of the same coin.

Necessity and possibility are philosophically perplexing. For one thing, if we never *observe* mights and musts, how can we *know* about them? This is one of the problems discussed in the branch of philosophy known as **epistemology**, the theory of knowledge. Even sticking to metaphysics, necessity and possibility give us plenty to puzzle over. When something must or might occur, what sort of fact is that? An actual event, such as the falling of a stone, is easy to understand. The world contains various objects in time and space, like stones. And certain events involving those objects occur: stones fall. But what kinds of facts are possibilities? In addition to the actual events we observe, is there also a realm of ghostly unobserved possible events and objects, ghostly dice coming up double ones, ghostly German military victories, ghostly unicorns, and 10-feet-tall humans? It is hard to believe that these ghostly entities exist. (And even if they do, why would they count as *possibilities*? Rather than making it the case that *unicorns are possible*, the existence of a ghostly unicorn would just mean that *ghostly things are actual*.) On the other hand, if possibilities are not ghostly entities, what are they?

Necessity, too, is perplexing. Necessary things are things that *must* happen. 'Must' suggests *rules*. But who made these rules, and who enforces them? On the other hand, if the rules picture is wrong, what is mustness? Consider the true sentence 'All bachelors are unmarried.' It is easy to see why this sentence is true: it is true because of certain facts about the physical world. The world contains certain objects (bachelors) and each of these bachelors has a certain property (being unmarried). But our sentence doesn't just *happen* to be true. It is necessarily true; bachelors *must* be unmarried. So there must be something over and above the physical world that changes our sentence from a mere truth into a necessary truth, that turns a mere *is* into a *must*. What is that something?

Let's begin by getting a grip on the very tricky words 'possible' and 'necessary' (and the related words, 'might', 'may', 'could', 'must', etc.). These words can be used to mean different things. Sometimes 'possible' concerns our *knowledge* of the world rather than the world itself. I once asked a friend: 'Have the Montreal Expos ever won the World Series?', and he replied: 'It's possible; I'm not a football fan.' My friend's reply was simply intended to convey his state of ignorance: he did not know whether the Expos had ever won. (His reply conveyed more ignorance than he intended.) These *epistemic* mights and musts are not particularly perplexing from a metaphysical point of view. They concern human knowledge, a part of the world of actual events. At other times, 'may' and 'must' concern *morality*. To say that you *must not* murder is to say that murder would be morally *wrong*. Unlike epistemic mights and musts, moral mights and musts raise interesting metaphysical issues. Where in the world of actual events can morality be located? Is morality merely a function of society, or does the moral realm transcend human practice? If the latter, what does morality involve?[1]

Fascinating as these epistemic and moral issues are, let us restrict our focus to *metaphysical* uses of 'possible' and 'necessary'. Even then, these tricky words can signify different things. The remainder of this chapter will focus on two metaphysical varieties of possibility and necessity: *natural* and *absolute*.

Natural Possibility and Necessity

Natural possibility and necessity concern the **laws of nature**. When a stone is dropped, it must fall. Burning methane and oxygen must react to produce carbon dioxide and water. Anyone with certain DNA must have blue eyes. The laws of nature governing the physical world—the laws of physics, chemistry, and biology (and perhaps other sciences)—guarantee certain behavior of stones, chemicals, and DNA. These laws say that certain outcomes *must* occur; those outcomes are *naturally necessary*.

Scientists try to discover the laws of nature. That is their job. Physicists seek the laws of physics; chemists, the laws of chemistry; biologists, the laws of biology. Learning the laws has a practical side: understanding nature gives us more control over it, and over our lives. But it also has a purely intellectual side. If you could interview God and ask her the truth about the world, you would not want her merely to list all the events that actually happened. You would also want to know *why* certain events

---

[1] Chapter 10 discusses the metaphysics of morality.

followed other events, what *principles* govern the unfolding of history.

By 'laws of nature' I mean the *real* laws of nature, as opposed to what scientists believe the laws to be at any given time. Scientists once thought the laws of physics allowed travel in excess of the speed of light. That was just a mistake (though a perfectly understandable mistake at the time). Superluminal travel is, and has always been, prohibited by the laws of nature (assuming today's physicists have got it right!).

Just what is a law of nature? Don't take the word 'law' too seriously. Laws of nature are nothing like the laws we institute to govern society. A few people break society's laws, but nothing ever breaks the laws of nature; no renegade stones fly up in the air when dropped, just out of spite. Also, unlike society's laws, the laws of nature have no legislators. No person or persons legislated the rule that dropped stones fall. It's not as if each stone has a little rulebook it consults. 'OK, I've been dropped; what must I do? Let's see, *Code of Behavior for Stones*, page 39, paragraph B. Yes, here it is: "when dropped, fall!". Ok, then, here goes!' That's silly.

Or is it? One might reply that laws of nature *are* legislated: by God. This theory of laws makes a big presupposition: that God exists. But even granting this presupposition, the divine legislation theory is problematic, for God legislates many things that aren't laws of nature. Suppose there is now an odd number of trees in North America. That is not naturally necessary; no law of nature insures it. It just turned out that way. But if there is a God, the number of trees in North America is just as much under her control as anything else. So we cannot define a law of nature as something legislated by God. When God created the world, she must have done something extra when she said LET DROPPED STONES FALL, as opposed to when she said LET THE NUMBER OF TREES IN NORTH AMERICA IN 2005 BE ODD. She must have done something extra to make the first, but not the second, a law of nature. And the divine theory gives us no clue as to what that something extra is.

A better theory is the **regularity theory**, according to which a law of nature is nothing more than a *regularity*, that is, a pattern in the world that holds at all times and places. It is a law of nature that dropped stones fall, simply because all dropped stones (here and everywhere, past, present, and future) in fact fall. Nothing more is required, because that's all a law is—a regularity.

The regularity theory has one very big thing going for it: it demystifies laws. No little rulebooks, or legislating God, are required to explain laws, if laws are just patterns in the events that actually occur. Recall you and your scientists observing the world. If the regularity theory is true, you really could observe the laws of nature, if you had genuinely unlimited time and resources and so could observe all times and places.

But the regularity theory conflicts, in a number of ways, with our ordinary conception of laws. First, saying that laws are just regularities seems to leave out the *necessity* of laws. How can a regular pattern of dropped stones falling, however uniform and long-lasting, make it true that a dropped stone *must* fall?

Second, consider the regularity that all dropped stones fall. Why do dropped stones always fall? What is the *explanation*? According to our ordinary conception, the regularity holds *because* of the law that dropped stones must fall. The law *makes* the regularity true. But if the law just *is* the regularity, the law can neither explain the regularity nor make it true.

Third, the regularity theory makes laws of nature too *global*. It says that a law is spread out over all of space and time, since a law is just an overarching pattern. We ordinarily think that natural necessity is more *local* than that. When a dropped stone falls, the fact that it must fall concerns only the stone and the surrounding circumstances, not the totality of stones throughout all of space and time.

These three problems show how the regularity theory conflicts with our ordinary conception of laws of nature. The defender of the regularity theory might respond by flatly rejecting our ordinary conception. Perhaps that conception comes from a mistaken picture of laws of nature as being like laws of society, or like little rulebooks that stones and other physical objects carry around with them for guidance.

But there is a devastating fourth problem with the regularity theory: some regularities are clearly not laws of nature. Here are two examples. First: let N be the maximum number of people that ever attend a single dinner party on a Thursday evening. Then the following is a regularity: *every dinner party on a Thursday is attended by N or fewer people*. If the regularity theory is true, then it is a law of nature that every dinner party on a Thursday is attended by N or fewer people. But that is obviously wrong. Suppose N is 15. It is obviously just *happenstance* that no more than 15 people ever attend a Thursday dinner party. No law of nature prohibits 16 people from attending a Thursday dinner party; larger dinner parties might easily have occurred. Regularities like this are just *coincidental*. Second example: suppose that I weigh exactly 160.35714 pounds, am exactly 68.56865 inches tall, and no one else in the past, present, or future is exactly that height and weight. (If by a miracle there is, surely this other person does not also have red birthmarks on his or her right index and middle fingers, as I do. We could then add information about these birthmarks to the height and weight, thus achieving a characteristic that is unique to me.) Let me tell you one more thing about myself: my favorite move in basketball is the jump shot. (Fake to the right, crossover dribble to the left, pull up for the shot. Swish, every time.) So, here is a regularity: *every person who weighs exactly 160.35714 pounds and is exactly 68.56865 inches tall has the jump shot as his favorite basketball move*. Since I am the only person in all of history with this exact height and weight, it is true that *everyone* in history with that height and weight likes this move. Yet it is obvious that, even though this is an exceptionless regularity, it is no law of nature. My liking the jump shot has nothing to do with my height and weight. I could just as easily have preferred the no-look pass instead.

Defenders of the regularity theory can try to revise their theory so as not to count just any regularity as a law. But instead of tinkering, let us consider a very different sort of theory. According to the **universals theory**, laws of nature arise from connections between universals.[2] First, what are universals? A universal is what is common to similar things. The universal *white*, for example, is what is shared by all white things; the universal *1 gram mass* is shared by anything that has 1 gram mass. The various *instances of white* are all the different objects that are white—white pieces of paper, white shirts, and so on. The universal *white* is a single entity that is common to all these instances.

Now for the universals theory of laws. Consider the following chemical law: methane and oxygen must react to produce carbon dioxide and water. Intuitively, this law is more than just the regularity that methane and oxygen always do react to produce carbon dioxide and water. The universals theorist locates the extra bit in a fact about the universals *methane, oxygen, carbon dioxide*, and *water*: these universals are related to one another in such a way that any instances of the first two react to produce instances of the second two. In short: the universals *methane* and *oxygen* **necessitate** the universals *carbon dioxide* and *water*.

This theory avoids the four troubles afflicting the regularity theory. Even though it is a regularity that every person who weighs exactly 160.35714 pounds and is exactly 68.56865 inches tall likes shooting jump shots, the universals theorist can say that this is not a law, since the universals *weighing 160.35714 pounds* and *measuring 68.56865 inches* do not necessitate the universal *liking the jump shot*. Regularities do not imply necessitations. So not all

---

[2] Chapter 8 discusses many issues about universals, including some of the assumptions about universals that are made by the universals theory of laws.

regularities turn out to be laws. That's good; the fourth problem for the regularity theory is solved by the universals theory. It's also good that laws turn out to be local rather than global. According to the universals theory, a law is a fact about the universals involved, not about all of time and space. When methane and oxygen combine to produce carbon dioxide and water at a certain place and time, the universals *methane* and *oxygen* are located then and there, and necessitate the universals *carbon dioxide* and *water*, which are also located then and there. No other places or times are involved. Third problem solved. And it's good that the universals theorist's laws can explain regularities. Unlike the regularity theory, the universals theory does not say that laws and regularities are the same thing. And while regularities do not imply necessitations, necessitations (i.e. laws) do imply regularities. If universal U necessitates universal V, then all Us must be Vs. So the universals theorist can say that U's necessitating V *explains* the regularity that all Us are Vs, thus solving the second problem. Finally, since the universals theorist's laws are not mere regularities, they seem intuitively to be more necessary than the laws of the regularity theorist. The first problem is solved too.

But remember the whole point of the regularity theory: to demystify laws. The universals theory takes a big step backward here. For the concept of necessitation is a mystery. What does it mean to say that *methane* and *oxygen* 'necessitate' *carbon dioxide* and *water*? Do these universals carry little rulebooks? Here is how I described the necessitation between *methane, oxygen, carbon dioxide*, and *water* earlier: 'these universals are related to each other in such a way that any instances of the first two react to produce instances of the second two'. This may have superficially appeared to be a good explanation, but in fact it is not. It just restates the fact we want to explain: the fact that methane and oxygen react to produce carbon dioxide and water. It does nothing to answer the question we are asking: what specifically about the relationship between these universals produces the regularity? An associate once gave me a similar pseudo-explanation. When I asked him how a silencer gun works, his answer was that 'the gun is constructed so that the sound waves don't escape'.

The question of laws of nature is a difficult one. Turning laws into regularities demystifies them by making them part of the ordinary world of events; on the other hand, doing so is incompatible with our ordinary conception of laws as local explainers of regularities. It is hard to know what to think.

Absolute Possibility and Necessity

On that uncertain note, let us turn now to our second metaphysical variety of possibility and necessity: **absolute** possibility and necessity. Recall two of our initial examples of necessities: if you let go of a stone, it must fall; and, any bachelor must be unmarried. These two examples are actually very different from each other. In addition to pointing out that necessity cannot be observed, David Hume also pointed out that exceptions to laws of nature are imaginable. It is easy to imagine a dropped stone hovering in mid-air, or levitating, or turning into Barry Manilow. But try as you might, you cannot imagine a married bachelor, since bachelors by definition are unmarried. The fact that bachelors are unmarried is necessary in a much stronger sense than the fact that dropped stones fall.

We can imagine worlds in which dropped objects turn pink, methane and oxygen combine to produce Gatorade, and eye color is determined by your date of birth. None of these events are *naturally* possible, since they violate the actual laws of nature. But in another sense they *are* possible, for the laws of nature themselves could have been different. These events are *absolutely* possible.

Absolute possibility is the broadest sense of the word 'possible'. Unicorns, flying pigs, and violations of the laws of nature are all absolutely possible. What is not absolutely possible? The clearest cases are contradictions in terms: a married bachelor, a round square, a person who is taller than herself, a day in which it both rains and never rains, an empty box with something in it.

Absolute possibility is the broadest sort of possibility, which means that it is very *easy* for something to be absolutely possible. Even violations of the laws of nature are absolutely possible, for example. The flip side of this is that absolute necessity is the *narrowest* sort of necessity; in other words, it is very *hard* for something to be absolutely necessary. Lots of things that are naturally necessary are not absolutely necessary, like stones falling when dropped. The only things that are absolutely necessary are things whose falsity is not absolutely possible. It is absolutely necessary that all bachelors are unmarried, and that it is raining if it is raining.

Absolute necessity and possibility are integral to philosophy itself. One of philosophy's distinctive features is that it investigates **essences**. And the essence of something is what is absolutely necessarily true of it. In ethics one seeks the essence of right and wrong; one seeks a theory of *what it is* to be right and wrong. That means finding a theory of right and wrong that is absolutely necessarily true. It is not enough to find a useful guide to right and wrong, a guide that is right most of the time. For if the guide ever delivers the wrong recommendation—if it is even absolutely *possible* for it to deliver the wrong recommendation— then it cannot capture the essence of right and wrong, and so is an unacceptable philosophical theory. Another example: in our study of personal identity, we sought to uncover the essence of personal identity—of continuing to exist over time. To succeed, we needed an account that was necessarily true. That was why it was appropriate to dream up thought experiments in which memories were swapped by evil scientists. Even if these exotic events never actually occur, they *might* have occurred in certain exotic circumstances. A good theory of the essence of personal identity should still correctly apply in those circumstances. If the spatiotemporal continuity theory is to be true, it must be absolutely necessary that a person persists over time if and only if that person retains spatiotemporal continuity.

Given the breadth of absolute possibility, the need for demystification is particularly acute. Nobody believes that the many and varied absolute possibilities float, in ghostly form, throughout our humdrum world of space and time! So: what are absolute possibilities?

One exciting idea is that they are **possible worlds**. Let's imagine a few possible worlds. World one: a world in which history went much as it actually did, but in which the Germans won the Second World War. World two: a world in which there exists nothing but a single rock, all alone, just sitting there, for all of eternity. World three: a world much like ours, except that every five days, at midnight EST, everyone on earth joins together and sings Barry Manilow's 'Copacabana'. World four: a world in which gravity works in reverse, so that massive objects repel rather than attract each other. In short, every complete alternative history that could have occurred is a possible world. The only things *not* contained in possible worlds are round squares, married bachelors, and the like—absolutely impossible things.

Flying pigs and planetwide songs are obviously absent from the physical world we experience. But according to the twentieth-century American philosopher David Lewis, they exist nonetheless: in other possible worlds. Figure 11 is a picture of reality according to David Lewis. The circles represent different possible worlds. These other possible worlds are not like distant planets. Mercury, Venus, Mars, and the rest are all in *our* possible world. Possible worlds are entirely separated from one another: each has its own space and time and its own objects (so you can't travel to another one—sorry). Our world, the actual world, is just one world among many. The others are just as real as ours.

ACTUAL WORLD

OTHER POSSIBLE WORLDS

Fig. 11. David Lewis's actual and possible worlds

A Lewisian possible world is a separate, self-contained realm of space and time.

Given Lewis's possible worlds, we can define absolute possibility and necessity. Something is absolutely necessary if it is true in *every* possible world; something is absolutely possible if it is true in *some* possible world.

The best thing about Lewis's theory is that it thoroughly demystifies absolute necessity and possibility. Lewis has no use for ghostly possibilities. He first confines flying pigs and other possibilities to their own possible worlds, so that they do not infest ours; then he removes their ghostly status by claiming that they are just as real as the objects in our world. Possible flying pigs are just as real and non-ghostly as our own actual pigs; the only difference is that they are *there* (in their possible world) and our pigs are *here*.

But the price is believing in flying pigs, planet-wide Copacabanas, and massive bodies that repel each other! In general it is irrational to believe in things without positive reason to do so. That is why adults don't believe in the tooth fairy or Santa Claus. So we should reject Lewis's worlds unless he gives us reasons to believe in them.

In fact, Lewis says that we *do* have a reason to believe in his possible worlds: only by believing in them can we demystify necessity and possibility. I personally find it hard to bring myself to believe in flying pigs for such a theoretical reason. Still, Lewis has a point: it is sometimes reasonable to postulate things for theoretical reasons. In a sense, no one has ever directly perceived an electron. Physicists postulate electrons to explain the results of the experiments they perform. But demystifying necessity and possibility may not be a strong enough reason to believe in Lewis's worlds.

The issue would be moot if one could demystify possibility and necessity without postulating Lewis's worlds. **Conventionalism** is an alternative theory of necessity and possibility that attempts to do just that. Conventionalism says that all absolute necessities are *true by definition*. Speakers of the English language have instituted a convention of using the word 'bachelors' for unmarried men. It follows from this convention that 'all bachelors are unmarried' is true. It similarly follows from the meanings we give to the words 'taller than', 'either … or', and 'not' that the sentences 'no one is taller than herself' and 'it is either raining or it is not raining' are true. According to conventionalism, something is absolutely necessary if it is true by definition; and something is absolutely possible if it is not true by definition that it is false. (Conventionalism is only intended as a theory of absolute necessity, not of natural necessity. The laws of nature are obviously not true by definition!)

Conventionalism demystifies possibility and necessity in a big way, by turning necessity and possibility into a matter of definitions. How we define words is clearly part of the natural world. No possible worlds or ghostly possibilities needed!

But are all necessities really true by definition? Here is a problematic case. Consider Bill Clinton. Clinton might have been different in many ways. Had things turned out otherwise, he might never have been impeached. In fact, he might never have been president; he might have lost the 1992 election, or even never entered politics. He might have been much shorter, or taller. He might have lived in a different country. He might have had electric blue hair. But now: could he have been a *flower*? We can of course imagine an eccentric person naming a flower 'Bill

Clinton'. But the question is not whether a flower could have been *named* 'Bill Clinton'. The question is whether a flower could have *been* Bill Clinton. Concerning the man actually called Bill Clinton (i.e. the actual 42nd President of the United States), could *he* have been a flower? And the answer seems to be no. There are limits on the kinds of changes we can imagine to an entity while having it still count as the same entity. Whereas we can imagine Clinton being taller, living in a different country, or having a different profession, we cannot imagine him being a flower. Any flower would not be *him*. Likewise, it seems that Clinton could not have been a table, or an antelope.[3] In short, Clinton could not have been anything other than a human being. That is, it is an absolutely necessary truth that Bill Clinton is a human being. But the sentence 'Bill Clinton is a human being' does *not* seem to be true by definition, for unlike the word 'bachelor', which carries a definition (unmarried male), the name 'Bill Clinton' has no definition. It just stands for Bill Clinton. We all *know* that Bill Clinton is a human being, but this isn't built into the meaning of the name 'Bill Clinton' by definition.

A second problematic case for conventionalism involves philosophical inquiry. As we noted earlier, philosophy investigates the essences of concepts, and thus investigates what is absolutely necessary. Ethicists seek the essence of right and wrong. Aestheticians seek the essence of beauty. Epistemologists seek the essence of knowledge. Metaphysicians seek the essences of personal identity, free will, time, and so on. According to conventionalism, these investigations ultimately concern definitions. It seems to follow that one could settle any philosophical dispute just by consulting a dictionary! Anyone with experience with philosophy knows it is never that easy.

---

[3] These limits on *possible* changes are somewhat like the limits discussed in Chapter 1 on what changes *over time* a person can undergo and still remain the same person.

Conventionalists may respond by adopting a new definition of 'true by definition', one not tied to dictionaries. After all, dictionaries are not the sources of meanings; they record pre-existing patterns of word-use. Evaluating this response could take an entire book on its own. There is a lot at stake here, and not just the status of necessity. If conventionalism is true, philosophy turns into nothing more than an inquiry into the definitions we humans give to words. By demystifying necessity, the conventionalist demystifies philosophy itself. Conventionalists are typically up front about this: they *want* to reduce the significance of philosophy. But their picture of philosophy is a far cry from its traditional aspirations.

FURTHER READING

Here are two books that discuss laws of nature. David Hume's book, especially section VII, defends a regularity theory, and is the classic source of the problem of laws of nature (and the related problem of the nature of causality). David Armstrong's book criticizes the regularity theory of laws, defends the universals theory, and is generally very readable.

David Hume, *An Enquiry Concerning Human Understanding* (1748).

David Armstrong, *What is a Law of Nature?* (Cambridge University Press, 1983).

Here are two books that discuss absolute necessity. A. J. Ayer's book, especially chapter 4, defends conventionalism. David Lewis's book defends the possible worlds theory of possibility and necessity. Though rich and fascinating, it is difficult and technical.

A. J. Ayer, *Language, Truth and Logic*, 2nd edn. (Dover, 1952).

David Lewis, *On the Plurality of Worlds* (Blackwell, 1986).

CHAPTER 10

The Metaphysics of Ethics

Earl Conee

Right and Wrong

Custodian

Tom was disappointed. He did not get the job he wanted. Custodian Cathy saw how he felt about it. Cathy made a special effort to give Tom a positive perspective. Cathy acted out of sympathy. She had no expectation of getting anything in return. Her consoling efforts brightened Tom's otherwise depressing day.

That was a kind thing for Cathy to do. It was morally right.

Coach

Mort was an unpopular insecure student. During a gym class Coach Curt ridiculed Mort's basketball dribbling. Mort felt humiliated. Curt did that just to get some cheap laughs from his players who were watching in the bleachers.

That was a cruel thing for Curt to do. It was morally wrong.

We are expected to endorse moral judgments like those. But don't they just parrot the conventional line? It is hard to see how there could be any real facts here. Aren't moral judgments just subjective?

That is not so clear. In fact it may be impossible for there *not* to be moral facts. Suppose that Roger believes that eating meat is at least sometimes morally permissible and Ralph believes that eating meat is never morally permissible. Those alternatives seem to be exhaustive; they seem to include all possibilities. But some possibility has to hold. So it looks as though one of those beliefs is *true*. A true moral belief is a *factual* moral belief; that is, a belief in a moral fact. Now it looks as though there have to be moral facts.

Here is something else that counts in favor of moral facts. If there are none of them, then the best-grounded moral evaluations are strangely mistaken. In the *Custodian* example it turns out that Cathy *didn't* do anything right, and in the *Coach* example it turns out that Curt *didn't* do anything wrong. What could prevent these evaluations from being true? It was definitely considerate and helpful of Cathy to do what she did. Why isn't that enough to make it right? It was definitely cruel and petty of Coach to do what he did. Why isn't that enough to make it wrong?

It is difficult to maintain that grounds like those are inadequate, *if anything is truly right or wrong*. But maybe morality is just a socially enforced pretense and it doesn't describe anything in the real world. What could make a moral evaluation objectively correct? If we think our moral judgments are genuine truths about people and their deeds, we'd better have a good answer to that question.

While the nature of moral reality may be obscure to us, we can note that the subjectivist side has its own trouble. For one thing, it is likely that denying moral facts is not even believable, when we take it seriously. No doubt we can fake it. We can say to ourselves, 'Nothing is really right or wrong.' But when it matters to us, we continue to believe in objective right and wrong.

To convince ourselves of that, all we have to do is to recall a time when someone who we love was treated meanly. We can't help but affirm, 'That was wrong.' That seems as true to us as any other fact. At least that's how it is for me, and I'll bet the same goes for you.

In the end, our resistance to giving up our belief in morality might be our problem, though. Maybe the resistance is a product of habit: we acquired moral values early, we were often encouraged to evaluate morally, and the tendency to moralize lingers on in us. But now we have no rational defense of it. If so, then our continued belief in morality gives no good reason to think that there are moral facts. Before accepting that conclusion, though, we can look for a way to defend our nearly irresistible thought that moral evaluations are sometimes correct.

Here is a basic metaphysical question about these moral judgments. What is it to *be* right or wrong? Is there an aspect of reality that some moral evaluations correctly describe? If so, what is it? If not, what are we talking about when we moralize?

Realism

We seek the substance of moral truths. We can try applying to moral judgments an attractive idea about truth in general. The idea is easy to understand. A judgment that places something in some classification is true when, and only when, the judgment is backed up by some *way that the classified thing is*. For example, a result of a car accident is correctly classified as a dent because one effect of the accident is a new way that part of the car is shaped: it is dented. A result of the accident is correctly classified as a headache because one effect of the accident is a new psychological way that someone is feeling: someone's head is hurting. These ways of things are properties that the things have. To make moral judgments is to attribute *moral properties.*[1] In the *Custodian* example, Cathy's act of consoling Tom has the property of being morally right. That is why it is true to say that the act is right. In the *Coach* example, Curt's act of ridiculing Mort has the property of being morally wrong. That is why it is true to say that the act is wrong. Generally, moral evaluations are about real properties that some actions and people really do have. This metaphysical understanding of morality is known in philosophical circles as **moral realism** because it claims that there are real moral facts and properties. Is it also realism because it harbors no illusions? We'll see.

Real Trouble

What are these alleged moral properties? They are not like the familiar properties of the natural world. Nature contains quasars, quarks, quakes, and queasiness. Evaluations of acts, such as being right and being wrong, don't belong on that list even after we expand it well beyond the 'q's. Moral evaluations are nothing like physical properties such as mass and charge, or biological ones such as being alive and having a gall bladder, or psychological ones such as hating the taste of cilantro and wanting to have a nap. They are not measurable conditions that things can be in. The following report by a medical technician in a white coat couldn't be true: 'We were monitoring Coach Curt's conduct with our morality gauge while he was making fun of Mort. Sure enough, the ridicule registered on the morally-wrong region of the scale.' Even the wearing of an official white coat wouldn't make that report credible. There couldn't be any 'morality gauge'. Right and wrong are not quantifiable qualities that could be detected by an instrument.

---

[1] For more about this see Chapter 8, 'Universals'.

Naturalism

Maybe we went too fast just now. Maybe it was hasty to dismiss *all* of the psychological properties as things that are quite separate from moral evaluations. Some emotional reactions are quite closely related to making moral judgments. When we think about Cathy's considerate good deed in *Custodian*, we feel approval. When we consider Curt's ridiculing in *Coach*, it repels us. In general, we respond with approval to morally positive things and with disapproval to morally negative things. Maybe something about feelings like these is *definitive* of the moral evaluations.

Moral and immoral acts don't have to get emotional responses from anyone in order to exist. Maybe right and wrong come from *tendencies* of conduct to elicit feelings such as approval and disapproval. In other words, maybe a tendency to prompt some favorable feeling is the true nature of being morally right and a tendency to prompt some unfavorable feeling is the true nature of being morally wrong.

This sort of view applies **naturalism**. It 'naturalizes' right and wrong. That is, this identification answers the question of where in the natural world are the conditions that make moral classifications correct. It tells us that these conditions are partly in the acts and partly in us. They are tendencies to bring about certain emotional responses. Tendencies like these are just as much parts of nature as the tendency of sugar to produce sweet flavor sensations when we taste it and the tendency of an extremely loud noise to produce discomfort when we hear it.

Natural Trouble

This naturalistic approach has a tendency of its own. It strongly tends to provoke objections. A couple of the objections are philosophical classics. Before we get to them, here are a couple of preliminary problems that make life difficult for this naturalism.

First, whose feelings count? Does every last person who considers an act have to feel the specified way about it? If so, that just isn't going to happen. Misanthropes aren't going to feel favorably toward some of the best things that people do. Sociopaths aren't all going to disapprove of some of the worst things that they themselves do.

This might seem to be trivial trouble. Why aren't most people's responses enough, leaving aside these outliers?

Deference to a majority would make trouble. The trouble comes from the sort of people who could have been in the majority. The naturalism is supposed to tell us what right and wrong really are. If it does, then it covers all of the possibilities. Yet the population of 'most people' could have been rigged with malign intent. A fiendish genetic modifier could alter the genetic make-up of the future population. Suppose that these altered people end up being most of the people who ever exist. Their alterations have them approving of the damnedest things. If the feelings of most people are what counts, then the theory implies that the feelings of that malicious majority would make the damnedest things right. That's wrong.

An Ideal Solution?

A fix for problems like this has been proposed. We can call someone an **ideal observer** if the person is optimally equipped to respond definitively. We can try to explain moral evaluations in terms of the feelings, pro or con, by which an ideal observer would respond, if an ideal observer existed. But what in the natural world is 'ideal' about an observer? The naturalistic hope is that some psychological properties will do the job.

The feelings of an ideal observer have to be perfectly informed if they are really to define morality. No factual omissions or mistakes can be made. To insure this, an ideal observer must be all knowing. All bias and self-interested favoring must be excluded. To insure this, an ideal observer must have a perfectly impartial perspective.

An ideal observer needs some further psychological features. Being all knowing and impartial does not guarantee having any feelings at all. According to the theory, it is an ideal observer's feelings that make things morally good or bad, right or wrong. So if an ideal observer felt nothing, then the theory would count nothing as good or bad, right or wrong. That would be giving up on morality, not showing us what its place in nature is. If the ideal observer had feelings but was emotionally troubled, then the feelings would be distorted rather than definitive. Also, emotive idiosyncrasies cannot count. Tastes are emotive attitudes. But the theory must exclude all such irrelevancies. An ideal observer could not establish genuine moral values by being a cauliflower connoisseur or a hazelnut hater. Any such accidents of taste couldn't be morally definitive.

What is the rest of the best emotional constitution for an ideal observer? It complicates the problem that naturalists have to avoid using any moral evaluations in specifying the psychological requirements. It would help a lot, for the purpose of getting the emotive responses that naturalists seek, to require an ideal observer to be 'virtuous' or 'ethically sensitive'. But that sort of requirement relies on ethical evaluations rather than explaining them in terms of natural properties.

It is not at all clear that a naturalistic specification of an ideal observer can require just the right feelings. And even if it can, the classic objections that we are about to discuss would still apply. So, having seen some hope of solving the preliminary problems for naturalism, let's proceed to those objections. It'll be harmless to pose the objections against a simple version of the general naturalist idea:

Prompting Attitudes (PA): For any act, A, to be morally right is for A to have the tendency to produce approval in those who consider it; for any act, B, to be morally wrong is for B to have the tendency to produce disapproval in those who consider it.

Classic Complaints Against Naturalism

PA says that being morally right is just the same thing as having the tendency to prompt approval in those who consider the act. The relation of rightness to the tendency is supposed to be a numerical identity.[2] The two classic objections to PA seize on this fact.

First Classic Complaint: Euthryphro

Recall Cathy in the *Custodian* example. She generously takes the trouble to console Tom. When we consider this act, we respond with approval. What is it about the consoling that prompts this reaction? Well, it was considerate and selfless. But that's only part of our reason. Someone could have been considerate and selfless in the service of knowingly aiding the murderous efforts of a cold-blooded killer. That would not have met with our approval. So there's more involved in getting our approval. The objection contends that part of the whole story about what secures our approval is that we think of the consoling as *the right thing* for Cathy to do. In fact, the critic contends, the rightness is the clincher for gaining our approval. This sets up the crucial point.

Suppose that thinking about the property of being right does help to prompt our considered approval of the act. Nevertheless, when we consider the act carefully and find that we approve of it, we don't think about how other people feel. We think about Cathy, Tom, and the consoling. The feelings of others are seldom,

---

[2] For more about this see the discussion of 'numerical sameness' in Chapter 1.

if ever, on our minds. So the property in PA of *being something that provokes approval in all upon consideration* does not play a role in that thinking. Yet the property of being right *is* on our minds. That is a difference—a difference in which property we are thinking about. That's enough. *Any* difference excludes their numerical identity. Hence, PA incorrectly asserts that these are one and the same property.

This is a version of what some philosophers call a 'Euthyphro problem'. Plato's dialogue *Euthyphro* contains the original rendition of this sort of objection.

The same problem affects other moral evaluations identified in natural terms. Here is a naturalistic identification about being good that has been used to illustrate the problem. It identifies the good with what we want ourselves to want.

> *Desire to Desire* (DD): For something to be good is identical to its being something that all desire to desire.

Happiness is good. According to DD, another way to state the same fact is that we all desire to desire happiness. Suppose we do. Why do we want that? Well, we know that happiness is often a pleasant condition. But we also know that a state of happiness sometimes isn't actively pleasant. Having happiness isn't being on a perpetual high. The pleasure of happiness isn't the whole story about why we want to want happiness. Eventually it becomes clear that at least many of us who want happiness want it because we appreciate this point: all in all it is a good thing to be happy. In this way the goodness of happiness is part of what gets us to desire to desire it. But the property of *being something all desire to desire* is *not* getting us to want it. We *do* think about the goodness of happiness and we *don't* think about how widespread any desire for it is. So again the properties differ. The property of being good played a psychological role that the property of being something all desire to desire did not play. Therefore, they cannot be identical.

The reasoning amounts to this. Suppose I want to want happiness, and I think about why that is. I think to myself, 'Because *it's good*'. I don't think to myself, 'Because *we all want to want it*'. Therefore, being good isn't the same thing as being what we all want to want. We have reached the conclusion that DD is untrue.

Second Classic Complaint: Open Questions

The other traditional objection to naturalistic identifications like PA and DD is called the Open Question argument. The twentieth-century philosopher G. E. Moore devised it. DD was one of Moore's targets.

Here are two questions:

Q1: Is each good thing something good?
Q2: Is each good thing something all desire to desire?

DD tells us that there is just one property that Q1 and Q2 are asking about, namely goodness, and they are asking the same thing about that property. If that is so, then clearly in English the property is invoked by the word 'good' and equally it is invoked by the phrase 'something all desire to desire'. They bring to mind the very same property in those who understand their meaning.

At this point the Open Question argument takes a seemingly modest step. From the observation that DD implies that Q1 and Q2 ask the same thing about the same property, the Open Question argument infers that given DD, there is *a mere difference in wording* between the question that is asked by Q1 and the question asked by Q2. In their substance, Q1 and Q2 ask the same thing.

The argument continues. When we step back from what DD alleges, it is clear to us that what Q1 asks is *strikingly different* from what is asked by Q2. Q1 is an idle question. Of course, each good thing is a good thing. There is no room for reasonably wondering about that. We can mark this rational emptiness of Q1 by calling it a 'closed question'.

Just as Q1 is closed to reasonable doubts, Q2 is open to them. It can be entirely sensible to wonder whether every good thing is something that everyone wants to want. Maybe not everyone has happened to think of all good things, much less have some desire about each of them. It is at least reasonable to wonder about that. Any such doubt about the answer to Q2 shows that Q2 could be a rational question to ask. It is an 'open question'.

So as a matter of fact Q1 and Q2 do differ in substance, not just wording. They differ in whether or not it is reasonable to wonder about the answer. So Q1 and Q2 must *not* ask the same question. The Open Question argument contends that this is where DD goes wrong. The argument has inferred from DD that Q1 and Q2 ask the same question and they differ only in wording. But we've just seen that they ask different questions: Q1 is closed and Q2 is open. The argument concludes that because DD has this erroneous implication, DD is untrue.

DD can be improved. A careful limit can be placed on the people who DD requires to want to want something in order for it to be good. One improved theory restricts these people to those who have thought about a full range of topics, so that they haven't overlooked anything good.

The same sort of Open Question argument applies against the improved account. It remains reasonable to wonder whether even the improved condition really does succeed in isolating exactly the good things. We can easily wonder: couldn't there be sensible reasons why people might not want to want good things like happiness? And anyway, why does everyone have to have any wants about wants? Maybe some people don't want to want anything, just because they have never thought about that. Also, don't Buddhists want *not* to want anything? Maybe in spite of themselves they also do want to want all of the good things... but why would they *have to* have his inner conflict? We are now sensibly wondering about the answer to Q2. Meanwhile, the closed Q1 remains as un-wonder-about-able as ever. The Open Question argument infers from this difference in the questions that goodness is misidentified by DD.

How could any naturalistic identification of goodness avoid this? How could it *not* introduce some new idea, an idea of something natural, an idea that is not just contained in the idea of being good? If they all do that, then they all make themselves vulnerable to Open Question arguments.

More on the Classic Complaints: A Misgiving

You might think that both of these complaints amount to nit-picking that doesn't threaten anything except your patience. You might think that pursuing verbal fine points about phrasings cannot show us anything about the nature of major ethical evaluations like right and wrong, good and bad. It might seem that this criticizing is just playing with words.

We should give these objections a fair hearing, though. It is in our own interest. Progress in metaphysics is difficult. We have to take full advantage of whatever intellectual resources we have. We know some things about words and their meanings, and we know some things about our own attitudes. The Open Question argument exploits this. The reasoning can seem petty. But it also seems crafty. It does have some apparent force. It appears that our verbal knowledge has a chance of getting us somewhere concerning the nature of moral evaluations. We've got to take seriously any reasoning that might turn out to make progress. If it does succeed, then we're getting some metaphysical work done with words and not just playing with them.

Non-Nature

Before looking more critically at the Open Question argument, let's think about what its total success would imply. Let's suppose for now that the reasoning shows that moral evaluations are not about any *natural* properties. Maybe they are about some other properties. How can we be sure that nature is the whole of reality? Many moral judgments do seem true. For example, it still seems quite clear that conduct like Cathy's in *Custodian* is right and conduct like Curt's in *Coach* is wrong. For now, let's stay with moral realism. So what makes moral judgments like these correct includes the existence of the properties of being right and being wrong. The new thought is that these are real properties that such acts have, but *non-natural* properties. That's what G. E. Moore thought. What's wrong with that idea?

Natural Dependency

Nothing is conclusively wrong with it. But it faces difficulties. One of them arises from something that is grandly called 'supervenience'. Fortunately, the idea behind the term is interesting and readily understandable.

The supervenience is something that we take for granted. Suppose that we think about Sidney. We know Sidney has a wonderful disposition. She is considerate, generous, brave, and honest. She is never intentionally harmful in any way. She has all of these good psychological characteristics and no negative ones. This tells us that Sidney is a good person. Suppose that in some distant part of the universe there is a Duplicate Earth that shares every natural feature with Earth. Duplicate Sidney is there. She is just like our Sidney in all natural characteristics. This tells us that Duplicate Sidney too is a good person. She must be, because she is the very same sort of person as Sidney is, in all the ways that matter for being good. It would be *loopy* to think that Sidney is good and Duplicate Sidney is just like her, except that she is not good. Now here's the point about moral supervenience. When we see that it would be ridiculous to count as good our Sidney but not Duplicate Sidney, we are relying on the natural characteristics of our Sidney to *determine* that she is good. In philosopher's jargon, we are relying on the moral status of being a good person to *supervene on* the person's natural features.

Whenever we find a moral difference, we take it to derive from some natural difference in the psychology of the people involved or their physical or social circumstances. This act was wrong, and that one was not, because this one had malicious intent and that one didn't, or this one was damaging while that one was harmless. It's always something like that. We count on the existence of some natural difference to induce the moral difference, because we see natural conditions of some sort as determining what the moral situation is. This determining by the conditions of people and their circumstances of the moral status of their acts is *not* cause and effect. It is more inevitable than that. The natural features completely settle the moral status, no matter what. It looks as though the same goes for all examples of *any* moral status: good or bad, right or wrong, permissible or forbidden, and so forth. That is:

> *Moral Supervenience* (MS): In any possible case of a moral evaluation, there are some natural conditions that are necessarily sufficient for the evaluation to apply.

It is worth pausing to think about whether we can come up with an exception to MS. MS asserts that a moral status is always determined by natural conditions. An exception to MS would be like this: two possible examples are exactly alike in every aspect that is part of the natural world—physically, socially, psychologically, and every other natural way. Yet something has some moral status in the one case—an act is morally right, someone is a moral person, or the like—while in the natural duplicate case that something is *not* morally the same. Could that happen? . . . On reflection, we don't find anything that could make the natural duplicates morally different. It seems impossible. No exception leaps to mind. On further reflection, no exception lumbers to mind.

MS is looking true. That's interesting. (It is!) And it will make a difference later, when we get to the view known as emotivism. What it does for us now is to prepare us for a criticism of non-naturalism—the view we are considering that says that moral properties are non-natural properties.

MS does not directly comment on non-naturalism. But MS shows us that non-naturalism creates a mystery. MS tells us that moral evaluations are necessarily settled by natural conditions. Yet suppose that non-naturalism were correct and no moral property was identical to any natural one. If that were true, then why would natural conditions always *determine conclusively* whether or not the moral property was there? Why couldn't the moral property get detached from its natural underpinnings? Moral properties aren't glued onto natural ones. Nothing like gluing would help us to understand the connection anyway. Even the best glue doesn't necessarily hold. In contrast, MS tells us that the natural-to-moral link is absolutely necessary. Non-naturalism leaves this as a total mystery. That is a liability.

Long Odds

As *Star Trek* fans know, the Borg is an immensely powerful collective of ruthless, relentless, ceaselessly adaptive invaders who are bent on universal conquest. Their well-justified slogan: 'Resistance is futile'. Science is the Borg of inquiry. It has been overwhelmingly successful at eventually explaining things, and it keeps getting better and better. It looks futile to resist the conclusion that moral properties fall within the realm of science, if moral properties exist at all. Nothing we know goes as far as to establish the impossibility of a non-natural realm of properties, out of the reach of science. But given the success of science, its existence would be a bad bet.

Back to a Classic Complaint: Questioning Open Questions

We should re-examine the reasoning that gives credibility to non-naturalism; namely, the Open Question argument. At a crucial juncture the reasoning makes a dubious inference. It starts from the safe thought that, given the naturalist identification DD, the word 'good' and the phrase 'something all desire to desire' brings to mind the same property. But the argument then takes a fateful step. It infers that according to DD, the phrase 'something that all desire to desire' is *just a rewording* of 'good'. Considered carefully, that looks like a misstep. It seems to ignore a possibility: the two phrases might bring to mind the same property, but *in conceptually different ways*. The concept that the word 'good' places before our minds can differ from the concept given by the phrase 'something all desire to desire', even if they are concepts of the same property.

This becomes a highly credible possibility once it's raised. The same sort of thing pretty clearly does happen when we have both non-scientific and scientific concepts of kinds of substances. Rubies are popularly thought of as being a certain type of red gemstone. Rubies are less often thought of as being red crystalline aluminum oxide with trace iron. But that's what it is to be a ruby. Science has discovered that being a ruby is having that molecular composition. When people first conceived of the gems as rubies, it would have been a completely 'open question' whether that molecular composition was the nature of a ruby, if anyone had happened to think of that composition at all. But the openness of that question cannot show that the science is mistaken. It just shows a difference between pre-scientific and scientific conceptions of what rubies are. There is no apparent reason why the same couldn't go for moral properties—different concepts stand for same moral property.

This is powerful evidence that the Open Question argument makes an invalid inference. The argument makes an inference from safe premises to the conclusion that given DD, the two questions about goodness, Q1 and Q2, have to be only *verbally* different. But we've seen that the questions could also be *conceptually* different. They could bring to mind different concepts of goodness, even if they were both concepts of the same property. That difference might be what opens up question Q2 while question Q1 is closed. If so, then the Open Question argument doesn't refute the identification of a moral property with a natural one.

New Naturalism

In the later part of the twentieth century, new ethical naturalists made use of this sort of rebuttal to Open Question arguments against naturalism. The new naturalists also applied another good idea. The idea is that some terms apply to something because they have the right *causal* link to it.

Names are prime candidates. For instance, suppose we have a friend named 'Mark'. The causal view is that Mark can have that name now because someone said, while pointing to newborn little Mark, 'We're calling him "Mark"'. When we now use 'Mark' to refer to our friend Mark, a series of past uses of the name goes back, by cause and effect, tracing through other minds and other mouths, to that first linking of the name to him. That connection makes all of those uses of the name refer to our friend Mark.

Here is a puzzle about names. Mostly we use the name 'Mark' for our friend Mark. Mostly we are thinking and talking only about our Mark. But lots of guys are named 'Mark'. So how do our uses of 'Mark' find their mark?

The causal view has a simple solution. A guy named 'Mark' gets referred to with the name when a particular use of the name causally traces in the right way back to that guy alone. Our 'Mark' traces to our friend Mark only. Problem solved. Score one for the causal view.

Terms for general kinds of things can operate like that too. It can be that an ark is called an 'ark' because the term was given to that kind of ship by pointing to one of them and saying something like this: 'Let's use "ark" for things like that.' This would be coining a term for arks by causally linking the word to some property that the example has—the property that makes it a 'thing like that'.

The **new naturalists** think that terms for ethical kinds, terms such as 'good', 'bad', 'right', and 'wrong', refer in this causal way. Being naturalists, they think that ethical terms designate things in natural kinds. Each ethical term applies to whatever has the natural property to which the term has been linked by some proper causal connecting.

Which natural properties are the moral ones? If the new naturalism is correct, then we cannot figure that out by just thinking about what we mean by the ethical terms. That thinking doesn't enable us to track down the properties that are at the beginnings of the causal series. Only investigating the causal lineage could decide conclusively the nature of the natural properties. We can make guesstimates. We have the close association between moral evaluations and feelings. It can guide us. One simple guesstimate is that 'good' is linked to happiness, 'bad' is linked to unhappiness, 'right' is linked to promoting happiness, and 'wrong' is linked to promoting unhappiness. Or maybe 'good' and 'right' are linked to kinds of things that we feel favorably toward; 'bad' and 'wrong' are linked to kinds of things that we oppose. These are among the sensible conjectures.

In any case, the natures of the linked properties are not at all obvious from our knowing the meanings of the ethical terms. So the new naturalism lets it be easy for us to make big mistakes about what really has the ethical properties, just as we can make big mistakes about what is a real ruby. And that seems quite true—people do sometimes make big mistakes about what is moral. You'll have your own favorite examples. They might not match mine. If so, then one of us is making one of those big mistakes. Providing this basis for the fallibility of our moral judgments is an asset of the new naturalism.

Trouble in the Twin Cities

The new naturalism seems very promising. So, you may ask—having noticed that philosophers apparently have objections to all philosophy—what do philosophers have against it? Well, the view suffers from a certain detachment.

The complaint can be brought out by a tale of two cities (a tale derived from one told by the philosophers Terry Horgan and Mark Timmons). The cities are much alike. The residents of each city speak a language that sounds exactly like English. A key social difference exists. In City One, happiness has a more central role in people's lives than it does in City Two. In City Two, giving and getting respect looms larger in people's lives than it does in City One. This social difference is just enough to have the following consequence. As residents of City One use the term 'right', it is causally connected so as to apply to acts that promote happiness. As residents of City Two use 'right', it is causally connected so as to apply to acts that attract respect.

Now suppose that a Resident Of City One, **Roco**, is discussing a certain scandalous act with a Resident Of City Two, **Roct**. (The act will not be further specified, to avoid needless wallowing.)

Roco and Roct both know that the act promoted happiness and attracted no respect. Roco says, 'Like it or not, that act was right.' Roct replies, 'So you say. I say that it was not right.'

It seems clear that Roco and Roct disagree. We are in agreement about that. But then the new naturalism is wrong. The new naturalism tells us that what Roco correctly calls 'right' is anything that promotes happiness. It tells us that what Roct correctly denies to be 'right' is anything that fails to attract respect. The scandalous act does promote happiness and does not attract respect. So by the new naturalism, both are telling the truth. According to the new naturalism, then, Roco and Roct are just telling different truths, not disagreeing. They *are* disagreeing, though—we agreed about that near the beginning of this very paragraph. Since the new naturalism wrongly implies a lack of disagreement in the exchange between Roco and Roct, it is untrue.

Troubling Emotional Involvement

Stepping back from this specific objection, we can see a general problem for moral realism. It tells us that moral evaluations attribute properties to their subjects, just as ordinary descriptions do. The general problem is this. Moral evaluations are more intimately entangled than that with feelings, intentions, and advice. For example, we might describe a nose punching as 'injurious' in order make a formal report of the fact that the punch injured the punched. That's a description that we could make with total indifference to what was done. But we wouldn't call the punch 'morally wrong' unless we cared about it in some way. We would have some negative attitude that would be engaged by thinking about the punch. It would get us to rate the act as wrong.

With this background in view, we can see that when Roco counts an act as 'right', we take it for granted that Roco's emotive attitudes are involved and they are in some way favorable to the act. When Roct responds by counting the deed as 'not right', he is registering that he is not on board with Roco about it—he does not feel favorably in that way. Their verbal exchange gives voice to a conflict of emotive attitudes. That would not be so, if they were just reporting on whether or not the act had some property. When we think of the exchange between Roco and Roct as being a 'disagreement', it may well be that some such conflict of attitudes is what we are discerning. Moral realism makes no place for that in its interpretation of what they are saying.

Emotivism

There are benefits to taking to a philosophical extreme the role of emotions in moralizing. The extreme idea is that moral evaluations are verbal outpourings of emotive attitudes. The evaluations have nothing to do with moral properties. The **emotivist** view says that there aren't any of those. So it denies moral realism.

Here is one asset of emotivism. Since moral properties don't have to exist in order for us to make moral evaluations, a problem that we've seen for moral realism is gone. Moral properties don't have to show up anywhere, either in nature or in some non-natural realm. That's good because we were having trouble finding any properties that seemed to be fully qualified for the job.

Simple Emotivism

When we morally evaluate, exactly what emotional thing are we doing according to emotivism? A radical thought is that we are not saying anything true or false, we are just giving vent to emotions. Some emotivists hold that when we call Curt's ridiculing of Mort in the *Coach* case 'wrong', for example, we are using the word to give verbal release to a negative sentiment toward the ridicule. We have some other terminology that uncontroversially does that sort of thing, words like 'boo' and 'eww'. That language can be recruited to illustrate this radical emotivism. It holds that what we mean by calling Curt's ridicule 'wrong' could be revealingly reworded like this: 'Curt's ridicule—hiss!' Similarly, our saying that Cathy's consoling in the *Custodian* case was 'right' is revealingly reworded like this: 'Cathy's consoling—hooray!' We aren't classifying the conduct by attributing a property to it. We aren't saying anything about how any part of the world is. What our moralizing does is to give vent to our emotions.

Expressive Enhancements

This is the simplest version of the emotivist approach. Improvements exist. First, when people moralize, they aren't often feeling the crude aversions and attractions that are expressed by hissing or cheering. Emotivism isn't limited to relying on any such simple feelings. Emotivists can say that we use moral language to express certain serious and careful forms of approval and disapproval.

With that elaboration, emotivism can cope with unenthusiastic moralizing. Suppose that you tell me: 'For Barney's own good, I morally ought to clue him in about his poor singing abilities, even though this will be painful all around.' You wouldn't be feeling anything like cheering when you made this positive evaluation of hurting Barney's feelings for his own good. Emotivists can agree. They can cite subtler positive or negative sentiments. In this case what you'd be feeling toward telling Barney about his singing would be some regretful sort of favoring.

A second improvement results from emotivists saying more about what gets us to make moral evaluations. This will help their view to accommodate something important that we've already noted: the highly plausible claim of MS that the moral derives from the natural. At first, MS looks bad for emotivism. Emotional reactions can be irrational. Nothing guarantees that every last natural duplicate of something that we moralize about will get us to feel the same way. Maybe we like some of the duplicates and dislike others, just on a whim. Emotivism tells us that without the same sort of feeling we wouldn't make the same moral evaluation. MS implies that things have got to be *the same* morally whenever they are the same naturally. Cases of irrationally differing reactions to natural duplicates seem perfectly possible, even likely, for the whimsical likes of us. Doesn't MS tell us that the moral differentiations that emotivism finds here are mistakes made by emotivism?

They are not mistakes if emotivism is supplemented as follows. Moral evaluations, when they are made sincerely and with full understanding, are made *on a certain basis*. When we sincerely and thoughtfully call something 'right' or 'wrong', this is because we take it to have certain natural properties, and they get us to have certain emotive attitudes. For instance, in the *Custodian* case what gets us to admire the conduct would be something like Cathy's considerate thoughtfulness in her consoling of Tom. In the *Coach* case what we deplore would be something like Curt's callousness and his cheap attempt at ingratiation in his ridiculing of Mort. We have some such natural properties as bases for our moral attitudes. Relying on these bases makes us all set to have the same attitude toward whatever we think has the same natural properties. So no wonder MS is so plausible. Our careful reflections don't turn up any examples that appear to violate MS, because in careful uses of moral terms the same natural basis gives us the same emotive reactions. According to the supplemented emotivism, it is this sort of reaction that we are voicing in making a thoughtful moral evaluation.

An improved version of emotivism like this is known as **expressivism**. The view is now looking pretty good. As you no doubt expect, however, some philosophers think that expressivism has some discrediting liabilities. Here are two of them.

Conditional Trouble

First, when we ethically evaluate we don't just engage in isolated evaluative outbursts. Sometimes we reason about right and wrong using more complicated claims. Emotive expressions don't seem rational enough for this task. Here's an illustrative piece of reasoning, with rational defenses of its premises in parentheses:

Deception Reasoning

Premise 1: Some intentionally deceptive lies are morally permissible (such as lies that harmlessly spare someone from great distress who is about to die).
Premise 2: If intentionally deceptive lying is sometimes morally permissible, then so are some intentional deceptions that are evasions but not lies (since intentional deception is the worst aspect of the lying and evasions are otherwise no worse).
Conclusion: Some evasions are morally permissible.

Deception Reasoning defends its modest conclusion pretty well. Expressivists must have some account of what is reasonable about it. All ethical reasoning poses a challenge to expressivism, just because it is reasoning. If moral evaluations are emotive expressions, not true or false claims about how things really are, then how can we *reason* about them? Isn't the point of reasoning to derive *truths* from *truths*? Expressivists owe us some explanation of truthless rationality.

Expressivists do have an explanation to offer. They propose that our reasoning about morality brings out our derivative emotional commitments. This is an emotional parallel to the standard view that reasoning about truth brings out derivative truth. Having noted this issue, let's set it aside and focus on a further problem that Deception Reasoning brings up.

The further problem is to explain what is meant by some compound moral sentences such as the second premise, P2. Expressivists can credibly say that a simple moral claim, such as the one made by premise P1, expresses some attitude like this: toleration toward some intentionally deceptive lies. But what emotionally expressive job is done by a conditional claim such as premise P2?

Notice that someone who sincerely affirms P2 need not feel any particular way about intentionally deceptive lying. For instance, Sasha *reviles* those lies because they are instances of what she regards as the loathsome practice of intentional deception. Still, she'd concede that some evasions *would be* sometimes okay *if* that sort of lying was okay. On that basis she affirms the conditional claim P2. Sylvester affirms P2 because he feels *positively* toward all lies. He thinks that they pose challenges that toughen us up in our intellectual lives. Sylvester affirms P2 when he notes the consequence that some evasions are helpful in this way too. Sasha and Sylvester seem to be basing their affirmations of P2 on drastically different attitudes. It looks as though no one emotive attitude could give P2 its meaning.

Expressivists do have proposals about what the attitude is. One leading idea is that affirming P2 is voicing a complex emotive attitude, something like this: opposition to the combination of a tolerance of some lies and an intolerance of all intentional deceptions. Those like Sasha who affirm P2, while reviling all intentionally deceptive lies, should be prepared to unite in having that complicated attitude with those like Sylvester who affirm P2, while liking all lies. Their feelings make them alike in this way: they are committed to opposing the combined attitudes of tolerance for intentionally deceptive lies and intolerance for intentional deception.

That solution isn't irresistible. Maybe Sasha and Sylvester should be *prepared* to share that complicated attitude of opposition, because by affirming P2 they are somehow *committed* to it. But is that negative attitude toward that combination of attitudes *actually present* in those of us who affirm P2? I am prepared to confess that the attitude didn't seem at all familiar to me, even after I convinced myself to affirm P2. It is doubtful that we who affirm P2 all have any such elaborate attitude toward attitudes. If not, then the proposed expressivist interpretation of P2 is in trouble. Expressivism asserts that our moralizing serves to voice some attitudes that we have; it serves to release them verbally. We can't verbally release an attitude that we don't have.

Pondering

Another problem for expressivism derives from another mental role that can be played by moral claims. Suppose that we simply consider the claim that lying is sometimes morally right. In doing the considering, we seem only to be holding that claim before our minds. We are just calmly focusing on the allegation that it makes. What emotional attitude toward lying might be at work when we coolly contemplate the claim?

Expressivists can propose that this pondering is taking an attitude of quizzicality. It would be an attitude we can put in other words by saying something like this: 'Some cases of lying, hmm.' But that proposal still seems too emotional. In order to consider the claim that lying is sometimes right, we needn't have any feelings stirred up at all, not even feeling quizzical about it. We can have it in mind without so much as a mild curiosity or any other sentiment about it. Cool contemplation just isn't emotionally engaged.

That goes against what expressivism tells us that moral claims do for us. Apparently we can bring to mind a moral claim without its serving any function involving our emotive attitudes.

Ethical Errors

We haven't found a fully satisfactory way to make good sense of moral properties, whether as natural properties or as non-natural properties. We haven't found a fully satisfactory understanding of moralizing without moral properties either. What's left? The last alternative that we'll consider is **error theory**. It says that morality is all a mistake. When we moralize, we are trying to tell the truth about how the world is. We make assertions about how things are morally. But no moral properties exist to enable us to assert moral truths. We are always in error.

For instance, here is a moral claim that it is difficult not to believe:

> *Wrong to Agonize Innocent People for No Reason (WAIPNR)*: It is morally wrong to subject innocent people to agony for no reason.

Despite the credibility of WAIPNR, error theory implies that it is untrue. *Nothing* is morally wrong. Claims about acts being wrong attribute a moral property, and there isn't any such property for the claims to tell the truth about (we'll see shortly why not).

Doesn't error theory render itself ridiculous right there? It seems to be affirming the *denial* of WAIPNR:

> *Not Wrong to Agonize Innocent People for No Reason (Not-WAIPNR)*: It is not morally wrong to subject innocent people to agony for no reason.

Yet affirming Not-WAIPNR seems preposterous. Out-and-out affirming that such terrible inexcusable conduct *isn't* wrong seems to be upholding a crazed morality.

One careful version of error theory does *not* affirm Not-WAIPNR. The version holds that all moral claims, both positive ones like WAIPNR and negative ones like Not-WAIPNR, *presuppose* the existence of moral properties. That is, all moral claims in effect allege that the properties exist, whatever else they say. WAIPNR tacitly says that moral wrongness exists while explicitly asserting that it characterizes agonizing innocents for no reason and Not-WAIPNR tacitly says the same thing while explicitly denying the same explicit assertion. As a result of their tacit allegations that moral properties exist, all moral claims are untrue. So both WAIPNR and Not-WAIPNR are untrue.

Another version of error theory *does* affirm Not-WAIPNR. The torture that it is about is not morally wrong, because nothing is. These error theorists urge those who doubt their view to be careful. If we hear Not-WAIPNR affirmed, we expect that something else is going on in the affirming person's mind too. We expect anyone to think that whatever is not wrong is permissible. So we expect anyone who affirms Not-WAIPNR also to hold that it *is* morally permissible to agonize innocents arbitrarily. Contrary to this expectation though, error theorists do not also hold those things. They deny them. Again, they say that nothing is morally wrong *and nothing is morally permissible*, because there are no such properties.

It also helps the plausibility of error theory to note that what the error theorists deny are specifically *moral* evaluations. This allows them to be consistent in variously vigorously opposing appalling conduct such as the arbitrary agonizing of innocents. They can find it repulsive. They can hate it. They can favor severely punishing it. They can be willing to die to prevent it. They just can't consistently *moralize* about it.

What convinces error theorists that moral properties don't exist? As they see things, all alleged moral properties have some fairytale-like aspect to them. For example, consider the alleged property of being morally obligatory. Error theorists think that for an act to have the property of being morally obligatory, the obliged person would have to be subject to some inescapable rule. It must be a rule that is built into the fabric of the universe that *demands* the act, whether or not it is actually performed. Yet nothing in the universe makes this sort of demand. Maybe laws of nature 'demand obedience'. But they do this only in the sense that they do get followed, no matter what. Error theorists point out that any other sort of 'universal inescapable demand' is just a fantasy. They say that nevertheless, that is what it would take for some act to be morally obligatory. Error theorists conclude that there's no such thing as being morally obligatory.

Similarly, some error theorists contend that for there to be any such thing as the moral property of being good, the property would have to make whatever had it *intrinsically attractive*. It would be appealing to all, regardless of psychology and background. But nothing is *that* irresistible. Error theorists conclude that the property doesn't exist.

Error theory proclaims that there is no truth in morality. We might feel that we must oppose this view because it seems to legitimate any conduct at all, however horrendous. But error theory definitely doesn't *morally* legitimate any conduct. It does deny that conduct is ever morally objectionable. But it does not encourage us to be indifferent to whatever is done. Error theory allows well-founded favoring of some conduct and well-founded opposition to other conduct. Error theory is consistent with our having good grounds for these attitudes because the conduct matters to us in any of numerous non-moral ways—we enjoy it or it disgusts us, we get inspired by it or depressed by it, we love it or hate it, and so forth.

Anyway, even if error theory did have dangerous implications, it might be that error theory turns out to be the most reasonable view of the metaphysics of morality. Before we accept it though, we should give it some critical attention.

Errors About Errors

One liability of error theory derives from the extreme credibility of the likes of WAIPNR. We don't get to be rational in believing things like WAIPNR just because they strongly strike us as being true. We are altogether too fallible about the facts, even when a claim seems quite true.[3] There can still be better reason to deny it. But if a claim has seemed as close to irresistibly right as has WAIPNR, for so long, to so many reasonable people, then considerable caution is warranted before we deny its truth. We run a great risk that some truth is there but it has been misinterpreted or it has been faulted for implications that it does not really have.

We should scrutinize how error theorists defend their astounding assertion of massive moral error. As we have seen, they assert something along these lines: alleged moral properties like being obligatory need unbelievable conditions to hold in order for the properties to exist, such as the existence of demands made by rules that are inherent in the universe. Plainly, no such rules exist.

Maybe moral properties seem unbelievable to error theorists because they exaggerate their requirements. For instance, does the existence of morally obligatory conduct truly depend on the existence of cosmic demands? Maybe saying that moral obligatory conduct is 'demanded' means only this: we *morally must* perform any morally obligatory acts. That is, it has to be that if

---

[3] For some locally available examples, consider the strong credibility of certain jointly inconsistent thoughts about freedom and about universals, as we discuss in our chapters on those topics. Despite their credibility to us, at least one of each of those groups of highly credible thoughts must be untrue, because they conflict with one another.

we do not perform those acts, then any alternative that we do take is immoral. This involves no literal demands. It says only that we must fail morally if we do not do what is morally obligatory. There is nothing fantastic in that. The error theory view that morality is a mistake might be undercut by errors like that one.

Conclusion

The metaphysics of ethics is not easy. Although the prominent approaches show some promise, they all face trouble. We could get exasperated and give up. But that would be hasty. For one thing, investigating the metaphysics of ethics is mind-expanding. For instance, we have seen possibilities that are good to know about. We probably wouldn't otherwise have noticed that there is a way for an act to be neither morally permissible nor morally impermissible. In any event, questions of the reality of morality are intriguing and important to us. That makes it wrong for us to give up investigating them. And there we have another ethical evaluation to try to understand metaphysically.

FURTHER READING

As a next reading about the metaphysical issues discussed here, a very helpful resource is the Stanford Encyclopedia of Philosophy article 'Metaethics' by Geoffrey Sayre-McCord: <http://plato.stanford.edu/entries/metaethics/>. Its bibliography includes the classic books and articles, and much more.

CHAPTER II

What is Metaphysics?

Earl Conee

Introduction

Biology is about life and art history is about the history of art.
Likewise, metaphysics is about metaphysics. But what *is* that?
Can we identify the subject matter in some more informative
way? We have some examples of metaphysics to guide us. In the
previous chapters we have considered ten main metaphysical
topics and numerous related metaphysical issues. What makes
these *metaphysical* topics and issues? Let's consider some candidate answers.

Being qua Being

One answer derives from Aristotle's book, *Metaphysics*. It discusses a field of inquiry that Aristotle calls 'first philosophy'.
This field seems similar to our metaphysics. Aristotle tells us that
first philosophy is the science of being qua being. Is that what
metaphysics is?

Well, first we have to figure out what is meant by 'the science of
being qua being'. To begin with, the term 'science' here means

theoretical knowledge. Counting anything as metaphysical *knowledge* is optimistic. As we've seen, controversy reigns in metaphysics. Established conclusions are quite rare (at best!). Fortunately, this optimism about knowledge is harmless for our purpose. We may have to gain metaphysical knowledge in order to *complete* a metaphysical inquiry. But we do not now seek to identify what it is to complete a metaphysical inquiry. We seek only to identify the distinctive *subject matter* of metaphysics. Whether or not we have knowledge of any metaphysical facts, we are now just asking what makes some facts metaphysical ones.

Concerning the subject matter, our initial answer from Aristotle gives us the phrase, 'being qua being'. Here is one interpretation of that. The first 'being' in the phrase identifies the topic as existence. The 'qua being' in the phrase adds that the focus of metaphysics is existence in general. It is not about the existence of fish, or the existence of things in the twenty-first century. It is about the general nature of existence. So if Aristotle's 'first philosophy' is metaphysics, then we have the proposal that the subject matter of metaphysics is existence itself. Metaphysics is not about any of the things that exist, or their existence under certain limited conditions. It is purely about existence.

The nature of existence is definitely a metaphysical topic, and a tough one at that. It is challenging to say anything informative about what it is to exist. One metaphysical controversy about existence concerns whether or not existence is a property. To see what is at issue, imagine a balloon that does not exist. Just imagine any merely possible balloon you like. Done? Okay, now imagine that same balloon, but try to add existence to the properties that you are imagining the balloon to have. What did you add? Nothing! Existence does not seem to be a separate property that can be added or deleted. Noting this, some philosophers are led to conclude that existence is not a property at all. Others think that existence is a special property that is required for having any other properties. Existence was already included in your imagining of a possible balloon, because you had to imagine it as existing to imagine it at all. This is a metaphysical dispute that is about existence itself.

We are considering the claim that existence is the subject matter of metaphysics. We have just looked very briefly at one metaphysical issue that is about existence. But much of metaphysics is not about existence. In effect, we have seen this repeatedly in the previous chapters. For instance, the problem of the nature of time is not focused on existence. In the case of the question of whether everything is fated to be exactly as it is, existence is not the topic. Investigating the nature of free will is not studying existence. The same goes for the nature of physical and absolute necessity. The question of whether universals exist does involve existence. But that question about universals is not focused on existence itself. The question is whether universals exist, leaving unexamined the nature of existence. The same comment applies to the topics of whether moral properties exist. Finally, a similar comment applies to the topic of the continued existence of persons. The topic is not existence, but rather the conditions under which the identical person retains existence, whatever existence really is.

Thus, if being qua being is sheer existence, then the subject matter of metaphysics is not limited to being qua being.

First Principles

Let's consider a new idea about what metaphysics is about. In Aristotle's *Metaphysics* he also tells us that the philosophy in that book concerns first principles and causes. The topic of causes seems more suited to the natural sciences. So let's consider the thought that metaphysics concerns just first principles. The first principles account of metaphysics suggests one improvement over our previous idea. The plural 'principles' goes some way toward acknowledging the plurality of metaphysical topics.

As it stands, though, 'first principles' is almost an empty phrase. The principles are 'first' *in what ordering*? There are many first principles. Metaphysical principles are surely not the first principles *in a code of ethics for real estate agents*! Likely the idea is that metaphysical principles are 'first' because they are somehow *most basic*. Okay, but now we have to ask: most basic *in what way*? 'Basic' sometimes means elementary. But of course the most elementary principles of accounting are not metaphysics. 'Basic' sometimes means important. But of course the most important principles of fire prevention are not metaphysics. Soon we'll consider a third way in which the topics of metaphysics might be most basic. But no matter what being 'basic' amounts to, we need additional help concerning the principles involved. What are the relevant principles *about*? The phrase 'first principles' does not really specify a subject matter at all.

Appearances vs Ultimate Reality

Let's try a different thought. Metaphysical investigations begin with initial appearances. For instance, one of the metaphysical issues that we have considered begins with the appearance that we act freely sometimes; another of our issues begins with the appearance that there are properties that many things share. Our other topics have their own appearances as starting points. In everyday life, these appearances are seldom questioned. In metaphysics, we investigate further. As we pursue a metaphysical topic, we seek to get beyond appearances. We consider arguments about how things really are. We seek to learn the reality of the situation. Reality may confirm initial appearances or it may undercut them. Either way, our goal is to find the ultimate reality. This suggests that the subject matter distinctive of metaphysics is ultimate reality.

There is something definitely right in this suggestion. The metaphysical facts about freedom, properties, and so on do consist in how things ultimately stand concerning these topics. The appearances are not conclusive. Only the ultimate realities give us the metaphysical truths of the matter.

We should think carefully about the idea of 'ultimate reality'. Suppose that something is real. Its existence is genuine and not a false appearance. Could anything be 'more real' than that, so as to be 'ultimately' real? How? Some things are more important than others in some ways, but that doesn't enhance their reality. When we see things in this light, it looks as though the 'ultimate' in 'ultimate reality' doesn't add anything. Everything actual is as real as things get.

If ultimate reality just consists in the things that actually exist, though, then an orientation toward ultimate reality does not distinguish metaphysics from any other factual investigation. In paleontology, for instance, the apparent nature of apparent fossils is not conclusive. Only the actual nature of actual fossils supplies the paleontological truths of the matter. The same goes for police detective work. The apparent facts about a crime are not the aim of a criminal investigation. Only when the actual facts of the crime are detected is the detective work truly done. Thus, metaphysics is not distinctively about ultimate reality.

Ultimate Explanations

The appearance/reality distinction may be leading us astray. There is another way to understand what is 'ultimate' about the subject matter of metaphysics. Another idea is that the aspects of reality that metaphysics is about are the 'ultimate' ones in that they are most fundamental in explanations.

This idea has a lot going for it. For one thing, the topics discussed in this book all seem to qualify as metaphysical ones by this standard. The questions why anything at all exists, whether or not everything is fated, what physical and absolute necessity really are, whether or not universals exist, whether or not God exists, these all seem to concern facts that are somehow fundamental to explaining reality. The same goes for the nature of freedom, personal identity, material constitution, moral reality, and time. In contrast, fossils and crimes seem more localized, less basic to explanations.

But metaphysics might not be completely alone in studying the fundamental explanatory realities. What about physics? Doesn't physics investigate elementary constituents of reality and how they account for all physical events and conditions? That sort of explanation seems pretty fundamental.

One reply in defense of the explanatory basics view of metaphysics reminds us about sharing. The reply says that a topic is not excluded from metaphysics just because the topic is also studied in another field. In this view, physics does include inquiry into the metaphysical topic of the elementary constitution of reality. This question is part of physics when it is pursued scientifically. But it remains a metaphysical subject too.

This defense of the proposal that metaphysics is about the most fundamental explanations is itself questionable, though. Physicists often wish to distance their work from metaphysics. They say that they are doing empirical science *rather than* metaphysics. Are they really doing both? Not necessarily. Maybe physicists are not *doing* metaphysics, because they are using scientific methods rather than philosophical ones. But they are scientifically investigating a *subject matter* that they share with metaphysicians.

So we have a promising proposal, although a question about its correctness arises from the overlap with physics. We'll look next at a revised version that avoids any such trouble. It turns out to be promising, but we'll soon see that both versions confront a harder problem.

Basic Necessities and Possibilities

The revised view is that metaphysics is about the most explanatorily basic necessities and possibilities. Metaphysics is about what could be and what must be. Except incidentally, metaphysics is not about explanatorily ultimate aspects of reality that are actual, but need not have existed. Metaphysics is about some actual things, only because whatever is necessary has got to be actual and whatever is possible might happen to be actual. This allows us to say that physics pursues the question of what the basic constitution of reality actually is, while metaphysics is about what it must be and what it could have been.

This new view may allow metaphysics to have exclusive claim to its topics. The view has its own liabilities, however. It seems to leave out much that goes on in the name of metaphysics. For instance, there is the question of whether or not we actually have free will. Answering this question seems as much part of metaphysics as answering the questions of what free will must be and what it might have been. Similarly, the question of why there actually is something rather than nothing seems to be about a contingent fact. Yet this question is as metaphysical as anything is.

These liabilities of the new view may turn out to be illusory. Perhaps the apparently excluded metaphysics does qualify by the present standard, because it turns out to be about possibilities and necessities after all. A metaphysician who seems to be investigating whether we actually have free will may not really be doing just that. Perhaps she is really investigating whether free will is possible for beings such as we are. Similarly, when metaphysicians consider the question of why there is something rather than nothing, maybe they are really seeking some possible explanation for the existence of contingent things. Of course, we are also interested in the actual facts about freedom, contingent things, and so forth. But maybe that important further aspect of our interest technically goes beyond pure metaphysics.

A different problem stems from the phrase 'most explanatorily basic'. The philosophical study of ethics is partly about the nature of morally right conduct. Many philosophers think about this as an inquiry into the nature of the property of being morally right. They regard this issue as squarely in ethics, not metaphysics. Yet the nature of right action seems as fundamental to explanations as, say, the metaphysical topics of fate and free will.

But maybe that's not too bad of a consequence for the current account. Maybe this is a case of overlapping topics, and the study of the nature of moral rightness is a metaphysical topic within ethics.

The problem seems worse when we consider the findings of logic and mathematics. These formal facts all seem to be necessary truths, and some of them seem quite basic to explanations. For one thing, the logic of an explanation—the connection between an explanatory theory and the facts explained—seems to be the most basic thing about it. The present view makes this connection a metaphysical subject matter. That is doubtful. It seems to belong to logic.

Again, this sort of objection may not be conclusive. Maybe logic and metaphysics share this subject matter. They differ by working on it in different ways.

There is a more difficult problem here, though. Both versions of the explanatory basics idea limit the metaphysical subject matter of math and logic to the parts of these fields that play a basic role in explanations. Yet all of the topics of math and logic seem to be metaphysically on a par. These fields study things such as mathematical objects like numbers and the logical features that make for valid arguments. All such things appear to be worthy subjects of metaphysical interest. Perhaps some of them are of special metaphysical significance because they are infinite or otherwise amazing. In any case, what seems to determine their status as metaphysical topics is their interest as entities in their own right, and not their role in explanations. The current idea about the subject matter of metaphysics says otherwise, and so it is in trouble.

Taking Stock

We have thought about the subject matter of metaphysics. We have discovered nothing conclusive. Ah well, that's philosophy for you. The stubbornly unresolved status of philosophical issues dissatisfies those who prefer to study the cut and dried. Philosophers find the status challenging, enticing, and even comforting (since they are unlikely to be rendered obsolete).

Some Concluding Questions

What have we been investigating in this chapter? In a way, we were explicit about that. We have been investigating the nature of the subject matter of metaphysics. But what sort of a topic is that? In particular, was our topic a metaphysical one?[1]

It is tempting to think that the obvious answer to this question is 'Yes.' But we should note that having as our topic the nature of metaphysical topics does not automatically make us have a metaphysical topic. This can be seen by analogy. Physics is about the physical world. So physics surely has a physical topic. But conceivably physics itself is an immaterial thing, perhaps because it consists in abstract propositions that constitute the theoretical truth about the physical world. If so, then physics is *about* the physical world but not *part* of it.

Thus, if we have the nature of physics itself as the topic of an investigation, then that investigation does not automatically have a physical subject matter. Analogously, our inquiry about meta-

---

[1] The questions conclude the present chapter and give rise to issues discussed in the final chapter.

physics in this chapter might have a non-metaphysical subject matter. So we should ask: if the topic of our investigation into metaphysical topics really is a metaphysical topic, why is that? And if this topic is not metaphysical, then what sort of topic is it?

Finally, now that we have taken up these questions, what is the nature of our topic now?

FURTHER READING

The best way to learn more about what constitutes metaphysics is to learn more metaphysics. Here are collections of essays on numerous metaphysical issues.

W. R. Carter (ed.), *The Way Things are: Basic Readings in Metaphysics* (McGraw-Hill, 1998).

Michael J. Loux (ed.), *Metaphysics: Contemporary Readings* (Routledge, 2001).

Jaegwon Kim and Ernest Sosa (eds.), *Metaphysics: An Anthology* (Blackwell, 1999).

Peter van Inwagen and Dean Zimmerman (eds.), *Metaphysics: The Big Questions* (Blackwell, 1998).

CHAPTER 12

Metametaphysics

Theodore Sider

Metametaphysics asks questions about metaphysical questions, questions such as:

Why care? Metaphysics won't help you build a bridge, or win an election, or save a life; so why care about metaphysical questions?

How can we know? Metaphysicians have no experiments to guide them to the truth, only armchair reflection; so how can we know the answers to metaphysical questions?

What's the difference? Metaphysics can seem like nothing more than semantics; are metaphysical questions about reality, or just about how to describe reality?

Actually, these questions can be asked about all of philosophy. (So this chapter might also be called metaphilosophy.) Why is that? What makes philosophical questions so questionable?

The answer is that philosophical questions are downright peculiar! 'How can I know that I'm not dreaming?' 'Do we have free will?' 'What is the nature of good and evil?' 'Does God exist?' 'Why is there something rather than nothing?' Questions like these are unlike other questions we normally ask. They are profound and important, but they are also abstract and difficult to answer—indeed, it's difficult to know how to even begin to answer them. The peculiar nature of philosophical questions is why they count as philosophical in the first place, and it's why there are difficult (philosophical!) questions about them.

Why Care?

Over two thousand years ago, Socrates, along with his student Plato and Plato's student Aristotle, gave birth to what is now Western philosophy. Socrates said that the unexamined life is not worth living, and he eventually chose to die rather than give up his principles. If you share any of Socrates' dedication to the life of the mind, you can appreciate the main reason to care about metaphysics: sheer intellectual curiosity.

To be sure, there is a more practical reason to study metaphysics, and other branches of philosophy as well. Because philosophical questions are so difficult to answer, philosophers have needed to develop distinctive, rigorous methods for answering them. When reading a work of philosophy, whether contemporary like this book or classical like a Socratic dialogue, one is struck by the way that philosophers *slow down* the process of inquiry. Whereas Socrates' conversational partners race ahead to conclusions that they find obvious, Socrates proceeds much more cautiously, making careful distinctions and examining each step of the argument. But Socrates is not only deliberate. He is also bold and powerful. He goes to the heart of the matter rather than side issues, and has an uncanny knack for asking just the right questions to enable progress. Studying philosophy teaches you this same intellectual deliberateness and power; and this has value for life generally. Not only can it help you to think more clearly about economics, physics, or literature, it can also be of great use outside the academy. Thinking clearly and powerfully can make you a better voter, a better decision-maker, and an all-around wiser person.

But the best reason to care about metaphysics and the rest of philosophy is the Socratic reason mentioned above: intellectual curiosity. If you are the kind of person who wants to know the truth about the world around you, you will want to know, if possible, the truth about freedom, God, morality, time, and all the rest. (You may even want to know the truth about the nature of truth itself—another metaphysical question!) Yes, this is an idealistic motivation. And there is more to life than investigating the truth, and more to investigate than metaphysics. But metaphysical questions are foundational, deep, and profound; and the fact that they're so difficult can make them even more enticing to a dedicated truth-seeker. Even if you don't take it as far as Socrates did, staking your very life on getting at the truth, if you care about the truth you may wish to find time in your life to ask the questions of metaphysics, just for their own sake.

How Can We Know?

I have advocated seeking the truth in metaphysics. But seeking something makes no sense if you have no way to find it. And some metametaphysicians are pessimistic about finding truth in metaphysics.

Their reason is that our usual ways of finding the truth don't work in metaphysics. Our usual ways rely heavily on the senses: vision, hearing, touch, smell, and taste. Sometimes we use our own senses, as when we look out the window to see whether it is raining; other times we rely on the senses of others, as when we listen to the weather forecast or read a book. The scientific method itself, the method of forming hypotheses and testing them by experiment, is merely a sophisticated version of using one's senses.

But using the senses, the pessimists continue, won't get you anywhere in metaphysics. Think of the metaphysical claims we have discussed in this book:

'Nothing could have happened differently from how it actually happened.'

'God exists.'

'A clay statue made by a sculptor is not a new object; it is the same object as the quantity of clay with which the sculptor began.'

'Whenever you have two objects of the same color, there also exists a third object: a color "universal" shared by those first two objects.'

It's hard to see how to use our senses, or experiments, to tell whether these or any other metaphysical claims are true. Take the first, for example. Our senses can tell us what actually *does* happen, but they can't tell us whether something else *could* have happened instead.

It isn't just metaphysics that is difficult to adjudicate with the senses. The same is true of philosophy generally. Take ethics, for instance; how can we use our senses to determine what is right or wrong, or good or evil?

'If at first you don't succeed, redefine success'—perhaps if we change our minds about what philosophical claims *say*, it will be easier to tell whether these claims are true. For example, if 'Murder is wrong' says nothing more than that *most people disapprove of murder*, then it's easy to tell whether murder is wrong: just do a survey.

According to the 'redefining success' approach to the problem, philosophical claims only seem to be difficult to evaluate if one makes grandiose assumptions about what they say. Yes, if claims about morality (such as that murder is wrong) are about object- ive standards of conduct, which are independent of what human beings do or say or feel, then the goal of learning the truth about morality will indeed be unattainable. But if we bring morality down to earth, by understanding it as just being about *us* (and what we do or say or feel), then we can learn the truth about it. By redefining success, we make success possible.

In metaphysics, the fan of redefining success might say the following:

> 'Something could have happened differently' says nothing more than that we can imagine it happening differently. 'God exists' says nothing more than that people believe in God. 'The clay statue is identical to the quantity of clay' says nothing more than that it serves our practical purposes to treat them as being identical. 'The universal of redness exists' says nothing more than that some objects are red. And we can tell whether we can imagine things happening differently, or whether people believe in God, or whether treating statues as identical to quantities of matter serves our practical purposes, or whether some objects are red, by using our senses and doing experiments.

By bringing metaphysical claims down to earth, we make it easy to determine whether they are true.

But achieving a redefined goal is pretty pathetic. What about your original goal? It's still out there, waiting to be achieved. Even if we agree that questions of right and wrong are just about what most people disapprove of (and thus are easy to answer), there remains the difficult question of how to tell what kinds of conduct (if any) are objectively permitted or prohibited. Similarly, even if the ordinary meanings of 'could have happened', 'God exists', and so forth are as mundane as the redefiner thinks, there would remain the difficult question of how to determine the answers to the loftier questions. For instance, even if the ordinary meaning of 'God exists' is simply that people believe in God (a bizarre claim about that ordinary meaning; but set this aside), we surely *can* ask a loftier question: that of whether some all-powerful being created the entire universe. The loftier questions are still out there, waiting to be answered. And surely they are what metaphysics was really all about in the first place.

What if the loftier questions somehow didn't make sense? Then the mundane questions would be the only ones we could ask, and redefining success wouldn't seem so pathetic. (Or anyway, would be a sad fact of life.) According to the **Logical Positivists**, an influential group of philosophers from the early part of the twentieth century, it is meaningless to ask a question that can't be answered with the senses. Why? Because of a claim about what sentences mean that the Logical Positivists accepted. They said that the meaning of a sentence is the way you can use your senses to tell whether it is true. Given this claim, if you can't tell with your senses whether 'murder is wrong' is true, then the sentence 'murder is wrong' is meaningless—no better than nonsense syllables. So according to Logical Positivists, the redefined, more mundane questions are the only ones that are meaningful. The loftier questions are nonsense, because they can't be answered with the senses.

Logical Positivists are hypocritical in a certain way. Look at their claim about when sentences are nonsense:

C: Sentences that can't be adjudicated by the senses are nonsense.

They go around chiding others for making claims that can't be adjudicated by the senses, but *their* claim C can't be adjudicated by the senses! C is a philosophical claim, after all, just like the claims that Logical Positivists chide others for making. Now, hypocrisy is a funny thing, since even a hypocrite's advice can be right. A hypocrite can say 'do as I say, not as I do'; what the hypocrite is saying to do might be exactly what we ought to do, even though the hypocrite isn't doing it. But the situation here is worse. The Logical Positivists aren't just hypocritical; also, their claim C couldn't be true. For suppose it were true. Then any sentence that can't be adjudicated by the senses is nonsense (that's what C says). But then, since C itself can't be adjudicated by the senses, C is nonsense. But if C is nonsense, then it can't be true, contradicting the supposition that C is true. So the supposition can't have been correct. So C isn't true.

Redefining success didn't get us anywhere; we need a better solution to the problem. A good start is to observe that the pessimists have too simplistic a picture of how we tell what is true. Using the senses is just one part of the story; *reasoning* is another. Mathematicians, for instance, use reasoning 'from the armchair' to reach their conclusions. Though they use pencil and paper to help them remember the steps, in principle these aids aren't necessary; mathematics can in principle be done without using the senses at all.

Another example of reasoning is using logic: inferring conclusions from premises. Scientists use logic all the time. To employ the scientific method, I said, we form hypotheses and test them by experiment. But scientific hypotheses can't be *directly* tested using experiments. Rather, scientists use logic to infer predictions from their hypotheses, and then they use experiments to test whether the predictions are correct. In the famous Rutherford gold foil experiment, for example, alpha particles shot at a thin gold foil rebounded in a pattern that supported the hypothesis that the mass of an atom is largely concentrated in its nucleus rather than being spread uniformly throughout the atom. The experiment didn't directly tell the scientists anything about atoms, since atoms are too small to observe. What they observed, rather, was the pattern of scattering; and they *inferred* using logic that this pattern could not have occurred if the mass of an atom were spread uniformly.

A final example of the need for reasoning also comes from science. An experiment can tell us that certain hypotheses are *not* true, by contradicting the predictions we have inferred from those hypotheses. But there generally remain many hypotheses left standing, no matter how many experiments we've done. The scattering pattern in the Rutherford gold experiment ruled out the hypothesis that the mass is spread throughout the atom, but didn't definitively prove the hypothesis that the mass is concentrated in a nucleus. Scientists did indeed regard that as the most reasonable conclusion to draw from the evidence, but in so doing, they employed reason. The point can be further illustrated by a silly example. When I look and seem to see a cat, the evidence from my senses is consistent with a whole range of hypotheses. It is consistent not only with the hypothesis that I'm looking at a cat, but also with the hypothesis that I am dreaming that there is a cat, that I am looking at a robot that is disguised to look like a cat, and so forth. Even if I do further 'experiments', such as pinching myself, dissecting the cat, and so forth, there still will be multiple hypotheses consistent with their results: I could be dreaming that I'm pinching myself, someone could have sneaked in and replaced the robot cat with a real one just before I dissected it, and so forth. These alternative hypotheses are getting more far-fetched, but that's just a way of saying that it's not reasonable to believe in them. Our senses don't on their own tell us that these ridiculous hypotheses are untrue; we need reason for that.

So in both science and everyday life, our method for reaching the truth isn't as simple as just using our senses. It's a combination of using our senses and employing reason. And that opens the door to metaphysics. If we have the ability to use reason, perhaps we can use that ability in the arena of metaphysics.

There's no guarantee that reasoning will work as well in metaphysics as it does in mathematics, science, or everyday life. Maybe reasoning is built for a certain domain, and won't work elsewhere. Then again, it doesn't have to work perfectly to make metaphysics worth doing; it's enough if we have some hope of reaching the truth. We knew from the start, after all, that philosophical questions are difficult; that's part of what makes them philosophical. If reasoning can raise us up from idle guessing to informed speculation about metaphysical questions, that's still progress.

What's the Difference?

Imagine a dispute over whether the Pope is a bachelor, or over whether martinis can be made from vodka or just from gin. These disputes would just be about words. Everyone agrees on the facts: the Pope is an unmarried adult male but is ineligible for marriage because of his station; some drinks are made from vodka and vermouth and others are made from gin and vermouth. The only question is how to use the words 'bachelor' and 'martini' when describing these facts. There is no dispute about reality, only about how to describe reality.

Some people think that metaphysical disputes are just like that. In chapter 1 we discussed an example of John Locke's in which the entire psychologies of two people, a prince and a cobbler, are swapped. Locke disagrees with the defenders of the spatiotemporal continuity theory over whether the person in the cobbler's body after the swap is identical to the original prince or the original cobbler. But according to some, this dispute is just about the words 'identical person', not about reality. After all, everyone agrees on how the people in the prince and cobbler's bodies look, act, and think at all times. Everyone agrees that the person in the cobbler's body afterward is spatio-temporally continuous with the original cobbler, and psychologically continuous with the original prince. So, according to some people, everyone agrees here about what reality is like; the only question is whether to describe this situation using the words 'the cobbler afterward is identical to the original prince' or 'the cobbler afterward is identical to the original cobbler'.

It's pretty obvious that the disputes over the Pope and martinis are only about words. Other disputes are obviously about reality, such as a dispute over why dinosaurs became extinct. How can we tell whether a dispute is about reality or just about words? Actually it can be quite difficult. I'll illustrate this by talking about space and time.

Suppose, when talking on the telephone to my friend Diana on the opposite side of the Earth, I point toward my feet and say: that's down. Diana points toward the sky—and thus in the same direction—and says: no, that's not down; that's up. Are we having a dispute about reality? Certainly not. 'Up' just means: away from the center of the Earth relative to where you are; 'down' just means toward the center of the Earth. The direction in which Diana and I are both pointing is up *for me*, and down *for her*; and there is no *objective* up or down.

Think of it in terms of pictures. If I had to draw a picture of Diana and me, I would draw it this way:

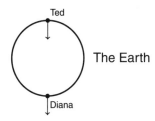

Diana, on the other hand, would draw it this way:

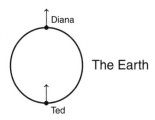

But the pictures are of the same thing; my picture becomes the same as Diana's if you look at it from her perspective, by rotating it 180 degrees. Pictures are always from a certain perspective, so they always include some information that isn't part of the objective reality of the situation, such as which direction is up and which is down.

Orientation is one element of perspective; another is location. Remember Cartesian coordinate systems from high school? In a Cartesian coordinate system, each position in (two-dimensional) space is represented by a pair of numbers: a number representing the position along a horizontal axis (the *x*-axis) and a number representing the position along a vertical axis (the *y*-axis). Any Cartesian coordinate system needs to make an arbitrary choice about which position to represent as the origin, point (0, 0). Changing the origin doesn't change what a Cartesian coordinate system represents about reality. For example, these two diagrams represent the same circle:

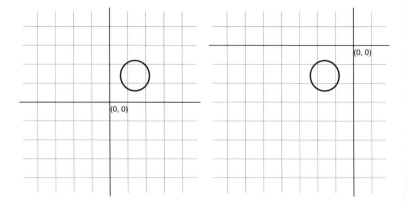

The only difference is that the origin has been moved. Think of the origin as being like a 'you are here' marker on a map displayed in a public place. The origin represents *here*, the position where the representer is located; and just as there is no objective up or down in space, there is no objective 'here' either.

Up, *down*, and *here* are not objective spatial features. They are not built into space; rather, they reflect perspectives on space. Other spatial features, on the other hand, are objective; think of shapes and relative sizes. The Earth is objectively a (near-) sphere; I am objectively larger than a flea.[1] But for still other spatial features, it is unclear whether they are built into space or merely perspectival. Are there *absolute* sizes, or is size always relative to a perspective? I am large compared with a flea, and small compared with an elephant; but is there any such thing as my absolute size? Here is a thought experiment. Suppose we doubled the size of absolutely everything in the universe. This wouldn't change any relative sizes, and so if there is no such thing as absolute size, this procedure wouldn't do anything at all. It would be like moving the origin in a Cartesian coordinate system: a change in how we represent things rather than a change in the things themselves. But if there are such things as absolute sizes, they would be altered. (No one would notice, though!—the instruments we use to measure size would double too.) It isn't obvious whether doubling everything's size would make an objective difference. Whether it would is a difficult metaphysical question about the nature of spatial size.

Here is another difficult metaphysical question, about time rather than space. Imagine that there is a distant galaxy that is *exactly* like our own Milky Way, down to the last microphysical detail, except for one big difference: everything happens in reverse order. In this galaxy there is a planet just like Earth, but in which events run backward. On this planet there is a person, whom we may call 'Det', whose life is just like mine, only reversed. From my perspective, Det's birth happens after his

[1] Actually this is a little more complicated. For example, given the special theory of relativity it is four-dimensional rather than three-dimensional shape that is objective.

death. But Det experiences his birth as happening *before* his death: his memories, for instance, are of his more youthful times, not of the times closer to his death. So Det would disagree with my statement that Det's birth is after his death; Det would say that his birth happens before his death. Is our disagreement about reality or about words? Is there an objective *before* and *after*, or are before and after like up, down, and here: somehow relative to an observer or perspective?

Before going further, I need to explain a concept from physics: **entropy**. Entropy roughly means 'disorder'. Suppose you have a vial of red-colored gas that you release in one corner of the room. It's *possible* that the gas would just stay put; but it's much more likely that it will spread out gradually over the whole room. The spreading out over the whole room is an increase in entropy. Or suppose you drop a vase, and it shatters. This too is an increase in entropy. Physics says that entropy tends to increase; and in all ordinary processes that anyone has ever observed, entropy does indeed increase (by which I mean: increase in the forward direction of time). Gas in a corner of a room always spreads out; spread-out gas never spontaneously concentrates in one corner of a room. Dropped vases always shatter; scattered shards of porcelain never spontaneously leap up and form themselves into an intact vase. But physics says that it's *possible*—although very unlikely—for entropy to decrease. Gas *could* spontaneously concentrate; shattered shards could form into a vase. Physics even allows that it's possible— albeit *incredibly* unlikely—that in an entire galaxy entropy always decreases. And the galaxy I imagined in the previous paragraph was precisely a galaxy in which entropy always decreases. Shards reconstitute vases, gases concentrate rather than spread out— everything happens in reverse.

Now let's return to the question of whether *before* and *after* are objective features of time or merely relative to perspective. Some philosophers (and physicists) say that there is no such thing as being objectively in the future. Rather, they say, 'future' just means: *in the direction of increasing entropy.* If this view is correct, and if entropy increases in one direction in some galaxies and another direction in other galaxies, then which direction counts as future depends on your perspective—it depends on which galaxy you're in. So my disagreement with Det over whether his birth is after or before his death is not about reality. Det's birth is before his death relative to his galaxy, but is after his death relative to our galaxy. Others disagree. They think that past and future are objective, built into reality just like shapes and relative sizes are; they reject the idea that the future is just the direction of increase of entropy. They think, in fact, that it would be possible for *everything* to happen in reverse, for this would simply be a world in which entropy everywhere always decreased in the true forward direction of time. (As with the example of everything doubling in size, no one would notice.) But if the future is just the direction of increase of entropy, on the other hand, then there would be no difference at all between things happening normally and absolutely everything happening in reverse. These would just be two different ways of describing the same reality. They would be like two assignments of Cartesian coordinates to places in the United States, one of which counts Philadelphia, PA as being at the origin (point 0, 0), and the other of which counts Hartford, CT as being at the origin.

Is Det and my disagreement over whether his birth is before or after his death about reality or words? If there is an objective future and past—if the distinction between past and future is built into reality—our dispute is about reality. If not—if the future is just the direction in which entropy increases—then our dispute is just about words; it depends on whether we define 'before' and 'after' using his perspective or mine. But notice what this means. It means that the *status* of our dispute—whether it's about reality or words—itself depends on the nature of reality. Thus the status of our dispute isn't about words! It depends on the nature of time, on whether the difference between before and after is built into it, which is a question about reality.

Something similar is true of other metaphysical disputes as well: whether those disputes are about reality or words depends on reality, not words. Is Locke's question about the cobbler and the prince about reality? It depends on the nature of reality. Specifically, it depends on how much is built into it: are facts about personal identity built into reality, or aren't they? According to some, the only facts about identity over time that are built into reality are the facts about the smallest bits of matter: subatomic particles. The identity over time of macroscopic objects—persons, tables and chairs, planets, galaxies . . . —is nothing more than the presence of certain kinds of continuities (just as, some say, the future is nothing more than the direction of increase of entropy). If this view is correct, then Locke's question is just about words; it's just about which kind of continuity is signified by the phrase 'personal identity'. But if, on the other hand, the facts about identity over time for macroscopic objects are built into reality—if there is such a thing as a macroscopic object's objectively continuing to exist identically over time—then Locke's question is about reality. It is about whether objective personal identity is correlated with psychological or spatiotemporal continuity.

How do we tell how much is built into reality? How do we tell whether there is such a thing as objective future and past, or objective personal identity? These are just more metaphysical questions. Like other metaphysical questions they are difficult to answer, but by applying reason we can at least arrive at educated guesses about the truth. And the truth concerns the nature of reality, not just how to describe it.

Conclusion

Every so often throughout the history of philosophy, someone comes along and argues that philosophy is, in one way or another, bunk. Sometimes it's bunk because there's no reason to care, sometimes it's bunk because we have no way of knowing, and sometimes it's bunk because it makes no difference to reality. But answering peculiar—difficult-to-answer and abstract—questions is just the philosopher's job description. Complaining about it is like a distance runner suddenly complaining about how long the races are. Philosophers are on a perhaps quixotic quest, trying to answer peculiar yet profound questions in a disciplined and rational way. Perhaps we'll never succeed, but it seems worthwhile to try.

Peculiar as philosophy is, it is actually not surprising that it exists. For it is only natural that we would test the limits of our ordinary concepts and our ordinary methods for seeking the truth. What would be really strange is if those ordinary concepts and methods worked perfectly smoothly no matter how they were twisted and turned. They presumably evolved, after all, in response to specific challenges in specific circumstances—to help us gather berries and escape tigers—and the world is a larger place than those circumstances.

There are very real questions about the nature of metaphysics, and indeed, about all of philosophy. This is not a defect of the subject. It is an inevitable consequence of the sorts of questions that philosophers aspire to answer.

FURTHER READING

Plato's *Apology* describes the trial in which Socrates was condemned to death, and includes Socrates' famous statement that the unexamined life is not worth living.

David Hume's *Enquiry Concerning Human Understanding* contains a famous argument that we cannot know the truth about metaphysics, in section 12, part 3. A particularly readable translation is available online at <http://www.earlymoderntexts.com>.

A. J. Ayer's book *Language, Truth, and Logic* (Victor Gollancz Ltd, 1936) defends logical positivism.

Laurence BonJour's book *In Defense of Pure Reason* (Cambridge University Press, 1998) argues that we need reason in addition to the senses to gain knowledge.

The issues in section 3 of this chapter ('What's the Difference?') are discussed further in chapters 4 and 5 of my book *Writing the Book of the World* (Oxford University Press, 2011), but those chapters are fairly technical.

Above I claimed that philosophers typically don't do experiments; but a recently emerging group of 'experimental philosophers' use the experimental methods of the social sciences to discover what 'ordinary people' (that is, non-philosophers) typically believe about various philosophical issues. What people believe about X has no direct bearing in general on the truth about X; but sometimes it can have an indirect bearing. For instance, if I learn that beliefs about X vary systematically from culture to culture, it would be prudent for me to be extra careful that my own belief about X is held for good reason, and not simply because of cultural inertia. Also, in some cases the truth about X might be partly constituted by what ordinary people believe about X (recall the discussion of 'redefining success'). *Experimental Philosophy,* edited by Joshua Knobe and Shaun Nichols (Oxford University Press, 2008), is a good place to learn more about the experimental philosophy movement.

ACKNOWLEDGMENTS

Philosophy is an ongoing and collaborative project: each new philosopher adds to what has already been done. We thank those philosophers on whose work we have drawn. We also thank those who helped by commenting on our chapters: Frank Arntzenius, Mark Brand, Seymore Feldman, Simon Keller, Alice Koller, Ned Markosian, Cei Maslen, Sarah McGrath, Daniel Nolan, Ron Sider, Brock Sides, Saul Smilansky, Mary Tinti, Gabriel Uzquiano, Brian Weatherson, and anonymous readers. Thanks to Frank Arntzenius and Tamar Gendler for the title. Ted Sider would like to thank Fred Feldman for his lectures on free will in his introductory philosophy course at the University of Massachusetts in 1990, which were an enormous help with Chapter 6, and would like to especially thank Eliza Block, Tamar Gendler, and Jill North for their extensive comments on his chapters.

INDEX OF TERMS
AND ABBREVIATIONS

It's easy to get lost in the shuffle. This book is a gift to those of us longing to find our way back to Him.

—JENNIE ALLEN, founder, IF: Gathering; author, *Nothing to Prove*

Sara's writing is exquisite. Her words remind us that nothing goes unnoticed by the God who delights in us.

—KATIE DAVIS MAJORS, author, *Kisses from Katie*

Listening in on Sara's conversations with God will call your heart, as it did mine, to want more time with Him.

—BARBARA RAINEY, FamilyLife; author, *Letters to My Daughters*

This book will prick your heart and encourage your soul. Let it rearrange your thinking in the most eternally beautiful of ways.

—KAREN EHMAN, speaker, Proverbs 31 Ministries; author, *Keep It Shut*

This book is exactly what my soul needed. Sara writes with profound wisdom and humble sincerity.

—SARAH MACKENZIE, author, *Teaching from Rest*

What a beautiful gift! *Unseen* invites us into the blessed center of what we were made for.

—CHRISTY NOCKELS, songwriter; *The Glorious in the Mundane* podcast

Sara exposes the beauty of abiding in the unseen and unrecognized, and we can't help but desire the same.

—RUTH CHOU SIMONS, author, *GraceLaced*; gracelaced.com

This journey into hiddenness will usher you to a place of newfound identity and intimacy with God.

—ALLEN ARNOLD, author, *The Story of With*

Sara winsomely models what we all desperately need: to long for the praise of God instead of craving the praise of man.

—DEE BRESTIN, author, *The Friendships of Women*

This book will inspire you to keep being faithful, to see beauty right where you are, and to rest in God's sweet love for you every day.

—SALLY CLARKSON, author, *The Lifegiving Home*; Sallyclarkson.com

With both wonder and practicality, *Unseen* will escort you to find that longed for place of joy and stability—hidden in His gaze.

—DANA CANDLER, author, *Deep unto Deep*

I'm desperate to "waste" more time with Jesus after reading *Unseen*, and I will recommend it over and over again.

—JEANNIE CUNNION, author, *Mom Set Free*

Sara shows us the power of wonder and stillness in the midst of crazy days. She gives us the courage to become unseen.

—SUSAN ALEXANDER YATES, speaker; author, *Risky Faith*

Because of this book, I have remembered who I truly am and what I truly desire. Sara's quiet story is transformative.

—CHRISTIE PURIFOY, author, *Roots and Sky*

You can't read this spectacular book without wanting more of Jesus, the one who always sees you right where you are.

—JENNIFER DUKES LEE, author, *The Happiness Dare*

Sara reminds us that being hidden with God is never time wasted. I desire a deeper friendship with God after reading her words.

—ESTHER FLEECE, author, *No More Faking Fine*

I will return to this beautiful and powerful book when I need a reminder of God's faithfulness, purposes, and love for me.

—AMY JULIA BECKER, author, *A Good and Perfect Gift*

Unseen is pregnant with the revelation that we can do nothing to earn God's love, a love we can experience when we are the least "useful" to him.

—SARA HALL, marathon runner; The Hall Steps Foundation

Sara turns our eyes to the beautiful reality that God is happily engaged in our everyday moments.

—CHRISTINE HOOVER, author, *Messy Beautiful Friendship*

If you are tugged by the allure of a life that makes a difference and are a bit disoriented by it all, *Unseen* is a must-read.

—RUTH SCHWENK, TheBetterMom.com; coauthor, *Pressing Pause*

UNSEEN

ALSO BY SARA HAGERTY

Every Bitter Thing Is Sweet:
Tasting the Goodness of God in All Things

UNSEEN

THE GIFT *of* BEING HIDDEN *in a*
WORLD THAT LOVES *to be* NOTICED

SARA HAGERTY

ZONDERVAN

Unseen
Copyright © 2017 by Sara Hagerty

Requests for information should be addressed to:
Zondervan, *3900 Sparks Dr. SE, Grand Rapids, Michigan 49546*

ISBN 978-0-310-33997-7 (hardcover)

ISBN 978-0-310-35053-8 (audio)

ISBN 978-0-310-33998-4 (ebook)

Published in association with Yates and Yates, www.yates2.com.

Cover design: James W. Hall IV
Cover photo: Shutterstock®
Interior design: Sarah Johnson and Kait Lamphere

First printing June 2017 / Printed in the United States of America

To Claire

Your life gave dignity to hiddenness long
before I knew what it was.
Until we meet again.

Contents

get the top-ramen, two-ingredient, sixty-second Jesus when the long game is where it's happening. A tree doesn't look like it's growing if you stare at it every single day. But if you water it, prune it, and take care of it, and every year compare it with the way it looked the year before, you'll see that all the growth happened in hiddenness.

When you walk with Jesus, the hiddenness is where you are seen the most. By Him. With ferocious, white-hot, piercing eyes. And his gaze of love is what changes us, what makes us, what we all are desperately searching for in the first place.

And that's why this book is so important, why we are so thankful for Sara. Not many people are shouting this message from the mountaintops, because not a lot of people have found this secret, but Sara has, and her story is compelling and inspiring. It changed us, and I know it will change you.

We are dying to be seen, but the good news is we can know we are already seen by the one who matters the most—Jesus.

—*Jeff and Alyssa Bethke*

one

Beautiful Waste

Opening Our Eyes to the Unseen

"Jesus came to Bethany."

—JOHN 12:1

I graduated from college unwaveringly convinced: I would change the world for God. As a college student, I volunteered with a high school ministry, sharing the gospel with hardened-to-Christ teenagers. And I was all in. When I wasn't studying, I spent time with students in their world. The deepest of time, one life pouring into another. I became addicted to seeing God influence the most unsuspecting lives.

The year I left college, I joined the high school ministry as full-time staff. I was on fire for God and ravenous to see what He could do. I believed there is no higher calling than to be used by God to love the lost. It was a belief that fueled me but also made me feel as if I were somehow critical to God's work. And in subtly assenting to this understanding of my role, I exchanged compassion for judgment of others who were going to waste their twenties on anything I deemed to be of lesser eternal value. After all, wasn't my work helping God change lives most important? I was filled with ambition.

The annual highlight of our ministry was the week we took a bus full of living-loud adolescents to camp. Every activity and experience was beautifully designed to illustrate the person and love of Jesus to our high school students. Outdoor adventures each day bled into evenings of sharing the gospel. We told the story of Jesus and gave teenagers the opportunity to invite Him into their stories. And many of them did. On the last night of camp, those who had decided to follow Jesus were given the chance to stand up and announce this life shift.

That final night was what I looked forward to all week long. It often remained suspended in my memory throughout the year like flakes in a snow globe: distant, dazzling, majestic. A few hundred sweaty teenagers who'd just spent their last hours at camp cramming dirty laundry into overstuffed suitcases, cleaning out bunks, and saying the kind of tearful goodbyes you typically say to lifelong friends, despite the fact that they'd met them just seven days before, gathered in the clubhouse. The room swelled with people and music and anticipation and new lives.

When the music was over and the final talk concluded, nervous varsity basketball players and homecoming queens and kids in the math club each stood up one at a time and shared that this week they'd given their lives to Jesus. "Let the redeemed of the Lord say so" (Ps. 107:2 ESV).

My heart raced on those nights because I knew it was just the beginning. I knew the bigger impact those dozens of yeses would have. In the year ahead, some of those teenagers in the room would open their Bibles for the first time ever and ask God to invade the world around them. Their changed lives would ripple out to influence families, friends, and football teams. Some would tell their children and their children's children that this was the night that changed everything. I looked around the room and tried to take it all in, as if my panoramic perspective could absorb the magnitude of such a night, of such a week. Reflected in the flushed faces of teenagers who wanted a fresh start, who wanted Jesus, I saw the face of God.

After camp was over, I came home to an even longer list of lives I wanted to influence. When teenagers are "on fire" for Jesus, their unchurched parents start showing up to church on Sunday, asking questions, and joining Bible studies. It was what I'd prayed for. It was everything I'd wanted when I started in full-time ministry. The work was sometimes hard and often exhausting, but the life-changing stories fueled me. They validated my calling and my passion. They kept me in it.

Until one year they didn't.

Lives around me were changing for Jesus, but my life had grown stagnant. My passion for ministry waned and a vague emptiness took its place. I'd have dinner with a teenager who'd just asked Jesus into her heart and find myself mindlessly repeating answers I'd said for years. I knew how to share about God's love with others, but I no longer felt like I was living in it myself. There was a voice in my head that wondered, *Am I just saying these things about God, or do I really believe them?*

So I'd come home and check in on my heart, carving out space to sit with God and ask that question out loud. Except when I got there, that space and time alone with Him felt awkward, like I was supposed to share the kinds of things you say mostly only in hushed tones to a close friend, but instead this was a conversation with a distant acquaintance. I didn't quite know how or where to start. More than thirty minutes with my Bible open, but without a Bible study to plan, and I didn't know who I was supposed to be. I wasn't sure who God was either, in my less productive quiet time and in the "nonessential" moments of life.

I knew Jesus as the one who'd walked on water and calmed the storm and healed a leper. I could describe that God in my sleep. But who was God to me during those ordinary days, the days when I didn't need Him to calm a storm or walk across the water or help me plan a Bible study? What about the days when I had to pay bills and clean the toilet and babysit a friend's children? I had no doubt He was the God of hardened teenagers, warming their cold hearts and drawing them closer into Himself. I knew He was the God of people who devoted themselves to ministry, to constant relationship with others, to speaking and leading. But who was He to me when I wasn't changing the world? When I was by myself? Who was He to me when I had nothing at all to give Him?

These questions would eventually guide my eyes to the unseen beauty of a hidden life in God. But as it is with most beginnings, first they were unnerving. I knew God was benevolently disposed toward me, but I'd always assumed His benevolence was also connected to my producing something for His kingdom. When I felt productive in ministry, it wasn't hard to imagine that God had loving thoughts toward me or that He looked at me with warm affection. I had a harder time trying to imagine what He might be thinking about me during the hours of the day when I wasn't doing anything tangible for Him—the hours of the day when I felt naked and exposed, unable to hide behind my productivity for the kingdom of God. What was the expression on His face when I didn't have a trail of changed lives behind mine? How did He feel about me on Saturday morning while I was lying on the couch in sweatpants, exhausted from the week?

But something inside of me knew there had to be more to my life with God than being productive and sharing the good news with others. Something inside of me craved the God I'd find when I wasn't changing the world. I'd always thought my craving for more in life would be satisfied with more ministry, more impact, more good works for God. But instead of filling me with more, the escalating effort I put into those things slowly left me feeling empty.

As I saw it, I gave in to burnout, but there was more to it than that. I'd been driven by a passion to see lives change, but I also craved the validation I received when my life made a notable impact on someone else's. Over time, the deep satisfaction I'd found in my work lessened. The nagging drive, albeit subtle, to which I'd responded to do more and more continued to leave me feeling inadequate. My expectations for myself increased as my ability to meet those expectations diminished. Even worse, I began to see myself as critical to God's success. But I just couldn't do it anymore.

So I left the ministry I admired.

I, the fiery-eyed, will-not-waste-my-life poster child, succumbed.

I took a break from telling others about Jesus and found a part-time job. For well into a year, I spent my afternoons amid bouquets of imported French lavender, handcrafted soaps, and Italian pottery at a boutique. I was instructed *not* to dust the porcelain guinea hens or stacks of plates—people feel at home in cottage dust, apparently—and sometimes I banked no more than five transactions in a day. Mine had become the wasted life I once judged, the person who ended most days without a single story of kingdom impact or even a spiritual conversation. Instead of raising money to dig wells for people without clean water, I spent my hours among decorative water pitchers priced at one hundred dollars a pop. It was a life I swore I'd never have—unproductive. A colossal waste of my time, energy, and gifts.

But to the surprise of my productivity-oriented heart, that quiet little storefront in the Barracks Road Shopping Center became a place where I met God.

I brought my Bible to work and cracked it open as I sat behind the register. I had hours unplanned for one of the first times in my life. I talked through God's Word with Him, and I did so slowly—less extrapolating a lesson and more absorbing who the person was within those stories. I circled the pottery-stacked farm tables with it, praying one passage at a time while the smells of French-milled soaps wafted in the air. And as I did so, I noticed things about Jesus I'd never seen while preparing to teach a Bible study or codifying a set of verses into a single palatable point. I was noticing more of Him as I read, and realizing that He too was seeing me in the minutia of my day. I was seeing the shape of the person who *was* this Word that I'd memorized and quoted for years.

He had eyes and a face.

His hands held a hammer, washed feet, cupped the faces of children. And adults.

He sweated.

I discovered layers of God's nature I hadn't considered when I was barreling through life, when He was only a leader and a coach to me. Slowly, my desire to see and feel who He is within the pages of His Word prompted me to look at the lines on His face. To take a long and thoughtful look at Him, and not just once. As I did so, I saw not only that He invited me to see Him—in the minutia of stories I'd read for years to gain broad themes and lessons—but also that He also saw me, right there in my middle minutes. For perhaps one of the first times in my life, I made eye contact with God.

His life on the earth and in these pages held a facial expression. Toward me. When I slowed, I saw that He too looked past my complexities to know and respond to my heart. He wasn't driving me to produce in such a way that all I saw was the back of His shoulders and His firm gait as He charged ahead of me; He was turned toward me and looking into me with a softheartedness and an ever-unfolding open stance.

His face held a gentle expression. *Loving* expression. Toward me, who was doing nothing for Him.

Just as little children need to be seen, need to see their reflection in the eyes of a loving parent, I needed to see God seeing me as I spent hours in the stillness of that store. I needed to see the twinkle in His eyes when He looked at me. I'd lived most of my Christian life in deficit, not seeing that spark and imagining His eyes to be dull and hardened toward me. I needed to know what He thought of me in my unproductivity, when I was doing nothing to advance His kingdom, just paying my bills, buying groceries, and making the bed. If God had tender thoughts toward me in my mundane moments, then those were moments in which I wanted to encounter Him. I wanted to believe that the same God who was pleased with me when I shared the gospel still smiled when I took out the trash or took a nap. If I could meet God's eyes in all those ordinary times—if I could just see the spark, there—then my assumptions about what matters most to God would have to change.

And I wanted them to change.

In a year that felt like failure by all my ministry productivity standards, I grew desperate to lock eyes with God and see His real expression toward me. I knew if on an average Tuesday afternoon I could see God as the Initiator, the one who gently draws me close and with tenderness, then I could finally find deep soul-rest. I wouldn't have to work so hard to get God's attention, because I already had it. Every single ordinary minute of my day would be an opportunity to encounter God's unwavering gaze.

This is hiddenness. It's not a natural concept for our human minds to apprehend. There are times when God tucks us away. He might hide us in a difficult job or an unwelcomed circumstance where we feel like no one gets us, where we feel misunderstood. He might hide us in a crowd where we feel lost—unseen—or behind the front door of our homes, changing diapers and burping babies. He does this all so that we might see another side of Him, this God who looks deeply and knowingly into us when no one else is looking or noticing, and come alive under that eye.

Sure, this hiddenness may feel undesirable at first. We resist it. We want out of the dead-end job and to be done with the ministry or church where we're not properly acknowledged for who we are and what we do. (And most of our friends might counsel us to do that, to get out.) We want to climb out from underneath burp cloths and laundry and serving in silence into a world where someone notices, where we're not only seen but appreciated, validated by those around us.

And yet even as we might naturally clamor to get out of these places, He continues to use the unwelcomed, unbending circumstances to show us that He sees, He knows—yes, even in this job we're praying desperately to be able to leave or this church that feels as if its people haven't yet discovered our capabilities. We feel like we're waiting it out or merely enduring hardship, but, from God's angle, these times are purposed.

In the words of Paul, these hidden times allure us to "think about the things of heaven, not the things of earth" (Col. 3:2).

In no way do we naturally fall into this way of thinking. We breathe and pay our bills and use our words, all in the temporal. We need help to look at the unseen, the things of heaven, not the things we can touch with our hands or gauge with a measuring stick. Our truest lives—once we come to know Him—don't reside in the temporal world. Hiddenness is God's way of helping us with this holy detachment, slowly releasing our clutch on "the things of earth," which we were never intended to grip.

Paul goes on to say, "For you died to this life, and your real life is hidden with Christ in God" (Col. 3:3 NLT).

It was in that cottage boutique—during a time when I also felt that I was experiencing the death of my dreams—that I first tasted this hiddenness. That's when I first practiced "wasting time with God." Up to that point, spending twenty to thirty minutes in the morning with God—my Bible and journal open on my lap—was all I needed and all I could justify. I'd never considered setting aside more time to spend with God. I'm certain I subconsciously saw that extra time to be wasteful, discarding otherwise productive hours and disguising sloth. But as my heart was resuscitated behind the storefront window, I started to see the worth of searching Him out in these undocumented, unproductive hours. And so I cautiously started to give Him access to the parts of me that no one, including myself, had seen before.

As my heart ebbed from a flurried life into the quiet of that store, the buried parts of my thinking surfaced. One day, the wife of one of my husband's college friends came into the boutique to browse. Instead of being excited to see her, I felt a flash-rush of unexpected shame. She'd caught me being insignificant—not sharing the gospel, not advancing the kingdom of God, not using my college degree, but selling pricey tablecloths—and I suddenly felt the need to justify my dormant existence.

No sooner had the glass door shut behind her than an urge to quit this job and do something significant with my life consumed my thinking.

In years past, I would have obsessed about that thought for days and weeks, but in the quiet of that store and the quieting of my activity, I was less threatened and more curious. Time and a newly tender brush with God created a safe space for me to see the layers within me. Initially after our twelve-minute exchange, she seemed successful and I felt foolishly stuck. She had real accomplishments to share, and I knew how to order her the correct color of tablecloth she wanted from our sister store. But I soon realized that the urge to quit that overtook me the minute she left wasn't one to guide me. Instead, it was an indicator of a deeper question I needed to ask of God: *How do You see me, especially now when I feel unproductive and unsuccessful? How do You see me when I feel naked without my life's impact to hide behind?*

These were the things that surfaced in the hours when I was on the clock but not changing lives. I started a new dialogue with God that didn't include a plea for Him to use me in someone else's life or to make my life matter. It was a conversation in which I saw that He cared for the inner workings of my heart. He cared about the insecurities that plagued me. I felt the pulse of His life in the biblical stories for which I had lost my passion. Not even whole sentences but mere phrases from His Word that had once been pat answers were transformed into poetry, renewing my mind and sparking fresh and intimate conversations with God. Not only was He becoming more real to me as I took time not just to study but to soak in Scripture, He was becoming personal. To me.

This age-old God was newly vibrant to me. And I was starting to think He might actually like me, right there in that store, where I was getting paid just above minimum wage and not using my college degree.

In the pages of His Word, I saw Him validate the hearts of those who sought Him in secret. God said to Samuel, "For the LORD does not see as man sees; for man looks at the outward appearance, but the LORD looks at the heart" (1 Sam. 16:7). I heard Him whisper those same words to me. I wanted to shame myself, and yet I felt oddly seen and known and enjoyed by God, simply because I had turned my heart and my conversation to Him in that moment.

Years before, I never could have believed that God would enjoy me in that state—or even tolerate me. But when the store was empty and the sun was fading, aslant on the floor amid farm tables stacked with overpriced tablecloths, I locked eyes with God anew. I sensed His pleasure. I was wasting time with God.

God liked me.

And He wanted to spend time with me.

When you're with someone who knows the quirks of your heart and enjoys you anyway, it's only natural that you want to spend more time with that person. When God was attentive to me—even the small, unseen parts of me—I wanted to reciprocate. I wanted to sit with Him and study the lines and contours of His face.

I was beginning to believe that maybe who I was in secret

was reason for praise. Maybe my unproductive, looking-up-at-Him life produced awe among the angels.

Now I was no longer unsticking the pages of my Bible out of obligation. Instead, I was driven by a desire to see and know more of God. In every passage, in every verse, I was clawing my way into what was life to me: the delight on God's face turned toward me. I'd been fiercely searching the crowd for that face for years, thinking I would find it only in the praise or approval among the masses, in the eyes of other people. But now I could see it manifest in God's face. God delighted in me even when I felt I least deserved it.

God was growing me, in secret, tucked well behind the display window in a Barracks Road boutique.

Rarely do I notice the roots of a tree unless my feet stumble over them. I may notice the way branches above me cut across the sky as I pull out of my driveway. I may sit with my toddler in the shade or pick apples at an orchard with my children in early autumn. I may roll a newly fallen leaf between my fingers. But most of the time I walk unaware right over the roots, the hidden life of every tree that makes everything else—branches, shade, fruit, and leaves—possible at all.

Often the obvious accomplishments of our days get most of our attention. Noticing the roots, much less tending to them, seems secondary when there are branches to climb and fruit to pick. We live for what is right in front of us, while God is ever so gently calling us toward the unseen. His unseen.

We come alive in the unseen.

We were made for it.

We are formed in it. .

I'd spent most of my twenties with a similar lack of awareness in my relationship with God. I envisioned growth to be outstretched branches—majestic when hit by the sun and seen against the pure blue sky—and mostly ignored the roots. But I could no longer grow tall in God without caring for my root system, without acknowledging that something buried beneath the surface gives life to the trunk and branches I showed the world. Noticing and tending to my roots—my inner and hidden life with God—seemed secondary when there were important ministry branches to climb and spiritual fruit to produce and pick. But God was ever so gently inviting me back to the soil. To hide in Him rather than perform for Him, to shift my attention from branches to roots, from my visible work *for* God to my unseen life *in* God.

It was as if He was patiently drawing my eyes away from the branches and down to my thirsty roots. *You don't have to try so hard to leave your mark on the world, Sara. Come back to the soil. Leave your mark on Me.* This was the whisper from God that emerged in that unproductive season. *Spend, pour out, right here, and I'll grow the tree.*

I hadn't before considered that I could pour out my life at His feet, caring only for what He thought of me. This was beautiful waste.

I was moving from merely a God-*follower* to a God-*lover* when I noticed Him seeing me and knowing me in the middle minutes of my day and enjoying me, right there. Squandering time with God in the hidden place was turning me into one who would do anything to bring Him glory on the earth. What I forged with God in secret led to a sweet partnership with Him, the kind of partnership that leads any of us into great impact in this world—not because of the magnitude of what we do or how we feel when we're doing it but because of who He is to us.

Those hidden exchanges with Him began to fuel how I interacted with the world around me.

We were made to be seen—to have our baby hair clipped and saved, to have our milestones noticed, to be celebrated. But at the end of almost every well-intentioned baby book you'll probably find the blank pages. Eventually, no one has time to count the number of our teeth or of the new words we've learned. As we grow, we swirl in a sea of other faces, other ambitions. We might feel we're drowning in lost moments, unseen for who we are and who we could be. We might feel that parts of our lives are wasted.

The craving to be seen is universal: we were made to be known. But there is only one who can know us. He is the one who created us to live with moments and hours that no one else can understand.

And that's where the mysterious beauty of hiddenness comes in. We who live most of our days in and around the people of this world don't naturally hide ourselves in God. We don't naturally look to His expression toward us to drive us.

We respond instead to the looks and applause and the direction of others around us. Thus, He hides us. And masterfully.

Like He did with me, God sometimes hides us in obscure circumstances. He takes us out of an up-front role so we can discover the beauty of falling in love with Him when no one else is looking on or applauding. We sit behind a desk, toiling at a job no one appreciates. We push a stroller, change diapers, and rock crying babies to sleep. We work behind the scenes, clipboard in hand, serving the person on stage. We attend a church whose mission isn't the perfect fit with who we are and how we're gifted, and we serve, quietly and unacknowledged, in the background.

Sometimes God hides us in hardship or suffering. We limp through a broken marriage, wondering if life will ever mend. We get a late-night phone call and a tragedy forever splits our life into a before and an after. We lose our routine to a flurry of appointments with pediatric specialists and settle in for another long night at the hospital holding our child's hand.

Other times, God hides us in plain sight, right in the midst of a life that keeps going full tilt, so we learn how to find Him while pursuing a career or leading a ministry or running a household. We earn a doctorate degree, each letter behind our name representing long hidden hours, undocumented measures of hard work, and sacrifices that no one will fully know. We cheer on our children from the sidelines, knowing there is so much more to their story than the goals they've scored this season. We carry great responsibility at work or heading up a foundation, wearing a title that brings burdens few recognize or understand.

Yes, *all* of us world-changers, made by God for His glory, experience being hidden, hidden on purpose. Perhaps hidden for now simply because God enjoys how we give our all to Him—our thoughts, our prayers, our focused devotion—in private. (Would that be enough, to simply pour ourselves out for Him alone?)

We spend the majority of our lives hidden from others. Our secret thoughts, our sleep, our parenting and driving and grocery shopping. God designed us to hide in Him, not perform for Him.

In my early twenties, I was hidden in a boutique among antique farm tables stacked with table linens and pottery while my ministry dreams languished in a worn journal somewhere in the basement at home.

As a young married woman, I was hidden behind a desk when the guy who had an MBA took credit for months of my work and never gave me a nod or a second thought.

Years later, I was hidden, childless, at baby showers in a room full of women swapping birthing stories and maternity clothes.

I was hidden under mounds of paperwork and the debt of adoption as my friends nursed their babies.

I was hidden in a guest home in Ethiopia with a newly adopted child who cried for hours, and realized that none of my friends back home would ever understand the sweat I'd shed in just a few days of motherhood.

I was hidden holding that same child as he cried anew over wounds from living abandoned for too many years, years I could not reach back and heal.

I was hidden when I stood jittery behind a podium to tell my story, opening vulnerable parts of my life to scrutiny and criticism, and giving others opportunity to comment and misunderstand.

Most recently, I am hidden in sweatpants at home with six children, children whose needs render my days a forgettable blur unless I document them online. I am hidden when I sit alone at the end of these days, too exhausted even to fold laundry or help little fingers hold a crayon.

There was a time I lumped all of these experiences together and labeled them unproductive. Wasted and lost. But now I see them differently. These are paramount days, the most important ones, each filled with hours in which I can choose to hide myself in God.

And I join throngs of other women and men placed purposefully in hiding, who are also in training to be passionate lovers of God. They are cleaning toilets, punching time cards, changing bedpans, fielding criticism, and battling fatigue. With the opportunity to find Him in the midst of it all. No moment is too small, too insignificant to hide in God and waste time with Him.

God loves to hide us. Behind circumstances and callings and misjudgments and scorn from even the dearest of friends, He hides us. We may feel veiled and unnoticed, but God is training us to turn our eyes toward Him, to find Him there.

Our hidden places aren't signs of God's displeasure or punishment. The psalmist says that the one "who dwells in the secret place of the Most High" has a refuge and a fortress in God (Ps. 91:1). God doesn't banish us to this hidden place.

He *invites* us. And finding God in the secret can teach a heart to sing.

Mary of Bethany.

Jesus said of her, "Wherever this gospel is preached in the whole word, what this woman has done will also be told as a memorial to her" (Mark 14:9).

She may not be one of the few we memorialize in the gospels or among Jesus' followers. In her lifetime, she likely wasn't a gregarious ministry leader who attracted a large following.

She simply touched one life.

And then her story was told. Forever.

When Jesus came to Bethany six days before Passover, He walked into the mundane swirl of Mary's world—the roads her calloused and tired feet knew by memory, the place she fetched water, the floors she swept. And it was in the familiar and ordinary that something extraordinary happened. An extraordinary waste.

As Jesus dined with his friends, Mary poured perfume on His feet and then wiped them dry with her hair. Though others were scandalized and quick to criticize her actions, Jesus dignified her with His words. The Son of God was grateful for what this woman did. He even said that she would be known and highly regarded for her wastefulness.

Hers was the story He came to tell that night.

And it's true. More than two thousand years later, we know Mary not because of the food she may have served earlier in the day, the elderly relative she may have cared for, or even the prayers she may have offered. We know her because of her reckless, loving extravagance for God. And yet this public display of affection was also a hidden one. Hidden not because no one else was watching but because no one else really mattered.

Mary had eyes for one. Her motives were oriented toward Him. She wasn't driven to His feet by accolades, and she stayed despite criticism. What she cultivated with this man, Jesus, in the quiet and ordinary became her greatest expression.

This is radical love, according to Jesus.

In Mary, we see what it means to waste ourselves on God. In situations we might otherwise avoid or resent—the fourth-floor cubicle, the back row of singers, the laundry room—God invites us, through Mary's forever retold story, into an expression of radical love. The kind of unhinged love that lays everything at His feet whether or not anyone else ever sees, approves, or applauds.

The pieces of Mary's wasteful moment are a prism through which to consider this idea of hiddenness. God used a moment meant for God alone to invite others to Him. A moment in which she lived out no desire for acclaim and no fear of others' opinions. A moment, rooted in dozens of others before it, when Mary's love for and devotion to Jesus fueled what she performed.

In the chapters ahead, we'll explore the rich, yet often buried, opportunities God gives us in our own moments of hiddenness and just how to lean in, there, with expectation. And to grow. Deep. *Continually.*

This invitation to embrace hiddenness grows from a seasonal, one-time invitation into the question of our lives: *When no one else applauds you, when life is hard and makes no sense or simply feels like drudgery in the still quiet, will you hide yourself in Me? Will you waste your love on Me, here?*

───────── *For Your Continued Pursuit* ─────────

1 Samuel 16:7 | Psalm 17:8 | Psalm 18:19 | Psalm 91:1 | Psalm 107:2 | Psalm 119:130 | Psalm 139 | Proverbs 25:2 | Song of Songs 2:14 | Isaiah 64:4 | Matthew 6:1–4 | Matthew 26:6–13 | Mark 14:9 | John 1:47–50 | 2 Corinthians 4:16–18 | Galatians 1:10 | Ephesians 3:17–19 | Philippians 1:6 | Colossians 3:1–4 | Hebrews 12:2

This section at the end of each chapter is for readers who, like me, want to dig deeper by tracing the teaching back to God's truth. Some verses are cited within each chapter and others are alluded to. I invite you to use these passages as starting points for hiding in God, for wasting time adoring Him, and for making His Word part of your everyday language.

two

SEEN AND CELEBRATED

Discovering Who We Are Apart from What We Do

"And Martha served."

—JOHN 12:2

I was seventeen and still a baby in my faith when, in a flurry of opportunity and impulse, I got on a plane for the very first time and flew to a Christian camp in the Adirondack Mountains to wait tables for free.

I'd never been away from home for longer than a week. I was the kid who still got homesick during slumber parties just a year or two before. And I grumbled when my mom asked me to vacuum. Yet there I was, flying several states away to serve others from seven in the morning until ten at night for a month.

Our work crew (thirty of us high school volunteers) set tables, served plates, and cleaned up at breakfast, lunch, and dinner for three hundred loud, ravenously hungry peers every day. We raced from one meal to the next, barely catching our breath. Lunch crumbs were still under our fingernails when the dinner bell rang.

The work was taxing, but what hangs out in my memories are the pranks we played in the thirty minutes before bed, the dances we choreographed while cleaning up lunch, and the ten-minute make-a-best-friend-out-of-you conversations with people I've now called the dearest of friends for more than twenty years.

Somewhere between the hard work, late nights, and crazy pranks, our work crew leaders also had us memorizing Scripture. The first verse we memorized upon arriving at camp was this: "For even the Son of Man did not come to be served, but to serve, and to give His life a ransom for many" (Mark 10:45).

This verse was new to me. I hadn't known that service was part of the whole Jesus deal I'd signed up for—that it was His very life witness—until I memorized that verse. But that summer I got a preview of what it means to lay down my life. I also have a photo album full of pictures of celebrated moments with thirty other people. We weren't exactly suffering that month, and we certainly weren't doing everything in secret, but I was getting a gentle first taste of service.

At the time, service, much less *hidden* service—the kind Jesus offered when He washed the soil-stained feet of His disciples—had little appeal to me. It didn't need to. In this early stage of my relationship with God, everything felt flashy and fun and new. I wasn't inclined to give much thought to the less glamorous verses of the Bible.

Instead, I had a way of reframing Scripture to fit what made sense to me. I read, "Whoever wants to become great among you must be your servant. And whoever wants to be first must be your slave" (Matt. 20:26–27 NIV). Now, I could have seen this verse as an invitation, a way to experience His best intentions for me by serving. However, when the sixteen-year-old version of me reframed it, I understood it to say something like this: *Buck up and serve. We're called to hang out in the lowest places.*

Back then I read, "The greatest among you will be your servant. For those who exalt themselves will be humbled, and those who humble themselves will be exalted" (Matt. 23:11–12 NIV). And I reframed it, *Stifle desires to do anything for yourself. Serving is the best thing to do and the only thing that really matters.*

But there was a clanging dissonance between my longing to be noticed and the messages I received that seemed to teach these desires were wrong. To reconcile my understanding of service with my desires for acclaim and acknowledgment (desires that weren't a byproduct of being sixteen and immature but were inherent in me before and after adolescence), I stifled my desires. I shoved them deep inside and came to loathe that part of me that wanted to be noticed. I felt disgusted by any part of me that didn't line up with my reframed understanding of what it means to serve. It didn't occur to me to ask myself, *Could it be that God has made me with a desire to be seen and to be celebrated, but my desires are merely misplaced?*

The truth is we are made by God to be seen and celebrated. We like to hear our own names. When we're noticed and affirmed for our accomplishments or character traits, we feel that internal sigh of satisfaction that says, *Yes, I matter. To someone.* It's God who gives us this craving to be known, to realize that we do matter. Author and pastor Dallas Willard says it this way: "Unlike egotism, the drive to significance is a simple extension of the creative impulse of God that gave us being. . . . We were built to count, as water is made to run downhill. We are placed in a specific context to count in ways that no one else does. That is our destiny."[1]

We mattered before anyone else knew us, before we even had breath. David knew this: "For You formed my inward parts; You covered me in my mother's womb" (Ps. 139:13). We were conceived and we grew in hiddenness: "My frame was not hidden from You, when I was made in secret, and skillfully wrought in the lowest parts of the earth" (v. 15). Yet even in our natal hiddenness, we had a set of eyes on us. We lived for that one set of eyes: "Your eyes saw my substance, being yet unformed" (v. 16).

From the moment we were created, we were seen. And it was marvelous. Even before we had words, our souls were encoded to know God's image: "I will praise You, for I am fearfully and wonderfully made; marvelous are Your works, and that my soul knows very well" (v. 14).

The one whose hands formed the intricately pieced-together parts of us also had thoughts while He worked. David marveled, "How precious also are Your thoughts to me, O God!" (v. 17). Many thoughts: "How great is the sum of them! If I should count them, they would be more in number than the sand" (vv. 17–18). And God doesn't stop thinking about us. He never stops looking at and into us. There is never a time when we are unseen by Him: "Where can I go from Your Spirit? Or where can I flee from Your presence?" (v. 7).

This is the intimate bond for which we were formed. We hunger for significance—to be seen and understood and loved, to be and live *marvelous*—because we are made not only to know God but also to be known by Him. David celebrates this truth when he writes,

> O LORD, You have searched me and known me.
> You know my sitting down and my rising up;
> You understand my thought afar off.
> You comprehend my path and my lying down,
> And are acquainted with all my ways.
>
> —VERSES 1–3

Even as we are known, we are nonetheless born into hiding. "God saw us when we could not be seen," writes Charles Spurgeon, "and he wrote about us when there was nothing of us to write about."[2] For the nine months we are encased in the womb, unseen even by the eyes of the woman whose body labors to give us life, we grow from the size of a seed to that of a watermelon. Unseen, we grow about 1,600 times larger than the tiny union of cells we started out as. In that secret place, we are incubated. Hand-hidden. Known. Witnessed. Concealed. Within the hiddenness of the womb, God gives us a glimpse of a forever truth, the truth that quickens and multiplies in secret.

The problem is not that we long for significance but that

we are shifty or misguided in where we look for it. When we crave most the eyes of others—their opinions and accolades—we break our gaze with the only eyes that will ever truly see us. We forget the beauty of the Creator-eyes turned toward us, the ones that saw the inception of our lives and loved what He saw.

We're *still* hungry for the thing for which we were made: to be seen, to be known, to be celebrated, to participate in something much larger than ourselves. But too often we settle for lesser things. It seems easier to get a like online than it does to get quiet before God, to seek His face and listen for His whispers. Especially if we're not sure what the expression on His face might be or whether His whispers will be kind. We wonder if God could ever like what He sees in us when no one is looking. And we forget it was in that same hiddenness that our selves took shape in the first place.

"He said He loves me, Mommy," my daughter told me as I tucked her in, her words whispered with her hand to her mouth and cupped around my ear. Apparently, it was a secret.

This was years after that summer in the Adirondacks, years after I'd paced the floors of that Barracks Road boutique, and several years into married life. Nate and I had four of our now six children at the time. Those four were adopted—Eden and Caleb from Ethiopia, and Lily and Hope from Uganda. Our children are shedding orphan skin, a process that isn't much different for the rest of us believers in Jesus, shedding their old selves to become who they truly are. We sometimes see our home as a laboratory of the human heart as we witness the transformation of orphaned spirits into true sons and daughters in family room afternoons and over dinner dishes and during soccer practice.

Adoption has a stigma, at times, of broken children being brought into intact environments. While that's partially true, the greater truth is that every one of us is fractured. And even after we find our way into God's arms, parts of us are still broken, still in need of the tender hand of a Father gently putting us back together. Whether twenty-three, forty-eight, or seventy-one, there are always newly vulnerable parts of ourselves that need the reassurance of this wild love of God.

The four hurting hearts in our house truly aren't much different from our own hearts, just less able to mask the pain. They desperately crave a carefree welcome into their daddy's lap and yet are terrified of such boundless love. They often find it easier to dutifully serve and be vigilantly careful never to make a mistake or always to prove their value and their worthiness for love. Their brokenness has taught them to scramble for security in how they perform rather than to find it with a sigh of relief in the stability of their daddy's arms.

As adults, we often accept the language of being a daughter or a son of God and yet still struggle—nearly daily and sometimes hourly—with the internal strife of not knowing how to rest in the safety of our God's arms. We live with Him, under His watch and in His family, and yet still behave like orphans—distant, fragmented, and serving tirelessly to earn our keep.

The Father's pursuit of us doesn't end at salvation. He is forever alluring us. Yet we often live as if we are more comfortable remaining fractured because that's all we know: serving well, and shaming ourselves back to good behavior when we don't. Author A. W. Tozer describes God's relentless faithfulness this way: "Psuedo-faith always arranges a way out to serve in case God fails it. Real faith knows only one way and gladly allows itself to be stripped of any second way or makeshift substitutes. For true faith, it is either God or total collapse. And not since Adam stood up on the earth has God failed a single man or woman who trusted him."[3]

At one time, this was all I'd known of how to relate to Him. But now I get to witness in my children the same healing work that is ongoing within me, the same healing work that I suspect is ongoing in you.

On this particular night, Hope couldn't yet give voice to what she was experiencing, but it was this: *she* was God's secret. This child had known horror in her early childhood. She had taken her first steps on the streets and without a home, dust under her fingernails. No soapy bubble baths in Mommy's bathtub for this wee thing. She couldn't count to ten, but she'd already climbed the mountain of fatherlessness on earth.

Yet God's gaze on her never wavered. She wasn't relegated to second-class status in His eyes when her traumatic early childhood left her developmentally "behind" the typical child. In a culture where babies are learning to read and toddlers are groomed for Harvard, Hope was being kept. By God. And she was starting to know it. She was breaking free from the lie that many of us believe: performance earns our keep.

Her brushes with God—and her awareness of His gaze on her—are my daughter's invitation out of an orphan spirit. They are her mile markers, more firmly charting her course than any SAT score or college acceptance letter or job promotion.

To understand that a Father with kind eyes *sees* us, even in secret, makes daughters and sons out of all of us who struggle to know what it means to call God Daddy. It makes hearts beat again. It turns prayer into intimate whispers between us and the one who made us.

"He said He loves me, Mommy," she told me. And I remembered her first dance recital, not long after she had come home to us. She had practiced her routine in and out of class for a semester. Every one of us in our family knew the steps. She'd spent weeks pirouetting through our kitchen with a dishcloth in hand, performing with confidence on our living room hearth.

But the night of the performance, I could feel her hand shaking in mine as I walked her down the hall to her lineup. I hurried back to my seat in the auditorium as she waited for her group to be called. I was nervous for her. I so wanted this night to be a win.

When she *relevé* out on stage among twelve other girls, I, like all the other parents, narrowed my eyes onto just my child. But several beats into the routine, I widened my scope and realized she was a step or two behind. Then three. Then four.

The other children moved in synchronized motion while my beautiful girl carefully performed her routine, too focused on her steps to notice how far behind she was. Too inexperienced to skip steps to catch up.

For seven minutes, I looked beyond her slippered feet—out of sync, arms moving in one direction while her classmates' moved in another—and fixed my mind on her story. Alongside the others, my daughter may have been out of step, but she was also stunning. Light and joy cascaded out of her with every twirl. She had come through the fire of loss and death and hardened dreams, and tonight she was *dancing*.

From my seat, I could see her counting steps, her expression serious and focused. But her eyes were alert and glistening under the stage lights, not dull and weighted as they were when we'd first met her at the orphanage months before. She wasn't posing as someone she'd learned to mimic—a common orphan survival skill. She wasn't dancing to impress others. If she had stopped to notice others, she probably would have frozen in panic. Instead, she was costumed in God. He was making a dancer out of a street kid. This was a child who was learning to be loved.

"He said He loves me" weren't words Hope had learned in a Sunday school song. They'd jumped directly from the pages of God's Word into her heart, and they came alive in her dance steps. This was His real love, welling up within her.

After the recital, her daddy and brother showered her with flowers and she chattered away the entire car ride home. She was the belle of the ball. This child who'd grown up a street-smart survivor and who had been called mischievous by orphanage workers became a glowing ballerina that night.

Her costume is now tucked away in a bin labeled with her name. She pulls it out sometimes, as if she can access that night all over again through the chiffon in her fingers.

I didn't show her the recording afterward, because it might tell a different story than the one I saw and the one she lived. Our human eyes can betray the truth of the story we're living. Even I, her mother, didn't see the whole of her that night. The God who formed her is the only one who saw it all.

To her teacher, my tiny dancer was out of step. To the parent sitting one row in front of me, she was one of two dark-skinned girls on stage. To the girl dancing next to her—being primed for a future in ballet—she wasn't good enough yet to be competition. To her mama, she was being restored. To her daddy, she was a doe-eyed princess.

To the one who made her, she was even more.

She was art.

She was fire and wonder.

Marvelous and worth His blood spilled.

She was His story.

She was His to hide. To keep.

And to tell.

My little girl lives in a world that might label her one way, but she is beginning to tune her ear to the one who tells her who *He* sees, who she truly is. She is destined for greatness, this child of mine. Destined to revel in the truth that she is seen even when no one else is looking. Destined to know the voice of the one who talks to her in the dark, even when no one else is listening.

∞

My children aren't the only ones who are surprised by uncon-ditional love. When I struggle to believe I'm loved, I find myself looking for ways to achieve more. (All of this is mostly subconscious.) If unfettered, I have a drive in me to earn love by being a star. When I'm not feeling deeply and uncondi-tionally loved, I try to keep others applauding, because I've forgotten how to listen for Jesus' sweet whispers in my ear.

Just like sweetly feverish Martha.

The night Mary poured perfume on Jesus' feet, her brother, Lazarus, was reclining at table with Jesus, and her sister, Martha, was serving. On a previous evening when Jesus was dining in Bethany, Mary had wasted not perfume but herself at His feet. She wasted time by wasting an opportunity to serve.

In contrast, Martha, the consummate hostess, "was dis-tracted with much serving" (Luke 10:40). Martha scurried to serve, to show her love—and likely to prove her worth—by meeting the perceived needs of her guests. No doubt she was overwhelmed. But she was also distracted from what truly mattered.

"Lord, do You not care that my sister has left me to serve alone?" protested Martha. "Tell her to help me."

But Jesus wasn't irritated with Mary, nor did He consider her lazy. To Him, Mary's choice was an act of radical love. "Martha, Martha, you are worried and troubled about many things," Jesus said. "But one thing is needed, and Mary has chosen that good part, which will not be taken away from her" (vv. 41–42). Mary was so confident in God's love for her that she sat at His feet and listened.

She wasted herself on Him.

So often in our scurry to serve, we forget our starting place, the one thing that is needed.

I had yet to learn this the summer I waited tables at that camp in the Adirondacks. My biggest crisis that summer was not having packed the right clothes to work in a stifling hot dining hall. So I called my mom from the pay phone in the center of the camp and asked her to send me new tank tops. What I didn't say directly but tried to imply was this: *don't send just any tank tops, but please, Mom, cute ones.* My one-month stint of serving behind the scenes gave me an invitation to flirt with tables full of cute boys from all across the country, and I was a bit dual-minded. Perhaps more obvious then was the struggle I still have: I wanted to serve, but I also wanted to be noticed.

But there was one small group on our crew of volunteers who didn't even have the option to be noticed. They were assigned to the affectionately (and appropriately) named area we called "the pits." This crew of six washed dishes in the back corner of the kitchen from just after breakfast until just before they crawled into bed at night. They didn't venture into the dining hall or flirt with campers. And theirs wasn't a rotating assignment—working the pits was their job for the entire month. Many of them had packed cute clothes and comfortable but trendy shoes in preparation for waiting tables. But now when they called home from the pay phone in the center of camp, they were asking their moms to send T-shirts and jeans that could get ruined. There was no time for stain-spotting in the pits' washing line.

I breathed relief when I was assigned to the dining hall. I felt pity for the people in the pits. For an entire month, hardly anyone knew they were there, except for the one night each week when the campers were introduced to our entire work crew. On that one night, our pits crew sat on stage among the one hundred high school and college-aged volunteers and merely stated their name and their job: "I'm Abby from Cincinnati, Ohio, and I work in the pits." In an entire month, they were seen just four times. The other forty-three thousand minutes of their thirty days went unobserved by all but one.

That crew of six fascinated me. I didn't understand the joy that erupted from them many times behind the swinging doors of the kitchen. How could one month in that job truly be fulfilling when they worked unseen? At the time, I didn't know about their early morning Bible studies or the conversations they had with God and each other. I didn't read their journals or see how their hearts for God grew during this month when their clothes dripped with well water and they reeked all day of dish soap and stale breakfast sausage. I just pitied them. And yet something tells me they had an experience that the rest of us in cute tank tops didn't.

I'd be naive to think those sixteen- and seventeen- and eighteen-year-olds on the pits crew loved the hidden corner of the kitchen when they started. Like me, they probably requested an assignment in the dining hall. Maybe they even muttered under their breaths during those first few days—or weeks—of elbows in suds, hearing laughter from the other side of the door where the cute boys and girls crushed on their waitstaff. But likely, they were indoctrinated early into wrestling with hiddenness and how to find Him and thrive there. They had thirty days of focused practice.

Hidden servanthood is drudgery when we're intent on praise from others. And it is also drudgery when we tell ourselves that our desires for recognition and praise don't matter.

How we respond when we are hidden by God is everything.

When we know we are seen by the one who created praise itself and He is the one who gives us a word of affirmation—when He is the one who notices us pouring ourselves out in secret—we realize that this is what we craved all along. We hear His applause. We are celebrated. And something inside of us comes alive. In that one moment, the underground hidden life looks and feels very different.

The pits—whatever they may be for us in any given moment—are no longer awful. Being elbow-deep in soapsuds and breakfast-sausage grease looks and feels different when we know God sees us there.

———————— *For Your Continued Pursuit* ————————

Genesis 1:26 | Job 28:24 | Job 34:21 | Psalm 90:4 | Psalm 119:32 | Psalm 139 | Psalm 147:5 | Proverbs 15:3 | Ecclesiastes 11:5 | Isaiah 46:9–10 | Matthew 10:30 | Matthew 20:6–7 | Matthew 23:11–12 | Mark 1:35 | Mark 10:45 | Luke 6:12 | Luke 10:38–42 | Luke 22:41–44 | John 12:2–3 | John 17:22 | John 17:26 | Galatians 4:1–7 | Philippians 1:6 | Hebrews 5:7 | Revelation 1:14

three

OPEN HANDS

Living a Story We Had Not Planned

> "A woman came having an alabaster
> flask of very costly oil."
>
> —MARK 14:3

It was long before morning when I woke up in a cold sweat. I felt as though I'd been chased in my dreams, except there was no villain and I wasn't a victim. My pounding heart was loud against the silence in the house.

The venue of my dream was a ten-year-old girl's birthday party. My daughter Lily had been invited at the last minute, and she responded with the youthful thrill that any birthday invitation incites. But just before she left, we learned that the event wasn't merely a birthday party; it was a slumber party, the stuff dreams are made of for preadolescent girls.

True to our waking selves, the dream versions of me and Nate, knowing Lily's makeup, decided not to let her stay the night. Most of her childhood had been one big overnight as she shared sleeping quarters with classmates and friends at the orphanage. She was still so new to our family that nights at home within the consistency of her bedtime routine and her father's arms as he tucked her in were necessary for her healing. In the dream, she was crushed by our decision. We spent the rest of the dream explaining to her why we wouldn't let her sleep over. Then I woke up, shivering and too agitated to go back to sleep.

Lying in bed and prayerful, I realized the dream was really about me. As I dreamed it, I'd felt all that Lily might feel. The rush of excitement, then the disappointment. The feeling of being the only one left out. The sting of your parents' betraying you, begrudging you something you want so much.

We were a family of seven by that time, and I treasured each of my children. At times, though, I caught myself feeling empty and dissatisfied. Those were the times I'd look more carefully at the bulletin board in our kitchen where we tack up Christmas cards and leave them up all year. The board was filled with photos of cousins and friends and neighbors, all with combed and styled hair and carefully picked and pressed clothes. Each family looked like what I had once thought my family would look like at this point in my life: Husband with his arm around his wife, children spaced two years apart, all with matching smiles, all secure and happy with albums of baby pictures at home. This was the Christmas card I envisioned when I was twenty-four and newly married. Back when I had a white-knuckled grip on my plans.

I was still pondering the significance of the dream a few days later when I woke one morning and noticed the early streaks of sunrise had just begun to show themselves beyond the woods lining our front yard. They highlighted the encroaching harshness of winter on a landscape that had been lush a few months earlier. Every tree looked dead.

Long dead.

Had I not lived here the winter before, had I not witnessed the routine seasonal transformations, I'd have assumed those trees had no life left in them. All I could see was what was *not* there.

But I knew the trees were not dead. They were merely dormant. In winter, the roots are quiescent. In winter, what we can see with our eyes is not the whole story. Winter gives birth to spring not just in the tree but in us.

At twenty-two and fresh out of college, I knew nothing about winter. I imagined my spiritual life as a tall and opulent tree, each year reaching new heights and bearing dazzling fruit as I grew toward mastery of my relationship with God. I lived to expect and exploit spring and summer—flourishing external growth—but autumn and winter soon followed.

There was frost when my fledgling marriage was chilled by anger and silence, followed by my father's death and—my longest, coldest winter—twelve years of infertility. I was no longer living in a hothouse, always growing taller, always producing fruit. God was winterizing me. His intention wasn't to leave me fruitless—God loves fruit. He hid me so that I would find Him in the hiddenness. So I would come back to my roots, so I would see His eyes on me in the hiding.

When what I see with my eyes doesn't come together like I hope, I tend to look a little bit longer at Him. When my dreams aren't being fulfilled, I'm invited to search the one who gives dreams in the first place. When I'm unproductive or when my greatest feats of productivity leave me empty, I grow hungrier for something more than what I can accomplish with my own hands and drive.

God hides me to show me His kind eyes toward me—gentler than the taskmaster I am toward myself. And He hides me to tell me my story—to remind me of Himself, the author. It is the greatest story my skin will ever know—God, in me, radiating through me, making glory for Him on the earth.

I have a version of my story, a shiny version fit to put on a Christmas card. But God's version is far richer. It's deeper and it's layered with purpose. His version of my story stretches beyond what I can see. It includes more twists and turns, goodness and glory, than my mind can construct.

Yes, I had plans as a college student and a new wife and an adoptive mother of four ready to build an ever-happy family. I have plans today, spoken and unspoken, that I want desperately for God to shape. But my plans often need dormancy. They need a winter—sometimes many winters—to rest. I need time to get caught up in God's seeing me in my unseen moments. Time so that when He breathes the warmth of new plans into me, I actually want them. And so I want Him more than I want the plans themselves.

Most of the time, we don't reach for God until we have to. Our hardest circumstances are often the ones God uses to call forth the deeper reach for Him.

Until I was in over my head with five children, I never needed to pray the Bible under my breath, up the stairs and down, from one bedroom to the next.

Until I sat feeling invisible in a crowd of peers, I never needed to ask God, daily, for strength to be unnoticed.

Until my friends' bellies were round and I was barren and felt forgotten by God, I never prayed the Psalms as if they were my own cries.

Until I was mothering four former orphans and wondering just how far God goes to restore a life, I never scoured the Word of God for truths about restoration.

Until the voices of accolades around me suddenly got quiet, I never saw a need to sit before God in the silence and wait for His whispers.

Until all the other words around me fell short, I never considered meditating upon God's Word, mulling it over and letting it dance around my mind for longer than a morning quiet time.

In all these experiences, it was as if God were the parent in my dream, the one slowly shaping my life from orphan to daughter. *You don't see it all like I do. I know what's best—I know you* best. *The story you want, though not bad, isn't the story I have for you. Will you let Me write your story?* This is the invitation God offers in the winters of my soul. An invitation to trust that my story is His story. And if I let Him winterize me, He will deepen my roots and help me to stretch my branches toward Him—for my good and for His glory.

Mary of Bethany also had plans, we might suppose. And planners don't like to leave things to chance. Mary carried her plan in a jar around her neck. She held dignity and extravagance near her chest. This spikenard oil was imported from India and cost a year's wages. This was no impulse purchase. It was her assurance—her savings account and her security. She'd likely had it long before she met Jesus, and so it was a part of her. Her scent mingled with the scent of this oil. It marked her. Until she saw a different function for its extravagance.

Yes, it was an extravagance that she carried, but it paled in light of the extravagance she experienced when she was with Jesus.

This man had comforted her when she grieved the death of her brother, had taught her truth and treated her with dignity in a culture that neither educated nor honored women. His kindness and His defiance of cultural norms emboldened her and prepared her to pour out brazen love as oil.

In a moment, her plans suddenly meant nothing to her. Letting go of them, while uncomfortable and unfamiliar, empowered her.

She'd grown safe within this otherworldly love He offered her, so an exchange of her story for His no longer frightened her. She moved from fear to desire. She wanted it more than anything else.

Even the oil.

Mary was so in love with the God who had seen her when no one else did, the God who knew her and whispered His secrets to her, the God who breathed fresh life into her dead brother, that she'd do anything for Him. She would crack open what had once been her treasure in exchange for a new story. It was a costly exchange, but it was worth it because she was His.

I cried when I found them, these two baby teeth carefully wrapped in a foam container, deep in my purse. They'd been there for months.

It had been a particularly hard set of months for my almost-teenager, who was now too old to lose baby teeth. And because it was hard for her, it was hard for all of us. Her struggles had become ours. She was once a photograph on our refrigerator for which we wistfully prayed, and now she was ours to hold and to help heal.

When we said yes to adoption, I said yes to a process and a person I couldn't yet hold or help heal and didn't know. I didn't realize we were also saying yes to mountains of paperwork, paperwork that documented every corner of our lives and invited social workers to comment on it all. The paperwork itself was mostly an inconvenience to my heart—all the systems we had to navigate and all the hoops we had to jump through made my entrance into motherhood feel like a mind-numbing bureaucratic procedure.

But when these heart-imagined children became names and toothy grins on our refrigerator, I started seeing past the paperwork. I also acquired a new ability to live stretched across two continents. When it was 3:00 a.m. in the Midwest, my children were just waking up across the ocean. *What are they doing? Who is shepherding their days? Do they think about us?* I routinely lived and loved and thought in two time zones— starkly and inconveniently parted from my very own children.

As the adoption process continued, I focused only on the

best possible outcomes. I closed my ears to stories of former orphans and their families who thought their biggest battles were the bureaucratic ones, only to discover later the real battles were just beginning when they brought their children home. I was naive when we said yes to adopting older children and outside of the birth order (older than our oldest child). I was convinced we would be different. Our fantastic family chemistry and love would wash over any lasting consequences from their years of loss.

But then that paperwork grew skin, and the stories had faces, and they weren't on the other side of the ocean—they were down the hall.

This particular child whose baby teeth wound up in my purse had lived many undocumented years before she came home to us. We didn't know when she'd lost her first tooth or taken her first step, and those were minor details compared with the pages we'd leave blank on the forms of doctors' offices requesting family history. Getting the twenty-seventh piece of adoption paperwork notarized was nothing compared with all that had gone undocumented in her life, everything from her first word and first step to family records of deaths and births.

By the time she came to us, she rarely wanted to be held. She'd long ago learned to push tears deep into her pillow. Years into having her in our home, loss still hovered over her. All her ouchies were on the inside, not ones a mama could kiss and make better.

So Nate and I spent a focused month praying mostly for her. All the children had their unique needs, but as is often the case in a big family with a lot of noise, you attend to the bell that rings the loudest. Though she'd been home for several years, different circumstances and life mile-markers triggered memories of her painful history. And often at unexpected times. Pain, through the body and life of a child, isn't always tidy. A simple correction could send one of our children spinning for days. An altercation with a sibling might trigger a child to retreat in silent anguish until she could be coerced into talking about the storm inside of her. Adoption amplifies the already-sown mystery of raising tiny, uniquely created human beings. Nate and I found that the first, best tending to the hearts of our children was done in secret with God. So we prayed.

As I watched this child writhe on the inside—in a way that conversation with God gives you an eye to see—I hurt along with her. I felt her loss, but I also felt mine. I grieved for all the life I had missed with my daughter. I grieved for all the times she cried without me there to hold her, without either of us knowing the other's face. I grieved for the story I wanted her to have instead of the one she was living.

I hadn't even been with her when all her baby teeth came out—at least, when most of them came out. A few months before this time of intense prayer, I had taken her to a dentist, who told us that while she had a mouth full of healthy teeth, it was too full. My not so little girl had gained all of her adult teeth while still holding on to two baby teeth. They needed to be removed.

After the extraction surgery (and subsequent rule that this squeamish mama does not witness the early aftermath of surgical procedures), I tucked those two teeth away. Deep enough that I didn't find them until months later, when all the years I'd lost with my daughter were haunting me.

I choked back sobs when I unwrapped that foam box. Oh, the timing!

Our youngest son at the time, the child of my womb, was a baby. He was learning to say Mama and leaving rings of drool on his shirt from cutting his own first teeth. Even as I celebrated his milestones, he was reminding me, day by day, of all I'd never had with my children who were adopted.

I finally admitted that I resented those lost years. I resented them for how they overshadowed my little girl and for the constant worry I felt about whether they always would. I resented that one day she might have a baby of her own and then struggle anew with questions about her birth and childhood I wouldn't be able to answer. I resented that no matter how much love I poured into her, it seemed to always bleed right out again.

There were times I doubled over in pain, haunted by unanswerable questions. *If I resent those lost years, how much more must my child resent them? What kind of pain must she be in? What kind of grief does she feel now that anyone who knew the early days of her life is gone?*

But her baby teeth.

Perhaps He'd been saving them for my finding. Because God was showing me through my child's story that what I'd considered lost was merely hidden.

And hidden—versus lost—changes everything.

There were *always* eyes on her life. Her early years may

not be recorded on pages I can see and hold, but she has a baby book. Every minute of her life has been not only witnessed but recorded. Noticed. Treasured. Loved. My baby, made for an eternal existence with God and held in my arms for the first time when she was seven, had not lost one single day.

I know that my child still needs healing. I know she will need to grieve and walk honestly through her losses. She will need to live into a different story than the one either of us might have chosen for her. And I am committed to be with her in all of it. To grieve with her. And to celebrate those times when she allows herself to be embraced, when we can share tears with one another rather than for one another. So her story is teaching me, her mama who never saw her first baby tooth.

She was made for a life that is witnessed. And though the veil fell thick on her childhood, her childhood wasn't unwitnessed. She was known. My little girl will heal and come to life as she sees herself in God's story.

As will her mama.

For Your Continued Pursuit

Psalm 1:3 | Proverbs 3:5 | Isaiah 43:7, 10 | Matthew 6:6 | Matthew 10:29–31 | Luke 10:38–42 | John 11:1–44 | John 15:1–2 | Romans 11:33–36 | 1 Corinthians 2:7–10 | 1 Corinthians 13:12 | Ephesians 3:20–21 | Colossians 1:26–27 | Hebrews 4:13

four

LOVE POURED OUT

Leaning into Our Call to Greatness

"Then she broke the flask and
poured it on His head."

—MARK 14:3

O*h boy*, I thought when I heard the conversation from another room. One child was shouting his math facts at the prompting of eager parents. Two plus two didn't require any computation from him. Five plus nine and twenty-three plus seven and sixteen plus three—this child was smart, easily adding numbers when most his age were barely counting fingers.

My children squealed and celebrated, too young to be concerned that another child knew more than they did.

Until one of my daughters chimed in, "Let me play!"

Her age on a transcript would suggest this game would be easy for her too. But I know her history. A simple equation isn't simple for the child who had the slums as her nursery.

"I can count to ten," she announced. "One, two, three, four, seven." She pauses. "Nine, eight . . . ten!"

All the children in the room cheered, celebrating anything said with a confident gleam.

But I wondered, *How many years does my girl have before she sees her life diminished by another's accomplishments? How many years do I have with her before what she can't do on the outside might wear like shame on her insides?* However, the very next day, my little girl displayed how two storylines can live simultaneously within one person.

It was an entire day full of cousin fun, my children's favorite kind of time. Dress-up clothes and dolls and croquet at Nana's house, in between giggly games of hide-and-seek. Somewhere in the commotion, though, my counting girl had slipped away. She'd holed up in the back office with tape and scissors and markers. She emerged hours later with a stack of love notes. She'd painstakingly made a card for each child, choosing to miss out on a play day she'd been looking forward to for weeks.

She passed out the cards like she was passing out hundred dollar bills, anticipating that each recipient would feel as full in the receiving as she did in the making and the giving. Cousins and siblings threw out a casual thanks for this construction-papered offering, but she didn't seem to notice. She radiated light. She was expressing who she was becoming.

If the sum of our daughter's identity were based on her outward life, Nate and I would be thinking only about her inability to count to ten. *Will she be able to balance a checkbook one day or read* Pride and Prejudice? *Will she study the Bible or give a public speech?*

But there are always two stories in a person—the visible

story and the invisible story—and only one set of eyes that sees them both. David knew the invisible truth: "My frame was not hidden from You, when I was made in secret" (Ps. 139:15).

God has created each of us for greatness. Not the greatness of a stage or a title or a degree, though He may use those things in our lives. He may even let the applause of others encourage us and help us grow. But the sweetest greatness starts with being rooted, being made and nurtured in secret, being seen by God alone.

I graduated from college *magna cum laude*, which is Latin for "with great honor" or "with great praise." I walked across the stage to receive my honors diploma with the pride of one who had turned people toward Jesus during college while still earning good grades. I'd graduated with greatness, or so I thought.

I *craved* greatness.

I vaguely understood that greatness has something to do with internal growth as well as outward accomplishments, but most of what I considered growth could be measured and documented: lives changed, movements started, goals met. If it mattered, I measured it. If I couldn't measure it, it didn't matter.

At the time, I didn't know I could also be great at two o'clock in the morning holding a sick baby or in graciously stepping away from a leadership position at church so someone else could take the limelight. I didn't know that greatness

could be had in a years-long journey of fielding the pain of a
former orphan or in quietly serving a friend who would never
thank me. I didn't know that I might find greatness in leaving
my task list unfinished so I could read to a child in my lap.
I didn't know at twenty-one with my diploma in hand that
I could be great in the dormant seasons—or what I would
have then considered unsuccessful seasons. I didn't know that
even my very desire for greatness was something that came
from God.

Jesus acknowledged this human craving for greatness
in the verse I memorized that summer in the Adirondacks:
"Whoever would be great among you must be your servant,
and whoever would be first among you must be your slave"
(Matt. 20:26–27 ESV).

For years, I assumed that this invitation to service—and
thereby greatness—was about bringing a meal to a sick friend,
volunteering in the nursery at church, or stapling information
packets for soccer practice. But the greatness Jesus describes
requires more than a slight strain on the pocketbook or the
occasional sacrifice of time. He was stating in no uncertain
terms that the path to greatness lies in hiddenness. And it's
a state of mind and a way of being, not a series of tasks to
perform and check off a list.

We become great when we genuinely, happily serve in
unacknowledged ways and places because that is where we
find the sustaining face of God, especially when no one else
sees us or applauds. Hearts that grow in God, that reach for
Him and receive His reaching back, become *profoundly* great.
Unshakable, even.

At such times, our biggest mistake is to call our hiddenness accidental. You've probably heard statements like these: "If I could just get out of this transition and into a role where I'm using my gifts . . ." or, "When the kids get a bit older and I can leave the house more . . ." or, "When he's not sick anymore, I'll really be able to give my life away for God's kingdom," or [insert yours here]. We forget that it's in the interruptions, the waiting seasons, the disappointments that we grow best.

It is in those times when we are "sidetracked" by a disheartening job, an unshared bed, or a leader who doesn't acknowledge our gifting that God whispers, *This is where you become great—on the inside.*

Content in all circumstances

Mary not only offered God her opportunity for greatness— that jar she carried around her neck—she broke it open. There was no going back. She was all in, and the oil was no longer hers for safekeeping. Mary was now Mary without the oil's musk that had marked her.

In an instant, what had signified security and recognition spilled through her fingers. Those dreams of moving comfortably into old age with financial assurance, and perhaps even thoughts of clothing herself in the finest linens, all fell away as she looked at Him. She was close enough to see the lines on His face. He was beautiful and powerful and safe.

Mary probably hadn't told a soul about this ahead of time. Perhaps she hadn't planned this moment at all. If she had and had told others about it, it's likely they tried to talk her out of it. But they didn't yet know what she knew—that when she got near to Jesus, the glow of everything and everyone else dimmed. When she got near to this man, her life became great. He reveled in her story and in her participation in His story: this was greatness.

There are two stories in a person—the visible story and the invisible story.

To Jesus, Mary's greatness was revealed in the very act that the onlookers called foolish. And in this weakened, wasted greatness, she got closer to Him—she participated in *His* story—and she grew.

Times have shifted. In this digital age, we might well wonder, "If it wasn't posted on social media, did it really happen?" We can't live for the beauty of the hidden life while feeding on likes and comments. As long as we don't make big impact synonymous with greatness, there's nothing wrong with it. But the unintended consequence may be that we think that anything that isn't big and observable isn't great, which renders the rest of life a waiting room. Wasted time. When we live a life of constantly reaching for the next big thing, we miss the greatness God is calling us to right here, right now. In the small, the ordinary, the hidden moments. The white space.

If the chief end of every human being is to glorify God and enjoy Him forever, shouldn't that glory and enjoyment be able to happen when no one is looking? Within the times when we don't seem to be influencing the world at all, the moments when we pour ourselves out at Jesus' feet?

Great kingdom impact comes not just from actions that

make a dramatic and observable impact but from all the accumulated moments we spend looking at God, bringing Him glory in private, and letting Him shape our insides.

We aren't forfeiting outward impact for private devotion to God. We are submitting to the understanding that life in God isn't about God's needing us to do His work for Him or to do it under our own power. It is instead about a glory we can't always measure. It is the work that happens beneath the surface, deep in the soil of our hearts, that in time produces a great harvest of fruit and growth.

Jesus tells us, "But the seed falling on good soil refers to someone who hears the word and understands it. This is the one who produces a crop, yielding a hundred, sixty or thirty times what was sown" (Matt. 13:23 NIV).

Yes, I *am* made to be great. I am made to produce fruit and to bring God glory. So are you. And that desire for greatness can help me start a new nonprofit or invest more in my marriage or adopt a child. Or prompt me to empty out my savings or open a room of my house to someone in need.

But later, when the nonprofit seed cash has evaporated, I'm going to need roots. When the person I've invited into my home leaves in the night and takes my wallet, I'm going to need roots. When the needs of a sick child feel like too much at three in the morning, or the hospital bills exceed my bank balance, I'm going to need roots.

"Some fell on rocky places, where it did not have much soil. It sprang up quickly, because the soil was shallow. But when the sun came up, the plants were scorched, and they withered because they had no root" (vv. 5–6 NIV).

In the context of greatness, we might say that this rocky-place seed accomplished something, at least. But without sinking deep roots into nutrient-dense soil—intimacy with God—it couldn't continue to grow and bear fruit. "But since they have no root, they last only a short time. When trouble or persecution comes because of the word, they quickly fall away" (v. 21 NIV).

Greatness begins underground. In secret. I have to sink my roots deep in the knowledge of God's love to grow branches that bear fruit in and out of season.

No one may notice if you exchange your earbuds and workout music for desperate whispers to God while you pound it out on the treadmill. No one except Him.

And your roots sink deep.

No one may notice if you curl up with your journal and spend time with God on the back porch before sticky-fingered children, just off the school bus, run clamoring through the front door.

But your roots sink deep.

No one may notice if you exchange your smartphone for His Word on your bedside table and check in with Him before checking email every morning.

Here, your roots sink deep.

No one may notice if you pray fiercely and secretly for a friend's ministry to grow, even though you crave the attention she is getting.

Your roots sink deep again.

No one may notice if you turn down a business opportunity in order to spend more quiet hours with God, or if you say no to an opportunity to serve someone in need because you ask Him and He whispers, "I have another plan to meet that need."

Our growing root system reaches and creeps and drinks, deeply, of a greatness that the world can't measure, a greatness that even some within the Christian community might not recognize or understand. But the long-term greatness of a tree is always found in the depth and health of its roots.

It was one of those 3:00 p.m. meltdowns that had become painfully familiar. I was in the laundry room, pulling wet clothes from the washer and shoving them into the dryer for the third time that day. Clothes that would be worn and discarded and back in the laundry room within the next twenty-four hours.

The laundry itself wasn't daunting; it was just a reminder of all of the other parts of my day that were on a vicious cycle: One child's sunken demeanor as she struggled to speak positive words (again). Another child's terse words and her sister's flashpot response. Another child who still couldn't read.

Then, like ticker tape through my head, in rolled all the things I'd hoped to accomplish that I still hadn't managed to do. I had been full of dreams for this year and had accomplished (maybe) one. I had intended to read a long book with each of the kids individually. I'd finished a chapter each at best. I had plans to teach them to cook and a stack of recipe books we'd not yet cracked open. My pantry was full of ingredients for the Saturday baking days we had never done even once. Weakness crowded into me in that tiny laundry room. No one but Nate knew how trapped I'd felt recently, sandwiched between my children's unrelenting needs and my greater hopes for our family.

Then came the interruption. A phrase, dropped into my mind from Him, softening me as I heard it: *I like you when you're weak.*

It was true. Biblical. "My strength is made perfect in [your] weakness" (2 Cor. 12:9). And now near.

God's power came when I had nothing left. It was perfected there in the cramped laundry room amid loads of wet clothing, loads of unmet needs in my house, loads of unrealized hopes. Loads of unwitnessed hours. Realizing that God saw me and even liked me changed everything about that unseen day.

On days like that, I want His Word more than soundbites I can read online.

On days like that, I crave conversation with God over texting a girlfriend.

On days like that, I see the thrill in searching Him out, knowing He longs to be found. I see spending time with Him—His Spirit breathing through the pages of His Word—as something I desire, not a duty. Verses I've read a dozen times or more become real to me when I have a brush with Him on a hard day.

"Pray without ceasing," writes Paul (1 Thess. 5:17). I want to talk with God throughout my day, even when I'm a mess, because I know He's not looking away from my story but whispering into it.

"Be still, and know that I am God" (Ps. 46:10). When His Spirit blows a light breeze into a stale and difficult day, I want to let it waft over me, refresh me as I sit still before Him.

In conversation with God, my thinking changes. Out of my desire to "be filled with the Spirit," speaking the truth of the Psalms helps me to let go of the vile lies I too often mutter over myself. And I don't have to force myself to do it. I *want* to make a "melody to the Lord with [my] heart" (Eph. 5:19 ESV). On days when I see God seeing me, the notes of a song naturally well up within me.

It's on these days that the places of my life that no one but God sees become the places for the greatest spiritual growth. Just like my baby has growth spurts at unexpected times—his ankles shoot right out from his pant legs—I find my love for God often grows most without noise or fanfare.

When our eyes are locked on our outward lives, we inevitably assess our growth by the "success" of our circumstances. But the heart can grow at any time. And God is all eyes for heart growth. "The Lord does not look at the things people look at. People look at the outward appearance, but the Lord looks at the heart" (1 Sam. 16:7 NIV).

Four more loads of laundry to do and evening is encroaching. Your underground heart in God can grow right here.

A presentation for work goes sour. Your internal life in God can grow, minutes after it's over.

Third date with a guy you've started to like and you realize that he wants this one to be the last. This is where your insides can reach for God and grow.

The dream of writing a book, shelved alongside your

rejected manuscript, another closed door. This may be your greatest chance to grow, when no one sees and no one applauds.

Or maybe you've achieved your big goal or gotten the big promotion but still go home from the celebration party feeling empty, anxious that you won't be able to do what others expect. Even in your greatest successes, you get to have secret conversations with God. He sees you offstage and on Saturdays, away from your position.

Our growth in Him can happen at any venue and in any season of life. Whether or not our tasks, our careers, our families seem to be successful at the time. And the times that God hides us, sometimes away from success or applauding hands, are often the times when our roots reach deeper into the earth. We grow, down.

"She could go far with this," my daughter's piano teacher told me. "She picks it up quickly. She's advancing fast."

Whether in piano or sewing or art or math, my Renaissance girl is a quick study. Nate and I put her in a unique class that taught both music skills and praying God's Word because we wanted to see a tuning in her heart. We wanted to stretch her ability to play the piano alongside her reach for God.

The other children in class were a head shorter than her and years younger, yet my daughter felt intimidated. She'd grown up among bullies scavenging for any piece of security the orphanage could afford them, often at the expense of the quiet ones like her.

Two weeks into the class, she was invited to play while others sang and prayed. She'd mastered her latest piece in one week at home, pouring herself out over the keys while I was across the hall in my office and her siblings were upstairs building Lego villages. She'd often walk past the piano on her way up the stairs, only to find herself pulled back to the chair to play for just a few more minutes.

This was all when she thought no one was watching.

So it was in a rush of uncharacteristic bravery that she agreed to play for a dozen sets of eyes. But when the moment came, those eyes became like the ones haunting her memory. That midwestern classroom became a dirt courtyard in Africa. She convinced herself that she saw the teachers roll their eyes at each other while she played.

My skilled piano player missed nearly every chord, according to her teary description when she got home. A teacher kindly rushed to her rescue, coaching her with basic piano instructions but causing her little heart to sink even farther into shame. *Maybe I really do stink at this*, she thought.

The class shifted and another child, three years younger, took the bench and played seamlessly.

She ran into my bedroom as soon as she came home. "It was awful," she said. "I'm so embarrassed." She told me how her fingers fumbled and a younger child got the applause. "Now everyone thinks I'm a terrible piano player," she moaned.

If she had played in public the way she does in private, the room would have swelled with applause. The other students would look at her differently when she came for class next time. They'd see her no longer as the shy child in the back but as the girl with great promise on the keys.

But God had another plan for that Friday afternoon. He was forging her in hiddenness, offering her a private invitation to sink her roots in Him and grow.

So my beautiful girl and I pressed pause on the ruckus in her head, the perceptions of others and the embarrassment and imaginary jeers. We asked God what He thought about that moment.

She quieted the internal noise and heard a whisper.

"I think He liked that I got up there to play," she said with the first smile I'd seen from her since the class.

What her human audience might have thought and what her wounded imagination perceived were both drastically different from what God thought of her. At the tender time of youth, she knew that God liked what He saw in her—yes, even her weakness. And she grew that day as both a pianist and a child of God. God had a message for my girl that afternoon that sank deeper into her soul than a round of applause. He used her weakness, the weakness she resented, to hide her. He spoke a whisper she could hear only if she leaned, just a little more, into Him.

Hidden behind fumbling fingers, she asked Him the question she might never have asked if she had wowed the crowd with her keyboard skills: *What does God think about that moment? What does He think about me?*

78

God shielded her from her own idea of greatness and invited her to know His thoughts of her instead.

Her roots grew deeper that day. And it was the beginning of true greatness.

—————— *For Your Continued Pursuit* ——————

1 Samuel 16:7 | Psalm 1:3 | Psalm 37:4 | Psalm 46:10 | Psalm 52:8–9 | Jeremiah 17:7–8 | Matthew 5:19 | Matthew 13:5–6 | Matthew 13:21–23 | Matthew 18:4 | Matthew 20:26–27 | John 15:1–8 | Romans 8:18–19, 24–25 | 2 Corinthians 12:9 | Ephesians 3:17–21 | Ephesians 5:19 | Colossians 2:6–7 | 1 Thessalonians 5:17

five

Uncovered

Becoming Vulnerable

"She wiped His feet with her hair."

—John 12:3

I *didn't realize we were going to a house party*, I thought, feeling uncomfortable even before I crossed the threshold of this home we were visiting just a few years after being married. The walls of the brownstone reverberated with song, and heat from dozens of warm bodies packed inside made the windows sweat against the winter air.

A local worship band was belting out a familiar praise song, and the living room furniture had been moved to accommodate sound equipment and standing guests. This was a homemade mashup of rock concert and church—a party among friends, except we knew only the couple who'd brought us. Nate and I glanced at each other, exchanging a wordless question: *You sure we should stay?*

That's when I saw her.

Eyes closed, arms raised, body swaying. She looked to be in her fifties or sixties, lost in a dance that reminded me of what I'd picture to be a 1960s rock concert. She was all "out there," seemingly with no awareness that she might be making a spectacle of herself. First, I judged her. Then I speculated. *Who is her audience? Who exactly is she doing this for?*

I was familiar enough with my unfortunate habit of rushing to judgment to know that I needed to pause from these thoughts. So I decided to pray for this woman in an effort to win over my critical thoughts. As quickly as the judgment entered my mind, another thought followed: *You don't know what she's been through.*

My prayer continued intermittently throughout the evening. For some reason, I couldn't take my eyes off this woman. Because my default mode was judgment, I'd recently begun to practice asking God to show me His heart for people. As I prayed for God's heart for her, one thought came: *She's like Mary.* It came to me as my own thought, but I suspected it was a whisper from God. After all, the woman who poured out her alabaster livelihood to anoint Jesus was one of my favorites, and this woman at the party—well, I wasn't seeing her actions in a favorable light.

But then I felt a divine nudge to tell this woman what I was thinking—that she reminded me of Mary. *Ugh. I don't want to do that,* I thought. *Wouldn't talking to her only validate her attention-seeking behavior?* (Another one of judgment's lies: that I was somehow responsible for correcting this woman's behavior.)

Even so, I hesitantly approached her at the back of the room where she now stood.

"I've felt a nudge to pray for you tonight," I said somewhat awkwardly, shouting above the worship band and not exactly looking her in the eye. "As I prayed, I saw you to be like Mary of Bethany."

She looked away, and then back at me. "You don't know what I've been through," she said.

I was speechless.

"In the past seventeen months, I've lost both my son and my husband," she said. "They both died. Worshiping God is the only place I find joy."

I was silenced, reminded again how getting even an inch deep into someone else's unseen story can change everything. Maybe I'd come to the party just for this, just for her.

In the decade that followed—the first decade of our marriage—I got to be this woman. Not because I learned to dance so freely in front of others but because I had my own story of loss and emptiness. I had a barren womb with little hope for healing, and reaching for God became the only way I could find joy. I canceled Friday night plans so I could stay home and pray. I rearranged my schedule so I had more time to cry and lament over my Bible. I propped up His Word on the treadmill at the gym, determined to use every available moment to soak in every line I could. I was falling in love with God through pain, caring less and less what others thought of me. Like the woman at the party, my response to my losses made me a little weird too. I was grieving and bleeding and needed a new sort of encounter with the God who is near to the vulnerable and brokenhearted.

Barrenness is about what you don't have, so it often goes undetected. I was sick—my body wasn't working—but I didn't have crutches or a sling. I had only my unchanging waistline. Like the grieving woman at the party, I had a story no one knew unless they took the time to ask. And few asked. My untold story forced me into a season of vulnerability before God, all while He hid me from the eyes of others.

The "Mary" I met at the party that night poured herself out at Jesus' feet not out of duty but because He was all she had left. Her circumstances had stripped her of everything but one truth: *He is all I have, He is husband to me, and His love is stunning.* She gave Him the kind of worship one can give only from a thin place—a place where the separation between this world and eternity seems to dissolve, a place where we believe and experience God's love in a visceral way.

My empty womb ushered me into that thin place, the place where I began to believe—not just say—that God's love is real. With every bleeding day, I was forced to reveal myself, in pain, before His eyes. And that's when I discovered how truly beautiful His eyes are. Only then could I pour myself out at His feet with unhinged, unembarrassed, extravagant devotion.

In Mary's day, hair was a woman's glory and her covering. Jewish women uncoiled their hair only for private moments within their own homes. To let down one's hair in public was scandalous behavior—and exactly what Mary did that night as Jesus reclined at the table. She not only let down her hair but also "took a pound of very costly oil of spikenard, anointed the feet of Jesus, and wiped His feet with her hair" (John 12:3).

Mary wiped Jesus' feet with her *hair*. She unwound the covering she'd hidden behind, her adornment, and used it to anoint Jesus' dirty feet. Her earthly glory brushed up against the Savior's humanity. Improper. Disgraceful. She used her covering and glory as a rag.

The men around the table judged her.

But the Son of God was moved.

Hers was an extravagant devotion. Adoration with God alone in mind. She chose to be vulnerable before the one who already knew her deepest longings. And Jesus called her vulnerability beautiful.

Mary did what few of us will allow ourselves to do: she disregarded both the approval and disapproval of those around the table so she could give the most outwardly beautiful part of herself to Jesus. Right in front them. Unashamed at her lack of restraint. She allowed herself to become unhinged in her expression of love. She lived out what she and all of humankind were created to crave: an unhindered, unashamed reach for God.

I was twenty-three. It was on a moonlit September night in Virginia, when the air still felt heavy like summer, that I told Nate I couldn't stop thinking about him. I blurted it out in an uncharacteristic rush of emotion. Our relationship changed in an instant with that admission, though we sat still in the car, letting the words hang as if they were echoing.

We didn't say much as time passed in his car, parked next

to my office, nestled in the windy streets of the old university town where we lived. I shifted and accidentally brushed his knee, and it was a touch as electric as those blurted words had been. I think I fell in love that night.

I'll never again make the turn onto Chancellor Street without remembering it as the place where everything changed. Where I surrendered to the vulnerability of love.

I have similar feelings about the dozens of places where I've surrendered to the vulnerability of love with God. Tender times when He cupped His hands around my story and hid me. My words to Him were raw, unfiltered, awkward. But He was tender and responsive. These were the ripest conditions for love to grow. When I was uncharacteristically vulnerable, He hid me in His love and drew me near.

Those vulnerable experiences with God have a way of sticking with us just like Chancellor Street does in my story with Nate. "In the secret place of His tabernacle He shall hide me," writes the psalmist (Ps. 27:5). Yet we still tend to avoid that kind of vulnerability with God. Our experiences of vulnerability with other flawed human beings too often leave us guarded and cautious. We shrink back from baring our souls. It's not safe. So we partake in the most elusive form of hiding: we hide from God.

We aren't the first.

Then the eyes of both of them were opened, and they knew that they were naked; and they sewed fig leaves together and made themselves coverings.

And they heard the sound of the LORD God walking

in the garden in the cool of the day, and Adam and his wife hid themselves from the presence of the LORD God among the trees of the garden.

Then the LORD God called to Adam and said to him, "Where are you?"

So he said, "I heard Your voice in the garden, and I was afraid because I was naked; and I hid myself."

—GENESIS 3:7–10

Adam and Eve were the first but certainly not the last to hide from God. Nakedness before God—the creator of blood, bone, sinews, and flesh—became the shared fear of humanity when Adam and Eve sinned. In their shame and embarrassment, they hid.

"Embarrassment is actually sin," says my husband, who knows my self-protective and self-preserving ways. I might say instead, "Embarrassment reveals sin." It might happen like this:

We've had friends over for dinner, and I've fumbled through expressing something near to my heart. I mixed words and misrepresented myself. I'm embarrassed the next morning, regretting that I doled out personal intimacies in a way that wasn't received. My embarrassment reveals that my highest goal is to preserve the image I've given of myself. I lash myself instead of talking to God.

I am afraid because I am naked. And I hide myself from God in self-condemnation.

I'm three minutes down the road from the house that held that baby shower, all those women corralled around one round belly, celebrating, and I want to defame them in my mind. I want to defend myself as a woman who still has value despite not being able to enter their rite of passage. I want to judge them for not recognizing my ache amid their cheers. I'm ashamed of what I don't have, so I criticize those who have it.

I am afraid because I am naked. And I hide myself from God in anger.

There are six small bodies in the car, but it feels like ten. The two in the far back have been bickering, and the babe is hungry and tired. One of my girls is hurting deeply, she stares blankly out the window, lost within her mind. I look behind the seat and discover remnants of last week's lunch molding on the floor mats. *How long until bedtime?* I wonder, eager for this day to be done. I'm resenting my role as a mother today, and even more, my response to it. How can I go to God like this?

I am afraid because I am naked. And I hide myself from God while simply waiting for this hard moment to pass.

These bare places are invitations. God invites us to exchange what feels raw and vulnerable for His strength. God never intended for us to hide from Him, to live with parts of us untouchable to Him. It's in those naked-place moments—the times we allow ourselves to be exposed before God—that He covers us with Himself, blankets us in His safe love, and replaces our exposed weakness with His strength.

"For Adam and his wife the LORD God made tunics of skin, and clothed them" (Gen. 3:21). Even after we've been exposed by our sin and failures, God covers us. He restores what feels like shards from the broken parts of our story and hides us in Himself, all so that we can take the risk to unveil ourselves before Him again.

Who told you that you were naked? asked the God who sees every part of us. And He teaches us the safe place to be seen.

Shortly after we'd adopted Eden and Caleb, a Christian counselor friend who'd worked with children for years observed them playing in his waiting room. We'd described to him their first few months at home with us, and he witnessed what we'd said and more. Even when we weren't within immediate reach, they played freely and without fear. They took delight in trinkets, but even more so in one another, as ones who were already siblings before they became our family. Their eyes were bright with curiosity and playfulness, not deadened or dull.

"There's a word for that," our friend said. "They are 'invulnerables.'"

He spoke to what we'd hoped was true—that Eden and Caleb showed little signs of the loss that had shrouded the years before they could even walk. Despite their traumatic beginnings, the souls of our children—former orphans—had been preserved.

I was relieved.

We'd said yes to them, our first two children to bring home, knowing full well what the experts said about the possible implications of early abandonment. We hung on to optimism more than we did to hope. Optimism is often naive, but hope is forged. (We were too new at this to have forged real hope.) Eden would always stand up for her little brother,

Caleb, and lean into me as Mommy. Caleb would trust. Their eyes would always be bright with expectation. They were the rare kind of "normal" that comes out of abnormality.

Phew. Both Nate and I knew we weren't cut out for deep-seated pain as new parents. So we called them the Invulnerables and exhaled in relief.

Until one day we couldn't anymore.

Growth and time and new siblings added to the mix a few years later revealed worn edges that two-on-two hadn't. One struggled to trust. Another to receive love. The brightness in their eyes waned for a time. A little bit of pressing and we saw tired years behind those wide smiles. Life had worked them over before we held them for the first time. They weren't as invulnerable as they once appeared. But really, is anyone?

I don't relish thinking of myself as vulnerable. I resent the tears I cry over missing my dad when something reminds me of him in the middle of someone else's birthday dinner. I cringe to think I may have "over shared" with a new friend over coffee. I blush when my child says something inappropriate in public. I don't want to send the text for the third day in a row that begs, "I need prayer." I feel naked before the friend with two older (more composed) children who stops by unexpectedly and sees my wreck of a house on a Tuesday afternoon.

Really, who *doesn't* want be an invulnerable? We've bought into the lie that exposing our hearts—in even the smallest of ways—brings only pain. And we take that lie into our exchanges with God.

The one who makes that 9:00 p.m. crisis call to friends

to say, "Our marriage is stuck. Can we come over and get some help?" wakes up to a morning-after "Why didn't we just deal with it ourselves?" gulp of shame. The fifty-year-old single woman who musters courage to whisper to her Bible study group, "I'd like to be married. Would you pray that I might meet someone I could love?" leaves the night feeling foolish for putting herself out there. The wannabe songwriter performs with passion the first song he ever wrote and receives only a smattering of polite applause. He steps off the stage promising himself he will never take a risk like that again. The woman with the baby in the NICU asks God—out loud and in front of the medical staff—to save her son despite his terminal diagnosis, only to wonder, *What if God doesn't come through? What will everyone say about my wild, foolish prayers?*

And yet vulnerability, to God, is beautiful. It incites Him. He moves *in* and near when we are vulnerable. "The LORD is near to those who have a broken heart," writes the psalmist (Ps. 34:18). We all have parts of ourselves that are broken. He invites us to expose those broken parts to Him. As authors Dan Allender and Tremper Longman describe it, "Brokenness is the antidote to shame."[4]

If I allow myself to be vulnerable with God only during the big crisis but not the morning-after embarrassment, whole continents of my heart will remain dark and hidden from the only light that can heal them. And God wants to heal them all. I pray for "more of God," but I rarely grow in personal, intimate understanding of Him without first becoming vulnerable.

To be an invulnerable is to be impenetrable. But those

who turn to God and hide their otherwise-shamed faces in His chest? Those are the ones who hear His heartbeat.

We haven't been hidden by God to suffer or to be punished; we've been wooed into hiding to meet with the God who turns vulnerability into communion. And, yes, this is true not just for our wounds but even in response to our sin. Many times it is our sin that causes us to erect walls and become hardened and distant to God. God draws us into the vulnerability of exposure that comes with repentance. And in the wake of our returning to Him, we find communion. We lean a little bit more into surrender.

God welcomes our most vulnerable selves not simply because He already witnesses every unseen moment of our lives. He welcomes us when we're vulnerable because He knows what it is like to be vulnerable.

Author C. S. Lewis states it this way: "God could, had he pleased, have been incarnate in a man of iron nerves, the Stoic sort who lets no sigh escape him. Of his great humility he chose to be incarnate in a man of delicate sensibilities who wept at the grave of Lazarus and sweated blood in Gethsemane . . . He has faced all that the weakest of us face, has shared not only the strength of our nature but every weakness of it except sin. If he had been incarnate in a man of immense natural courage, that would have been for many of us almost the same as his not being incarnate at all."[5]

Jesus' body broke. He subjected Himself to weakness, though without sin.

Jesus experienced perhaps the most severe form of hiding as He was laid in the "dust of death" (Ps. 22:15). He was naked, disrobed, and mocked by men His hands had formed. Hidden from their understanding. The Son of God who had no sin within Him was vulnerable to the death.

The God whose Spirit enables the breath inside my chest endured a far worse rejection than I ever will. From that vulnerable place, Jesus cried out words through the mouth of David: "Do not be far from Me" (Ps. 22:19). And these are the words He invites us to pray from the depths of our own vulnerability. In His weakness, when He was poured out like water, He gave us permission to be vulnerable, undone. And our vulnerability, only a mere shadow of His, can call up the same cry within us: *God, be near.*

This nearness is most brilliant when I am most weak, here at the nexus of hiddenness and vulnerability before God. He redefines my circumstances even without changing them. When that happens, I no longer resent being hidden, because now I share with Jesus the devastating pain of human rejection. He is no longer just familiar to me. He is the one whose callused, earth-stained fingers gently hold the tender parts of my heart, the raw and bleeding parts of me. He is the one who loves for me to be exposed before Him, leaning in.

∞

Soon after having kids, Nate and I decided that Saturday, not Sunday, would be our day of Sabbath rest. And Saturdays are my weekly reminder of just how much I resist being vulnerable.

We stay in our jammies on Saturdays. We boil the teapot,

several times. Nate and I read our Bibles and books while the kids build forts in the woods and upstairs. We go for walks and let the laundry sit and leave the kitchen a mess—for just a few hours. We breathe, soaking in new ideas and old truths about this God who loves us and hides us close. I read poetry.

It sounds like bliss, but around 2:00 p.m. every Saturday, that same dreaded feeling creeps into my chest. The respite of unplanned hours wears off, and I move into the empty space of the afternoon. I start to wonder, *Who am I with all this time and nothing accomplished with it?*

On Saturdays, I'm reminded of why Sunday through Friday's schedule tempts me to fill it. Too much space and time not filled with boxes to check and tasks to accomplish and worlds to change leave me feeling naked. Exposed. *Who am I without my accomplishments? Who am I without my to-do list?*

As with Adam and Eve in the garden of Eden, our humanity requires coaxing to come out of hiding before God. It is often much easier to obey God's rules than to allow our souls to lean into a fuller surrender of ourselves unto Him. Surrender is vulnerable, and this choice to risk vulnerability with God takes practice. Observing a Sabbath makes this practice frequent. And frequently painful.

I come to those afternoons feeling a combination of empty, squirmy, and uncertain. But He always slides His hand into mine and opens a new world to me—my deeper thoughts, my true feelings, the undercurrent of emotions I've kept buried underneath busy.

I used to say, "Life stops on Saturday in the Hagerty home." This was when I still held on to vestiges of the belief that productivity is the marrow of life. But the empty feeling that persisted on the days when life unproductively "stopped" made me vulnerable and eventually opened a new side of me to God, the side that was safely inviting me to do more than just obey, but to surrender. Now I say, "Saturdays are when life happens in our home." Saturdays are when I am less busy, more weak. Less accomplished, more present. Saturdays are when I fall a little more in love with God. Saturdays are a step toward a deeper surrender.

We have a petri dish of a home. Having eight different bodies doesn't mean only eight different personalities and eight different body types. In our house, we have eight different beginnings, started in three different countries and cultures.

Some people call my toddler son, Bo, or my newborn daughter, Virginia—the ones my body gave birth to—"my own," but all of my children are my own. However, even as I notice each of my children in their uniqueness, I sometimes use Bo as my benchmark to better recognize and understand any differences between how he and his siblings relate to me and reach out for connection.

Several summers ago when I was away from my children for a night, I lay on a hotel room bed and talked to God and had a rush of understanding about my kids—and about beautiful, confident vulnerability.

"Up, please." In my mind's eye, I saw Bo's wide eyes and outstretched arms.

My babe looks up at me with expectation and says this one phrase more times in a day than I can count. It's the first one he learned. At 7:30 a.m., he's squeaking it, his voice rusty from sleep and his body ready to be held. At 9:30 a.m., it's a cry for relief. He's been in the sibling-care rotation and needs the steadiness of Mommy's arms. Sometimes it's said with a quivering lower lip and eyes brimming with tears.

"Up, please"—the incessant plea of the well-tethered child. Up from the world of blocks and puzzles and rowdy siblings and back into the place of sure safety. All day long, I'm reminded that I have one who needs me. One who _knows_ he needs me.

Four others need me too. But they never got to say, "Up, please." Instead, they bury their "up, please" behind eyes that don't cry or that cry as a way of trying to manipulate love. Shame and rejection can shove that vulnerable "up, please" way down, as if to say, _I never again want to feel that ache of needing and not receiving, so I won't ask the question that leaves me with my arms in the air and no one on the other side to pick me up._

"Up, please" is a dangerous request for any of us who question love. Somewhere after saying yes to Jesus, life taught us that "up, please" is for babies. And we don't want to be babies to God.

"Truly I tell you," Jesus said, "unless you change and become like little children, you will never enter the kingdom of heaven" (Matt. 18:3 NIV). This verse is on our grandmother's wall and in cartooned storybooks. We know it by heart. But if we're honest, we don't really like it.

I'd rather not be like a child. I don't want to fumble over my words in a crowd. I don't want my eyes to be red at church from a "discussion" I had with my husband in the car. I don't want to be pushing forty and needing to ask, *What broke at fifteen to make me still keep struggling with that same issue?*

I don't want to be diapered and drool.

To be honest, I don't really want to need God.

Instead, I want to crawl out of weak skin and take notes on a five-point lecture on how to grow my love for God, because wouldn't we all rather learn the hard lessons about love in a tidy sermon than in the rough-and-tumble of our lives? Yet He keeps inviting me to be bare with Him, to sit before Him and let down my heart and ask the questions and wait on His answers. *Be vulnerable and stay vulnerable* is quite the invitation in a world that praises and rewards the invulnerables. The dozen moments in a day that I resent because they remind me that I'm weak are the ones when God wants to hear my faltering voice: "Up, please."

Needy tears have become a treasure in our house. When pain spills out through eight- and ten- and eleven-year-old versions of "up, please," we celebrate. We give long cuddles to reaffirm that raw, vulnerable hearts are hearts on their way to coming alive.

Hey, you in hiding, where are the places you're working hardest to be strong? What causes you to shut down on a given day? What is it that makes you want to send a panicked text to a friend or to escape behind a screen or to rummage in the fridge for something to eat? Where are the places you're coaching yourself to be tough?

Invite God there.

Sometimes we are all too familiar with those places in our lives, but other times it takes practice to recognize them. Search His Word and ask Him to teach you about *you*, and to teach you about Him, right in the midst of the rawest, weakest parts of your life.

Mary let down her hair and elicited a gasp from those around her as she did. Yet with this one act, she inched herself away from self-protection and into the presence of God. Into a deeper surrender to Him. Her moment can be ours, every day. Ask God to help you let down your hair in vulnerability, in adoration. For Him.

My babe cries an "up, please" about as often as I need to say an "up, please" of my own. My vulnerable heart, and your vulnerable heart, needs routinely to climb into God's lap. The more we reach up for God, the more we'll grow, and in the hidden corners of our hearts, the more willing we'll become to choose vulnerability again. To inch toward a deeper surrender to Him and to His story for our lives. When we acknowledge our frailty before God, He offers us wisdom and strength. The psalmist understood this truth when he prayed, "Behold, You desire truth in the inward parts, and in the hidden part You will make me to know wisdom" (Ps. 51:6).

Stop hiding from God. Come out, vulnerable and raw before Him with new strength. *His* strength. Sit at His feet and allow the warmth of His tender eyes to bore through you, to see what's most vulnerable in you, and to respond to it.

—————— *For Your Continued Pursuit* ——————

Genesis 3:7–11 | Genesis 3:21 | Psalm 5:3 | Psalm 7:9 | Psalm 18:6 | Psalm 22 | Psalm 26:8 | Psalm 27:5 | Psalm 31 | Psalm 34:18 | Psalm 51 | Psalm 63:5–7 | Psalm 91:4 | Psalm 119:151 | Psalm 145:18 | Hosea 2:14–15 | Matthew 18:3 | Matthew 27:35–37 | John 1:16 | John 12:3 | John 15:9 | Romans 8:1–2 | Romans 11:17–18 | 1 Corinthians 11:15 | 2 Corinthians 4:7–12 | 2 Corinthians 5:16–20 | 2 Corinthians 12:7–10

six

INVITATION TO WONDER

Training Our Eyes to See God's Beauty

"And the house was filled with
the fragrance of oil."
—JOHN 12:3

Hope had been working for days on a project that was nondescript and yet time intensive.

She carried her colored pencils in a pouch that she pulled out whenever she had spare minutes. She discreetly slid her work into a basket of books beside her bed when we came to tuck her in at night. She seemed as giddy about the secret creativity as she was about the upcoming reveal.

Finally, the day came when Hope tiptoed into my bedroom with her hands behind her back. It was as if her person was so linked to this project that both the art and her body needed to carry this sacred surprise in a whisper.

"See, Mommy?" she said as she held out a collection of folded pages in front of her. Her face beamed with the sweet confidence of a child who knows she created something beautiful. She'd spent weeks working in anticipation of my delight—she knew I'd love it. And of course I did—in that way that a parent sees focused attention and sweat and persistence as the real prize of any project.

Hope had written a book—a book! My child, still in early readers, had copied drawings from other books and cobbled together phrases to "tell the story of Jesus." The gospel story was intermingled with sketches from *Little House on the Prairie* and *Paddington Bear*—a child's version of how God stretches across all of her scenery.

She wanted to be just like her mommy: a writer. Never mind that she was still sounding out three- and four-letter words, my child wanted to be just like me.

Children often mimic their parents. At five, I wanted to be a teacher, just like my parents. Our son Caleb used to push an overused and ailing baby stroller alongside Nate while he mowed the lawn. Three of our older girls have clanked across our bathroom tiles in my high heels, talking about dates with their husbands and weddings they're attending. At nearly two, Bo made a baby out of a plush pig. He held the pig like I hold him. While I type these pages, eleven-year-old Lily sits beside me with a stack of poetry books and a sketchpad, just like her mommy.

We are, all of us, created to be image bearers. It is written into our DNA.

God made us to wear another's likeness.

His.

"Then God said, 'Let us make man in our image, after our likeness'" (Gen. 1:26 ESV).

So we naturally search within our stories for images to

bear. And then we mimic what we see. Our mimicking begins when we are infants and continues as we age. During the metamorphosis from child to adult, we either begin to see God within our story or we begin to work the room in search of another image to bear. Often it's a little of both.

Daily, these little decisions to look up at God or look around at everyone else might seem insignificant, but only until we get backed into the corner of our circumstances or placed in a season of hiddenness. Then whatever image it is that we've been mimicking reveals itself for what it is—lasting or temporal, truth or facade.

"The lamp of the body is the eye," Jesus says (Matt. 6:22), and my eye can look many directions in one single day without ever leaving home. It's possible for me to see my best friend from first grade winning a mother-daughter footrace and another friend's op-ed in the *New York Times*. I can see my sister traveling to Europe and my cousin's first sale in the business she launched. I can see that an acquaintance from church spent her morning with her Bible and a cup of tea. All in a brief glance at a screen.

Offline, I can see a mother who's ushered her four children under five (all in matching outfits with their hair combed) into a coffee shop, and a neighbor who's come back from a five-mile run. I can see a lawn with fewer weeds than ours and a car with less rust and a home that has a pool. I can see a physically fit mom pushing a stroller effortlessly and another wearing a cute pair of new pumps.

These are all fine things to notice and admire as long as I'm already certain of the one whose image I'm bearing, if I'm certain of His thoughts about those hundreds of minutes in my day that no one else sees.

But it's all subtly destructive when I scan these images and fail to turn my eyes back to God. They too often become a checklist of all the ways I am less than: less than organized, less than responsible, less than spiritual, less than athletic, less than beautiful.

We become what we behold. When we're eager to mimic or to catalogue what we're missing, the way out isn't in internal chastisement or creating a rigorous self-improvement plan. The escape hatch is in where we set our eyes. God invites us to turn our eyes back to Him, to bear His image.

God is not just the creator of beauty. He is beauty itself. We become what we behold, and that beauty swells within us whenever we choose to behold Him.

I imagine that even though the jar of perfumed oil Mary wore around her neck was tightly sealed, it still released a fragrance. I picture her warming the bottle between her palms and holding it close, tracing the seal with her fingers, inhaling even the faintest whiff of scent.

Mary herself may have been something like that sealed container. Perhaps she kept her heart just as locked, doling out only small fragments of herself to friends and family.

Until she met Jesus.

As she had grown to know Him, she wanted only to know Him more and to be known by Him. She wanted to be like

Him, and she wanted to give Him more of what she'd tucked away to keep safe from others.

On the night her trembling hands broke the neck of the flask, her senses awakened. This woman whose days knew duty and practicality, sat in awe, enraptured. Her heart raced in love as the smell of the pungent oil, no longer a trace scent, enveloped her. Flooded her. Extravagance seeped from one room into the entire house.

The exchange was intimate and ravishing, rich for the senses of any who had eyes for what was truly happening as this woman gave herself away in the breaking of her jar, as she not only saw beauty from a distance but imbibed it.

She adored Him with the oil, with her hair unkempt. He was now even more beautiful to her. And she was becoming her true self as she moved nearer to Him.

Everyone there inhaled the anointing. All present could choose to look at Him—humbly radiant—or at her and at each other, criticizing her wasteful choice.

But her eyes were only on Jesus.

I'd barely sat down in the reading nook off to the side of our bedroom when I paused to look out the glass doors that open to our back porch and yard. The sky was suddenly aflame with color. Auburn with streaks of burnt gold illuminated my back yard, making silhouettes out of my favorite trees. I'm so unfamiliar with our landscape at dusk that I actually gasped when I saw it.

Most days as the sun goes down, I'm catering a meal for several voracious eaters or corralling children into pajamas and beds. But on this particular night, Nate had taken the kids to basketball practice and I'd tucked myself away, enjoying the stillness that fell on the house after the flurry of tying shoes and snatching water bottles and shoveling in "one more bite."

For the five minutes it took the sun to fall, I was rapt. Tearful, even. *You painted the sky for me*, I whispered to remind myself. And to acknowledge Him, because this was His doing.

His love notes are stashed everywhere. Every day in my back yard, there is a sunset. Every day in my back yard, there is riveting beauty. God's beauty is made for beholding. For *receiving*.

"If you want true beauty, look into the face of Jesus," writes preacher Charles Spurgeon.[6] Beauty is in the lines of His face, the humanity He wore for you and for me. But we tend to be a people of quick glances—even with God. Life at warp speed allows for little beholding. We are increasingly accustomed to three-minute waits and one-click purchases. And in our approach to God, we follow the same pattern. We want the soundbites. Or we wait in expectation for barked, impersonal orders. Or we expect to barrel through life and then sit down for thirty minutes and somehow find focus, though our hearts were racing for the other twenty-three and a half hours of our day. We want to gaze on God's beauty, we want to look into Jesus' face, but speed and beauty rarely coexist.

Hidden seasons invite us to slow down, to notice the beauty too often blurred by hurry, to cultivate the same wonder a toddler experiences watching a butterfly for the first time. Life's "little things"—the sunset behind the winter treeline, the flock of geese in perfect formation overhead, the aspens blazing in fall, the chicken-scratched love note left by a spouse under the coffeepot—all of these are mere reflections of another beauty. "God had created lower things to be signs that pointed to higher spiritual realities," writes George Marsden of Jonathan Edwards' perception of reality. "The universe, then, was a complex language of God. Nothing in it was accidental. Everything pointed to a higher meaning."[7] That we so often miss them reveals that we're also missing beauty in His truest form: Jesus.

Whether or not we are in a hidden season, whether or not we are in a busy season, we have to pause long enough to *look*. This look is not a passive look. Looking at God's beauty increases our desire for more of Him. It can grow our desire to look again. And again.

When we approach God with an open, mindful, hungry heart, we position ourselves not only to see His beauty but to let it change us.

I got a glimpse of God's beauty when Hope was baptized—submerged in water, wearing a dress over her bathing suit, exposed and still hidden as she told a dozen sets of eyes that she'd given her life to Jesus. I inhaled on that Sunday afternoon, receiving that this child and her life rested more deeply in God's grip than I had assessed.

I saw God's beauty when Lily leaped out of the car that brought her to our guest home in Uganda and squealed, "Daddy!" as she looked at her father's face, in person, for the first time. That night I lifted my eyes away from the fear of how this adoption might turn sour. Seeing a glimpse of what God was doing in it all infused faith into me.

I saw God's beauty on the day Nate proposed to me, and on the day, months earlier, when I knew I would marry that boy. I never thought I wanted the kind of love Nate offered. It threatened me and often caused me to retreat. But God showed me He knew my needs better than I did when I took time to look at the beauty behind this boy's pursuit of me.

I saw God's beauty in the countenance of a rough-worn teenager who bowed her heart to the love of God for the first time. In pausing to look in, as much as I could as an outsider, I started to believe that His beauty could overshadow any darkness.

I saw God's beauty in the lunar eclipse last night, on which millions of eyes were fixed. And that look changes me when I realize there is a Creator behind it, inviting me to see His creation and Himself as the best investment of my eyes.

But it's harder for me to see God's beauty late in the afternoon, in the thousands of minutes in the middle of my days that don't seem worthy of photographing or scrapbooking or sharing with others. He tells us in His Word that His glory is ever available, and it's tucked inside every day. Every single one.

> The heavens declare the glory of God,
>> and the sky above proclaims his handiwork.
> Day to day pours out speech,
>> and night to night reveals knowledge.
> There is no speech, nor are there words,
>> whose voice is not heard.

Their voice goes out through all the earth,
and their words to the end of the world.

—PSALM 19:1–4 ESV

It's my eyes that need training to see it in the middle minutes.

Too often, we relegate things like silence and wonder to others, such as monks or poets—the naturally contemplative, the ones we consider either social misfits or spiritual giants. We assume that these quiet, hidden times with God aren't for the extroverts, the social, the normal. We aren't that kind of odd or that kind of deep, and so we just don't go there, as if spending time looking long at God is only for weird loners or spiritual superheroes.

But when we cut ourselves off from attending to God in the quiet and the small, we're cutting ourselves off from soul food, starving ourselves of our life source, which is the unconventional sitting at His feet and seeing Him throughout every messy, wonder-filled moment of our day. We choose wonder when we look at God and talk with Him—even, and maybe especially, at the odd times. Author and pastor Eugene Peterson writes, "In prayer we intend to leave the world of anxieties and enter a world of wonder. We decide to leave an ego-centered world and enter a God-centered world. We will to leave a world of problems and enter a world of mystery. But it is not easy. We are used to anxieties, egos and problems; we are not used to wonder, God and mystery."[8]

Wonder means cracking open our eyes to see God, who is seeing us, *all the time*.

But wonder is sometimes shy. It slips the notice of hearts that refuse to look for it in the minutia of life.

Thus, God hides us.

Yes, even after the family skirmish and the flat tire and the visit to the doctor's office for the third time in one week—all things no one outside our world would know about—God calls us to wonder. We can ask Him to speak to us, then. We can find life in His Word, then. We can reach for His nearness, then. A life trained toward scanning the day for His wonders at *those* times is a life sinking its roots, strong, into love.

The moon has become our nightlight. The children are in bed, but not asleep. I open and close the front door with my hand on the latch so little ears can't hear.

I slide out into the evening, slippered, blanketed by a blue sky fading into dark black. I pad slowly around the circular drive in front of our house. I relish the quiet and the walls that separate me from the hum of the dishwasher, the rumble of the dryer, and the mindless thumps of Caleb's feet against the wall as he lies on his back and reads in bed.

I start praying, my insides filling the quiet with internal noise. I'm now both talking to God and listening to myself. It's never simple to get quiet.

After a few laps around our circular drive, I notice something, hear something I'd missed when my mind was still full from the day.

The crickets are loud, a synchrony to their hum. Something else is buzzing. I turn my head to listen. *What else in creation is awake at 8:00 p.m.?*

I hear movement on the hardened crabgrass that edges the woods—deer or coyotes, perhaps. And then an owl hoots in the far distance. The breeze picks up and the leaves skitter, awakened from their dormancy, and make their presence known. In some ways, the night outside is louder than dinnertime inside my home. There is a world out here, refusing to be quiet, refusing to be still and rest.

I smirk. I understand that kind of refusal. Cacophony is the soundtrack for my days. Even the nondescript parts of my day make noise. There is the constant buzz from the dryer producing piles of laundry that needs to be folded, the squeals and hollers of giddy children, and even the background hum of ocean waves from the white-noise machine in the upstairs bedroom—we often forget to turn it off, even when no one is asleep.

Quiet doesn't just happen. Ever.

Not even out here.

Internal stillness takes practice. It is the fruit of hiddenness—a life that's lived looking at God, a life of wonder in Him—and it needs to be cultivated.

Our fast-paced culture, our growing connectivity to friends all over the country, our endless to-do lists, and sometimes even the quietest of nights that allow for our unfettered and weighty thoughts to get loud oppose the communion that makes our hearts grow wildly deep. Perhaps all that goes against our calling to gaze at God's beauty only reinforces the need to look for it.

Elizabeth Barrett Browning says it aptly in her epic poem "Aurora Leigh":

> Earth's crammed with heaven,
> And every common bush afire with God:
> But only he who sees, takes off his shoes,
> The rest sit round it, and pluck blackberries.

Only those who see this beauty of His tucked within the ordinary are able to receive it as holy.

God loves to interrupt our days with Himself. He is always speaking, calling us back to our senses—back to what truly makes us come alive—inviting us to pause long enough to turn our eyes His way.

When my daughter Eden shouts from the yard on a busy afternoon, "It's a dove!" I peek out from the upstairs window to see a bird perched on our front walk, and something inside me stirs. A hummingbird that could fit inside my palm hovers over my zinnias out front, and the routine spin of my day stops. The sun catches Bo's hair as he looks up at Nate, and in that sweet, ordinary moment, I feel God call me to attention with this whispered love note.

I didn't always notice these things. I noticed birds when they left droppings on my car, and trees when their leaves clogged my gutters. They were things that needed my tending, my cleaning, my managing. The sunrise in the early morning blinded me on my morning run, and dusk was merely a transition to bedtime.

God was speaking, but I was too busy tasking to listen.

But when God hid me in difficult circumstances and the misunderstandings of others and within the confines of what many would call the mundane, I had time to notice these stealthily planted love notes. I began to see Him speaking with more than just instructions for good Christian living.

He wanted my affection, not my work. My willing lean into surrender.

The heavens were declaring the glory and the wonder and the beauty of God, and in these hidden seasons, I was aware that the deepest craving of my heart was to see Him. Everywhere.

Two years ago, I entered a season with a new baby and a new book, both needing my time and focused attention. It was in the midst of the flurry of responding to these needs that I realized I was waiting for life to somehow slow down so I could fully engage with God. Sure, I gave Him my time, but my mind and my heart weren't all there. I wasn't fully present with Him.

I had a mental list of things we'd talk about, God and me, when I finally had time to rest. I wasn't ignoring the need to rest before God and sit at His feet. Instead, I was working hard to get there. Once all the items on my list were checked off, I'd be in. I was looking at spending time with God as something that happened when all the work of life was complete, not something I could choose right in the middle of barreling through it.

So I instituted what I called my "wonder hour." In the midst of tending to my children's growing needs and book publicity and piles of winter laundry—extra socks and coats and gloves, every single week—I started to carve out time to wonder, to look at God.

I wrote "wonder hour" into slots on my calendar several times a week. This time was separate from my morning quiet time, and right in the middle of when I could be otherwise productive. And I did it as a way to make my schedule say what my heart wanted to say: *Jesus, sitting at Your feet is never a waste of time.* During wonder hour, I chose to trust God with a part of my life I clung to most tightly: my time.

I closed the bedroom door, hung an antique brown key on the handle to signal to all the little people on the other side of the door that I was not to be disturbed, and I opened my mind to God. Some days I read the Psalms, and other days the gospels. Some days I read poetry that lifted my eyes to Him or a book that might stir me toward a greater understanding of His hand in my life.

I said with my schedule, *You, God, are the best thing I have going today.* My to-do list might be stymied, but my wonder hour was a concrete way for me to hide myself in God, to choose holy wonder over productivity. It was a reach toward surrendering my story to God by surrendering my schedule and squandering my time—with Him.

I still schedule wonder hours into my weeks, and it still isn't easy. I have to fight for it. The days are full. And when I say fight, I mean the battle that goes on inside myself. It always seems a lot easier to tackle grocery shopping for the week than it does to settle quietly into conversation with God. But one movement in that direction, no matter how small (even ten minutes), creates a pathway for wonder over time. As life gets even more full—more laundry, more "can I lie across your bed and talk to you, Mommy?" minutes, more ideas brewing to put on a page, more friends in deep need—I am continuing, ever so slowly, to pattern my life toward what I first began to learn when I canceled plans to cry over my Bible after yet another baby shower: tucked away in a hidden place, looking to God is what brings me back to life.

Still in the fog of morning sluggishness and with a thinly veiled air of motherly annoyance, I dropped my four older children at soccer practice with water bottles and balls and snacks in baggies. I thought perhaps I could use a few laps around a field to clear my head. So I put two-year-old Bo in the stroller with no plan for where to walk, just knowing I needed to pound it out on the pavement. The chaotic early morning rush to get everyone ready and out the door had shredded my nerves. I struggled to like my kids in that single moment, and I surely didn't like myself. I was remembering why we didn't do these early morning activities very often.

On days like this, I have to whittle life down to one passage, which is part of training my eyes to see wonder: "On the glorious splendor of your majesty, and on your wondrous works, I will meditate. They shall speak of the might of your awesome deeds, and I will declare your greatness" (Ps. 145:5–6 ESV).

I pushed and pounded harder than necessary to move the stroller, but with as much exertion as I needed to work out the morning's frustrations. I recited these verses in my head a dozen times while replaying the last forty-five minutes of trying to hustle everyone out the front door. The flustered child whose water bottle didn't have as much ice as she wanted. The missing shin guard. The squealing baby and the car seat stained from last week's takeout that I'd forgotten to clean.

Then this one phrase interrupted my venting: "I will declare your greatness."

The morning wasn't great. They were grumpy. I was terse. They were late. I was unforgiving. They joined a field of players who had lily-white skin and families that from the outside certainly looked more intact than ours. This morning held so much more than soccer, and very little of it was great by my standards. But I would find Him, here.

Is this a time to reach back and remember? I wondered. *To declare the greatness of the God who hurdled mountains of paperwork impossibilities to bring our children home? The God who brought them today onto a soccer field with breakfast in their bellies and a mommy who would ask their forgiveness when practice was over? The God who made this toddler in the stroller in front of me, after my womb was empty for twelve years?*

A small flash of color on the path caught my eye, and I swerved the wheels of the stroller to miss a brilliant blue eggshell.

"Look, Bo!" I said pointing, still halfway lost in my thoughts. "A birdie was in that egg!"

"Egg. Egg. Eggie!" Bo's voice grew louder with each repetition. I set my feet back on the path and my mind back on the Psalms: "On the glorious splendor of your majesty, and on your wondrous works, I will meditate . . . I will declare your greatness."

With each phrase of the passage, the erratic pounding of my heart was recalibrating, finding its steady rhythm again. I was telling my soul what was true as if it were undergoing CPR. The morning still felt messy. I was relieved our long-term houseguest hadn't witnessed my behavior, and I didn't really want to tell Nate about it later. But I did want to repent to my children. I had spent long years without ever asking for forgiveness from Nate in our early married days, so my desire to repent was significant. God was doing a work in me.

As we continued on the path, Bo intermittently interrupted my thoughts with "Oh!" pointing in childlike wonder to a tree and then a car and back at the eggshell as we passed it on our return trek. And now I couldn't seem to get my mind off it. This shell struck me as so much more than a discarded home for a baby bird. This small piece of God's created order evoked a question I'd been asking with my life but hadn't put into words until this morning: *What is greatness to You, God? What* are *Your wondrous works?*

I'd seen God's greatness in the miracle ruling in the Ugandan court system that granted two children a home in our family. My marriage is a wonder—we made it through the rise and fall of a business and the rise and fall of our stubborn hearts. My children, though I might have thought them ruffians that morning, were having parts of their broken hearts restored. All of these were glorious wonders.

But the eggshell. And the soccer practice down the street. Wonders?

God was inviting me to reconsider the ever-unfolding opportunities for wonder around me. There were opportunities for awe at God in even the most unlikely moments, and my eyes needed to be trained to see them as much as my heart needed to be trained to engage them. God was available, infused into my every minute, but my flesh was bent toward independence. I hadn't been trained to see Him in the eggshell. Or at soccer practice.

I could see the wonder of God in the knowing look Nate gave me across the kitchen island the night before when he heard me encouraging a child he knew would be easier for me to critique. I was in awe of God as my daughter, who has a painful history, slid her hand into mine at church while we sang, "I see heaven invading this place." I was invited to wonder later that day when I shut the door to my bedroom to ask Him for help with a different (presently difficult) child. He was wondrous when I didn't have time to text friends for prayer but paused to talk to Him in the midst of chaos and felt that permeating peace that could be attributed only to God. And wonder was in my children who were merely players on a field to most spectators of the game, but who were beginning to understand that they are a son and daughters when no one but God, Nate, and I are looking.

Yes, the eggshell and the soccer practice are wonders. These things are beautiful because they point to a Creator God who both sees and orchestrates the glorious details of life. Who reaches *into* my minutes. These things have the power to cause me to look at Him, if I step back and let them. They have the power to move my heart, if I let it engage.

Dozens of minutes every day are shot through with this wonder, pregnant with potential to draw our eyes up to God. Our flitting eyes, with just as many opportunities to behold things that won't nourish our souls, need to be trained to see them. They need to be trained to see the face of Jesus.

The house fills with the fragrance of oil. The whole earth fills with His glory. My soul fills with awareness of His wonder. Today.

And before long, I'm unwinding, sitting before Him in the small moments of the day, sliding my watch off my wrist and looking up to Him alone.

—————— *For Your Continued Pursuit* ——————

Genesis 1:26–27 | 1 Kings 19:11–12 | Psalm 5:3 | Psalm 16:8 | Psalm 17:6 | Psalm 19:1–4 | Psalm 27:4 | Psalm 45:10–11 | Psalm 65:1 | Psalm 81:10 | Psalm 139:1–6, 16–18 | Psalm 145:5–6 | Song of Songs 2:14 | Isaiah 55:1–2 | Hosea 6:6 | Matthew 6:22 | Luke 22:39–45 | John 11:28–37 | 2 Corinthians 3:18 | 2 Corinthians 4:16–18 | 2 Corinthians 10:12

seven

SECRET EXTRAVAGANCE

Wasting Ourselves on God

"Why this waste?"
—MATTHEW 26:8

I'd been in a suit and heels since 5:00 a.m., and after a full morning, I was at the airport for an early afternoon flight home—home to a husband, but no children. It was a couple of years after my season at the boutique on North Barracks Road, but still a few years before the grief of infertility had settled into my soul.

I'd recently started to crave *more*. I wanted more from my sales support job. I wasn't tired of doing it or even tired of the deskwork and the travel, but I was tired of working for little more than sales goals and a paycheck. I wanted more than productivity and success. I wanted brushes with God and meaning and almost anything that mattered but wasn't easily measured.

My work for the day was done and I was tired, but my heart was hungry, and I was beginning to like heart hunger. So I prayed: *God, I want to meet with You in this airport.*

Meeting Him required quieting my insides enough to hear and respond. The kind of dialogue I was learning to have with God burgeoned when I saw it as an exchange—my mind for His thoughts, my fear for His assurance, my whispers for His response. As I made my way to a restaurant near my gate, I noticed an elderly gentleman who was being pushed in a wheelchair. I prayed for God to breathe life and strength into his frail body. I saw a man running as fast as my mind usually worked, and I prayed his racing heart would come to know Jesus. I saw a young woman with vacant eyes, and I prayed she would find the filling her heart most needed. I realized afresh that the people all around me weren't merely interesting. They were God-created. I wanted to talk to Him about what He had made.

God, what do You see in the man who is late for his flight? And the one in the wheelchair—how do You see the heart buried underneath that broken body? Rather than looking at people as faces among the masses, I asked for His eyes for them and responded with minute-long prayers: *God, I want to meet You in this airport.*

No one knew this conversation I was having in my head with God. And I was starting to like these secret exchanges.

At the restaurant, I grabbed the last available seat at the bar, which was full of day travelers with carry-ons. As I scooted up onto my stool and glanced at the laminated menu, I noticed the gentleman sitting next to me. He looked to be near retirement, but he was dressed for business. I was drawn to him in the way you're drawn to someone who is not at all like you, but with whom you feel a strange connection.

Maybe I'm supposed to share the gospel with this man, I thought. I ordered my food and opened my book, trying to concentrate on reading while staying aware of what felt like a nudge from God.

Ten minutes later when the waitress brought out my order along with that of the man next to me, I noticed that we both had ordered the same meal. I awkwardly mumbled a comment about it, looking for a way to begin a conversation. But my voice, perhaps too quiet from nerves, got lost in a salvo of loudspeaker announcements. He hadn't heard me. I went back to my book, resigned that I'd misread God's cues.

The book I was reading explored the concept of abiding in the vine from John 15. The author used the notion of tree grafting to illustrate this abiding. After hours of client presentations on throbbing feet, my mind couldn't absorb the words. I read and reread the same paragraph, but without comprehension. And then this prompt dropped into my mind: *Ask the man sitting next to you to explain it.*

Uh-oh, I thought.

As much as I wanted to hear from God, I knew that we humans sometimes mishear Him and mistake our mental wanderings for His voice. *What should I do?* Talk to the man and risk awkwardness and embarrassment? Or not talk to him and risk missing what might well be God's answer to my prayer to meet with Him in this airport?

Well, at least I'll never see this guy again, I thought. So I went for it.

"Sir, excuse me," I said, much louder this time, almost shouting to compensate for my nerves.

He startled. "Yes?" he said, raising his eyebrows like the authoritative boss of a fresh college grad.

"Do you know anything about grafting?" I coughed out.

"What?" he asked.

Oh no. I had to say it again. This business exec didn't even seem to know what the word meant.

"Grafting, sir. Do you know anything about grafting?" My face was red hot.

"It's funny you should ask," he said. I noticed tears welling up in the corners of his eyes.

My heart started racing.

"I majored in agriculture in college and I minored in grafting. I run a farm equipment business but have gotten away from what I once loved."

Now I was sure I could actually hear my heart, not just feel the pounding.

He stretched back on his stool, took off his glasses, and rubbed his eyes. Then he enthusiastically explained the details of how the branch of one tree is grafted into another as if he were telling me a page-turning story. I showed him the paragraph in my book and asked him questions. He made it all so clear.

I'm not sure if I was more surprised that the prompt to talk to this man really was from God, or that God was personal enough to meet me at an airport barstool. Apparently, God was meeting this man too, right over his hamburger and French fries. He thanked me after our exchange as if he'd been reminded of his boyish love for trees and for grafting, a love that needed rediscovering.

Twelve years later, this conversation remains my most memorable business trip. Still. I can't remember where I'd gone or even who I met with on that trip. I remember it only because I'd felt seen and heard by God.

God showed up when I was in my suit and heels, and He winked. We shared a secret. During those days of client presentations, excel spreadsheets, and conference calls, He was whispering, *I want to meet with you, here.* What I might once have considered a waste of time—conversation with Him in the midst of a demanding day—became, instead, food for my hungry heart. It was a gift of hiddenness during a season when my work required me to be on during the workday.

God's currency is communion—a relationship that *grows*, nearer still. A relationship that is cultivated when no one else is looking. A relationship accessed not just when we feel we need His help but at all the odd times that punctuate our agenda-driven days. A depth of relationship that feeds the recipient in the way that productivity and accomplishment just cannot.

What a waste. What a beautiful waste.

"Why this waste?" A condemnation wrapped in a question. It is among the most powerful lines in Mary's story, spoken by onlookers as she poured a fortune on Jesus' feet. She'd grown accustomed to the scornful looks of the religious leaders, but these bystanders were Jesus' friends—their condemnation perhaps, then, more jarring for her.

But Mary had been here before, frustrating those who valued her productivity over her passion. She had already been chastised by her sister, Martha, for wasting time at Jesus' feet, but Jesus had praised Mary's choice. She'd found what mattered. And she was developing a habit of this, uncapping her love and offending those who couldn't handle the waste.

"Why this waste?" they asked. Their words shielded them from an expression of love they likely feared as well as craved. They too had been close to Jesus. They'd known there was something wildly different about this man, but they apparently were trapped in an old standard of measurement that dismissed devotion like this as waste. Now that she'd shown what she valued most, everyone knew she was different. Surely such extravagance must be a waste. After all, what would she have to show for it?

Wasteful. By their standards.

Precious. By His.

"Wherever this gospel is preached in the whole world," Jesus said, "what this woman has done will also be told as a memorial to her" (Matt. 26:13). Jesus acclaimed Mary's choice then, and He invites us to make the same choice now: to live by a reckless love—even, and perhaps especially, in our hiddenness.

Extravagant, hidden giving to Jesus at the expense of publicly productive Christian service will always offend. Yes, even Christians. Yet it is all over the Word of God. Read these verses with an eye for this uncorked, abandoned, and extravagant love that happens perhaps even at the expense of producing something for Him:

LORD, I have loved the habitation of Your house, and the place where Your glory dwells. (Ps. 26:8)

His house is rich. It's where He is. Stay there for just a little while longer than you're used to and, over time, it will no longer feel strange to orient your schedule around being in that place.

One thing I have desired of the LORD, that will I seek: that I may dwell in the house of the LORD all the days of my life. (Ps. 27:4)

When we cross over to heaven, we won't discover a new, mysterious craving for God. It is here that we practice. We cultivate. We are made for this: to waste time simply being with Him. Sitting at His feet enjoying him isn't a foolish expenditure of time. It's strength training for heaven.

But one thing is needed, and Mary has chosen that good part, which will not be taken away from her. (Luke 10:42)

Jesus said this about a woman who chose to forfeit productivity and to risk judgment to sit with Him and learn from Him.

You shall love the LORD your God with all your heart, with all your soul, and with all your strength. (Deut. 6:5)

Hiddenness turns dutiful workers into lovers of God. To stay in love, we must resist the culture. To resist the culture, we must stay in love. Author Henri Nouwen says it this way: "The farther I run away from the place where God dwells, the less I am able to hear the voice that calls me the Beloved, and the less I hear that voice, the more entangled I become in the manipulations and power games of the world."[9]

At some point it became an easy decision for Mary to pour out her life savings on Jesus' feet. To surrender herself there. She didn't do it out of guilt or obligation. She did it out of a wildly extravagant love.

She was *wastefully* in love.

A decade and a half after my summer at the camp in the Adirondacks, the routine of my mothering days hasn't changed all that much. It is just as patterned and just as circular. Wake, prepare breakfast, clean up breakfast, prepare lunch, clean up lunch, plan for dinner. Set the table for several hungry bodies, clear the table. Reset. The same pair of Eden's jeans goes from worn to washed to folded to worn multiple times in a week. We empty the diaper bin on the same day the next shipment of diapers arrives.

Some might use a word like trapped to describe such an existence. I confess there are some weak days I might be tempted to also.

Tears of former orphans fall and hearts move ever so slightly and the babe learns a new word—all in the eight hours that no one else sees. But these are just the little minutes between long hours of sweeping floors and turning off lights and tying shoes and wiping up drool.

Is this all there is? pokes at me.

My day might look different from yours, but I suspect the same question haunts you.

At twenty-two, before children, I was telling high school students—future world-changers—about Jesus. Stories of transformed lives made the long summer hours in the dining hall and weekday afternoons of ministry administration worth it. My life had purpose, purpose I could measure one life at a time.

Today, with six children, I could coach myself in the same way and find the stories that make the tedium worth it. That point in the afternoon when I catch my little girl at the piano writing a song from her Bible makes me think, *Something besides diapers is being changed around here. At least I'm not wasting my time.* When I see four of them, with different histories of brokenness, spread out on their backs on the trampoline laughing between fits of jumping and squealing, I forget how long it took to prepare their dinner.

Maybe you do the same. We scout our days, you and me, for these stories that make it all worth it. We're forever on the lookout for new ways to infuse our otherwise mundane lives with measurable impact. We troll for tiny signs that what we're doing matters, a mark on the earth, whether in the glowing successes of our children or the business promotion or the ministry we launched. Parenting feels most like it's worth it when we see our child thrive, and the business or ministry seems to most warrant our outpouring when it's growing.

But what if our real mark on earth was meant to reverberate in heaven? What if there is a possibility for impact—impacting God's heart with our hidden devotion to Him—that far supersedes these this-made-it-all-worth-it moments?

The mundane hours can outweigh the one this-made-it-all-worth-it moment in a week if we are meeting God and pouring ourselves out at His feet, there. What if right in the middle of that mundanity we could *waste*? Like Mary at Jesus' feet.

Without a vision for what's available to us in sitting at His feet in the hidden place, we become restless. This restlessness is powerful enough to make us start new projects, sign up to volunteer, begin foundations, delve into new ministries. Many a small group is launched, blog written, and book published by ones who are itching to climb out of the hidden place. All these things can be beautiful within God's timing. But out of time, they will only perpetuate the restlessness, the craving for the next "soul hit." We become thrill seekers who miss the biggest thrill. We train ourselves to be satisfied with so little.

And so God whispers to us, *Don't climb out of this hidden, mundane place*—don't start the foundation, run after a new ministry, defend yourself to your critics, start the next blog—*just yet. Find Me. Here.*

Every single minute of the day is available for us to feel His hand resting, firmly, on the small of our backs and His breath brushing like a breeze against our skin, softly awakening us. His beauty is close, disruptively near.

Every single minute is available for wasting ourselves at His feet. To reach the dwelling place, to see and know Him there, we need to allow for the quiet, the questions. We need to lean into, and not away from, what can come out of the aching hiddenness with God.

We've been sequestered.

The closet, the corner, the place where we've been hidden from the crowd is where God's whisper becomes a life-changing brush with His love. All the waiting rooms in life, the wasteful places where the only question is, "When will I ever get out of this place?" are the places God loves to show us Himself.

The waste of extravagant love we pour at Jesus' feet is never squandered. That love expands us, it doesn't diminish us. We weren't made to ration our love. We were made for extravagance.

―――――――― *For Your Continued Pursuit* ――――――――

Deuteronomy 4:29 | Deuteronomy 6:5 | Psalm 26:8 | Psalm 27:4 | Psalm 41:12 | Psalm 119:130–32 | Proverbs 8:17 | Jeremiah 9:23–24 | Matthew 6:33 | Matthew 26:8–9 | Luke 10:39–42 | John 12:43 | Galatians 1:10 | Ephesians 3:17–19 | Colossians 3:23

Adoration:
   Characteristics of God
   Watch wait see - invitation of God.
   Ps. 18 Honest w/God. Do we believe this
   about God.? What side of God that we don't
   believe.?

   Ps 62

eight

THE NEEDS AROUND US

Changing the World at Jesus' Feet

"For this fragrant oil might have been
sold for much and given to the poor."

—MATTHEW 26:9

The earth is still covered in night, but I am waking. I hit the snooze button on the alarm for just a few more moments of rest, but my mind is already racing into the day, dragging with it the missed opportunities from the day before.

I think of a woman we bump into from time to time. An adult orphan and still without family, she is in need of more than just an occasional conversation and a smile. *Should I have invited her over for dinner when I saw her yesterday?*

I had skimmed a blog post on the plight of Syrian refugees: *Should we open our home?*

I remember a neighbor's brother who is in the hospital: *Someone else is coordinating meals for them. Should that have been me?*

I had received a text image of a child in foster care: *We have one extra bedroom. Should we adopt again?*

The needs are unending. And all before breakfast. All before even getting out of bed.

I have time and resources and the world has needs. Isn't this an equation with only one correct answer: me?

My resources are at God's disposal. He may sometimes ask me to take a risk to meet those needs, to do more than I think I can. But I err when I think of resources, whether time, money, or spikenard oil, as merely transactional. As if meeting needs alone is the only thing, or the most important thing, God desires of me. If meeting needs is my primary focus, I've missed a foundational step: friendship with the King. To meet any need, I first have to hear God's whisper about that need.

"No longer do I call you servants," Jesus said to his followers, "for a servant does not know what his master is doing; but I have called you friends, for all things that I heard from My Father I have made known to you" (John 15:15).

Friends talk. They share hearts and get their fingernails dirty in one another's stories. They carry the load for the other. And sometimes they are simply present.

We often assume that God, however, is somehow pining away for just one thing: our A+ effort so this broken world can *finally* be fixed. As if He is anxiously waiting to see which one of us will respond and how well we will do. We make our relationship with Him transactional. We give, He gives in return. We mess up, He withholds His love from us.

We make our worth dependent on our ability to meet

the needs around us. And when we're honest about the darker parts of our hearts, we have to admit our actions for others can sometimes be an attempt to feel good about all we can do for God.

But to a friend, time is an investment of the heart, not just the hand.

Friends spend. Time.

Every day I am flooded by opportunities to change the world by meeting the needs around me. Any servant can meet a need, but what about sons and daughters? Do beloved children exchange chores for room and board or even for affection? Or how would parents respond to children who gladly cleaned the house and mowed the lawn but refused to spend time talking with and enjoying them, the very ones who have loved and cared for them their whole lives? We know this isn't the way things should operate in a healthy family, and yet we often and subconsciously relate to God in this way. We give Him what we perceive to be our obedience yet internally resist a deeper surrender.

On any day, I am overwhelmed by the needs of the world, but my greater need is to interrupt this kneejerk cycling between the cries of the world and my response so that I can cultivate friendship with God. It's there that I learn that it's the friends of God who truly change the world. It's there that I have the depth of friendship that informs the way I respond to the world's needs.

When I let friendship with God become my first priority— talking to Him, hearing from Him, letting His Word shape my thinking—I align myself with an agenda that does, in fact, help meet the needs of others. But instead of being driven by my limited cost-benefit analysis, I get to tap into the wisdom of the greatest king of the earth and heavens. And as I scoot nearer to Him, my senses are awakened. I move from being an efficient and productive worker to a friend who can touch and see and engage with God. I grow to love the things and the people He loves—with my actions, with my time, and with my presence.

 Lovers will always outwork workers.

As Mary did with her fragrant oil, I want to spend myself on Jesus. I want to move His heart with an extravagant out-pouring. The world changes from an exchange such as this. Instead of frantically scurrying to meet the latest need, I slowly pattern my life toward pouring myself out at His feet—toward giving Him the best of my affection, sometimes in a hundred small glances a day. It's from that place of connection that I hear His heartbeat for the needs around me and see His per-spective on my role. It's from there, that place of carrying His heart, that I learn how and when to respond to others' cries.

We're training for a lifetime of friendship with God, an eternity. Yet training and friendship may seem to be opposi-tional words. We train for road races and learning the piano and acquiring new job skills. We take parenting classes and computer classes. But friendship? Shouldn't that just *happen*?

Not exactly.

When transactional beings who live in a world focused on productivity meet a relational God, we *do* need training for how to settle into friendship with Him. Repatterning. Spending time with Him in hiddenness orients us toward that repatterning.

Responding to the needs of the world from the foundation of friendship with God takes practice. This is not natural to us, but it is possible for us. Here are some thoughts on how to grow toward what might not feel natural: friendship with God.

Look at Him first thing. Each day.

For me, training begins in the morning while I'm still in bed, even before the morning light splinters through my bedroom blinds, before I am subjected to the vulnerability that accompanies a fresh day. I am most raw in these transitional morning moments, just after waking from six or seven hours of sleep and dreams. Left unfettered, my morning thoughts are first populated by all the not-God voices clamoring for my attention, from my insecure heart's wanderings to a replay of a conversation from the day before to the thoughts about the latest needs of others who are right in front of me. Or sometimes my mind simply fixates on how I need a chai latte if I'm going to function at all.

But I've learned that the morning is for Him to hold—to hold me. I love these words from the psalmist: "My voice You shall hear in the morning, O LORD; in the morning I will direct it to You, and I will look up" (Ps. 5:3).

The morning is often when I feel most susceptible to the thoughts flying through my head. I could wake on the defensive, but God loves to receive my most vulnerable self.

For nearly a year, I woke up every single morning with the hymn "I Need Thee Every Hour" playing in my head, ushering me into alertness. It was as if God was reminding me I was *that* needy. I had masked my weaknesses for so long that it was freeing to finally admit—and first thing in the morning, almost as the pronouncement over my day—how much I needed God.

Now, whether or not I wake up with that hymn ringing in my ears, my first words nearly every morning are, "God, I need you." In the rawest, most vulnerable part of my day, I position myself as needy and attentive. I decide to listen to Him, to look at Him, rather than chase after the myriad things clamoring for my attention.

These are the gentle but intentional acknowledgments of friendship with God. Instead of settling for a transactional relationship, I see Him entering into the still, small minutes of my day. The almost undetectable moments. And I want Him there—not just because I need help but because I like His presence.

If I go for too long during the day—too many minutes of checking my email or padding through the house lost in thoughts or hanging out in anger over a scuffle with my children or with Nate—without anchoring what I see and how I see it in biblical truth, the day shows it, and I wear it. I am anxious, the clamor of needs around me speaks louder than His voice, and circumstantial peace becomes my goal. So instead, I learn from my toddler how to be like a child.

My toddler, Bo, sweetly warm in his footie pajamas as he wakes up, can't quite rip through the house with his normal confidence until I've held him close, read him a few stories, and combed my fingers through his bed-worn hair. I'm the same way with my heavenly Father. I need to be held, to be weak, to be secure in the arms of someone who loves me no matter what the day brings. I need to be cuddled. I wake vulnerable, and I want to give that vulnerability to Him.

I give Him my best affection. First.

And my roots go down.

Give yourself permission to start where you are and to start small.

One year when I was in full-time ministry, our staff team set aside an entire January day for prayer. We piled into cars, drove a few hours to a retreat center, and spent the day fasting and praying for the lives of high school students and their families.

We scattered ourselves throughout the cavernous meeting room, carving out our own spaces to ask God to move in and through the people He'd put in our lives and ministry. Hour by hour, the topic for prayer changed. We knelt. We stood with arms raised. We huddled in groups and then walked the outside perimeter of the building, breathing into our hands to keep them warm. With our hearts and our bodies, including our empty stomachs, we wanted to say to God, *We seek You first for this ministry.*

It was an intense and memorable day, but perhaps not in the way it should have been for me. What I remember most was my apathy and agitation.

I was restless, checking my watch after an hour. My body wasn't used to fasting and my mind wasn't used to praying for one hour, much less the long hours of an entire day. I felt like a junior varsity cross-country runner at the Olympics.

I knew prayer is the real work of God, but I couldn't cut it. I didn't fit here. I was bored, and God felt distant, all while my stomach grumbled.

I guess I'm more cut out for the actual work of God, not the conversation with Him, I decided as I glanced around at my teammates, who mostly seemed engrossed in prayer and not hungry at all.

For years after that day, when something came up about an extended period of prayer, I told myself, *Some people can pray a lot and some can't. I'm one of the ones who can't.* My mind kept going back to that day of being bored and distracted and indifferent.

A decade later, I was tucking Lily into bed and kissing her cheek, silently breathing a prayer: *God, heal this broken heart of hers.* I had four children, and spending a day, much less an hour, in prayer wasn't planned for the next week or the next year. The next day, I'd be doing laundry and clearing dishes and facing exactly what I'd faced that day—the same hurdles of being a tired mom with more needs than I could meet.

But at that point in my life, my minute-long prayers were multiplying, consistently and covertly escorting me into longer conversations with God, conversations that were moving beyond my morning quiet time and into the parts of my day where I was most inclined to produce something.

I remembered that long-ago January day of extended prayer, and it made more sense to me why I couldn't spend the focused time with God that seemed to come so easily to others in that room. A full day of conversation with God—at a time when my mind was oriented toward impact and God was my coach, not someone I wanted to be with—was too intangible to my immature heart. I wasn't there yet. I had eyes for ministry impact and related to God as the one coaching me to get there, not as someone I wanted to spend time with and enjoy. And so He was unfamiliar to me, a mere acquaintance.

But somewhere between that January day and the night of my breath prayer for Lily, I had begun relating to God as a friend. Slowly, imperceptibly, I'd moved from seeing Him as a coach who constantly pushed me to work harder, to seeing Him as a loving Father who wants to share His heart with me. As a result, my conversations with God changed from once-a-day requests for help with tasks and assignments, to moment-to-moment breath prayers throughout my day. A string of tiny prayers. This is how you talk to friends, after all: frequently and openly.

And so I became more intentional about those tiny prayers. I prayed phrases of Scripture up the stairs and down, chopping onions, walking to the mailbox. I allowed myself to make small requests as well as big ones, reminding myself that God cares just as much about this one ordinary moment as He does the big moments.

Strengthen me on my insides, I prayed from Ephesians 3:16 when anxiety and fear clouded my thinking.

Open my eyes, that I may see wondrous things from your law, I prayed from Psalm 119:18, especially when His Word felt more like a textbook to me than the love letter my eyes had read dozens of times. I wanted a new start the next day.

Create in me a clean heart, O God, I prayed from Psalm 51:10

when I was terse with my children and grumpy about my lot in life.

Other days it was, *Lord, please change her heart*, over a child's attitude. Or, *Strengthen the weak parts of Nate*, rather than an internal complaint about him. Or, *Help her sleep, God*, as I closed the bedroom door after tucking Eden in.

I exchanged anxious thoughts—wondering what a friend thought of me, fearing the outcome of my children's behaviors, worrying about the unpaid bill—with tiny prayers from His Word. (He was beginning to infuse the minutia of my day.) I started these conversations just as I might initiate a conversation with a new friend. *Here's a tidbit about me. Tell me a little about You.*

Whereas my prayer life had once revolved around asking God for the big things—salvation for a teenager, funding for an adoption, greater impact for a ministry endeavor—now I was all about the small things. *God, I'm tired. Would You meet me in this exhaustion and lift me up?* Or, *I'm feeling overwhelmed by my list today. Would You bring me peace in this moment?*

Tiny prayers assume more of God than they do of us. They acknowledge that He is big enough to receive a small request and respond. He starts where we are, and sometimes we need to start small. In our footie pajamas, even. Childlike. And yet God always seems to respond with more than we even know to ask for. Through my tiny prayers, I noticed subtle growth, a new and fresh hunger for God. My tiny prayers were carving new space in my spirit to hear God's voice and to expect an enjoyable exchange, not a monologue.

When the needs of the world were clamoring loudly, I

could see these nascent, minute-by-minute reaches for God as a waste of time. Or I could see them as partnering with a Friend who can do exceedingly abundantly above all that I ask or imagine—through me and with me as we do life together.

Follow Jesus' example of being tethered to God.

Jesus talked to God.

The one who *was* God's image—made from God, carrying all of God, wearing the fullest expression of God in skin—talked to God.

Often.

- "Now in the morning, having risen a long while before daylight, He went out and departed to a solitary place; and there He prayed" (Mark 1:35).
- "But Jesus often withdrew to lonely places and prayed" (Luke 5:16 NIV).
- "In the days of his flesh, Jesus offered up prayers and supplications, with loud cries and tears, to him who was able to save him from death, and he was heard because of his reverence" (Heb. 5:7 ESV).

We so often approach prayer as mere discipline. While discipline is a starting place for conversation with God and a tool for those of us who need structure, discipline wasn't Jesus' foundation for communicating with God.

For Jesus, conversations with God began with desire, not discipline. He stayed close to God. Tethered.

They were already one—God and Jesus—united with the Spirit, and yet Jesus loved being with the Father, who loved

Him. Jesus invites us to share in this oneness with Him. He prayed this for us: "I do not pray for these alone, but also for those who will believe in Me through their word; that they all may be one, as You, Father, are in Me, and I in You; that they also may be one in Us, that the world may believe that You sent Me" (John 17:20–21).

Jesus prayed that our unity with God would be like His unity with God, born not of duty but of desire. Of friendship.

We get a small infusion of God—a spark of an idea, a dream that could impact the world around us, a nudge that might change circumstances—and we run with it without tracing it to its source. We believe that the work of God, in and through us, to meet the world's needs is the greatest demonstration of Him in our lives. Though that work is significant and often substantive, we can chase it with such fury that we miss the dozens of opportunities for friendship-like conversation with God along the way, for stillness to hear God's whispers as we work.

We feel the same discomfort with a story like Mary's that the others in the room did that night. Discomfort turns to judgment turns to dismissal—until we look at the concealed parts of our lives and acknowledge, *I feel better when I'm producing, and I feel best when it's noticed.*

Yet God continues to bring us back to friendship with Him and to the layered understanding of the motives behind our pursuits.

Jesus, whose assignment was to save the whole world, took time out to be with God. He regularly separated himself from the crowds and their needs—the unhealed bodies and the leprous skin and the broken families—to communicate with His Father, His friend. And the Father didn't merely need the Son. The Father loved Him. Jesus said, "As the Father loved Me, I also have loved you" (John 15:9).

This is the kind of relationship, the love exchange, into which we are invited.

This kind of scoot-up-close-to-me-and-let-me-share-myself-with-you relationship isn't a quick burst of affection we're given so that we can do what God wants of us. It's a love that can seep into our core and change us if we look at Him and receive what He offers as He reaches back to us. Then we will see our families, our neighborhoods, our world with new eyes as He imparts more of Himself to us.

Speak the Word of God. Out loud.

I hadn't seen Nate pray the Word of God out loud like this before we got to Uganda.

We'd gone on an impulse, a strong nudge from the Lord, and spent money we didn't yet have, all in an effort to adopt two children that the Ugandan legal system might not even release to us. We were there for almost six weeks but had packed for months, unsure of when we might return.

These were the craziest days of our married life. Nate was enflamed with holy determination, and I was afraid. At a glance, the whole thing looked like a foolish crusade to save children who didn't yet know us and who might be even further scarred if the adoption process failed and fell apart, slaying their hopes. Our future was in the hands of an unfamiliar judge and a mostly unbending system.

We met with our lawyer in the lobby of our guest home.

He was pleasant, but frank. This didn't look good for us. He'd told us not to come, and we'd lived up to his expectations of irrational but determined Americans who hoped their dollars and good intentions would force circumstances to work their way. But here we were. The likelihood was high that we would soon return to the States, thousands fewer dollars in our pockets and without the children we longed to make our own.

So I lay awake at night under the mosquito net (which seemed to trap mosquitoes in, rather than keep them out) and obsessed about all the possible outcomes while Nate snored beside me. But in the mornings, he prayed. Bible in hand, he walked the perimeter of our guest home, speaking aloud the Word of God. I'd heard Nate teach the Bible and had seen him spend many mornings with his well-worn Bible open across his lap and a cup of coffee in his hand. But I hadn't heard him pray like this—out loud, as if he were preaching a sermon to himself.

Around he went: in front of the unruly and easily agitated watchdog, underneath the lines of laundry drying out back, and between the fence and the guardhouse. Again and again, morning after morning. For almost six weeks.

The judge's office was closing early this season, we learned.

Nate paced and prayed God's Word.

Two more pieces of paperwork were missing from our file.

Nate circled the house with his Bible in hand, his mouth open, preaching the Word back to himself.

No new verdict on our case on the day they promised to deliver it.

Around the guest home again.

"The words that I speak to you are spirit, and they are life" (John 6:63).

Before we went to Uganda, Nate and I had approached parts of God's Word as if they were merely platitudes and rules for clean living. They'd been moral guidelines—until we were desperate for them to be so much more.

When Nate began to speak the Word of God, our relationship to Scripture changed and deepened. These words and passages weren't edicts or codes of conduct handed down by a distant and intangible God. These words were living Truth, loving Truth, *the* Truth, and we mainlined every morsel as Nate spoke them around the guesthouse and into his heart.

As I watched Nate from the guesthouse window, I starting saying under my breath the same words Nate was speaking as instigators for my own conversation with God. And with each passing day, I noticed a subtle shift. I wasn't just hearing these words preached, I was metabolizing them. They were life-giving food, nourishment for my roots in God's love.

The Word of God takes new shape when we don't just read it but *hear* it, and from our own mouths. "So then faith comes by hearing, and hearing by the word of God" (Rom. 10:17). *The Message* puts it this way: "The point is: Before you trust, you have to listen. But unless Christ's Word is preached, there's nothing to listen to."

Night after night, I had been lying in bed blanketed by the muggy July musk of Africa, lost in my thoughts and fears and expectations of what might happen based on what our lawyer said. During our days, we heard unfavorable speculations from the judge's office staff. We read sobering and sometimes heartbreaking articles and posts from others who'd been in our situation. But when Nate read the Bible aloud, we were grounded by a wholly different input. In his book *Psalms: The Prayer Book of the Bible*, Dietrich Bonhoeffer writes, "The richness of the Word of God ought to determine our prayer, not the poverty of our heart."[10] Nate and I both learned how deeply true it is that "the word of God is living and powerful" (Heb. 4:12). It is powerful enough to shift a heart, to change a situation, to shape our thoughts and perceptions. There is only one Truth, one source of input, that enables us to truly see beyond the limitations—and sometimes the lies—of our circumstances. And we can replace those limitations and lies with truth, spoken.

One minute at a time.

There are days when I circle the outside perimeter of our house in the early morning hours and speak the Psalms back to my heart, just as Nate circled our guest home all those years ago. Inside and fast asleep are the two little ones we brought home from that prayer-filled trip. I lift up their hurting hearts with words of truth, again and again.

As a family, we sometimes sing God's Word too. Though not all of us are singers, there's something about setting a passage of Scripture to a tune that allows those words to sink deep. Nearly every top-forty pop song that came out when I was a teenager has worked its way into my permanent memory bank. I'm at the grocery and find myself singing along with songs on the PA system that I haven't thought about for two decades. Music can sneak past our rational thinking and work its way into our operating system. This is why we sing God's

Word, even if we're off key. I not only want to remember these truths twenty years from now, I want them to become part of me. I want them to shape my thinking.

You can do this. Take a phrase from God's Word. Speak it aloud in the shower or as you pull out of the driveway for work. While in the carpool line or running errands, quiet the noise around you with the sound of your voice saying His Word. Win back your day one minute at a time with the truth of God's Word, or with a little ditty that sticks, and watch what happens to your heart as His truth begins to speak louder than all the other noise of the day. "Left to ourselves," writes pastor Eugene Peterson, "we will pray to some god who speaks what we like hearing, or to the part of God we manage to understand. But what is critical is that we speak to the God who speaks to us."[11]

Growth in God—reaching for Him and sinking our roots deep—doesn't happen passively. We have God's truth, and we can *wield* it. We can put it in our mouths and speak it, sing it, and declare it, because it is true.

Adore God.

If we sit sideways in the oversized leather chair, the one that was already faded and cracked before we got it, two of us can fit. Caleb's little body, tucked into last season's mismatched pajamas, presses beside mine as we all sit around the fire before the children go to bed, and I wonder just what might come out of this kid's mouth tonight.

He's still a mystery to me, this child. He was a toddler when we adopted him, and thus he has no memories of his life before becoming a Hagerty. He smiles and pops his collar like Nate and spends hours using his sisters' thread to string up plastic toys and Legos so he can hang them from the second-story banister. He's goofy and loud and all things boy, but some days the clouds hang low behind his eyes. They threaten to disrupt his young-boy lightfootedness. He has a history that one day will be fodder for his conversations with God, but right now he's not ready or able to talk.

I think my son is a mystery to himself too.

Those clouds of loss and grief hang low some days, and he can't wrap words around what feels so hard, so he grumbles. Something hurts. It's that dull ache again, but how does a young child process the kind of loss he faced before he even walked?

Each of my children processes their grief in different ways. One crawls into my lap, near weekly, and says, "I'm just having a hard, hard day." She makes the connections to her past without me. Her grief is tangible to her. Another cries in secret while I spend months readying myself for the small piece of her heart that she'll sanction for exploration when she's ready to talk.

But Caleb, he climbs trees and scouts for hawks and makes pets out of field mice, and one day he will discover that bravery is found in a bare heart. Until then, I wait with him. And we adore together. We take a phrase or sentence of God's Word that demonstrates who He is, and we tell it back to Him and to our own souls.

One evening, as Caleb's seven-year-old body sidled up to mine on the leather chair, we were adoring God based on Luke 2, the part when the heavenly host of angels announces God's joyous Christmas secret to poor shepherds.

"God, You didn't give Your secrets to just the wealthy or the kings," Caleb said. "You told them to people nobody cared about."

Caleb isn't yet old enough to verbalize his grief, to ask God questions about why his story has unfolded as it has. But he can recognize himself in the biblical story of others who lived a seemingly forgotten existence and yet were noticed by God. Through adoration, Caleb can try on a language about God that describes His love and His eye on the unnoticed. His words of adoration are leading his heart, making a way for him to process what he will one day feel and experience more directly. This is the crazy, transforming power of adoration. We use our words to praise God and in the process find ourselves getting healed of false perceptions of Him.

Caleb and I are teaching our souls to look up at God in wonder and awe, to give Him the praise He deserves and loves, even when we don't feel it. This is, perhaps, one of the most critical parts of adoration: *even when we don't feel it.*

In adoration, we take a phrase or sentence of God's Word, we see what those words say about who God is, and we speak them back to Him and to our own souls. We pattern our words toward praise in the midst of whatever we are feeling.

Our emotions can tell us a lot about how we see God, but if our emotions are left unfettered or unexamined, they can become a barrier to adoration. When we choose to practice adoration anyway in the midst of whatever we are feeling, our words lift us over that barrier and into a deeper connectedness with God. That's why we start our adoration right where we are—no platitudes or "Christianese" that paints a gloss over reality. We start from the grit of life, whether we're grumpy or overwhelmed, tired or angry. Adoration says, *Yes, my heart is just barely willing to praise, but that's okay. I'll start here.*

Adoration is a way to remind our souls who God is according to His Word. We take our eyes off of what we are not and where our circumstances are lacking and form words around His beauty and His truth. Adoration waters our friendship with God. He loves when we use our mouths to praise Him, and we train our hearts to look at Him, rather than what we're not, when we adore.

Recognize the truth about yourself in light of who God is.

A simple and gentle correction had sent my near-teenager into a downward spiral of shame right back to a dark part of her heart that questioned her worth and her value in God's eyes. And it wasn't the first time. Former orphans often wear what the rest of us get good at hiding. She's too young to have learned how to shove down shame, and Nate and I don't want her to. We want shame up and out, exposed before God and ready to be tended gently by His hands.

So on this night when she is once more cowering in shame, I have her stay up later than the other children. Together, we pull out sketchpads and colored pens and Scripture. Her inroad is art.

I open the Bible to the Psalms, to a verse that steadies me, rights me, when I feel most raw and ashamed: "He delivered me because He delighted in me" (Ps. 18:19).

She's writing it out, hand-lettering, and I'm praying, realizing as I pray how impossible it feels that an eleven-year-old girl with her history might understand God's delight. We'd all rather be workers, earners, than lovers of God. Working feels easier, more within reach, for the former orphan and for me.

As she carefully inks down the verse with her pen and I can tell her mind is wandering, I start to list out loud all the things I love about her, things I'm sure God loves about her too.

"Did you know that He loves when you dance in the kitchen and you think no one is looking? He loved the painting of the Blue Ridge Mountains you made for Daddy. He loves when you sing in the shower."

She's still sketching but also listening. I move on to "like," more akin to delight, yet harder for the achievement-seeking heart to understand.

"He likes when you play basketball in your rain boots. And that day when you tried out your bike in the snow, He really enjoyed you."

She cracks a smile, maybe starting to like this part of herself too, if God does.

"He likes that you read under the covers of your bed, late at night. He likes how neat you keep your drawers. He made you to love order."

"Mommy," she says, looking up at me, "am I the only person on the planet who has a hard time believing that God likes me?"

"Nope," I tell her. She's tapping into the deepest cry of the human heart, the heart that can preach a sermon on God's love one moment and flog itself in private over a single mistake the next. We all struggle to believe His delight. Might this be one of the greatest barriers to our communion with

God—believing that the one who made us barely likes us, the one we assume finds us barely tolerable?

I don't read Psalm 18:19 and immediately believe that God delights in me. But when I speak that verse back to Him—like my girl and I did that night as she sketched and I prayed after we talked—something inside me shifts a little more closely toward belief.

So much of the distance between God and us could be spanned if we'd let His Word inform us about who He is and who we are in Him. When we see God more clearly, we see ourselves more clearly.

My sweet daughter is learning to delight in what God loves and realizing a bit more every day that it is her.

They grumbled, critical. "For this fragrant oil might have been sold for much and given to the poor" (Matt. 26:9). They criticized Mary not only for what she did but for what she didn't do, and labeled her omission a moral failure.

This may have been the most sharply painful comment for her to hear, especially from ones she likely loved and trusted. Words that made her the most vulnerable, pained, if she caught herself caring more what others thought than what Jesus thought. Although her outpouring came from deep within her, it certainly would have been easier to offer it if no one else had known about it. Subjecting herself to the eyes of others in such a private moment was a sacrifice in itself.

Perhaps their comments echoed her own fears: *Should I*

have done something more worthwhile with this oil? Perhaps she second-guessed herself in a flash of insecurity. But she'd done it. She spilled a life savings over feet and floor. Gone. Done.

She might have noted scowls on their faces seconds before she poured the oil out, but it no longer mattered. She'd tasted the good thing. Again. She squandered the best of herself for love. And He received her as a friend.

She would be one who told others about Him. Who served. Who gave. But on that night, her service began with waste for God alone. And I like to think that in pouring herself out at His feet, she changed the world.

———————— *For Your Continued Pursuit* ————————

2 Chronicles 16:9 | Psalm 5:3 | Psalm 18:19 | Psalm 25:14 | Psalm 51:10 | Psalm 86:12 | Psalm 105:2 | Psalm 119:18 | Psalm 141:8 | Psalm 147 | Psalm 149:4 | Hosea 2:16 | Matthew 26:9 | Mark 1:35 | Luke 5:16 | John 6:63 | John 10:27 | John 10:30 | John 15:9 | John 15:15 | John 17:20 | Romans 10:17 | 2 Corinthians 4:18 | Ephesians 3:16–21 | Ephesians 5:18–20 | Colossians 3:16 | Hebrews 4:12–13 | Hebrews 5:7 | James 4:8 | Revelation 2:2–5

nine

VOICES

Hearing God's Truth above the Criticism and Chatter

"And they criticized her sharply."

—MARK 14:5

Several years ago on my birthday, we took the whole family out to dinner. With a young crew and a bank account freshly depleted from adoptions, a dinner out was no small thing. I felt my age this particular year but also felt a giddy anticipation akin to what most eight-year-olds might feel on their birthday. This meal was going to be good. The kids had been prepped that this evening was not about them. And I had curled my hair. I wasn't wearing sweatpants.

We arrived early for the dinner rush and were seated in a nearly empty restaurant. But the waitress assigned to our table was unhappy at hello. She rolled her eyes at our requests, muttered under her breath, and placed our drinks on the table as if she were a beleaguered official stamping passports. She didn't know this was my day to be celebrated. She didn't know I'd already fed my four children, twice, that day and bathed and dressed each one of them before getting there. We'd even clipped all sets of nails. *Toe*nails.

Our waitress was too consumed by her own story to attend to mine. Our children's eyes were wide as they witnessed her undeniable irritation roiling around behind that drink tray. Between water refills, we whispered to the kids, "This is where we practice God's love."

They smiled big and called her ma'am and used an unusually high level of manners. Nate left her double his standard tip and told the children about it. It was easy for them—and for us—to love well that night because this waitress had no emotional hook in our hearts.

But what about when the emotional hook *is* there? Loving others who mistreat us is harder when our hearts are wrapped up tightly in the relationship, when the harsh words play directly to our fears, or when the mistreatment lasts for years and we're spinning in anger and hurt.

I've had both. The ache of someone I trust and look up to bruising my heart in their calloused hands, and the harsh words from one not as dear to me that played right into the center of my fears. I've faced waves of misunderstanding and judgment, often the kind that are especially hard to let go of. But I've also learned that hidden beneath those pounding waves is one of the best places to seek God.

How do You *see me, God?* isn't a question we consider asking when the world treats us as we feel we deserve.

Who am I from Your *perspective, God?* isn't a game-changing conversation when the relational mirrors around us make us feel good.

Jesus' instruction to turn the other cheek is all well and good until we're criticized or misunderstood and need to understand how God sees us in that moment.

When I've been wronged or unjustly criticized, I want to fight back. I want to grit my teeth and defend. Find justice. I want people in my circle to bend a sympathetic ear and to be on my side.

But when another human being doesn't see me clearly, I get to ask God who I am. When I'm on the receiving end of judgment or mistreatment, I get to carve a space in my prayer closet where only one voice matters. When rough hands hurt what is tender within me, I get to scoot up next to the one whose hands formed me.

And so, in some ways, the one who mistreats me gives me a gift: the gift of collapsing into the arms of God. What happens in the secret place between God and me is out of that person's reach, making it even sweeter.

Sometimes when I'm under God's kind eyes, I see that my opponent isn't all that wrong. And I'm not all that right. Other times, I still feel wounded and misunderstood. The real battle here isn't for a winner, for me over the other person, but to win over new places of my heart to God's gentle perspective on me.

When we believe that a life poured out for God is our most beautiful expression, every accusation and misunder-standing carries within it an opportunity to step into that beauty, just in a way we might not have chosen.

If we can find a place to pause from the swirl, the answer becomes clear: the ones who oppose us when we need championing the most are also the ones who send us into the hidden conversations with God, conversations that change us. God champions us like no human can, but we don't often see that unless we have nowhere to look but Him.

I can allow those who misjudge me to help me become more of a daughter, one who comes to her Daddy in a whole new needy way when she's been mistreated. I can bless those who curse me because of how He whispers to me when I'm mistreated. In the light of Him who loves me, I can face my fear of not being loved. Thomas Merton says it this way: "If we are to love sincerely and with simplicity, we must first of all overcome the fear of not being loved."[12]

Why wouldn't I give them—the critics, the judgers, the misunderstanders—my other cheek, my favorite coat, my tired extra mile?

"Blessed are you when they revile and persecute you, and say all kinds of evil against you falsely for My sake," says Jesus in the Sermon on the Mount. "Rejoice and be exceedingly glad, for great is your reward in heaven, for so they persecuted the prophets who were before you" (Matt. 5:11–12).

We read these words and yet too often still experience surprise when our best efforts at Christian living result in something other than Christian applauding. *Do the works of God and people will see and they will celebrate*, we think. We forget that the map for following God was given to us by a man who was routinely persecuted by the religious leaders of

His day, who was abandoned by virtually all of His followers at the end of His life and then brutally murdered.

We want our work to be known and our impact to be memorialized. And it will be, but by God alone. No human can give us accolades that will satisfy the deepest longings of our hearts. We search vainly from others for the acclaim that only God can give.

This is why we need to reframe the way we view and respond to mistreatment. If we can see it as a form of hiding in God, it takes on new significance. In God's hands, it becomes a tool He uses to redirect the human heart toward finding its value in Him rather than in other human beings. When we learn to relish what happens in the hidden place, we lean into what He wants to offer us in mistreatment.

We all face routine human misunderstandings and relational challenges, the scuffles that happen as our lives brush up against another. Your best gift today may be the one who misunderstands you or even opposes you. Your adversary may actually be your advocate, the one moving you closer to God.

What did Mary think others would say about her when she undid her hair and wasted her inheritance on Jesus' feet? Perhaps she had to overcome days of fear, knowing that she was about to do something unwelcome and strange. Perhaps she was so focused on adoring Him that she never considered what other voices would say. Perhaps her thoughts of doubt were her biggest enemy. Or what if her action wasn't planned at all? What if her impulsive rush of devotion overshadowed even the thought of onlookers' opinions?

Mary had already unfurled her heart before this Savior along the dusty road, talking with Him after the crowds went home. She'd developed a history with this man in the private spaces of her heart and in the private pockets of her day. His voice had become bigger to her than any other voice, any other noise.

But the criticism that night was sharp. Biting. These were not strangers. They were people she knew well. People whose opinions she valued. Out of the weakest parts of themselves, they spoke words that lodged in the weakest parts of her. They knew how to hurt. They knew how to play on the criticisms she likely already told herself.

But Mary had developed the habit of valuing Jesus' voice above all others.

She knew she'd come for Him alone.

"I just can't hear God," my ten-year-old told me after facing her sin. She'd participated in an unfettered rant toward her siblings and was having a hard time turning her heart and repenting. She was simply mad, and the suggestion I'd made for her to quiet herself for a few minutes and talk to God only positioned her to field more of her desperate anger. She was both defensive and defeated, not wanting to admit fault yet feeling irrevocably flawed and stuck on the inside. I guess this line of thinking isn't age discriminate. This young one was discovering that sometimes accusations and criticisms come not just from outside voices but also from voices on the inside. When the accusation is internal, we can't merely acknowledge it and move on. We need to challenge it by putting up a fight.

My daughter's thoughts had been brewing for hours after a morning altercation in the kitchen with her sister over a skillet of eggs. I could see in her eyes that her dark thoughts had taken over. She'd become their slave, responding to what ricocheted around her mind. No wonder she'd had difficulty with a simple request to set the dinner table.

And she couldn't understand His offer of kindness for her repentance, gently inviting her to turn. This incident only proved to her what she'd already felt on the inside: she was wrong. Just bad.

Trying to think quickly, I pulled out a notebook and began sketching. I drew an outline of her head, leaving the space within empty, void of the voice of God just as she described it and just as she felt it, though I knew her mind was full of other voices.

"Tell me exactly what thoughts have gone through your mind this afternoon," I said. "Let's take a closer look at what's inside of there."

After some coaxing, we made a list. On it were statements like, "I'm a bad person," and, "I'm not a good sister," and, "I keep messing up." For every thought she mentioned, I made a hash mark across the head of this rough sketch. When we were finished, there was no white space left. No room in her mind for anything but her own accusing thoughts.

"Now, where's the room to hear God?" I asked, holding up the notebook.

She smiled, coyly.

"I get it, baby girl," I said to her as I scooted up close to her. "I'm almost thirty years older than you, and in one single day I can lose all the white space in my head too. My mind can get full of all sorts of things that keep me from hearing God."

Maybe you can relate.

She is just beginning to learn what I still need to practice to stay alive in God: every single thought matters. The thoughts that don't bow to God will give permission to another god. But a barreling life leaves little room for evaluating these unfettered thoughts. It leaves little room for letting God's rest and His peace seep in and His truth invade the cacophony in my mind.

Responding to the clock and reacting to our to-do lists and chasing the latest thrill in front of us—yes, even the good-work-of-His-kingdom kind of thrill—keeps the mind that's not at peace in motion. The quick decision to forfeit quiet to read another's status update keeps our minds racing, with no space to consider which thoughts of ours are aligning with God and His Word. Just like my daughter hears *I keep messing up*, we let the noise take charge of the uncertain parts of us, often without even knowing it.

The white space of the day is God's gift to us. Discovering the white space of our minds on which He can write is what we're invited to find, there. The hum of the washing machine as we fold our load from the dryer. The still of two o'clock in the afternoon before the bus unloads children and backpacks and giggles. The sigh of a prayer as we sit down to a good meal. All of these moments remind us, by comparison, of the noise that happens within our minds the rest of the time.

It's one thing to get rid of the noise. It's another thing to know how to invite Him into the white space.

It's Tuesday afternoon.

The babe's down for his nap, the children are building forts in the backyard woods, and Nate is working from home with one eye on the computer while answering to shouts of "Daddy, we found a turtle. Come see!" and "Is it time for a snack yet?" and "Can we ride bikes down the hill?" The baby monitor drones in the background at home as I get in the car to drive a few miles to a coffee shop. Tuesday afternoons are my time to write.

As I pull away from the house, my thoughts go something like this: First, I remember all the things I've left undone at home. *Is the oven on? I forgot to check Lily's reading. Ooh, the bread for dinner is still in the freezer.*

If unchecked, that line of thinking can escalate from a simple question, *Should I just turn around?* to questioning my worth and my calling: *What I am thinking, trying to add writing to my life? Who do I think I am?* By the time I walk through the door of the coffee shop, order a chai, and sit down, I'm in a slump, less enthusiastic about my writing now that I've reminded myself of all that I "should" be doing and all the ways I'm unqualified to do anything at all.

Then I glance at the young woman two tables over, writing away on her computer. A school paper, maybe, or a book? She looks intent. Having entered my rut of unfettered thoughts, I'm susceptible to more: *The world doesn't need another writer. There are so many people saying something, anything. Why do I want to add my voice to that noise?* The writing idea that had been bumping around in my mind for days suddenly seems foolish. I cross a line through it on my page of handwritten notes.

I'm better off just getting lost in a book today, I reason, and so I join the throngs of writers and painters and accountants and schoolteachers and photographers who forfeit God's display of glory through them in exchange for a lie.

I join the mothers who kiss their children goodnight, only to walk back into the kitchen in shame at the tone they'd used five minutes earlier. *I knew I'd never be a good mother.* The painters who get their equipment together for an afternoon of playing with God only to end the day with an empty canvas. *If I can't get it just right, I'm not ready to try.* The bankers and lawyers and architects who spend every commute berating themselves for not hitting the achievement marks they think they should. *I'm just an unqualified faker underneath this suit.*

The accusations in my head and yours aren't just personal report cards. They are arrows from an enemy who is hounding our lives and our pursuit of God. "For we do not wrestle against flesh and blood" (Eph. 6:12). The enemy is exploiting our weak spots, the ones that have the potential to bring the greatest glory of God into our lives, and we've been duped. The enemy is, after all, a destroyer of what is good. When we let shameful lies speak louder than vulnerable expressions of our true selves, we are missing a meeting with God. When we hear Satan's lies and respond with an acceptance letter, God is still inviting us: *Engage with Me in the place where you feel less-than or ashamed. I'll breathe My truth over your dark thoughts.*

When we hear the cacophony of accusing voices on the inside of us, we don't have to surrender to them. We fight those lies with spoken truth: "For we do not wrestle against flesh and blood." We recognize that God made us to fight the battle against our untruthful thoughts: "Therefore take up the whole armor of God, that you may be able to withstand in the evil day, and having done all, to stand" (v. 13).

In the hidden places, we realize that the Word of God is a powerful weapon, not something created just for a cross-stitched wall hanging or as generally helpful advice. It reaches into our insides, into our inner thoughts and intentions, and exposes us before the God who has made us to partner with Him and against the internal lies we battle. "For the word of God is living and powerful, and sharper than any two-edged sword, piercing even to the division of soul and spirit, and of joints and marrow, and is a discerner of the thoughts and intents of the heart. And there is no creature hidden from His sight, but all things are naked and open to the eyes of Him to whom we must give account" (Heb. 4:12–13).

So how do we battle these accusing voices? Start by jotting down the self-defeating thoughts you entertain, the ones with which you often agree. Thoughts like, *I'm never going to change*, as you look at parts of yourself that long have been sedentary and unbending. *I'm not worth sticking with*, after a vulnerable moment with a friend. *I'm just setting myself up for another big failure*, when stepping out into something new. These thoughts will dictate your emotions and your actions if you let them. These are the enemy's accusations and lies. When they creep in and you see them for what they truly are, renounce them with God's truth. Refuse to agree with them. Fill your mouth with life, recognizing that "death and life are in the power of the tongue" (Prov. 18:21). Power is in speaking what is true.

Instead of saying to yourself, *I'm never going to change*, renounce the lie that a heart is forever unbending. Repent for agreeing with these thoughts that do not line up with God's Word. Lean into God's power to work in you, even though your fears speak otherwise. As you pray for yourself, repeat back to God, "He who began a good work in [me] will carry it on to completion until the day of Christ Jesus" (Phil. 1:6 NIV).

Instead of, *I'm not worth sticking with*, renounce the lie that you are unlovable and unworthy. Repent of agreeing with this lie and ask God to hear the cries of your heart to have a friend who knows you in your pain. Use the words of the psalmist: "In the day when I cried out, You answered me, and made me bold with strength in my soul" (Ps. 138:3). The Word of God equips you to fight back when you hear those toxic mutterings.

Instead of, *I'm just setting myself up for a big failure*, renounce the lie that the worst is yet to come. Repent of disregarding the hope of Jesus for your life and agreeing with hopeless expectations. Ask God to awaken your life in prayer and to show you, afresh, how He hears you. Use the words of the psalmist:

Many are they who say of me,
"There is no help for him in God."

But You, O LORD, are a shield for me,
My glory and the One who lifts up my head.
I cried to the LORD with my voice,
And He heard me from His holy hill.

—PSALM 3:2—4

In His Word, we have help, especially for the lies many of us have just accepted as part of life. I often find the help I need in the Psalms, which is sometimes called the prayer book of the Bible. The Psalms includes prayers that run the gamut of human experience from prayers of thanksgiving and praise to prayers of lament and confession. God gives us these prayers not only to help us express our thoughts and emotions to Him but also to help us hear His truth above the world's chatter. Author and pastor Tim Keller says of the Psalms, "We are not simply to read the Psalms; we are to be immersed in them so that they profoundly shape how we relate to God . . . [They] are the divinely ordained way to learn devotion to our God."[13] The Psalms demonstrates that we can bring to God all of ourselves—with all of our emotions—and trust that He has the power to change us.

When I feel helpless and hopeless and alone, I pray, "My soul clings to the dust; revive me according to Your word" (Ps. 119:25).

When I've messed up big, I pray, "Purge me with hyssop, and I shall be clean; wash me, and I shall be whiter than snow" (Ps. 51:7).

When I'm filled with anxiety, I pray, "In the day when I cried out, You answered me, and made me bold with strength in my soul" (Ps. 138:3).

And when I start to feel worthless, unnoticed, and over-looked, I pray, "Keep me as the apple of Your eye; hide me under the shadow of Your wings" (Ps. 17:8).

I pray when I feel helpless and hopeless and alone. I choose with my words to lay myself bare before Him instead of standing at a distance from Him and chastising myself for how I've fallen short. My emotions—the ones that a full schedule and an outwardly productive life can help prevent me from feeling—are a road to conversation with God. The hidden places of my heart get exposed and He responds.

When we let the Psalms or any biblical truth sink into the white spaces in our lives and minds, we are winning one of the most significant battles of our lives. We learn to lean into Him for a win. Just as it was with my daughter, our minds are often full of myriad unfettered thoughts, such that there is little room to receive God's thoughts. When these words go beyond falling lightly within our hearing, when we allow them to sink deeply into us—reading, memorizing, speaking, singing, and praying them—we find that our white space expands. "[The Psalms] are written to be prayed, recited, and sung," Keller writes, "to be done, not merely to be read."[14] We work less to crowd out the noise in our minds and realize that the white spaces aren't the empty times of our day or vacant parts of our minds waiting to be stuffed. They are pregnant, full in themselves. And expansive.

At the break of day, noon, night, and a dozen times in

between, God's Word is your ally. Read it. Say it. Sing it. To live and thrive in God amid all the competing noise and voices of this age, we have to engage with His Word. Not just once a day or once every few days. We can't live without this Word.

So we lean into God, in hiding. We lean into Him in the late afternoon when we see the sun illuminate the dust on our coffee tables, speaking the Word of God against the lies that have been infecting our day. We lean into Him on the Saturday without any plans, asking Him to speak into the void and remind us that there is no void in God.

The Word of God is powerful against our internal traffic. It pierces through our souls, even to the parts of us we've hidden from ourselves. It reaches into our spirits with His Spirit, breathing life as He moves in. It replaces the internal chatter of life—the criticisms, the comparisons, and the shoulds—with the truth of what God sees and thinks and feels. And that's a beautiful sound.

It's just after dusk and the children are in bed. I can hear the clock that's been ticking, unnoticed, all day. I can hear the quiet.

I have much I could be doing. But I also have an invitation: *Let yourself hear My voice. Express your emotions through the Psalms. Be silent with Me. Let go of the voices, the noise, the chatter.*

I don't write a blog post about the exchange. I don't snap a picture. Only God and I know the details of our conversation. And an hour later, the only evidence that it was time well spent is hidden underneath my skin. My heart grew. He loved my private reach at an unplanned time. He responded. He loved the opportunity to marvel at His own craftsmanship in me.

It's time for bed on a Tuesday and I have nothing to show for it.

Tonight has been wildly successful.

───────────── *For Your Continued Pursuit* ─────────────

Psalm 17:8 | Psalm 51:7 | Psalm 119:25 | Psalm 138:3 | Proverbs 18:21 | Song of Songs 2:14 | Isaiah 26:3 | Zechariah 3:1–5 | Matthew 5:11–12 | Matthew 5:39 | Mark 14:3–9 | John 10:10 | Romans 2:4 | 2 Corinthians 10:4–6 | Ephesians 6:10–20 | Philippians 1:6 | Philippians 4:8 | Hebrews 4:11–13 | 1 Peter 2:21–25 | 1 Peter 4:12–14 *ten*

THIRSTY SEASONS

Learning to Long for God's Presence

"Me you do not have always."

—MARK 14:7

We were warned before adopting our kids that adoption might ruin us. If you walked into my kitchen at 5:00 p.m. the first winter after one of our adoptions, you might have indeed thought we were ruined. I surely did, then.

The sun sank earlier every day, and my daughter sank right with it. The cause changed daily. Not enough food at dinner, too many crumbs to sweep from the kitchen floor, and a sibling's accidental elbow bump all made her wail. Night after night we fielded the sobs, knowing it was easier for her to cry over spilled milk than to go into the crux of her pain, loss that no five-year-old should ever have to face.

So we held her in the tears and wondered if we'd ever know normal again. As I ushered children into their jammies each evening, I prayed a new kind of prayer—short and desperate. I was tired and needy and confused. I had no book to tell me what to expect from a child with her history, her particular cocktail of losses and grief. Even the best parenting strategies were not sufficient. I needed God.

Our family struggled so much during this time that, yes, some might have said we were truly ruined. But a change was taking place inside me that had started years before and is still working its way through me. Instead of running from my weaknesses, I started to lean into them.

I began to like the benefits of unraveling my heart at the feet of Jesus, who never promised I would have strength of my own. I studied His expression toward me when I brought nothing but tears to our conversation. He promises in His Word to care for the brokenhearted. I began to realize that the brokenhearted weren't the ones I pitied from my cushioned life. They were me. I was brokenhearted.

My children didn't ruin me. I was ruined long before they came along. However, my children did bring me into circumstances that God used to show me how weak I really am. Terribly weak, it turns out. I am no more ruined now than I was when life ran on time, the laundry was always immediately folded, and I knew what to expect out of each day. It's just that now I can see my ruination more clearly. I can see how much I need God.

Out of my weakness, and yours, can come a glorious thirst for God. What some may call the end of us, the ruin of us, can bring us closer to God than any one of our strongest days. We think, *When I get there [to that elusively strong place], then I'll rest, be satisfied, be confident, change the world, [fill in the blank].* And then we go to embarrassing lengths to claw our way out of any situation that leaves us feeling helpless. We do anything to feel strong again, even if that strength is a shadow. But God's invitation to us is and always will be, *Die to this illusion of strength you've created. That's when you'll find what you've been thirsting for.* God created us to want more of Him. He created us to thirst for Him. He created us to need Him, even when all we want to need is ourselves.

Today, Hope pirouettes through the kitchen and Caleb stores books under chairs so he can read them between chores and Lily paints us a picture of a boat for our bedroom that's better than anything I've ever bought from a store. Eden belts out hymns in the shower and Bo is learning to snuggle close and pat my hand when I'm sick. I love these banner moments when my children are happy and enjoying life. But these best moments with my children are not what truly bring out the best in me. It's in all those not-shining moments that these beautiful children have made me want to rest on God's chest, that place where I've crumbled and where He moved in with power. I'm weepy and He's gentle. I'm burdened and He's kind.

I'm reaching. Thirsty. And He responds.

The degree to which I allow weakness to become thirst for more of God, and the degree to which I allow myself to lean into that thirst rather than run from it, is the degree to which I am becoming my best self.

It's a verse you've likely seen in a church foyer or cross-stitched on your grandmother's wall: "As the deer pants for the water brooks, so pants my soul for You, O God" (Ps. 42:1). Perhaps it was written in calligraphy beneath an image of a majestic deer quietly drinking from a sun-dappled stream. It's an idyllic, peaceful scene. But what if the psalmist had a different scene in mind? What if the deer had a desperate thirst? A deer that *pants* for water might be running from death, nearly frantic for water.

Maybe you've experienced a version of that desperate physical thirst. Perhaps you were in intense heat and without any water for hours or miles. It's a terribly uncomfortable condition to be in. It's also incredibly vulnerable. When you're dehydrated and thirsty, thirst is all consuming.

What if this desperate thirst is the scene the psalmist had in mind? A soul full of such longing for God that nothing else matters. And a thirst that is actually a good thing, an indicator of present and coming growth.

Though it seems counterintuitive, the spaces in our lives where God seems to be absent are sometimes the places where we grow the most. If we can tolerate the thirst long enough, staying in our weakness and our need, we will find more of God.

Every few years, I circle back to the same reminder, the same invitation. Each time, it's with a little more clarity and a growing readiness to lean into Him in my weakness.

Just after I birthed our first biological child, who was the fifth child in our family, I remembered that familiar feeling returning, the one where I felt I was sinking while those around me remained afloat. My "bigs" had growing heart-needs alongside their growing bodies, and yet there was only one me, one mommy, for all of them. Now I had *five* of them. I found myself making a daily mental record of their needs and my gaps, allowing a steady drip of self-resentment about my human weakness to leak into my thinking. I was tempted to despise this season in which I felt mostly weak and incapable.

But God reminded me to allow for the thirst. I heard Him while I nursed the babe and between all the heart-needs that surfaced in a day. I heard Him when I slowed down to evaluate, and not just imbibe, my thoughts and fears. This was an invitation: to lean. In.

It took hidden times, desperate times, for me to practice leaning into my weaknesses rather than despising them. Whereas I once responded to experiences of weakness by adding another spiritual discipline or seeking a new ministry opportunity or chiding myself for my discomforting thirst, now I was praying prayers like this:

I want more of You, God.

Grow me, on the inside.

I'm thirsty. Fill me, God.

I could have slaked my thirst with temporary fixes. Every day was filled with dozens of distractions that tried to woo my attention away from this uncomfortable void inside me. I was a God-follower who did not and could not *feel* God, and all I wanted was not to feel that way any more—not to be so vulnerable and parched. *What is wrong with me?* But I kept seeing thirst come up in His Word:

- "You, God, are my God, earnestly I seek you; I thirst for you, my whole being longs for you, in a dry and parched land where there is no water" (Ps. 63:1 NIV).
- "I spread out my hands to you; I thirst for you like a parched land" (Ps. 143:6 NIV).

177

- "Blessed are those who hunger and thirst for righteousness, for they shall be filled" (Matt. 5:6).
- "Ho! Everyone who thirsts, come to the waters; and you who have no money, come, buy and eat. Yes, come, buy wine and milk without money and without price" (Isa. 55:1).

"Feel the gap and fill it" had been my approach to life in God up to that point. But now I was in a desperate situation, and I needed freedom to say, "I'm empty. It's okay to be empty and stay empty for a little while." That admission led to this prayer: *I really do want more of You, God. I want more than what I am experiencing and knowing right now.* And I let myself feel the dryness of thirst without trying to fix it on my own.

Realizing that my thirst wasn't wrong but could instead increase my reach for God surfaced an eagerness in me. I read His Word and prayed with greater expectation. I waited with eyes open. I noticed Him in places I hadn't seen Him before and in ways I hadn't allowed Him to come to me before.

In the early years after our adoption, I was alarmed when my children's deep wounds manifested themselves in some way. I felt both ill-equipped to respond and skittish about what might lie ahead—for them and for me. Their weakness made me acutely aware of my own. I wanted to crawl out of my skin, here. I certainly didn't feel a staying power as I faced these chasms in myself.

"Do something, *anything*, God, to change this. To change them," I'd pray, desperate not to feel so vulnerable. Desperate to stop the pain in them and in me. But God used this desperation to intensify a thirst in my soul. A thirst I didn't have when my children and our home felt normal, when I didn't feel so exposed. A thirst that offered an opportunity to reach. To lean in. To stay in that place of internal floundering want.

In a culture that's full—full of commitments, full of tasks, full of opportunities and people and digital windows into lives that aren't our own—God calls us to resist succumbing to readily available distractions and instead to press into these thirsty moments, our weakest seasons. Thirst is our ally. We want to be thirsty for God.

This is a beautiful paradox of the spiritual life. Jesus invites us to come to Him and then makes this promise: "But whoever drinks the water I give them will never thirst. Indeed, the water I give them will become in them a spring of water welling up to eternal life" (John 4:14 NIV).

Yet there remains this conundrum: we still feel parched for Him.

Thirst = Need of God

Before heaven, before completeness, before the end of lack, we can rest in our thirst, in this longing for God. When our thirst for more of God deepens our awareness of how much we need Him, our capacity for Him grows. We not only see Him as the spring of water, but we develop a continued and ever-growing thirst for *that* water. Our thirst is how God allures us. The thirsty don't just find God, they *thrive* in God. They drink with deep satisfaction. And this drink makes them thirsty for all that will one day be.

"Me you do not have always."

Jesus had just acknowledged His impending death. In polite company and over dinner. He often upended social mores.

He spoke not to Mary but to the dinner guests who'd criticized her. Yet it was within her hearing. And on this night of her outpouring. Here, in one of her most vulnerable moments, Jesus made it clear He was not long for this earth.

Perhaps His statement shocked her. Or maybe it simply confirmed the sad truth she already suspected. She would know His face, His smile, that look He often gave her just a little longer. Then she would know the sharp pain of His absence, sharper still because she had stared into that face. It was her love for Him that made the longing for Him so great. The memories she had with this God-man as she sat at His feet would fuel an ache for her reunion with Him that would never quite subside until it happened.

Mary was made to move from thirst to fulfillment to thirst again, only to look toward a forever fulfillment one day still to come. Thirst and being satisfied in God would be interwoven for the rest of her days.

These were her growth spurts in God.

And this night, though thirst would come again, she found herself overflowing as she emptied her love at Jesus' feet.

Bo has six teeth, and only Nate gets a full toothy reveal.

All seven of us were around the dinner table laughing at

the antics of our one-year-old. Deep belly laughs and a single one-syllable word (at varying decibels) to describe just about everything. For his siblings, this babe is better entertainment than an electric train. And at the dinner table, Daddy draws out the best of that kid.

So there he was, the spitting image of his father and sitting four seats away, showing off all those teeth in one direction.

"I saw your baby pictures, Daddy, and he looks just like you," said Hope casually between bites.

"His hair is turning out to be the same color as yours, and his eyes are blue too," says Eden. "You know, Daddy, I think he looks just like you."

"Nah," says Nate. "We'll have to just wait and see what he looks like." In other conversations like this, he's reminded Caleb how many people say he and Caleb look alike but for the color of their skin. I do the same thing. Partially out of habit and partially to pacify the terrible ache of their loss.

As the girls move on to talking about hair color, Nate jumps in: "Your hair color is the same brown as Mommy's." They disagree. Mine's lighter, they argue.

Everyone is taking bites and weighing in on hair color and eyes and the varying skin tones of one another (a common discussion in our home). I join the conversation with uneasy laughter, and yet this moment, for me, feels supercharged.

Nate and I want each of our kids to know and experience the God whose face is set fiercely toward them. This is the God who wants to heal their hearts, the hearts that may soon ache over the blank pages of their baby books—the ones unnaturally at the beginning. When that day comes, we want them to know they can cry at His feet. They can pour out the grief they feel when they realize that they may never see on earth the faces of the beautiful women who birthed them.

When the pain makes them want to pretend all that loss never happened, we want our children to feel the hands of God as He cups their chins and looks into their eyes with limitless understanding of their pain. We want them to have a tender brush with the God who came to not just reset the bones of their brokenness but make their broken hearts sing. But for that to happen, we have to let them feel the hurt, to feel the longing for something more. If we insulate them instead or somehow teach them to avoid the ache and the thirst of their history, we're giving them permission to overlook the most enrapturing parts of their God.

The same applies to you and me. If I constantly try to avoid how spiritually parched I feel, I'm missing the infilling nature of God, the one who doesn't just acknowledge my desert but gives me a stream, right there. Laughter is an incredible gift, and we as a family grab it when we can. It is healing. Yet if Nate or I or any one of these beloved children around our table refuses to look at and grieve our losses, we may also miss our most profound story in God.

As long as we're on earth, we *will* thirst for God. And He will respond. It may not be in the way we expect or within our timing, but He promises to respond to the thirsty. It's His way with us. Not just intellectually assenting to this but being willing to live in it, with Him, is what releases us from resenting the places that reveal how thirsty we are.

My children's wounds and needs remind me how much I need God. *I'm thirsty for more than a quick fix.*

An unexpected afternoon alone makes me feel barren in a way that I didn't notice the day before in a packed schedule. *I notice now that I need Him. I'm thirsty for Him to come and meet me.*

Being an indistinct face in a large crowd makes me want to be seen. *I'm thirsty for acknowledgment of the little movements of my life. But I'm really thirsty for His eyes, on me.*

I can welcome thirst when it prompts me to reach for God in the driest places.

Tenderly.

"I will lead her into the desert and speak tenderly to her there" (Hos. 2:14 NLT). These are God's words about His wayward people, spoken to the prophet Hosea, who had a wayward wife named Gomer. God's plan required a desert—an arid, dusty, inhospitable climate. Today, our desert equivalent could be our corners of hiddenness. Our anonymous cubicles. Our support roles. Our 3:00 a.m. baby feedings. Our fifteenth sojourn in the doctor's waiting room with an ill child, condition still undiagnosed. Our 136th day in the carpool line. Our crowded church sanctuaries. Our Friday nights alone. Our monotonous shifts in the grocery store that barely pay the bills.

It is there, in whatever this desert is, that He promises to speak tenderly.

What feels like a wilderness, a desert—the hidden seasons

and the hidden spaces throughout our day that expose how dry we are on the inside—cannot thwart the maker of rain. These are the times our roots forge deeper through the earth to find the water source. It's the only way to survive drought.

> For I will pour water on the thirsty land,
>   and streams on the dry ground;
> I will pour out my Spirit on your offspring,
>   and my blessing on your descendants.
> They will spring up like grass in a meadow,
>   like poplar trees by flowing streams.
>
> —ISAIAH 44:3–4 NIV

Our water is Him. This beautiful God. His eyes, they know us—all the parts of us. His arms, they're strong and they hold us. His whisper speaks life and breathes dust off what's old and needs reviving.

We drink of Him—this living water—and we want to drink again. It's that good. This God-man is *that* surprisingly good, better than any other single thing with which we've tried to slake our thirst. We're not trapped in these parched and hidden moments where no one sees us; instead, we're invited to sink our roots deeper into God right there. To stay long enough to hear God's tender voice over that specific moment, for us.

Thirst makes us reach for God not just as *the* Healer but as *our* Healer. And we watch the water pour on desert lands.

For Your Continued Pursuit

Psalm 33:16–22 | Psalm 34:18 | Psalm 42 | Psalm 63:1–8 | Psalm 81:10 | Psalm 84:1–4, 10 | Psalm 119:20, 81 | Psalm 143:6 | Psalm 147:3, 10–11 | Proverbs 27:7 | Isaiah 41:18–20 | Isaiah 44:3–4 | Isaiah 55:1 | Isaiah 61:1–3 | Hosea 2:14 | Matthew 5:6 | Matthew 9:15 | Mark 14:7 | John 4:1–26 | John 6:33–35 | John 7:37 | 2 Corinthians 12:8–10 | Ephesians 3:19 | 2 Timothy 2:13

eleven

GOD IS FOR US

Healing in the Hiding

"She has done what she could."

—MARK 14:8

"Mommy, I think God wants me to tell you why I don't like Ethiopia," my five-year-old told me, so matter-of-fact.

I'd been waiting for this day. It just came about five years earlier than I'd anticipated. Over the course of the few years since she'd come home, any mention of Ethiopia left my little girl eyes-to-the-floor.

"We love Ethiopia!" I once declared to an Ethiopian coffee-shop barista as I slid a sleeve over my cup of tea. She had noticed my kids, recognized something familiar in their faces, and they had noticed her. But as we walked away, my little one said under her breath, "I don't love Ethiopia."

As her language skills and cognitive development advanced, I asked questions, trying to understand her disdain, but to no avail. We prayed in private, Nate and I, knowing that the secrets her little body held would become toxic if not brought into the light.

It wasn't until all four of us were in Uganda chasing papers for our two other daughters that I sensed God's prompting: *Now. She's ready to talk now.*

It happened to be the day we'd set aside for a mommy-daughter date during those waiting days after finally meeting the two older girls. I held my little one's hand as we walked on the dusty road from our guesthouse to the nearest spot for a cup of tea. She rambled about anything that came to mind, excited to have Mommy all to herself.

As she sat sipping her milk from a straw, she cracked open what she called her prayer journal to a picture she had drawn of a brown hut. She remembered. I wasn't sure that she would.

The minutes that followed felt like years as I listened to my little girl speak about big girl things—things I'd never taught her, things she saw in real life, not on a television or movie screen. It was as if she had grown up in one morning, suddenly able to articulate her pain, loss, and disappointment—and all the scenes that brought them about—with a coherence that didn't fit her age.

I choked back tears, just listening. I was stunned equally by her vivid account and her ability to communicate it. So many pieces of her puzzle came together in that one conversation. Gaps in our understanding of her suddenly filled.

When she was through, we talked. We prayed to ask Jesus to reveal how He felt about her and how He saw her during those lonely years.

I sat there praying: *What do I do now with these shards of glass, the remnants of her pain?* Then I saw the answer on her face. It went something like this: *Now I've told you everything,*

Mommy, so what are we having for lunch? It was finished, at least for now—wrapped up, handed to Mommy for safekeeping, and finally off five-year-old shoulders never meant to carry such a burden.

Since that conversation, her steps have been lighter. After that point, in her pretend play, she was often a transcontinental traveler, Ethiopia being one of her main stops. "I want to go back to Ethiopia one day and tell them about Jesus," she said to me recently.

God took this part of her burden. "He heals the brokenhearted and binds up their wounds" (Ps. 147:3). My little girl was climbing her way out, early, of brokenness. She was remembering, and acknowledging, the pain—the pain that creates space and emptiness and looks to God for healing.

This is, too, what the process of climbing out of brokenness looks like for me some days. A friend says something that stings, and instead of mentally rolling my eyes at her or looking for ways to defame her in my thinking, I ask God, *Why does this hurt?* I turn my attention away from my friend and toward God. I ask Him about me: *What is it in me that You want to heal? What is it in me that needs Your touch because these words hurt?*

As I lift my hurts, big and small, to God, I've often been surprised by how God shows up to heal everything. Even the parts of me I thought were unfixable, sedentary, "just part of my personality," or "just part of my story."

So many little aches or obstinate quirks that we accept about ourselves are places in our lives that God can heal, into which He can breathe His perspective. But for Him to

speak a healing word over old wounds, we have to acknowledge them.

My girl started young. He led her there. This was the first
of many conversations just like it she will have with Him in
the years ahead.

He loves to heal what has broken.

One Sunday after church, I was talking to new friends—new
to me, to us, and to our story. I knew that when they looked
at our family on Sundays, they saw colorful headbands and
cute boots on this one day of the week when we all looked
fairly well kempt. They saw rescue and redemption in the
intermingled line-up of light and dark skin, and they saw
my babes taking turns being lifted into Nate's arms during
worship. But I saw what they couldn't. I knew what simmered
beneath the patterned dresses and pressed shirts. I had held
those same babes the night before when one complained of
the nightmares again and the other cried for no identifiable
reason—and for every reason.

One of my girls sidled up beside me in this conversation
with new friends. She was brewing with pain from the
day before but dressed as if the American dream was hers.
When my new friends asked her a few questions, she looked
down and then away. She mumbled something under the
hand she uses to hide herself when she is shaky and unsure.
She was weary, and this invitation to chat with smiley
strangers only exacerbated her fatigue. But if you didn't

know her history, you might have written her off as a rude preadolescent.

A few minutes later, the conversation was over and we were putting on gloves and coats and walking to the parking lot. I slid into the car, embarrassed and sulking.

My daughter hadn't "performed."

In just a three-minute conversation, I felt trapped by imagined judgment from people I barely knew.

How do I get her to stop this? I grumbled about my apparently sullen child. *What if she still can't look someone in the eye when she's thirty? How can I ever take her anywhere if she continues to do this?*

That morning, I felt like I'd failed to live up to the image of a stellar parent who was facilitating redemption in her child's heart. Instead, I looked like I was aiding and abetting disrespectful children, clearly indulging self-centeredness by not addressing it on the spot.

Three minutes after a three-minute conversation and I was sunk. I perceived another's perspective and received it as truth—for my daughter and for me.

On the drive home, I took deep breaths and felt even worse about what was bubbling out of my heart than about what had actually happened. Hours later, I finally sat myself before God, asking Him to bring wisdom and healing to these hidden parts of me.

My response to that brief conversation at church showed me my fears. I was afraid of the opinions of others, and I was afraid of the trajectory of my daughter's life. I cared more about the opinions of others than I did about the opinion of God. I believed more in my fears than I trusted Him. My reactions weren't just a reflection of my tendency to worry. They were a reflection of my needing God.

Healing starts with acknowledging we're broken. Seeing God as Healer starts with seeing ourselves in need of healing.

And so God hides us. He takes us into a place where the opinions of others fail us. Where we can't see through our fears. That's where He speaks to us. And the longing that comes from being hidden makes us more aware of our brokenness, more receptive to His healing, than we'd ever be in the light of the world's applause.

The perfume was, indeed, a waste. As Mary's critics pointed out, she could have sold it and given the money to the poor. But Jesus defended Mary's sacrifice.

"She has done what she could," He said to the skeptics in the room. These are the words of a Savior in flesh who saw Mary's actions—and her woundedness—in a different light. He saw her not as one forever broken but as someone in need of healing who reached for that healing, beautifully. And He healed her as He spoke of her, transforming her sacrifice from waste to beauty.

Mary had an offering for Him who was healing her with Himself. We don't know the specifics about Mary's brokenness or the ways she needed this healing, this wholeness of Him. Perhaps in relationships, in destructive choices, in jealousy or fear. But Jesus had seen it all before that night. He sheltered her with how He spoke of her. He made her story part of the gospel story and gave her a leading role in His resurrection. And so it was Mary, with all of her history and all of her lack, who anointed Him for burial with her wasteful outpouring of fragrant oil. This once-broken woman now being healed prepared the Savior for His own healing—and for the healing of the world.

I was in my thirties before I ever acknowledged one of the most significant broken parts of my story: the loss of my dad.

My dad was my hero. He watched me run across a playground one day and told me over dinner that night, "Kid, you've got a stride. Let's teach you how to really run." A decade and a half later, I was still lacing my shoes for races. My dad drove ten hours to watch me finish my first marathon.

A vivid memory I have of my childhood living room is of my dad sitting with me and listening to my teenage angst. I didn't tire him. My dad loved processing life with me. As he drove me to drama class and voice lessons, he never once tried to talk me out of my dream of becoming an actress. My dad dreamed with me. He made life seem limitless.

But everything changed one hot August day when I was fourteen years old. I biked home from my best friend's house and found my dad slumped on the couch. A back injury had returned with a vengeance. Many surgeries later, my dad was no longer hitting the tennis ball with me or running laps with me around the block. He was wheelchair-bound and sleeping in a bed we'd lugged down to the first-floor family room.

I seemed to take it all in stride, as most of us do when our childhood tilts. "Children are resilient," they say. What they mean is, "Children learn to cope, until they can't anymore."

My dad and I stayed close. He could barely sleep the night before I got on a plane to backpack across Europe on a college summer break. He lived my adventures along with me, whether or not he was physically with me.

Dad died a young death from a quickly growing cancer a month after I turned thirty-two. But it wasn't until years later when I had five children and a full schedule and a mortgage that I realized what had happened when I was fourteen, how that time when my dad's body first broke had affected the way I saw my life from then on.

It was the hiddenness and loneliness of motherhood that slowed me down enough to notice. With five boisterous kids and no one else noticing my days, I saw it—that my search for approval from older leaders was a hunger for my dad's validation, something he wasn't able to give in the years I needed it most. I had spent much of my early-adult life running harder, working to achieve more, and pushing myself further—all in an effort to get the smile I wanted from my dad, who was gone. Even years after his death, as a new mom, I was still reaching out for approval and validation, but at two o'clock on a Tuesday afternoon, no affirming adults were around to give it. God hid me from the approving eyes I sought so that I could find His.

Over weeks and months of talking with God about the loss I'd learned to stuff deep, God spoke into my wounds. (It doesn't always happen in a single afternoon like it did that day with my daughter under the Ugandan sun.) He reminded me that He saw me during those years of my dad's broken body. He had words of validation for me in Scripture that made my heart come alive. They far surpassed words that even the most trusted leader might say or the approving nod of the one whose affirmation I most wanted.

God called me to healing even after I thought I was already healed. *Hadn't I grieved my dad when he died?* I wondered. I'd always said I'd grieved for my dad even before he died, as he endured a long and painful decline. What I couldn't see, and what was perhaps more accurate, is that I had never grieved for my dad's *life*.

The tears came. How was it possible that my dad had been out of my life for so many years and it wasn't until now that I desperately wanted to remember everything about him? The scents of sweat and fried eggs that filled our kitchen on childhood Saturday mornings after my dad returned from playing tennis with his buddies. The safety I felt as a young girl having him kneel beside my bed and fill my mind with stories that gave flight to my imagination. The thrill of sharing a raft with him in the ocean, riding waves twice my size but not feeling the least bit fearful because of who I was with.

Why did this happen to me, God? I choked out with guttural cries.

And God peeled away a layer from the part of my heart where I'd buried my dad without grieving him, where I'd never grieved the parts of my childhood and young adulthood that were lost to the injury that took him—as we knew him—from us.

God wasn't working to heal me so that I could "be healed"

and be more readily useful to Him. He was healing me so that I would know Him as Healer. He was moving in, to me, in the healing. I was raw in this place of experiencing old pain that had hung like low clouds over my life. But when I saw God as Healer, my broken pieces didn't feel so daunting or heavy. I wanted to bring them to Him because I saw Him respond out of who He is. I wanted more of the nearness I felt when I broke before Him.

When our wounds meet the Healer, we begin to live from new places of restoration instead of just working to avoid these old aches. Isaiah wrote this of the Healer:

> He has sent Me to heal the brokenhearted . . .
> To give them beauty for ashes,
> The oil of joy for mourning,
> The garment of praise for the spirit of heaviness;
> That they may be called trees of righteousness,
> The planting of the LORD, that He may be glorified.
>
> —ISAIAH 61:1, 3

We grow tall as we heal, as we recognize our need for healing, as we allow ourselves to be thirsty, digging our roots deep into unseen places.

I'm a frequent and vivid dreamer, but I hadn't had even one dream of substance of my dad since his burial until years later when I finally allowed myself to grieve him.

I dreamed I was meeting with an influential person about my first book, which had recently been published. I'd gone to this person's estate at his request and was nervously answering his questions. From across the room, I spotted a man in his thirties with a familiar head of red hair, young and handsome and confident. He looked at me and in an instant I knew it was my father—my dad, the tennis coach and teacher and vibrant grasper of life I remember most. He was the age that he had been when I was seven or eight, during my golden years of childhood when the carpet beside my bed was permanently indented by his knees from tucking me in at night.

When my eye caught his, he didn't say a word. He moved no closer to me. He just smiled the knowing yet proud smile that a father gives only to his daughter or son.

And he winked.

Then he was gone, along with the dream. I was fully awake at three in the morning. Undone. I'd seen my dad again, the dad I remember. He'd entered into the conversation in my life that was most vulnerable at that time—my creativity, my story, set out for others to see and criticize as they wished.

This is the dad who set up a folding chair at every one of my footraces, yet wasn't there when my book was published five years and one day after his death.

In my vulnerable expression of creativity, I needed a daddy's approval. I needed God's approval. But I didn't realize my need for God's affirmation right here, my desperation, until I received it through that dream. God responded to my grief, to my blubbering laments, in a way that brought healing to a whole stretch of life my dad hadn't seen on earth.

When we acknowledge the parts of us that are broken, we have significant growth spurts in God. As I grieved the loss of my dad, God was tender, personal, and patient. I grew as I gave myself permission to grieve—long past the time I'd allotted for grieving—and God healed with His presence over that moment and that slivered part of my heart. The long-broken parts of me don't disqualify me from His love. Instead, they catch His eye. He heals us—from the inside out.

—————— *For Your Continued Pursuit* ——————

Psalm 19:12 | Psalm 34:18 | Psalm 51:1–17 | Psalm 139:1–10 | Psalm 147:3 | Proverbs 23:10–11 | Song of Songs 2:3 | Isaiah 55:8–9 | Isaiah 61:1, 3 | Ezekiel 47:12 | Mark 14:3–9 | John 1:4–5 | Revelation 22:2

twelve

HOLY WHISPERS

Embracing the Mysteries of God

"She has kept this for the day of My burial."

—JOHN 12:7

It is 4:09 p.m. My children are quiet, tucked away in the back loft playing. The babe is sure to sleep another thirty minutes at least. I'd penciled in four o'clock as my time to step away and breathe, my "wonder hour." But now it's nine minutes past four and my tasks are haunting me. These are the two busiest weeks of my spring. I'd been watching them approach on the calendar for months. Easter is a tick away, and twenty people will be joining us for our annual Passover Seder dinner. There are two impending speaking engagements to prep for and a manuscript deadline just around the corner. Rest feels like an undeserved luxury.

But I close the laptop and close the office doors and step outside, away from all the reminders of what is left undone. I lace my running shoes and hit the trail for a walk through the nature preserve adjacent to our house.

It is 70 degrees in March, and I hear the noises of spring:

My feet crunching against wintered crabgrass speckled with new green. The woodpecker hammering somewhere above me. The rabbit moving through the brush.

I hear my heart too.

I feel God here. Rather, I feel *known* here, tromping through the woods without a soul in sight. I pass the stream near our property and I'm fairly certain that, other than a hunter or two, no one but us has looked at that stream in the past year. It's hidden, and so am I.

I notice the Bradford pear is in bloom on the other side of the loop I'm walking. The tree is striking against the brown of winter, holding thousands of white cotton balls from its limbs. I didn't notice it last year as it produced its fruit alongside the rest of the forest's compatriots. This year it is a loner. And brilliant.

We're all hidden, together, under His eye, these winterized trees and me. Masked, tucked away this afternoon, yet seen and thriving. He sees me and I know He sees me, and *this* reality, made clearer in the quiet of the afternoon, makes me want to talk to God. I want to participate in what was once discipline and is now the tender cord, drawn tighter and tighter, that connects me to the one who made me and knows me.

Waiting back at home is a hungry toddler, starting the roll call he does after every afternoon nap. "Mommy, Daddy, Caleb, Lily . . ."

Waiting back at home is an impossible list of tasks. I'd be superhuman to complete it, yet it's still written in Pilot ink on a notecard on my desk.

Waiting back at home are all the ingredients for dinner. The meat has been thawing for hours, dripping off the counter and onto the hardwood floor. I stepped over the pooling red to walk outside.

So many untended pieces of my life are waiting for me, just as they'll be waiting again tomorrow. I'll handle each one better because of what is happening on my insides out here in the wilderness of the walking trail.

These times of peace and conversation with God in the midst of a full-tilt life are not the waste I once thought they were. I started talking to God when I was hidden and hungry, and found the key that unlocks the deepest joy of any life: secret prayer. Whispers with God. My faith hinges upon this. His Word doesn't work its way inside of me unless it becomes my dialogue with Him. The gospel doesn't spread from my heart to my hands unless He's directly informing it. No relationship, covenanted or not, can grow without time, face to face.

I come alive in this conversation. I hear His heart here. And I change here. These moments have become the greatest thrill, the greatest adventure, of my life.

As I walk, I unload my heart to God. Phrases from His Word echo through my mind, intersecting with my sighs before God, reminding me that He knows what He made in me. I can't imagine that responding to one more email or getting a head start on dinner or finally scraping off of the pantry shelf the dried honey that's been driving me crazy could be as good or as needed as this. One more social media post can never settle me as much as exhaling my thoughts before God. I want—I need—to talk to God when no one is looking. I thrive on what happens there. *I do love this Jesus.*

Some things that I will ask of Him, no one will ever see or know or hear. "The secret of the LORD is with those who fear Him," we read in the Psalms (Ps. 25:14). Pouring out my thoughts to Him and carrying the thoughts of His heart toward me, and toward my family and the people in my world, is not merely a part of life in God. It is *all* of life in God.

Just before I make the last turn on the trail and head back to our yard, I pass the back side of the lonely Bradford pear. There, in the middle of what is still winter wilderness, is glorious spring. Hidden and beautiful.

I've come to believe that familiarity is the enemy of anyone who wants to fall in love with God.

The faith leaders in Jesus' day were so familiar with and attached to their version of religion and their expectations of the Messiah that they put nails through the hands of the best thing that ever happened to them. Even Jesus' closest companions were trapped in their ways of thinking and seeing things. He repeatedly gave them insights about the kingdom and what was to come, but they couldn't see beyond the temporal—the visible and the familiar. Only a few had a sense of what His words really meant and of the darkness, and the light, to come. Mary was one of the few.

We don't know whether Mary chose to pour out the oil at Jesus' feet because she knew His death was certain and imminent. We do know that Mary was immersed in the traditions of her culture, including the respectful anointing of honored guests and the anointing of the dead in preparation for burial. Feasting and grieving. Mary would know the rituals and cultural expectations for both.

"She has kept this for the day of My burial," Jesus said of Mary and her fragrant oil (John 12:7). His words suggest that Mary understood His heart and His future in a way that only those who are intimate with God can.

Mary's connectedness to Jesus was both private—love spilled—and public. Soon, the Son of God would shed His humanity, the humanity He took up for everyone around that table, for Mary, and for her family's forever-descendants. The oil Mary poured was His transitional robe.

Mary participated in God's biggest story by following a holy nudge inside her, one that grew from her time with Him. It was all she could do. It is all God calls us to do.

Much like the faith leaders and even those nearest disciples of Jesus' time, we too are at risk of missing Jesus, of failing to see who He really is, because of our attachments to the safe things we think we already understand about Him. Pastor Eugene Peterson describes it this way: "Left to ourselves, we will pray to some god who speaks what we like hearing, or to the part of God we manage to understand. But what is critical is that we speak to the God who speaks to us, and to everything that he speaks to us."[15] We allow ourselves to be lulled into a dull familiarity with the parts of Jesus we've experienced, the passages in His Word we've studied most, the truths about Him we can explain and understand. Then we string all of these familiar things together and call them God. And when we pray from this place of familiarity, instead of being alert for how the truth of how He really is will likely upend our human understanding, we end up watching for confirmation of what we already know.

It's here that prayer becomes stale and sends us searching elsewhere for adventure. But God brings us back to the simple accessibility of prayer—the hinge of our relationship with Him—and invites us to pray like wide-eyed children.

An airplane in the sky is a "jumping car" to my two-and-a-half-year-old, who is just beginning to make sense of the world. In God's invitation for us to come to Him as children, He understands that we likely will behave in similar ways by using what we know and recognize to make sense of what we don't yet know and can't yet see about Him.

This is how finite humanity approaches the infinite God.

Yet true growth in God requires that our perspective of Him grow with us. Progressively, prayer becomes less about relating to Him as we're certain He must be and more about seeing His bigness in light of how small and limited we are. We ask more questions, expect more mystery, leave more room for God to overturn our understanding. It's in this growth that we gladly exchange familiarity with God for the unknowns and His surprises.

The ones who lean into hiddenness begin to see that conversation with God has more to do with a growing connectedness to His heart and less to do with getting the answer we want. These prayers often begin with words like, "God, I barely know You and I want to know You more. My life is found in connecting to You, not in following what I think I already know about You."

That's when we know we've left milk behind and are dining on the meat of maturity in God.

"I just heard the baby's heartbeat," she whispered as she scooted from the church aisle into a seat just next to mine.

This mom-to-be had just graduated from her first trimester and was bubbling over with new data points on her unseen little one. But as her words and her enthusiasm moved past my mind into my heart, grief crowded in. At the time, we were still waiting for our older two daughters to come home.

With Eden and Caleb, I'd never before known parenthood. I hadn't thought I'd care about things like baby yawns and toddler babble, the silly observations children make and the wide-eyed way they navigate ordinary life. I lived in the present as I anticipated their arrival, wondering when the next piece of paperwork would clear so that we could travel to get them.

After these beloved two were home, a whole new sensory side of parenting opened up to me. I loved the smell of Eden's skin and the softness of her hair after a bath. I loved rubbing each of Caleb's unusually pliable ears between my fingers. These children were *mine*, and I was growing to love the parts of them I'd not considered when I held only a glossy photograph in my hand.

With Lily and Hope, it was harder to wait because now I knew what I was missing. Each day they lived across the ocean was another day I wasn't holding them. I wasn't tending to their little-girl skin. I couldn't picture how tall Lily would stand against my shoulders or how much of Hope's body I could enfold within my arms.

So I made a new kind of baby book for these two who had already left babyhood behind. I started talking to God about what I didn't know. I made what was unfamiliar to me the starting point for our dialogue. I asked for His heart for these girls.

What would You have me pray?

This God had made our girls in secret, when no one was watching or recording or perhaps even celebrating. He knew every single moment of my children's undocumented lives. So I asked Him for insights about their personalities. This dialogue with God wasn't one of many parts of my relationship with my children—it was the only bloodline I had. I learned motherhood of them by talking to God first. Through words of Scripture, He showed me their heartbeat. I prayed into what I couldn't see, and because of what I couldn't see, I prayed with His eyes.

Lily and Hope were spending their nights in cramped rooms lined with beds without anyone to kiss them goodnight. I was on another continent asking God for prayers about them to pray back to Him. I prayed His Word, His promises, His ideas for my girls. As I prayed for children I'd never met,

I developed a new depth in my relationship with God. Instead of a growing girth, I had a growing connectedness to God.

God was teaching me about the weight that prayer holds in His unseen world. No one saw those prayers. I couldn't take snapshots of my inner life in God to post in social media feeds. Even on these pages, I can only reference them. I can't truly share them.

What was masked, what was unfamiliar, was unveiled in my private conversations with God. My prayers directed toward the unseen, my prayers in hiddenness, were as real to me as a heartbeat on a sonogram screen.

We'll mature without effort into wrinkles and gray hair, but our hearts won't mature deep into God by default. We have to desire more and more of God. Paul prayed for such greater fullness in our experience of God: "[I pray] that you, being rooted and grounded in love, may be able to comprehend with all the saints what is the width and length and depth and height—to know the love of Christ which passes knowledge; that you may be filled with all the fullness of God" (Eph. 3:17–19).

There is a *further* filling to those who already have committed their lives to following Jesus, a filling that comes as a result of sinking our roots ever deeper into Him—His is a love our minds can't fully understand.

Prayer—conversation with God—is how we sink our roots into what is real and will last forever. Prayer fights against the vaporlike existence of a life rooted only in what others see, which is gone just after we show and tell. Prayer laces our hearts to the unseen mysterious God, to whom we say, *Who You are, God, is more important than what I see in front of me and what others see of me.*

No one but God sees in full this glorious exchange that produces deep and lasting growth. Prayer tethers us to the truest reality, one that will never change. His.

I published my story on paper a few years back and entered into a whole new world of metrics. I bled on the page, and now I saw there were ways to measure its impact or lack thereof.

Had I wanted to, I could have compared the sales rank of my book with that of every other published author at any given time of the day. A few more clicks and I could count all the reviews as they came in. I could read the words of those who loved the book and those who felt otherwise. I could click through social media tags and images and comments to analyze from every angle what people were saying about the outpouring of my heart. And by any of these metrics, my book would have been merely that: what I could see and measure with my eyes.

But I wanted another measure. I wanted to birth this book with my nervous hand in His, leaning more into what I couldn't see than what I could. So I prayed prayers that only God and I (and sometimes Nate) knew about. I prayed wild prayers for this baby book, much like the ones I prayed for my girls when they were still in Uganda (which is when I learned that prayers make the best kind of baby books).

This exchange with God became more important to me than His answers. I knew He *could* answer—He was able—and I was also beginning to trust His leadership enough to know that when He didn't answer, it was all right.

Most of all, I wanted to dream *with* Him. *His* dreams, His way. Bigger dreams than I could conceive from looking around me.

I wanted to just talk to Him about the *whole* thing. I wanted to talk to Him about the eyes that might read the pages and the people who would pass dogeared copies on to friends. I wanted to pour out my fears to Him and hear His tender response, to find the gentle side of Him in His Word and carefully affix it to each one of my crazy nerves. I wanted to ask big things of Him, and I wanted to pray for the tiny details—the cover, the design, the font. And I wanted to align with Him: I wanted to know His heart, His thoughts, His dreams for this book.

It's what you do with a best friend and a father and an invested coach. God was all of these to me and more. I wanted to pray my way through God's nature and not just read about it in the pages of His book. I wanted to see it cropping up all over my own story.

I did. And He did. I cry-prayed and talked and gushed and fretted, out loud and right to Him. And He winked. Just like my dad in my dream, God winked. He responded in ways I wouldn't have had an eye for had I not prayed them first. Prayer positioned me to notice. *Him*.

Some of these conversations with God on the inside happened as I faced the critical eyes of others on the outside, eyes that made me want to quit and never write another word because it hurt too much to take creative risks like this.

But what kept me moving forward was that there was this second storyline, the most important storyline. The first might have been "Sara published a book," peppered with pretty images of the teal cover and people's stories of how they'd been touched by it. But the second storyline has a title that I can't share even here or it might lose its weight and beauty. And all the images that stretch across my mind as I write about it are mostly to be shared between God and me.

I needed the second storyline in order to walk out the first.

The wink of God: It comes when we believe He is capable of reaching tenderly and knowingly into our story. It comes when we believe He wants to intertwine His story with ours and tell our story back to us, His way.

This is prayer. It is coming to God, opening His Word, expecting His whisper and dialoguing with Him, knowing that there are myriad sides of Him yet to be explored.

Prayer is sinking deeply into the soil of God and expecting to be nourished in ways that are mostly undetectable to the human eye.

God made us in secret. We grow in secret. But that secret space is not a void. He stays in the secret, right there with us. That's where we grow, deep.

When I was newly on full-time staff with the high school ministry and just out of college, I gave my first gospel presentation in a new city to a roomful of sweaty teenagers from all over the city. While I was speaking, most of the two hundred kids stared at me blankly or cast zoned-out looks elsewhere or flirted with their neighbors. Only a few of the leader-types in the room looked like they were actually listening. I was upfront, passionate, and felt virtually unnoticed.

I can still feel the heavy weight that lodged in my stomach as I lugged the overhead projector back to our ministry office after the night was over. I spent the drive back to the office analyzing my twelve-minute talk from twelve different angles. I knew I had bombed.

For weeks afterward, my face flushed when I thought about it. *Never again*, I vowed. I'd work ten times harder for the next one, ten times harder to ensure I wouldn't say something stupid or repeat words that weren't received.

This talk was about them and me. I hadn't considered, at twenty-two, that it was the power of God, not my words, that could change a human heart, or that fruit came from my abiding in Him, not from my perfect delivery.

So I worked hard on my delivery, mostly so that I wouldn't ever again feel the shame of vulnerability. I didn't consider then that God uses foolish things to make His name known. I just wanted never to be foolish again.

Fifteen years later, I was speaking to another crowd. I was talking about a passion for pursuing God in the midst of family life. I'd spoken publicly many times before, but I'd not yet fully shed the fear that I might walk out of a room having bombed.

I'd spent weeks in advance praying about this particular conference, asking God to relieve the fear of failure, the fear of saying it wrong or missing His leadership or finding myself shamed. It'd been a long time since I was twenty-two, but there was still this thread of fear entwined in my preparation to speak.

After my talk, I stepped off the stage, spoke with a few people, and then walked to the car with Nate. I was feeling increasingly drawn to hiddenness since I'd felt more and more exposed after writing my book. I wanted to get back to those secret conversations with God. I wanted to live hidden, no matter how my talks and interviews and the book might expose me.

As Nate and I climbed into the car on that overcast afternoon, my first thoughts were leading me into shame. But instead of allowing them free rein, I asked God, *What did You think?*

This was about us was the phrase I felt rise up within my spirit.

God told me what I already knew, but what I needed to hear again: the story of God and me is my most significant story. His eyes on me and into my life are the source from which I draw everything else. Whether I am folding laundry or speaking from a platform, my exchanges with God are always about His reach for me and my reach for Him in return, again and again. The rest of life is the overflow.

Prayer, this internal exchange with God, is where it all happens.

Underground.

Rooting down deeper still in Him.

And eventually growing up.

──────── *For Your Continued Pursuit* ────────

Psalm 25:14 | Psalm 81:7 | Psalm 139 | Ezekiel 36:26–27 | Matthew 6:4–6 | Matthew 18:3 | John 15:1–7 | 1 Corinthians 1:27–29 | 1 Corinthians 2:9 | Ephesians 3:16–21 | Hebrews 5:12–14 | Hebrews 6:19–20

thirteen

THE HIDDEN WAY

(Becoming a Friend of God)

"Wherever this gospel is preached
throughout the world, what she has done
will also be told, in memory of her."
—MATTHEW 26:13 NIV

The darkness of the Christmas Eve sky contrasted with the streets below, all of them aflame. Strings of multicolored lights and inflatable snowmen and light-skinned Marys and Josephs lit the night.

This was Lily and Hope's first American Christmas, and part of me wanted to keep them inside, to keep their eyes innocently fixed on a miraculous birth and the unsuspecting shepherds and the world's greatest gift of God come as a human. We drove to the Christmas Eve service, and their mouths formed steam on the windows as they ogled plastic Santas and luminaries and LED icicles.

This was the first Christmas Eve service I could remember in which the children were invited to come forward, mid-service. I hadn't prepared mine. Things that most children handle easily can dislodge children like mine, whose lives have already had a deeper dislodging.

All but one of my children went up front, joining one hundred of their peers, many of whom looked a bit nervous as they faced an audience of onlookers and parents snapping photos and mouthing "smile" to the little people they had made.

There was a boisterous dad up front, leading the children, coaching them with questions through a retelling of the nativity story. Arms shot up and out even before the next question was asked. Kids were loaded, ready. Each child wanted his or her voice heard.

The designated dad closed with one last question: "Now, what did the angels say?" And my child, who had raised her hand to answer every single question just like every other eager-to-participate little one, finally had her number called.

The dad in charge pointed to her, my little girl who'd been in America for only a few months and who pantomimed more than she spoke. I still wasn't sure if she understood that the plastic snowmen weren't a part of what happened that first Christmas.

She responded confidently by reciting verses we happened to have spent the last few months memorizing—the only complete sentences in her memory bank, and full of words whose meaning she didn't know: "Then the angel said to them, 'Do not be afraid, for behold, I bring you good tidings of great joy which will be to all people. For there is born to you this day in the city of David a Savior, who is Christ the Lord'" (Luke 2:10–11).

The room full of parents and grandparents and friends

erupted with cheers. My little girl about burst out of her dress. She did it! Whatever *it* was.

She ran back into my arms and I cried.

I wasn't crying because I was the proud mama whose child had given the winning answer. This wasn't a moment to display the stellar memorization skills we'd imparted or even the fact that we were memorizing Scripture in our home.

The others in that room didn't know where my little girl had been eating her meals a year before or that she'd missed more than a few. They weren't close enough to see that I still had African dirt underneath my fingernails from a summer of clawing through paperwork walls to get her home. They didn't see what I saw. They couldn't have. They weren't meant to, at least not in that moment.

But the thirty seconds between when the crowd erupted around her and she bolted back into my arms were holy moments. Through my daughter's words that evening, God reached into the deepest part of me and said, *I see you.*

No one in that room, apart from Nate, knew the inner dialogue I'd been having recently. Overnight, we had gone from two children to four, and sometimes it felt like we were carrying the burdens of twelve with all the years of loss they bore. Most days, I felt like I was drowning in their brokenness. Hearts take time to heal, certainly more time than I had allotted or expected.

As I reeled from the body blows of all the ways their losses impacted everything from our dinner times to afternoon play dates—and what it would mean for them in the years ahead—I wanted other people to feel the pain too. I wanted friends to know how hard it was to show up to church on time or to convince this young one to step away from the wall during ballet class or to teach another one to look adults in the eye (after she'd spent an orphanage lifetime learning to look away). I wanted family to see that typical gatherings sometimes couldn't run as planned, that I couldn't prepare for what might trigger an angry reaction or when grief might suddenly overtake a child.

Someone, anyone, please notice. Or rather, *Someone, anyone— know.*

I wanted to shout it everywhere we went: "Behind this child is a story!" And maybe the truer statement I wanted to shout was, "Behind this woman is a story!"

But that Christmas Eve night, the ancient announcement rolling off my daughter's lips was a better gift than a whole throng of onlookers who *noticed* and *knew.* "And your Father who sees in secret will reward you openly" (Matt. 6:18) speaks both of the one who sees in secret and the parts of us that were made for rewarding.

He *does* reward.

It would be disingenuous for me to say that I didn't want any reward for the outpouring I'd given to these children who, in their aches and losses, sometimes boiled over with anger and other times stewed in sullen unresponsiveness. I'd be dishonest if I said I didn't need anyone to notice that I'd been cleaning up emotional wreckage I didn't cause, only to do it again the next day. I'd be superhuman to say I could thrive for days, much less hours, mending heart-ouchies without an acknowledging nod in my direction.

At the very least, I wanted someone to thank me for making dinner.

I'm adult enough to know that the proverbial nod from even the most respected person is a vapor that soon vanishes, but I'm child enough to feel the need for an eye, an intimate whisper of acknowledgment, a "Way to go!" note from a friend. So I can get stuck between these two: serving without a desire for recognition, all the while clamoring internally for my outpouring to be known.

My daughter's words that night were God's way of saying to me, *I saw the hundreds of minutes before this one when she bristled against your loving leadership, and I'm at work in her.*

This is God, my friend. The one who *knows* me. The one who *gets* me.

"How precious also are Your thoughts to me, O God! How great is the sum of them!" (Ps. 139:17). When I don't realize what I'm truly craving, God's thoughts toward me will get lost while I seek affirmation from a sea of other eyes. But when I listen in hiddenness, God's thoughts reveal themselves and become precious. My hearing, trained in that hiddenness, becomes attuned to the best kind of sound: the voice of my friend.

Throughout history, God related to many of His people as friends. He sought friends too. God searched the earth for those who *got* Him.

"And he was called the friend of God," James says of

Abraham, after stating, "Abraham believed God, and it was accounted to him for righteousness" (James 2:23).

Abraham's descendants were identified as those who came from the forever friend of God: "descendants of Abraham Your friend forever" (2 Chron. 20:7).

John the Baptist referred to himself as the "friend of the bridegroom" (John 3:29).

And lest we think this friend status is reserved for the superheroes of the faith, we can turn to Jesus' words to all His followers: "No longer do I call you servants, for a servant does not know what his master is doing; but I have called you friends, for all things that I heard from My Father I have made known to you" (John 15:15). A friendship that started between Father and Son expanded to include you and me.

Yes, we want to be known. But how often do we consider that God wants to be known too? The unsearchable God does invite our searching; friendship is formed in this seeking. God wants to be our friend in the way that friends share more than high-fives and occasional help. He wants to share hearts and stories and inner lives.

This friendship with God isn't just about the winks He gives to us when no one is looking. He's also searching the earth for ones who will look back, who will *know* Him, who will carry His heart.

I first discovered that I wanted to be one of those friends when He met me in my hidden years of barrenness. Over time, the women around me who had experienced barrenness for as many years as I had grew fewer and fewer. Yet as human friends who understood this pain diminished, I found an understanding friend in God, the kind of friend who made me want even deeper friendship. More reaching.

I wanted to be a friend *to* God.

They clamored for Jesus, perhaps more desperate for healing than for a Healer.

The curious and accusatory and hungry, they thronged Him.

Those nearest to Him, the ones He invited close, fought for a seat at His right hand. Even the ones who knew Him best glommed on to His fame.

To some, He was a miracle, and to others a fraud. But wherever Jesus went, opinions and needs followed Him. He came to save the world, and the world let out its cry when it saw Him.

But Mary was different.

Wasteful with her love.

The others around the table likely counted their money and ministry impact, but she had thought that she might carry His burden with Him. She reached toward Him in friendship. And He spoke on her behalf. He chose her, the woman from the back row, to memorialize.

This is the memorial, told throughout all of time: Mary befriended God.

And the gospel would no longer be told without sharing the story of the woman so enraptured by God that she wasted all she had on Him. That she became His friend.

A few years ago, I was invited to speak to a house full of women for an overnight retreat. I'd held a microphone a few times in the year or two before then, but I still had nerves when I stood up in front of people. It had been a long time since the ministry days of my twenties, when I was frequently speaking or leading a Bible study in front of a crowd.

Now I was about to spend a weekend speaking to twenty or so women I didn't know, young adults in trendy jeans and fortysomething moms who could still hang with those half their age, all congregated in one lakehouse over food and stories and a shared hunger for God.

I arrived that first night with a nursing babe and my eldest daughter as a helper. I was tired from traveling and uncertain how I'd do the next twenty-four hours with two children in tow. I tucked in Bo and meandered with the women down to the lake for the first session. We'd meet waterside as the sun set.

With the chairs circled up, I began to speak. As I moved through my notes, the sun dropped behind the treeline at my back on the other side of the lake. The day went from dusk to dark in what felt like minutes. This transition left me feeling suddenly alone.

I could see nothing but the dim lights from the kitchen of the lakehouse up on the hill. I couldn't even make out the silhouettes of the women around me. My notes, too, were lost in the darkness.

I had no idea whether my audience was moved by this

message or if they were quietly nodding off. I had no eye contact cues to guide my words. And I had no idea how much was left in what I'd planned to say. I was winging it from memory and by the whispers of God inside of me. The only lines in my Bible I could use were the ones I'd memorized.

So I delivered a talk to the crickets and the bullfrogs and the owls, the most responsive of the crew around me.

Afterward, as I walked up the hill and back to my room, my mind launched into critique mode, combing through my talk for any mishap or hiccup. Just a few more moments of this and I would go under. I knew this shame spiral routine by heart. I'd been here before.

So I stopped. I asked the Lord to breathe His love into this perplexing night. And then it hit me. In an instant I knew this night would be the image I'd carry with me into every public speaking engagement for years to come.

The pitch-black night had given me a new light.

God let the night drop over my vision so that I would search His heart alone, so I would seek His thoughts for these women. Their nodding expressions, warmly encouraging me as I spoke, were not as significant as His heartbeat for them, a heartbeat He might share with me if I turned my eyes toward Him instead.

This is friendship with God.

He sees me when no one is looking, and I search Him in response.

Perhaps God initiates friendship with a desire that we might befriend Him, eagerly, in return.

John the Baptist, in calling himself the "friend of the

bridegroom," qualifies this friendship as one who "stands and hears him." Who "rejoices greatly because of the bridegroom's voice" (John 3:29–30). Friendship with God means hearing. We become God's friend when we listen for His heart and His soft whisper in His Word.

Like Mary, we can tend to God—listening, tuning our ears to the cadence of His heartbeat, and spilling out our lives in response to what we hear. This is communion. Surrender of our lives, unto Him. He made us for this.

Author Jon Bloom writes that Mary's pouring out her perfume wasn't a waste but a windfall: "A poured-out life of love for Jesus that counts worldly gain as loss displays how precious he really is. It preaches to a bewildered, disdainful world that Christ is gain and the real waste is gaining the world's perfume while losing one's soul."[16]

I want to be another Mary.

I want to know God as a precious friend.

My sweet daughter was recently praying for my book. *This* book. Though she didn't know what it was about, she knew I sometimes took time away to write. She asked God for His eyes for me as she prayed. Then she looked up from underneath those dainty eyelids and said, "Mommy, you're like a morning glory, except you open in the night when no one sees you but God. And you're hidden and closed during the day."

The morning glory in our yard has always enamored my kids as they've tried to catch it when it is closed and figure out exactly when it opens. Now this mysterious flower was a picture for me. Of me.

I want God to get the best of me. Unfurled and reaching. Exposed but tender. Whether in the dark or light. Open to Him.

I sat in another circle of women in a different state and a different setting and heard one woman say about prayer, "I know I *should* pray more, but it's so hard to live that out in the middle of the day." She is right, both about the call to prayer and about how most Christians see that call.

We're not merely invited to pray, but we are called to pray unceasingly. Always. In every circumstance and in every setting. On our back patio pruning geraniums and in the laundry room loading the washer with whites and taking a shower and stretching at the gym and during that quick afternoon grocery stop and in the drive-through at Starbucks and sitting on the metal chairs at the DMV.

That's praying without ceasing. That's the kind of conversation with God that Paul says is possible: "Rejoice always, pray without ceasing, in everything give thanks; for this is the will of God in Christ Jesus for you" (1 Thess. 5:16–18).

As you read, do you feel your pulse rising? Just like the woman in the circle, are you pleading in defense of yourself in the way we often do when we see a gap, *This is really hard! I should have prayed more today, but how am I supposed to remember and find the time?*

But there is no need to plead or to defend. The gaps in our prayer lives are simply reasons to pause. To examine.

Though discipline is not a bad word, and certainly there are many times when discipline carries us when our fickle hearts won't, our prayerlessness reveals much more than a lack of stick-to-itiveness.

Paul, who wrote these words about unceasing prayer, was a friend of God. He wasn't a stalwart follower, more disciplined than the rest of us. God had been *near* to him. Near enough to share His secrets with Paul. God had to be such a close friend to Paul, perhaps at least in part because this man was out of other options: "From the Jews five times I received forty stripes minus one. Three times I was beaten with rods; once I was stoned; three times I was shipwrecked; a night and a day I have been in the deep; in journeys often, in perils of waters, in perils of robbers, in perils of my own countrymen, in perils of the Gentiles, in perils in the city, in perils in the wilderness, in perils in the sea, in perils among false brethren; in weariness and toil, in sleeplessness often, in hunger and thirst, in fastings often, in cold and nakedness" (2 Cor. 11:24–27).

Comrades turned traitors, accusing words, hurled stones, hunger, sleeplessness, brutal treatment by his countrymen, and untold perils. When he had no one and nothing else, Paul found a friend in God. God, in return, shared His secrets with His friend. Paul speaks of himself here: "And I know such a man—whether in the body or out of the body I do not know, God knows—how he was caught up into Paradise and heard inexpressible words, which it is not lawful for a man to utter" (2 Cor. 12:3–4).

Paul carved a friendship out of those mysterious whispers. This is holy and other, and yet Paul's true friendship with God was forged in circumstances that hid him and made him (in the world's eyes) not only an absolute fool but also a target for abuse—and worse. Paul didn't pray because he *should*. Paul prayed because he'd grown—*grown*—to want nothing more.

Maturing in our friendship with God, the place where somewhere down deep we all want to be headed, means wanting nothing more than to talk to Him because of who He is to us in our weakest, most confounded moments. This is what fueled Paul's passion for God: "That I may know Him and the power of His resurrection, and the fellowship of His sufferings" (Phil. 3:10).

Unceasing prayer can grow to be something we do not because of discipline but because of friendship. Desire. It's where we're headed, if we'll let Him take us there.

This God bent low to gift a son into thirty years of obscurity. It isn't beyond Him to stretch His hand of friendship into the middle minutes of our day, the "Hey, can I open myself to you for this moment?" kind of friendship, so that we might see engaging with Him as the preeminent prize of our lives.

One day you just may *want* to pray without ceasing.

Who knows what you might hear.

It was a normal Tuesday morning, and I was relieved. The day before, I had just finished what I thought would be the last chapter of this book. I slid out the door into a chorus of birds. My shoelaces were double-knotted for one of my first spring runs—off the treadmill belt and onto the road.

The dark was still hovering. I wore my reflector vest as I crossed the street and turned right out of my driveway. I would run one mile and stop to stretch and then another mile before turning back. Habit.

On my way back, I hit a patch of water and mud and fell hard and awkward, my limbs flying in opposite directions. I lay crumpled on the sidewalk, unable to walk, surprised and embarrassed. Nate had to come drive me home.

Days and doctor appointments later, I got my diagnosis: broken ankle. I was charged not to drive or walk for two months. One little run, one little fall, and all my plans for spring were suddenly muddled.

I tried to keep things in perspective. I hadn't gotten a midnight phone call that someone I treasured was gone. The storm didn't lift my house off its foundation. The time expected for my ankle to heal was only eight weeks, after all. These are all things I told myself to quell the internal fit I was throwing about not being able to go on long Saturday morning runs or take meandering walks with my children or scoot away to a coffee shop for a couple of hours to write and sip chai. I was trying to coach myself to see things another way.

Except it wasn't working. Self-coaching never makes a lasting shift.

But something else did.

I remembered *her*. This woman who still intrigues me. This woman who didn't grudgingly spill her livelihood onto Jesus' feet while biting the inside of her cheek in resentment but quite literally poured out all that she had for Him.

She *wanted* to give it all.

Of course, everyone else in the room called it waste. Human nature can't comprehend this kind of surrender—a relinquishing of the things that matter most to us—to a mysterious God. We can't coach ourselves up to a better perspective, just a little bit higher until we reach something holy. (Though we try.)

We need a new way.

We need a new way to endure pain, both acute and mundane, to face the daily deaths we're offered in broken ankles and broken dishwashers and broken relationships when we wish we could just walk away. We need to journey through the hidden spaces of our lives with an expectation of victory, as if we really believe that these unnoticed moments matter.

We need a hidden way.

This way God has given us looks like waste from our earthbound perspective. It always will. The outpouring at His feet will never make sense to human eyes. No, not ever.

But what strikes me most about Mary is that she had practice. It appears from earlier biblical accounts that she had created what might be called a lifestyle of waste: "There is only one thing worth being concerned about. Mary has discovered it, and it will not be taken away from her" (Luke 10:42 NLT).

Mary found it: the *only* thing worth being concerned about in this life.

She found Him.

Mary didn't have one wild brush with God and run to tell this world about it. She got near to Him and she stayed. We might say it this way: Mary practiced being wasted. She made a lifestyle of it. Something kept her there.

In the days after breaking my ankle, I managed my home and was a mom to my children and maintained relationships, all from my couch and crutches. I also mentally catalogued all the things I was missing. First, I thought about how I was losing about a dozen Saturday morning runs. But then I realized that even bedtimes were on the list. I wouldn't be able to walk up the stairs to my children's bedrooms or lift my toddler into his crib. Nor would I be planting the garden we'd been planning for weeks.

I'd half wished I could say something like, "But I realize these losses were so small compared with what my children faced in their early years and what my girlfriend in another state is facing with her cancer and what my dear friend lost when her dad died." But those words were empty self-coaching for me.

The only thing that effectively lifts me out of the rut of complaint is knowing that Jesus isn't calling these unproductive two months in a cast a waste. He is calling them an invitation.

With a broken ankle and a house to run, there is still only one thing worth my greatest concern, according to Jesus. Insert your own story here: with a child who is behind in school, with a best friend who has betrayed you, with a promotion you didn't get, with a promotion you won only to find yourself in over your head, there is only one thing truly worthy of your concern, only one thing that will deeply satisfy you and thrill you, at times, beyond measure.

Jesus didn't refer to this one thing so that we would shove

our emotions and lift our chins and stiffen our lips. He said it of a woman who looked up at Him, weak and vulnerable and thirsty, and likely uncertain and nervous in her thirst. He said it of a woman who was simply trying to get close to Him, to the one thing she thought might meet the deepest craving of her heart.

He said it of me, in His invitation, an almost-forty-year-old finally quieting down after the newest internal tantrum: *Sara, remember Me, the one thing always available to fill you. Even this change won't take it from you.*

You could pattern a lifetime around this one. Because as we look deep into His eyes, nothing is wasted.

Like so many in middle America, I grew up under the Friday night lights.

First, I was the wide-eyed little sister, tagging along behind my big sister to the games and congregating with friends under the bleachers, taking mental notes on how older girls acted. Then I was the ardent fan, barely watching the score but making youthful celebrities out of the best players, shouting their names and their numbers. Then (finally) I was the uniformed participant, cheering the team all the way home to Cougar Lane on musky fall nights while the parking lot lights served as smoke machines against the fall frost, welcoming back our small-town heroes.

When I outgrew the stands as a student, I returned in the

name of ministry. On these nights, I was just another member of the community rallying in the city's centrifuge, loving my bundled-up neighbors in between shouting the names of seventeen-year-old athletes.

As a young married woman without kids, I had a different sort of Friday night lights. I spent Friday nights with friends, all of us circled around the table of our favorite restaurant under low lights, sharing lives between bites.

For all those years, Fridays were the social metronome of my life.

But then, several years into marriage, came one Friday that was different.

I was alone, but now by choice. My husband was out of town, and I wasn't afraid of the night or myself or who I might find when the house was empty.

I brewed a cup of tea and I opened the back door. Only the screen separated me from the intermittent sounds of the night.

I cracked open my Bible, except this time it wasn't out of duty. I wanted to be here. I was drawn to Him, this God-man who had seen me in my weakness and heard my whimpering and saw my reach for Him, amid all my flaws. I wanted to talk to God. Not because of a looming decision or a penance I felt was overdue. I was hungry, craving more than what even the best of hot appetizers or the town's fanfare or a night with my best friend could give me. God was new to me, ever unfolding. With every new glimpse of Him, I wanted more.

And something in me knew that this raw and desiring side

of me is what God wanted too. Desire drew me—and who I was when I desired Him. I was beginning to like who I was under His eye. The raw me. The real me.

I liked Him, and He liked what He'd made in me.

Perhaps it was similar to the desire that drew me to spend years of Friday nights with best friends. We're drawn to where we come alive, to where our passion takes flight. To where we are known. We want to be with those who know us and remind us of what we like about ourselves. Those who invite us to consider our lives as much bigger than what our eyes can see.

I knew that I once would have called this time—God, me, my Bible—a terrible waste. I wasn't making plans to change the world or contemplating a major decision or even asking for a personal breakthrough. I was sitting with God just to enjoy Him. And I wanted to stay just a little bit longer.

It was a night of mutual affection, and yet it still felt a little awkward, just like the beginning stages of any true friendship. Of course He knew all of me, but I was just beginning to learn that I was comfortable being known.

And I wanted more. More of Him. More of that version of me.

This night was both emptier and fuller than anything I'd experienced on a Friday night. No lights, no fanfare, no victory celebration. Just me, squandering time with God, picking up a conversation we'd build upon over a lifetime.

Wasting time.

I'm not sure I had ever felt His pleasure more.

——————— *For Your Continued Pursuit* ———————

1 Samuel 13:14 | 1 Chronicles 16:11 | 2 Chronicles 16:9 |
2 Chronicles 20:7 | Psalm 14:2 | Psalm 19:12 | Psalm 26:8 | Psalm 80
| Psalm 139:17 | Proverbs 25:2 | Ezekiel 36:26 | Matthew 6:16–18 |
Matthew 20:20–28 | Matthew 26:1–13 | Luke 10:38–42 | John 1:5
| John 3:22–36 | John 14:26 | John 15:15 | Acts 6:4 | Acts 13:22 |
1 Corinthians 1:20–31 | 1 Corinthians 15:58 | 2 Corinthians 5:17 |
2 Corinthians 11:24–27 | 2 Corinthians 12:3–4, 7–11 | Philippians
3:10, 12–14 | 1 Thessalonians 5:16–18 | James 2:23 | Revelation 21:5

Acknowledgments

I saac Newton wrote, "If I have accomplished anything of value it is because I have stood upon the shoulders of giants." My thinking on the notion of hiddenness has inadvertently been influenced by so many, even from centuries past, whose stories populate our bookshelves—writers, giants of the faith in shepherd's clothes, missionaries, common people who bled for Jesus with their lives and did it in hiding, all because they loved Him.

I owe much to these, and to the parking lot attendants, the grocery store baggers, and the sage mothers of many children (like my late friend, Claire DeLaura), and to Sue, Pat, Dara, Cindy, Val, Anne, Betty, Tonya, Jina, JoAnna, Katie, Joan, Cathy, Susan, Amy, Betsy, Julie, Beth, Andee, and many others who loved Him profoundly when no one was looking and of whom God gave me a glimpse.

In addition, not so ironically, my name is on the cover of this book because of so many others who served and loved fiercely, with only a few (if any) noticing.

To everyone at Yates and Yates, especially Mike Salisbury and Curtis and Karen Yates: I had no idea what an ever-unfolding gift you would be. You pastored us while advocating for this book and its message.

And the team at Zondervan, to name just a few: Alicia Kasen, Brian Phipps, Jennifer VerHage, Sandy Vander Zicht. You all have taken a process that could have been merely transactional and laced it with thoughtful ingenuity and heart. I'm honored to have had such a dream team not once but twice.

To Jana Muntsinger and Pamela McClure: Thank you for making this fun, while not at the expense of being professional and determined.

Elisa Stanford: I'm not sure I could write another book without you. I've learned more from you about writing than any degree could have afforded me, and have formed a treasured friendship in the meantime.

To Jefferson and Alyssa Bethke: Having your voice accompany this message is an honor. Your thoughtfulness with your lives demonstrates a layer of beautiful hiddenness that some might dismiss. But not me.

To Dave and Tracey Sliker: I know I'm not the only one who has benefited from your cheerleading, but I sure feel like I am. You have infused more courage into me than I could sufficiently give credit for. Thank you, Dave, for reading the manuscript with your gifted critical eye.

To Kristy Reid, Kelly Raudenbush, and Rachel Medefind: for offering gentle input early and helping to sharpen this message.

Lisa Jacobson: I prayed for years for a sage in my life who understood both of my passions—for writing for His glory, and for keeping precious the value of motherhood and home. What a gift to have had you mentoring me from a distance.

MT girls: Hannah Robinson, Cherish Smith, Annie Kawase, Mary Arntsen, Rachael Steel, Erica Nork, Telma Weisman. It's early as I write this. You've only gathered in my family room a few times, and I'm already feeling the fruit of your partnership. Your hearts and your hunger for Him make this team significantly more than I could have envisioned.

And of course, Mandie Joy Turner: Your eye and your skill are only part of what I love about working with you. Thank you for bringing humor, gravity, and friendship to this work.

Tim and Chris Willard: You live this message, and our dialogue has given fuel to my writing it. Here's to many more fireside chats—you by yours, and we by ours, across the telephone line—about Him and beauty and hiddenness.

Jen Stutzman, Elizabeth Wilkerson, Abby Anderson, Nicole Rice, Molly Harrington, Trina Rogers: Each one of you has graced my life with pieces of Him that I wouldn't know or hadn't seen without you. You make me belly laugh, and you give flight to these crazy writing dreams of mine (even—especially—as I face my fear of it all) at the most needed times. This book has your fingerprints all over it.

Sarah Markman, Eliza Joy Capps, Kinsey Thurlow, Amy Wicks, Heidi Meythaler: Girls, you've demonstrated with your lives what happens when friendship and prayer intersect. You truly have fought for my heart in my writing, my marriage, and my motherhood.

To Kelly Tarr: I can think of no one else who lives the

message of hiddenness in Him more earnestly and fervently than you. You are one of God's greatest gifts to me.

Mom: Your friendship is one of the very best parts of my life. I want to be like you when I grow up.

To the ones under my roof who see it all—my sin, my languishing over my writing and speaking, my long, scruffy days in pajamas and a topknot, my kitchen dance routines—and still cuddle with me: Lily, Hope, Eden, Caleb, Bo, and Virginia. You are my absolute joy, my favorite part of life. My world would be dull without each of you.

And Nate: Sixteen years in and it just keeps getting better. You give me courage to write, over and over again. This book is ours, and this message is one that you live more wildly than I could ever hope to myself.

Last and greatest in my heart: Jesus. You've bored through my soul with the safest eyes I've ever known, and I keep wanting more. Your undoing is healing me.

NOTES

1. Dallas Willard, *The Divine Conspiracy: Rediscovering Our Hidden Life in God* (San Francisco: HarperSanFrancisco, 1998), 15.
2. Charles H. Spurgeon, *The Treasury of David*, vol. 3 (Massachusetts: Hendrickson, 1869), 263.
3. A. W. Tozer, *The Root of the Righteous* (Harrisburg, PA: Christian Publications, 1955), 50.
4. Dr. Dan Allender and Dr. Tremper Longman III, *The Cry of the Soul* (Colorado Springs: NavPress, 1994), 213.
5. C. S. Lewis, *Letters of C. S. Lewis*, ed. W. H. Lewis (New York: Harcourt, 1966, 1988), 383.
6. Charles Spurgeon, *Gleanings among the Sheaves* (Philadelphia: Lumen Classics, 1864), 44.
7. George M. Marsden, *Jonathan Edwards: A Life* (New Haven, CT: Yale Univ. Press, 2003), 77.
8. Eugene H. Peterson, *Answering God* (San Francisco: HarperSanFrancisco, 1989), 23.
9. Henri J. M. Nouwen, *The Return of the Prodigal Son* (New York: Image Books, 1992), 47.
10. Dietrich Bonhoeffer, *Psalms: The Prayer Book of the Bible* (Minneapolis: Augsburg, 1970), 15.
11. Peterson, *Answering God*, 5.
12. Thomas Merton, *No Man Is an Island* (Boston: Shambhala, 2005), 213.
13. Tim Keller, *The Songs of Jesus* (New York: Viking, 2015), vii.
14. Ibid., viii.
15. Peterson, *Answering God*, 5.
16. Jon Bloom, *Things Not Seen: A Fresh Look at Old Stories of Trusting God's Promises* (Wheaton, IL: Crossway, 2015), 186.

Every Bitter Thing Is Sweet

Tasting the Goodness of God in All Things

Sara Hagerty

Taste the Goodness of God in All Things

Sara Hagerty found Him when life stopped working for her. She found Him when she was a young adult mired in spiritual busyness and when she was a newlywed bride with doubts about whether her fledgling marriage would survive. She found Him alone in the night as she cradled her longing for babies who did not come. She found Him as she kissed the faces of children on another continent who had lived years without a mommy's touch.

In *Every Bitter Thing Is Sweet*, Hagerty weaves fabric from the narrative of her life into the mosaic of a Creator who mends broken stories. Here you will see a God who is present in every changing circumstance. Most significant, you see a God who is present in every unchanging circumstance as well.

Whatever lost expectations you are facing—in family, career, singleness, or marriage—*Every Bitter Thing Is Sweet* will bring you closer to a God who longs for you to know Him more.

Going beyond the narrative to offer timeless insight, Hagerty brings you back to hope, back to healing, back to a place that God is holding for you alone—a place where the unseen is more real than what the eye can perceive. A place where every bitter thing is sweet.